R. Capurro, K. Wiegerling, A. Brellochs (Hg.)

Informationsethik

Schriften zur Informationswissenschaft
Band 18

Herausgegeben vom Hochschulverband
für Informationswissenschaft (HI) e.V. Konstanz

Herausgeber dieses Bandes:
Gesellschaft für angewandte Informationswissenschaft
Konstanz (GAIK) e.V.
Rainer Hammwöhner, Josef Herget, Rainer Kuhlen

Mitglieder des wissenschaftlichen Beirates für die Schriftenreihe:

Nicholas Belkin	Rutgers University
Hans Peter Frei	ETH Zürich
Norbert Henrichs	Universität Düsseldorf
Harald Killenberg	TH Ilmenau
Alfred Kobsa	Universität Konstanz
Jürgen Krause	Universität Regensburg
Rainer Kuhlen	Universität Konstanz
Klaus Dieter Lehmann	Deutsche Bibliothek Frankfurt
Hans-Jürgen Manecke	TH Ilmenau
Erich Ortner	Universität Konstanz
Wolf Rauch	Universität Graz
Gerard Salton	Cornell University
Thomas Seeger	Hochschule Potsdam
Dagobert Soergel	University of Maryland
Gernot Wersig	FU Berlin
Harald Zimmermann	Universität Saarbrücken

R. Capurro, K. Wiegerling, A. Brellochs (Hg.)

Informationsethik

UVK · Universitätsverlag Konstanz

Die Deutsche Bibliothek – CIP-Einheitsaufnahme

Informationsethik / (Hrsg. dieses Bd.: Gesellschaft für Angewandte Informationswissenschaft (GAIK) e.V. Hochschulverband für Informationswissenschaft (HI) e.V.). R. Capurro ... (Hg.). – Konstanz: UVK, Univ.-Verl. Konstanz, 1995
(Schriften zur Informationswissenschaft; Bd. 18)
(UVK-Informationswissenschaft)
ISBN 3-87940-507-7
NE: Capurro, Rafael (Hrsg.); Gesellschaft für Angewandte Informationswissenschaft <Konstanz>; 1. GT

ISSN 0938-8710
ISBN 3-87940-507-7
© Universitätsverlag Konstanz GmbH, Konstanz 1995
Druck und Bindung: Siegl-Druck GmbH, Friedrichshafen
Einbandgestaltung: Riester & Sieber GmbH, Konstanz
Papier: Chlorfrei gebleicht

Inhalt

1	Einleitung	7
2	**Grundfragen der Informationsethik**	**21**
	Norbert Henrichs: Menschsein im Informationszeitalter.	23
	Klaus Wiegerling: Medium und Verhalten.	37
	Daniel Bougnoux: Qui a peur de l'information?	73
3	**Ethische Fragen in der Informationspraxis**	**83**
3.1	**Ethische Fragen auf Makroebene**	**83**
	Rafael Capurro: Moral issues in information science.	85
	Thomas J. Froehlich: Ethical Considerations in Technology Transfer	105
	Ronald D. Doctor: Information Technologies and Social Equity: Confronting the Revolution.	135
3.2	**Ethische Fragen auf Meso- und Mikroebene**	**165**
	Robert F. Barnes: Ethical and Legal Issues Raised by Information Technology: The Professional-Producer-Product Mix.	167
	Thomas J. Froehlich: Ethics, Ideologies, and Practices of Information Technology and Systems.	175
	Rosemary R. Du Mont: Ethics in Librarianship: A Management Model.	195
	Robert Hauptman: Ethical Concerns in Librarianship: An Overview.	211
	John Swan: Ethics Inside and Out: The Case of Guidoriccio.	219
	Martha M. Smith: Infoethics for Leaders: Models of Moral Agency in the Information Environment.	237
3.3	**Ethische Fragen in Lehre und Forschung**	**257**
	Barbara J. Kostrewski, Charles Oppenheim: Ethics in information science.	259
	Bernd Frohmann: The Power of Images: A Discourse Analysis of the Cognitive Viewpoint.	273
4	Ein- und Weiterführende Bibliographie	287
5	Ethik-Kodizes	289
6	Die Autoren	305

1. Einleitung

Die Reflexion über informationsethische Fragen gewinnt immer mehr an Bedeutung, wie man anhand der Literatur unseres Fachgebietes beobachten kann. Thomas Froehlich hat die wichtigsten Ergebnisse in seinem Bericht Ethical Considerations of Information Professionals- (Annual Review of Information Science and Technology, Vol. 27, 1992, S. 291-324) zusammengefaßt. Eine Reihe von Monographien (siehe Anhang) sowie das Erscheinen des Journal of Information Ethics, herausgegeben von Robert Hauptman, bestätigen in jüngster Zeit das wachsende Interesse an der Diskussion dieser Fragen, vor allem im angelsächsischen Bereich. Mit dem vorliegenden 'Reader' sollen einige dieser Beiträge in der jeweiligen Originalversion präsentiert und damit wichtige Stationen dieses Reflexionsprozesses aus den letzten Jahren exemplarisch wiedergegeben werden. Natürlich bleibt diese Auswahl, die sich an Forschung und Praxis des Informationsbereichs richtet, nur ein Torso.

Die Idee zu dieser Zusammenstellung entstand bei Gesprächen mit Kollegen, insbesondere mit Rainer Kuhlen und Josef Herget (Universität Konstanz), Thomas Froehlich (Kent State University, USA) und Bernd Frohmann (The University of Western Ontario, Canada).

Losgelöst vom für diese Auswahl leitenden Kontext 'Bibliothek, Information und Dokumentation' (BID) wird der Titel 'Informationsethik' zu einer umfassenden Bezeichnung für ethische Fragen im Medienbereich (journalistische Ethik, ethische Fragen der Massenmedien), in der Informatik (Computerethik) sowie im soziopolitischen Bereich (Informations- und Kommunikationsökologie, Verhältnis von Information und Demokratie). Wie bei der Lektüre der hier ausgewählten Beiträge deutlich wird, stehen diese Bereiche in Wechselwirkung mit dem BID-Bereich, so daß eine zu enge Auffassung der Informationsethik weder möglich noch sinnvoll erscheint.

Dennoch bleibt die Bibliotheks- und Informationswissenschaft in der vorliegenden Textauswahl im Zentrum, wenngleich das Verhältnis zwischen diesen beiden Disziplinen seit nahezu einem halben Jahrhundert Gegenstand kontroverser Standpunkte ist. Der vorliegende 'Reader' deckt nicht das gesamte Spektrum der ethischen Fragen im bibliothekarischen Bereich ab. Der Schwerpunkt wird hier auf ethische Probleme der elektronischen Informationsverarbeitung und -vermittlung sowohl innerhalb als auch außerhalb von Bibliotheken gelegt. Wir meinen, daß diese Fragen einen zentralen Gesichtspunkt bibliothekarischer Praxis ausmachen.

Information, so lautet die Konstanzer Devise, ist Wissen in Aktion. Sie ist also untrennbar vom Handeln menschlicher Subjekte. Dieser anthropologische Informationsbegriff stellt die Grundlage der hier erörterten Fragen einer 'Informationsethik' dar. Sie reichen vom Handeln individueller Subjekte auf der Mikroebene, über das Agieren von Informationsunternehmen (Bibliotheken, IuD-Stellen, Hosts, Netzwerke, Consulting Agencies) auf der Mesoebene, bis hin zu den makroethischen Fragen wie zum Beispiel die Rahmenbedingungen nationaler und internationaler Informationspolitik sowie die 'epochale' Frage nach einer neuen 'Wissensordnung' (Helmut Spinner).

Information ist Wissen in Aktion. Wissen kann zum einen Gegenstand einer Wahrheitssuche um ihrer selbst willen, zum anderen aber auch als Mittel zum Zweck aufgefaßt werden. Diese instrumentalistische Sicht menschlichen Wissensstrebens ist vor allem seit der Neuzeit vorherrschend und sie gipfelt in der allgemeinen Mediatisierung allen Wissens in der Informationsgesellschaft. Wissen wird zum Gegenstand, den man 'verarbeitet' und zur Ware, die einen Preis hat. Träumte die Aufklärung von einer allgemeinen Demokratisierung des Wissens und von einem zensurfreien Raum des Gedruckten, so erwacht sie heute inmitten einer medialen Welt, in der die Menschheit einerseits der Idee einer ideellen Zusammengehörigkeit mit Hilfe technischer Mittel näher zu kommen scheint, während andererseits der Streit der partikularen Interessen um die Macht über Mitteilungsinhalte und -kanäle ein planetarisches Ausmaß annimmt. Mitten in einem nie dagewesenen Reichtum an Wissen und Medien herrscht bei einem großen Teil der Menschheit der Analphabetismus, nicht zuletzt durch die Massenmedien selbst verursacht. Die Abhängigkeit der Informationsarmen von den Informationsreichen scheint gerade aufgrund des technischen Fortschritts zu wachsen. Der hemmungslose Kampf um Informationsmärkte zeigt deutlich, daß nicht nur Wissen, sondern eigentlich erst Wissen in Aktion Macht ist. Die heutigen Medien erhöhen den zeitlichen und räumlichen Aktionsradius des Wissenseinsatzes in einem solchen Maße, daß die Handlung des Informierens und des Informiert-werdens als eine Machtäußerung von globalen Ausmaßen erscheint. Das führt zu einer weiter steigenden Ökonomisierung der Medialität. Das demokratische Recht der allgemeinen Informationszugänglichkeit gewinnt an Brisanz.

Gegenüber der Einschränkung des Wissenszugangs auf bestimmte gesellschaftliche Gruppen (Universität, Adel, Klerus), proklamierte die Aufklärung das Ideal eines zensurfreien Raumes der gedruckten wissenschaftlichen Mitteilungen. Dieser Raum - garantiert vor allem durch die

Schaffung von öffentlich zugänglichen Bibliotheken sowie durch die Enthaltung von Kontrolle oder Zensur seitens politischer und religiöser Machtinstanzen sollte zugleich eine von ökonomischen Privilegien unabhängige freie Zugänglichkeit gewährleisten. Mit der Veränderung der politischen Verhältnisse im 19. und 20. Jahrhundert wurden allmählich aus privaten Sammlungen öffentlich zugängliche Bibliotheken.

Das Ideal der Aufklärung, das dem Auftrag der Bibliotheken, Wissen der Allgemeinheit zugänglich zu machen, zugrundelag, scheint, am Ende des 20. Jahrhunderts, in sein Gegenteil umzuschlagen. Die Informationsgesellschaft wird immer mehr von der Informationswirtschaft bestimmt. Information ist nicht mehr primär ein allgemeines Gut, sondern eine Ware und diese hat einen Preis. Diese Subsumierung der Kategorie der Information unter die Ökonomie hat Rückwirkungen auf das menschliche Verhalten, sofern dieses als ein bloß mediatisierbares Verhältnis aufgefaßt wird. Es gerät dabei leicht in Vergessenheit, daß auch und gerade im Informationsverhalten der andere niemals bloß (!) als Mittel, sondern jederzeit zugleich als Zweck zu gebrauchen ist (Kant). Die steigende Vorherrschaft der Ökonomie über die Information muß parallel zur sozialen Marktwirtschaft durch eine soziale Informationswirtschaft ausbalanciert werden.

Eine gelebte Moral trägt den veränderten technischen Entwicklungen Rechnung, indem sie neue Sitten einführt oder vorhandene verändert. Uns aber Rechenschaft darüber zu geben, ob und wie diese neuen Sitten zu rechtfertigen sind, ist Aufgabe der Ethik.

Eine Informationsethik als Theorie und Kritik der Entwicklung moralischen Verhaltens im Informationsbereich umfaßt individuelle, kollektive und menschheitliche Aspekte. Als deskriptive Informationsethik fragt sie nach der Entstehung der verschiedenen Strukturen und Machtverhältnisse, die das Informationsverhalten in verschiedenen Epochen bestimmen. So war zum Beispiel die Macht des religiösen Mythos in der Antike oder die des Christentums im Mittelalter maßgeblich für die Entwicklung von Institutionen und Praktiken, die der Konsolidierung von Informationshierarchien dienten. Heute sind es vor allem ökonomische Machtmonopole, die Formen und Inhalte menschlichen Miteinanderseins bestimmen. Eine Kritik des Kapitals ist heute ohne Kritik der Information nicht denkbar. Sie steht als Aufgabe noch vor uns. Eine Informationsethik müßte aber sowohl eine Kritik der bestehenden Verhältnisse als auch der neuen Informationsmythen leisten. Sie müßte zugleich analytisch und dekonstruktiv sein, d.h. sie müßte die scheinbare Selbstverständlichkeit herrschender

Sprachnormierung durchbrechen und die dadurch verdeckten Widersprüche offenlegen. Als normative Informationsethik müßte sie das anthropologische Phänomen der Information sowohl unter materiellen als auch unter formalen Gesichtspunkten analysieren.

Denn Information gehört zweifellos zu jenen Gütern, die erst in neuester Zeit einen hohen gesellschaftlichen Stellenwert erreichen, ja sie erscheint als notwendige Bedingung des individuellen und sozialen Handelns überhaupt. Waren bisher Begriffe wie 'Tugend', 'Gesinnung' oder 'Konsens' paradigmatische Wendepunkte der Ethik, dann scheint es so, als ob heute die ethische Qualität menschlichen Handelns wesentlich von einer neuen Informationsordnung abhängt, denn, wie sollen wir unsere Urteilskraft ausüben, wenn wir nicht vorher ausreichend informiert sind? In Abwandlung des Kantischen Diktums können wir sagen, daß Urteilskraft ohne Information leer und Information ohne Urteilskraft blind ist. Wie vollzieht sich aber Urteilskraft im Informationszeitalter?

Dieser 'Reader' versteht sich als Anregung zur Diskussion dieser Fragen. Wir haben Beiträge versammelt, die einen Einblick in die Grundfragen und eine Übersicht über die Problembezirke der Informationsethik verschaffen. Sie sind in drei Abteilungen gegliedert, wobei eine eindeutige und ausschließliche Zuweisung zum jeweiligen Problemkreis kaum möglich ist. In der ersten Abteilung - Grundfragen einer Informationsethik - werden anthropologische Probleme im Informationszeitalter, mediale Neudimensionierung aller Lebensbereiche, Fragen einer neuen Wissensordnung und die Frage nach der Bestimmung des Informationsbegriffs behandelt. Die zweite Abteilung - Ethische Fragen der Informationspraxis - umfaßt Beiträge über ethische Fragen auf Makro-, Meso- und Mikroebene. Bei der ersten Ebene handelt es sich um allgemeine soziale und politische Fragen, vor allem um Fragen der Gerechtigkeit in Zusammenhang mit dem Verhältnis zwischen den informationsarmen und -reichen Ländern. In einer zweiten Gruppe, welche Fragen auf Meso- und Mikroebene anspricht, haben wir Beiträge ausgewählt, die sich sowohl mit ethischen Fragen elektronischer Informationsvermittlung als auch bibliotheksbezogener Ethik-Beiträge befassen. In der dritten Abteilung - Ethische Fragen in Lehre und Forschung - bringen wir zwei Aufsätze, die sich in einem Abstand von zwölf Jahren kritisch mit der Informationswissenschaft, ihrer Forschung und Lehre und ihrem Jargon auseinandersetzen.

Einleitung

Norbert Henrichs eröffnet mit „*Menschsein im Informationszeitalter*" die Diskussion der ersten Abteilung über Grundfragen der Informationsethik. Er behandelt das Thema einer anthropologischen Fundierung der Informationswissenschaft. Ausgehend von der Veränderung der Lebens- und Kommunikationsformen durch die Informationssysteme und -netze weist Henrichs auf die unmittelbaren Auswirkungen für die Verwirklichung menschlicher Grundrechte hin. Das wird am Begriff des menschlichen Handelns aufgezeigt, in dem dieser durch die Möglichkeit weltweiter unmittelbarer Wirksamkeit eine neue Qualität gewinnt. Das hat Auswirkungen auf die bisherigen Formen der sozialen und politischen Partizipation, der Organisation, der Arbeit und des Denkens. Die Kommerzialisierung des Informationswesens führt, so Henrichs, auch zu einer neuen Form des 'homo oeconomicus' sowie zu neuen Strukturen kollektiven Daseins in immer engerer Symbiose und in wachsender Abhängigkeit mit dem Funktionieren oder Nicht-Funktionieren technischer Systeme. Die Mediatisierung des Geistes steht der unserer leiblichen Kräfte nicht nach. Die Frage des „Menschseins im Informationszeitalter" bildet den Kern einer Informationsethik, und diese ist wiederum ein überfälliger Titel für das Nachdenken über die ethische Rechtfertigung der herrschenden (A-) Moralität in einer informatisierten Welt.

In seinem Beitrag „*Medium und Verhalten*" definiert *Klaus Wiegerling* den Begriff des Mediums als informelle und zugleich ethische Prägeinstanz, mit der sich menschliche Personalität ausbildet. Medien sind also prinzipiell keine neutralen Gegebenheiten. Er verzichtet dabei auf die zu Verwirrungen führende Scheidung von ideellen und materiellen Momenten, betont dagegen, daß Medien Sinn und Wert von einer bestimmten Weise ihrer Einrichung erfahren. Der transportierte Inhalt erweist sich als den jeweiligen medialen Bedingungen angepaßt. Information ist keine vom jeweiligen Träger und seinen Werthierarchien unabhängige Größe. Sie läßt sich niemals ohne Sinn- und Werteverlust von einem in das andere Medium übertragen. Dies hat grundsätzliche Bedeutung für ihre Wirkung auf das menschliche Verhalten: Wenn Informationen in einem medialen Wertzusammenhang formiert und transponiert werden, dann ändern sich mit dem Auftreten eines neuen Leitmediums auch menschliche Verhaltensweisen. In der Gegenwart heißt das, daß mit der Dominanz der visuellen und rechnergestützten Medien eine zunehmende Mediatisierung der Welt- und Lebenserfahrung stattfindet: Der Verlust eines unmittelbaren Verantwortungsbezuges und die Auflösung von gemeinschaftlichen und individuellen Wertehierarchien in einer gleichgeordneten, entropischen Welt sind die Folgen.

Daniel Bougnoux schränkt in seinem Beitrag „*Qui a peur de l'information?*" den Informationsbegriff anthropologisch ein: Es gibt keine 'Information an sich', sondern Information ist immer bezogen auf ein erkennendes Subjekt, mit bestimmten Interessen, einer bestimmten Vorbildung usw. Er zeigt, wie wir Informationen nach dem Grad unserer Offenheit oder Verschlossenheit filtrieren und selektieren, und wie unsere individuellen und sozialen Stereotypen die Zirkulation von Information, die Kommunikation also, ermöglichen. Dies geschieht indem sie den Neuigkeitswert reduzieren und einen leichteren Lernerfolg bewirkt. Dementsprechend zeichnet sich Information dadurch aus, daß sie einen Unterschied oder eine Veränderung verursacht und dadurch, im etymologischen Sinne des Wortes, 'informiert'. Nach Bougnoux unterscheidet sich der Vorgang der Information von dem des Reiz-Reaktions-Verhältnisses durch eine Undeterminiertheit des Bezuges zwischen Sender und Empfänger, die einen Raum der Interpretation und somit der Kritik offenläßt. Dieser kritische Raum verringert sich, so Bougnoux, wenn - wie bei den Fernseh-live-Übertragungen - der Abstand zwischen Sache und Zeichen, wirklich oder nur scheinbar, nicht gegeben ist. Anhand dieser und anderer Analysen, zum Beispiel zur Frage der Manipulation, zeigt Bougnoux, daß Information als anthropologisches Phänomen eine fundamentale ethische Dimension einschließt, die sich auf den Ebenen ihrer Produktion, Vermittlung und Nutzung aufgrund der dabei stattfindenden Selektion aufweisen läßt.

Die zweite Abteilung befaßt sich mit ethischen Fragen der Informationspraxis auf Makro-, Meso- und Mikroebene. *Rafael Capurro* verweist in seinem Aufsatz „*Moral issues in information science*" auf die Verankerung des Grundsatzes der Informationsfreiheit in der UN-Charta der Menschenrechte und im Grundgesetz der Bundesrepublik Deutschland. Dieser Grundsatz stellt die Basis für die Erörterung von ethischen Prinzipien in den Bereichen der Informationsproduktion, -vermittlung und -nutzung dar. Capurro geht zunächst auf die umstrittene Frage nach Sinn und Grenzen der Kodifizierung von ethischen Maximen ein. Makro-ethische Dilemmata in den Bereichen: Sicherheit, Beschäftigung, Industrie, Planung, Dezentralisierung, 'Informationsüberflutung' werden identifiziert. Er verweist aber auch auf ethische Fragen auf Meso- und Mikroebene. Das Paradigma der „idealen Kommunikationsgemeinschaft" (K.O. Apel, J. Habermas) bietet nach Capurro eine zwar notwendige aber nicht

Einleitung 13

hinreichende Begründung der Informationsethik. Denn eine solche Basis verweist letztlich auf eine Totalität, die dem offenen und kontingenten Charakter menschlichen Mitteilens widerspricht.

Thomas J. Froehlich diskutiert in *„Ethical Considerations in Technology Transfer"* Fragen des Informationstransfers im Verhältnis zwischen der 'Ersten' und der 'Dritten Welt'. Dabei versucht er die Probleme sowohl aus der Kantischen als auch aus der utilitaristischen Perspektive zu beschreiben, um am Ende zu einer Art Synthese beider Positionen zu kommen, mit der die Transferfrage einer Lösung zugeführt werden soll. Doch während der Utilitarismus das Moralische dem politischen und ökonomischen Kalkül opfert, gibt der Kantianismus keine Handhabe, um die Handlungsmotive zu objektivieren. Das Grundproblem des Informationstransfers ist die Orientierung an kulturellen, ökonomischen und politischen Standards der 'Ersten Welt'. Der utilitaristische Ansatz führt zu ethischen Konflikten zum Beispiel im Falle einer landwirtschaftlichen Bibliothek in einem Land der 'Dritten Welt', wo die Faktoren der sozialen Verantwortung, der sozialen Nutzung und des institutionellen Überlebens nicht im Einklang gebracht werden können. Froehlich zeigt die Schwierigkeit solcher Abschätzungen beim Transfer von Informationsdiensten und -technologien aus der 'Ersten' in die 'Dritte Welt'. Am Ende greift er Ideen einer feministischen, antirigoristischen Vorsichtsethik auf, die ihre Basis in einem fürsorglichen, familiären Verhalten hat, welches allerdings den Sinn für die Kleinheit des Planeten und die gemeinsame Geschichte verliert. Froehlich sieht letztlich in einer Balance von Rechts- und Vorsichtsethik das entscheidende Mittel, moralische Fragen im Informationstransfer zu handhaben.

Ronald D. Doctor behandelt in seinem Beitrag *„Information Technologies and Social Equity"* das innergesellschaftliche Informationsgefälle. Die bereits existierende Kluft zwischen denjenigen, die über Informationen verfügen und denjenigen, denen Kompetenz und Möglichkeiten fehlen, um an Informationen zu gelangen ('information rich'/ 'information poor'), könnte durch die Verbreitung von Computer- und Telekommunikation noch verschärft werden. Doctor schlägt ein Konzept vor, in dem regionale und gesamtstaatliche Institute eng kooperieren, um Probleme der Informationsvermittlung, Ursachen und Charakter von Informationslücken, sowie Informationsbedürfnisse zu erforschen und Wege aufzuzeigen, wie Informationsungleichheit abgebaut werden könnte. Doctor beruft sich dabei auf ein Konzept, das Harold Sackman in den frühen 70er Jahren unter dem Titel „Experimental Mass Information

Utility" (EMIU) entwickelt hat. In diesem Konzept sollen in einer experimentellen Verfahrensweise für eine Kommune maßgeschneiderte Masseninformationssysteme, die die bestehenden Informationsbedürfnisse befriedigen, herausgefunden und geeignete Schulungsprogramme - zum Beispiel an Schulen und öffentlichen Bibliotheken - v.a. für sozial Schwache angeboten werden. Doctor macht konkrete Vorschläge für ein solches experimentelles Evaluierungs- und Schulungssystem in den Vereinigten Staaten, wobei viele Ansätze durchaus als Anregungen für eine vielerorts ins Stocken geratene nationale und internationale Informationspolitik verstanden werden können.

Der zweite Teil der zweiten Abteilung, der sich mit ethischen Fragen auf Meso- und Mikroebene befaßt, beginnt mit dem Beitrag *„Ethical and Legal Issues Raised by Information Technology"* von *Robert F. Barnes*, der die Frage der Haftbarkeit ('strict liabality') des Informationsspezialisten gegenüber seinen Produkten erörtert. Sicherlich problematisch, wenn auch aus utilitaristischen Prämissen verständlich, ist Barnes' Auffassung, daß rechtliche Streitfragen letztlich ethische sind. Nimmt man Information als Produkt, so ist zuerst der Hersteller dafür haftbar, wenn ein fahrlässiger Umgang ('negligence') damit nicht nachzuweisen ist. So klar dieser Sachverhalt für die Hardware ist, so problematisch ist er für die Software, da die Produktdefinition hier schwierig und eine ökonomische Absicherung problematisch ist. Das gilt vor allem für den Fall einer maßgeschneiderten Software, die aufgrund ihrer Einmaligkeit nicht als 'Produkt', sondern als 'Dienstleistung' bezeichnet werden sollte. In diesem Fall wären die Haftungskosten im engen Sinne des Wortes ('strict liability') nicht durch den weiteren Verkauf gedeckt. Bei Mischfällen - wenn also eine Standardsoftware nach individuellen Wünschen verändert wird - ist das Problem schwieriger, wenn eine Nachlässigkeit bei der Veränderung bewiesen werden muß. Schließlich erwähnt Barnes die Frage der Sicherheit und Vertraulichkeit seitens des Informationsspezialisten. Auch wenn viele dieser Fragen rechtlicher Natur sind, stellt sich die Aufgabe, die Gesellschaft dafür zu sensibilisieren als eine echte ethische Herausforderung dar.

Thomas J. Froehlich untersucht in seinem Beitrag *„Ethics, Ideologies, and Practices of Information Technology and Systems"* die Frage nach der ethischen Neutralität von Informationstechnologien. Er geht zunächst von der im informationswissenschaftlichen Bereich üblichen Unterscheidung zwischen den „intellektuellen Technologien" - d.h. jenen Technologien,

Einleitung 15

die der Organisation, Speicherung und Verbreitung von Informationen dienen - und den „Technologien" selbst - im Sinne einer Gesamtheit von Werkzeugen oder Prozeduren, die der Erfahrung der Informationssuche zugrundeliegen - aus. Beide greifen in der Praxis ineinander. Er zeigt, wie Computertechnologien, wenn man sie aus einer konkreten sozialen Perspektive analysiert, ihre angebliche Neutralität verlieren. Ihre Möglichkeiten und Grenzen treten gegenüber den Nutzern, ihren Werten, kulturellen Gewohnheiten usw. offen zutage. Das gilt um so mehr für die 'Informationstechnologien', wie er am Beispiel von Erschließungsmethoden (Klassifikationen, Thesauri) und Online-Retrieval-Systemen aufweist. Aus einem Mangel an Einsicht in diese Fragestellungen ergibt sich eine zunehmend instrumentalistische Perspektive, wonach Technologien bzw. Informationstechnologien nur als Mittel betrachtet werden, während sie tatsächlich Wertzusammenhänge verkörpern und herstellen. Das führt zu Vorurteilen, wie zum Beispiel zu der Vorstellung, daß mehr Daten zugleich besseres Verstehen bedeutet. „Computer literacy" wird zum Euphemismus für „consumer training", unter Vernachlässigung der kritisch-hermeneutischen Fähigkeiten bei der Auswahl und der Nutzung von Computertechnologien und ihrer Verbindung mit den „intellektuellen Technologien".

Rosemary Ruhig Du Mont schlägt in ihrem Beitrag *„Ethics in Librarianship"* ein Management-Modell für ethische Entscheidungen in der Bibliothekspraxis vor. Sie geht vom Unterschied zwischen Recht und Ethik aus: Nicht alles, was illegal ist, ist notwendigerweise unmoralisch, und umgekehrt; nicht alles, was moralisch geboten ist, wird auch vom Gesetz garantiert. Zugleich gibt es aber so etwas wie eine Kodifizierung von moralischen Normen, die in Zusammenhang mit der Diskussion über Fragen der Verantwortung entsteht. Diese Diskussion flammte im bibliothekarischen Bereich vor allem in den 60er Jahren wieder auf, und rückte die Verantwortung gegenüber den Nutzern in den Mittelpunkt. Du Mont sieht dabei eine Entwicklung, in der der Begriff der 'sozialen Verantwortung' immer deutlicher an Bedeutung gewinnt. Dieser Entwicklung gehen zwei Etappen voraus, nämlich die Zeit vor 1930, als die Zeit der Verantwortung für den Aufbau und die Erhaltung des Bestandes, und die Zeit zwischen 1930 und 1950, als die Zeit, in der ein Bewußtsein über die Verantwortung des Bibliothekars für die eigene Institution entsteht. Eine vierte Etappe läßt die Gesellschaft als Ganzes, und nicht nur die tatsächlichen Nutzer der Bibliothek als Horizont bibliothekarischer Verantwortung aufkommen. Demnach werden ethische Dilemmata der bibliothekarischen Praxis immer mehr in einem gesamtgesellschaftlichen Kontext reflektiert. Während der

Grundsatz der Denkfreiheit in der dritten Phase im Sinne von Neutralität verstanden wurde, wird er heute immer mehr im Sinne einer zu fördernden pluralistischen Gesellschaft verstanden. Die neue Richtung in der Debatte zwingt ausgehend von Fragen des Bestandsaufbaus bis hin zu Fragen der Kriterien für die bibliothekarische Erfolgsmessung zum Umdenken.

Für Du Mont ist Management wesentlich eine ethische Aufgabe. Bibliothekarische Entscheidungen haben Auswirkungen auf die individuelle Ebene der Individuen und auf der Ebene der Organisation und der Zugänglichkeit zum System. Schließlich schlägt Du Mont einen Handlungsplan für die Weiterentwicklung und praktische Anwendung dieser Perspektiven - beginnend mit ihrer Vermittlung während der bibliothekarischen Ausbildung - vor.

Robert Hauptman befaßt sich in seinem Beitrag *„Ethical Concerns in Librarianship"* mit ethischen Konfliktfeldern in Bibliotheken. Ein klassisches Beispiel ist das Dilemma zwischen der Informationspflicht seitens des Bibliothekars und der Nachfrage nach 'gefährlichen' oder 'unmoralischen' Informationen. Hauptman favorisiert den Vorrang der persönlichen gegenüber der beruflichen Verantwortung. Er hebt drei Bereiche der bibliothekarischen Praxis, in denen ethische Überlegungen eine wichtige Rolle spielen sollten, hervor. So zum Beispiel beim Aufbau und bei der Erschließung des Bestandes - man denke an die Verwendung von diskriminierenden oder verharmlosenden Schlagwörtern, bei der Benutzerberatung und bei der elektronischen Informationssuche.

Hauptman befaßt sich insbesondere mit ethischen Konflikten der Benutzerberatung bei medizinischen und juristischen Anfragen. Er fragt sich dabei, ob eine restriktive Praxis seitens der Bibliotheken weniger den Benutzern als den speziellen Berufsinteressen, zum Beispiel der Juristen, dient. Fragen der Vertraulichkeit, der allgemeinen Zugänglichkeit, der Fachkompetenz u.a.m. gehören für Hauptman zum Kern einer lebendigen bibliothekarischen berufsethischen Reflexion.

Auch *John Swan* befaßt sich in seinem Beitrag *„Ethics Inside and Out: The Case of Guidoriccio"* mit Fragen bibliothekarischer Ethik. Er analysiert einen Fall, bei dem zwei Kunsthistoriker - nämlich ein Amateur (Gordon Moran) und ein Fachmann (Michael Mallory) - in Frage stellten, ob ein berühmtes Fresko - die Darstellung des Reiters Guidoriccio da Fogliano im Rathaus von Siena tatsächlich von Simone Martini stamme, wie die Fachwelt bisher annahm. In einem Aufsatz aus dem Jahre 1977 behauptete Moran, daß das ursprüngliche

Einleitung

Fresko vernichtet und durch das nach dem Tode Martinis bemalte und bis heute erhaltene ersetzt wurde. Bibliotheksethik fängt, so Swan, mit dem Informationsprozeß selbst an, nämlich dort, wo Entscheidungen darüber fallen, welche Information erzeugt und wie sie an vorrangiger Stelle präsentiert wird. Und so kam es, daß aus einem Gelehrtendisput ein Fall von Zensur mittels Verschlagwortung wurde. Denn man vertrat von offizieller Seite im Kunsthistorischen Institut zu Florenz die herkömmliche Auffassung, so daß seit 1980 eine 'selektive' Indexierung der Aufsätze von Moran und Mallory stattfand. Sie wurden ohne Verweis auf Simone Martini in einer Mappe mit der ominösen Aufschrift „Miscellanea Moran" aufbewahrt. Die Aufschrift diente also tatsächlich der Verdeckung eines Sachverhalts ('concealment by subject heading'). Im Sach- und Autorenkatalog konnte man allerdings diejenigen Veröffentlichungen wiederfinden, welche die herkömmliche Auffassung vertraten. Swan analysiert im weiteren Mortons Fall als einen Konflikt mit dem wissenschaftlichen Berufsethos, dem Prinzip der Kollegialität, das eine scharfe Trennung zwischen Fachkollegen und Außenseitern schafft. Nach Swans Auffassung sind Bibliothekare ethisch verpflichtet, über beide Seiten, Amateure und Fachleute, qualitativ und quantitativ zu informieren. Das Verhältnis der Bibliothek zu Zensur und Kontrolle hat eine eminent sozialethische Bedeutung. Durch die Nutzung der elektronischen Informationstechnologien in Bibliotheken können zwar Fragen der Erschließung und des Zugangs leichter gelöst werden, sofern man das Problem wahrnimmt. Swan artikuliert mit seinem Beitrag die Frage nach dem Verhältnis von ethischen Normen zwischen wissenschaftlichen Bibliotheken und der 'scientific community'.

Martha Smiths Beitrag *„Infoethics for Leaders"* behandelt Fragen der ethischen Verantwortung von Informationsspezialisten in führenden Positionen. Sie gebraucht den Ausdruck Infoethik ('infoethics'), der so unterschiedliche Bereiche wie Computerethik, Medienethik und Bibliotheksethik umfaßt. Ihr Ansatz stellt das moralische Selbst als Handlungsinstanz in persönlichen, privaten, professionellen und öffentlichen Verantwortungskontexten in den Mittelpunkt. Dementsprechend gibt es zahlreiche Loyalitätskonflikte, die sie mit Hilfe eine vierstufigen Modells analysiert: 1) Problemdefinition, 2) Analyse der Werte, 3) Bestimmung der involvierten ethischen Prinzipien, 4) Prioritätensetzung bezüglich Loyalitätsverpflichtungen. Smith unterscheidet ferner fünf Ebenen für die ethische Orientierung am Arbeitsplatz, die sie mit Beispielen aus dem Bibliotheksbereich erläutert, nämlich 1) allgemeine ethische Werte, die von der Gesellschaft insgesamt getragen werden, 2) institutionelle berufsethische

Ziele, die der Bibliothekar bei seinen unterschiedlichen Tätigkeiten anzuwenden hat, 3) private Ziele oder Situationen, die unter Umständen in Konflikt mit der Institution treten können, 4) Gruppenbildung innerhalb des Berufes, um bestimmte Ziele durchzusetzen, 5) reine individuelle oder persönliche Ziele, die zur Isolierung des Betroffenen führen könnten.

Die dritte Abteilung des Readers betrifft ethische Fragen in Lehre und Forschung. *Barbara J. Kostrewski* und *Charles Oppenheim* haben vor fünfzehn Jahren die neuere Diskussion vor allem im Hinblick auf die sich akademisch etablierende Informationswissenschaft eingeleitet. In ihrem Beitrag „*Ethics in information science*" gehen sie zunächst auf die vorausgegangenen Kontroversen um den professionellen Ethikkodex der American Library Association und anderer Organisationen, vor allem in den USA ein. Sie heben zwei Aspekte moralischer Konfliktfelder in der Forschung hervor, nämlich das 'publish or perish'-Syndrom und die Frage der mehrfachen Autorenschaft. Aufgrund des Veröffentlichungsdrucks ist die Gefahr des Betrugs in der Forschung insgesamt groß, aber die Autoren sehen, zumindest im Jahre 1980(!), dieses Problem in der Informationswissenschaft als nicht gravierend an, und zwar weil sie die Informationswissenschaft eher als eine praktische Kunst auffassen, die relativ wenig Forschungsergebnisse produziert. Auch verfügt die Informationswissenschaft über keine eigenen theoretischen Grundlagen. Bezüglich der Veröffentlichung von Forschungsergebnissen sollte, nach Meinung der Autoren, einem Nachwuchswissenschaftler erlaubt sein, allein zu publizieren, wenn er die Untersuchungen weitgehend selbst durchgeführt hat, sein Betreuer aber die Veröffentlichung unter seinem eigenen Namen nicht wünscht. Kostrewski und Oppenheim befürworten, in Anschluß an Belkin und Robertson, eine Grenzziehung gegenüber Forschungsbereichen, die zu Manipulationszwecken eingesetzt werden könnten. Ethische Fragen in der Lehre der Informationswissenschaft unterscheiden sich nach Meinung der Autoren nicht wesentlich von denen in anderen Bereichen, sie betreffen vor allem intellektuelle Rechtschaffenheit und Selbstkritik. In diesem Beitrag werden auch ethische Fragen der Informationspraxis behandelt. Die Autoren vertreten dabei die Ansicht, daß Information nicht neutral ist und stets eine sozialethische Dimension einschließt.

Bernd Frohmann untersucht in „*The Power of Images: A Discourse Analysis of the Cognitive Viewpoint*" die dem kognitivistischen Ansatz in Bibliotheks- und Informationswissenschaft (N.J. Belkin, S.E. Robertson, B.C. Brookes) zugrundeliegenden Machtimplikationen, die mit diesem wie auch mit jedem anderen angeblich rein theoretischen Diskurs verbunden sind. Ziel seiner von Michel Foucault inspirierten machtanalytischen Kritik des kognitivistischen Diskurses ist es, nachzuweisen, daß dieser Diskurs Information als Ware konstituiert und Personen als berechenbare Informationsverbraucher innerhalb marktökonomischer Bedingungen bestimmt. Information wird wie ein Gegenstand naturwissenschaftlicher Untersuchung behandelt, und deren metaphysische 'Aufhebung' kulminiert in Karl Poppers 'dritter Welt'. Der kognitivistische Ansatz gibt vor, die einzige und zugleich globale Theorie des gesamten Bereiches der Bibliotheks- und Informationswissenschaft zu sein. Ihre Rhetorik von 'Bildern', 'Modellen', 'Wissensspeicherung', 'Abbildstrukturen' als 'mentale Ereignisse' im Innern von 'Individuen' usw. steht in krassem Gegensatz zu einem von diesem Ansatz ausgeklammerten Diskurs von Informationsprozessen als soziale Praktiken. Durch diese strikte Reglementierung der Weisen, in denen über Information gesprochen wird, erweisen sich die konstituierten Gegenstände eher als Auswirkungen von Macht denn als 'objektive' und 'naturgegebene' Phänomene. Dieser Diskurs spiegelt die Macht von bestimmten Machern und institutionellen Größen, die den Informationsmarkt einrichten und beherrschen. Die Verwandtschaft zwischen der Diskursstrategie des kognitivistischen Ansatzes und der kapitalistischen Konsumtheorie ist offensichtlich, trotz oder gerade wegen der vordergründigen Betonung der 'Nutzerzentrierung'.

Die Frage nach Sinn und Zweck von *Ethik-Kodizes* ist umstritten. Hier liegt ein offenes Feld für künftige Untersuchungen. Wir haben einige Beispiele ausgewählt. Der Reader enthält schließlich eine *ein- und weiterführende Bibliographie*. Da die ausgewählten Beiträge jeweils ausführliche bibliographische Angaben enthalten, soll diese Bibliographie lediglich eine Anregung für eine weitere Vertiefung dieses Themas oder für den Bestandsaufbau sein. Der 'Reader' erscheint nicht zuletzt mit der Absicht, daß die hier erörterten Fragen Gegenstand der Diskussion in Forschung, Lehre und Praxis werden. Wir meinen, daß Informationsethik zum Pflichtkanon in der Ausbildung von Informationsspezialisten - Bibliothekaren, Dokumentaren, Informatikern, Journalisten usw. - gehören sollte. Didaktische Ansätze dazu sind leider Mangelware. Kein Wunder! Die Vermittlung dieses Stoffes findet noch kaum statt. Hier besteht wohl akuter Handlungsbedarf, zumal wenn die Gesellschaft und vielleicht auch unser Zeitalter immer mehr durch den Bezug zur Information bestimmt werden.

Danksagung

Besonderen Dank sagen wir Frau Anne Gros und Frau Claudia Zartmann, die uns bei der technischen Bearbeitung unseres Readers unterstützt haben.

Wir danken auch Herrn Prof. Dr. Rainer Kuhlen für die freundliche Unterstützung des Projekts.

2. Grundfragen der Informationsethik

Menschsein im Informationszeitalter[*]

von Norbert Henrichs

1. Zwei Vorbemerkungen

Das Thema „Ethik in den Informationswissenschaften", dem der folgende Beitrag zugeordnet ist, erfordert zwei Vorbemerkungen. Einmal ist zu klären, was der relativ junge Begriff „Informationswissenschaft" meint, - ohne hier freilich in detaillierte wissenschaftstheoretische Erörterungen eintreten zu können. Zum anderen ist ein Wort zum Stand der Ethikdiskussion in diesem Wissenschaftsbereich zu sagen, um die nachfolgende Argumentation verständlich werden zu lassen.

Kommen wir zum ersten Punkt. Was der Begriff „Informationswissenschaften" umschreibt, ist hierzulande nicht festgelegt. Faßt man den Begriff weit, nämlich als Sammelbegriff, überspannt ein weiter Bogen eine Reihe von Disziplinen: die Kommunikationswissenschaften, die Medienwissenschaften, nachrichtentechnische Disziplinen (heute vielfach unter der Bezeichnung „Telematik" zusammengefaßt), die Informatik (im Sinne von Computerwissenschaft) mit ihren zahlreichen Töchtern (sogenannte „Bindestrich-Informatiken": wie Wirtschafts-Informatik, Rechts-Informatik, medizinische Informatik, geisteswissenschaftliche Informatik, Sport-Informatik etc.) - und schließlich die Informationswissenschaft im engeren Sinne (singularisch, englisch: information science).

Informationswissenschaft - darunter verstand man vor einigen Jahren noch im wesentlichen die Archiv-, Bibliotheks- und vor allem Dokumentationswissenschaft (englisch: library and information science). Unter Einbeziehung des Benutzungsumfeldes von (archivarisch, bibliothekarisch, dokumentarisch fundierten) Informationssystemen, zumal in organisationellen Umgebungen (in Unternehmen, Behörden, wissenschaftlichen Einrichtungen etc.), definiert sich diese Informationswissenschaft im engeren Sinn zunehmend als Management Wissenschaft („Information als Ressource", „Information als Produktionsfaktor", „Information als Führungsgröße" sind diese Entwicklung charakterisierende Schlagwörter). Ich werde mich im folgenden - dies legt zudem das thematisch vorgegebene Paradigma „Datenschutz" nahe - auf

---

[*] In: Steigleder, K.; Mieth, D.: Ethik in den Wissenschaften. Ariadnefaden im technischen Labyrinth? Tübingen: Attempto Verl. 1991 (2.Aufl.) S. 51-64. Mit freundl. Genehmigung des Attempto Verlages.

einen pragmatisch eingegrenzten Begriff „Informationswissenschaft" beziehen, der sich auf jene Disziplinen konzentriert, die sich mit elektronischer Informationsverarbeitung befassen, das sind also: die (angewandte) Informatik, die Telematik, die Informationsmanagement-Wissenschaft.

Lassen Sie mich diese Gruppe von Disziplinen inhaltlich als solche verstehen, die sich

- mit methodischen Fragen der Wissenschaftsorganisation und der formalen wie materialen Informationsverarbeitung befassen; die sich
- mit ingenieurtechnischen und verfahrenstechnischen Problemen der Konzeption, Konstruktion und des Aufbaus von Informationssystemen und Informationsnetzen beschäftigen und die schließlich
- organisatorische und ökonomische Probleme von Informationsprozessen, Informationssystemen, Informationsnetzen und Informationseinrichtungen untersuchen.

Das sogenannte Informationszeitalter ist eben nicht nur ein Zeitalter der Informationstechnik, sondern ist insbesondere auch durch ein spezielles und explizites Informationsbewußtsein charakterisiert, mißt nämlich Information eine herausragende Wertigkeit bei. Die hier ins Auge gefaßten Informationswissenschaften zeichnen sich gerade darum durch eine integrierte Sicht dieser beiden Momente aus, also durch eine integrierte Sicht von Informationstechnik und der Rolle der Information selbst als wichtiger gesellschaftlicher Größe. Gegenstand und Erkenntnisinteresse der Informationswissenschaften sind demnach also viel weiter zu fassen, als dies bei der (allgemeinen) Informatik der Fall ist.

Diese Informationswissenschaften - und damit komme ich zum zweiten Punkt meiner Vorbemerkungen - sind auf ethische Fragestellungen bislang kaum vorbereitet. Zum Stand der Ethikdiskussion in den oben genannten Disziplinen ist also schnell mitgeteilt, daß bislang erst vereinzelte Arbeiten vorliegen, die sich mit der Notwendigkeit und Möglichkeit verantwortlichen Handelns in einer informatisierten Welt auseinandersetzen. Unübersehbar ist zwar die Zahl von Untersuchungen zu erkennbaren oder für die Zukunft zu erwartenden (gesellschaftlichen) Folgen der mit großer Ausbreitungsgeschwindigkeit fortschreitenden Informatisierung. Aber zum einen haben jene Arbeiten ihren Ursprung außerhalb der Informationswissenschaften und werden auch eher dort - also vor allem im Bereich der die Informatisierung gewöhnlich mit Argwohn beobachtenden Sozial- und Erziehungswissenschaften sowie der Psychologie - diskutiert und erreichen diejenigen Disziplinen, die an der Informatisierung unmittelbar konzeptionell beteiligt sind, nur oberflächlich. Zum anderen muß aber vor allem deutlich festgestellt werden, daß diese vorliegenden Beiträge zur Technikfolgenabschätzung die eigentlich ethische Dimension dieser Thematik überhaupt nicht erreichen. Sie können als Vorarbeiten gelten, sind aber selbst - dahin ging ja die Frage - noch kein Beitrag zur Ethik der Informationsgesellschaft. Eine solche Ethik steht noch aus.

2. Das Fehlen einer Informationsethik

Wo Informationswissenschaften sich aber auch dieser Folgendiskussion gegenüber nicht blind und taub verhalten haben, haben sie die aufgeworfenen Fragen jedoch bislang als eher politische bzw. wirtschaftspolitische und juristische Fragen oder gar als nur technische Fragen verstanden und kaum als Fragen, die einen den informationstechnischen Möglichkeiten künftig besser angepaßten Katalog von neuen Handlungs- und Verhaltensnormen erfordern. Ich will solche auf die Folgendiskussion bislang nur vordergründig erfolgte Reaktionen nun kurz an wenigen Beispielen erläutern.

Für rein technische Interpretationen von Technikfolgen steht beispielsweise der Komplex „Bildschirmarbeitsplätze". Die Reaktion der Informationswissenschaften beschränkte sich bisher auf die Beschäftigung mit arbeitsphysiologischen Auswirkungen und bestand in der Entwicklung strahlungsärmerer, möglichst flimmerfreier Bildschirme, verbesserter Tastaturen, angepaßter Mobiliare und Raumausstattungen. Psychische Konsequenzen der Bildschirmarbeit (etwa ein vermehrter Leistungsdruck bei Mensch-Computer-Interaktionen, Veränderungen von Kommunikationsgewohnheiten etc.) wurden bislang nicht diskutiert, geschweige denn in informationswissenschaftlich neue Systemkonzepte mit einbezogen. Auch Fragen der Neuordnung von Arbeitsabläufen und die Reformulierung von erforderlichen Qualifikationen wurden höchstens von der Arbeitswissenschaft aufgegriffen. Den Informationswissenschaften fehlt offensichtlich noch das Bewußtsein, daß die Probleme einer Humanisierung der Computerarbeitswelt weit über Fragen eines oberflächlichen Systemdesigns hinausreichen.

Rein technisch-organisatorisch angegangen wurde von den Informationswissenschaften bislang auch der Problemkomplex „Datenschutz". Man kümmerte sich um Zugriffsschutzverbesserungen für Informationssysteme bzw. um entsprechend wirksame organisatorische Maßnahmen zum Zugangsschutz von Rechenzentren und Datenarchiven. Im übrigen überließ man die Problemklärung natürlich juristischem Sachverstand, was aber auch für die im Zusammenhang mit der Datenbankbenutzung und mit Verfahren des elektronischen Publizierens neu auftretenden Fragen des Urheber- und Kopierschutzes gilt. Daß nicht erst oder sogar nur bestenfalls Anwendungen von Systemen ethische Probleme aufwerfen, sondern bereits deren Entwurf bzw. die Konzeption bestimmter Datenstrukturierungs- und Informationsermittlungsverfahren, liegt bislang noch außerhalb informationswissenschaftlicher Betrachtungsweisen.

Für eine rein politische bzw. wissenschaftspolitische Interpretation von Informatisierungsfolgen steht schließlich auch die Frage der Zugänglichkeit von Informationssystemen. Hier haben es die Informationswissenschaften völlig den politischen Instanzen überlassen, darüber zu befinden, ob ein organisiertes Informationswesen als Instrument staatlicher Daseinsvorsorge, also im Sinne staatlich organisierter, finanzierter und verantworteter Infrastruktureinrichtung zu gelten hat oder dem Kräftespiel eines freien Marktes zu überlassen ist, woraus womöglich unverantwortliche Angebots- und Zugangsrestriktionen resultieren. Für Fragen der Zugangsgerechtigkeit zu Informationsressourcen und -systemen haben sich die Informationswissenschaften selbst bisher nicht zuständig gesehen.

Nochmals: Für die ethische Dimension jener beispielhaft erwähnten und weiterer Konfliktpunkte, die man bislang ausschließlich vordergründig mit technischen, juristischen oder politischen Mitteln zu lösen suchte, sind die Informationswissenschaften auch gegenwärtig kaum sensibilisiert. Vor allem kann für die Notwendigkeit ihrer eigenen Mitwirkung an der Entwicklung von Orientierungshilfen und zumal an der Beseitigung von Konfliktursachen erst wenig Bereitschaft erkannt werden. Je weniger allerdings Informationswissenschaften sich - wie oben als Trend skizziert - allein von der Technik her definieren, je holistischer sie sich planend, entwickelnd, implementierend und kontrollierend mit den vielfältigen Aspekten von Information, Informationsprozessen, Informationssystemen sowie deren Teilnehmern und Benutzern befassen, desto weniger werden sie künftig das Veränderungspotential des modernen organisierten Informationswesens außer acht lassen und sich verantwortlichen Reflexionen entziehen können. Doch, wie schon gesagt, vorläufig bleibt zu konstatieren, daß informationsethische Untersuchungen höchstens ganz vereinzelt und auch nur zu Einzelfragen vorliegen - und dies mit bisher nicht nennenswerter Wirkung. Ansätze zu einer notwendigen systematischen (materialen) Informationsethik sind leider noch nicht erkennbar. Sie müßten sich wohl auf die folgenden fünf Zielgruppen beziehen:

- auf Entwickler und Hersteller von Informationstechniken (Informationsindustrie),
- auf Vermarkter von Informationstechniken und zumal von Informationen (Informationswirtschaft),
- auf Entscheidungsträger über den Einsatz von Informationstechniken und Informationssystemen (Informationsmanagement),
- auf Anwender und Benutzer von Informationstechniken, -systemen und Informationen,
- auf Instanzen der Legislative und Exekutive (Informationspolitik).

Schließlich fehlt in den Informationswissenschaften auch noch die Ausbildung eines entsprechenden Wissenschaftsethos im Sinne einer „informationswissenschaftlichen Standesethik".

Solch eine „Standesethik" soll uns im folgenden nicht beschäftigen. Aber auch um die geforderte materiale Informationsethik - und sei es nur skizzenhaft - kann es hier noch nicht gehen, solange nicht die Fragen der anthropologischen Fundierung einer solchen Ethik diskutiert sind, d.h. bevor nicht klarer ist als heute, ob und in welchem Maße menschliche Lebens- und Kommunikationsformen in einer von Informationssystemen und -netzen bestimmten Welt tiefgreifenden Veränderungen ausgesetzt sind. Aus dem Blickwinkel ethischen Interesses steht indes auch in diesem Punkt die Diskussion noch am Anfang. Immerhin sind Ansätze dafür erkennbar, daß diese Fragestellung künftig wohl doch aufgegriffen wird.

3. Ansätze einer anthropologischen Fundierung

Wo heute schon solche ersten Schritte zu einer (letzten Endes an der Klärung ethischer Probleme interessierten) neuen Qualitätsbestimmung des Menschseins im heraufziehenden Informationszeitalter getan werden, lassen sich zwei unterschiedliche Grundeinstellungen ausmachen. Vereinfacht gesagt, geht es bei dem einen Ansatz um die Behauptung des traditionellen, immerhin auch formal gültigen, weil grundrechtlich abgesicherten Menschenbildes und daher um eine möglichst engeführte Adaption der Technikentwicklung an dieses Menschenbild. Verantwortbar und akzeptabel erscheinen nur solche Nutzungsformen der Informationstechnik, die sich mit den dieses Menschenbild bestimmenden Wertvorstellungen (bezogen z.B. auf die Arbeitswelt des Menschen) in Einklang bringen lassen.

Der andere Ansatz versucht zunächst, möglichst vorverständnis- und vorurteilsfrei das Veränderungspotential der neuen Informations- und Kommunikationstechnologien zu ermitteln und zu gewichten, und schließt danach als Konsequenz - im Unterschied zum ersten Ansatz - eine eventuelle Anpassung anthropologischer Grundkategorien an die festgestellten Entwicklungen nicht prinzipiell aus. Andererseits will er traditionelle Wertvorstellungen durchaus nicht leichtfertig preisgeben und auf der gewonnenen empirischen Basis, falls erforderlich, auch gezielte Abwehrstrategien formulieren.

Die zuerst genannte Argumentationsrichtung knüpft - wie etwa bei den Bemühungen der UNESCO um eine sogenannte Weltinformationsordnung erkennbar - an jene anthropologischen Grundeinstellungen an, auf die sich auch die Regelungen rechtlicher Konflikte der Informationsgesellschaft (vgl. die Datenschutzgesetzgebung, das Urheberrecht etc.) letztendlich beziehen. Es sind dies - wie schon angedeutet - die Grundrechtsbestimmungen nationaler Verfassungen und zumal auch die allgemeinen Menschenrechtserklärungen, da die weltweite Informatisierung eine supranationale Lösung im Sinne der genannten Weltinformationsordnung erfordert.

Nun ist aber der Novellierungsbedarf der erwähnten Rechtsregelungen auf Grund der ungemein schnellen Technikentwicklung immens groß. Das kodifizierte Recht hinkt den tatsächlichen Entwicklungen bekanntlich stark nach; zum einen, weil die Novellierungskommissionen angesichts der angesprochenen Entwicklungsgeschwindigkeit weitgehend überfordert sind, zum anderen aber, weil die an der Technikentwicklung hängenden wirtschaftlichen und politischen Interessen Einigungsprozesse zumindest stark verzögern. Daß diese Sachlage für die Rechtssicherheit in konkreten Konfliktlagen nicht gerade förderlich ist, liegt auf der Hand. Es erscheint daher diese im Grunde immer nur reagierende und reparierende Form der Auseinandersetzung mit den Informationstechnologien wenig befriedigend.

Informationsethische Wertungen, die in analoger Weise zum juristischen Vorgehen zustande kommen, also formuliert werden mit dem Rücken zur Wand jener Grundrechtsordnungen, werden daher - das steht zu befürchten - ebenfalls wenig grundsätzlich wirksame Orientierungshilfe bieten können. Eine Ethik, die sich auf die Rolle beschränkt, einer die Gesellschaft bedrohenden Hydra nur immer wieder nachwachsende Köpfe abzuschlagen, und glaubt, daß ihr dies jeweils rechtzeitig gelingt, bevor Schaden entsteht, kann der Gesellschaft keine Maßstäbe setzen, die Herausforderungen durch das Neue konstruktiv anzunehmen.

Der erwähnte zweite Ansatz, der vermutlich erfolgversprechender ist als der erste, stützt sich nicht auf eine von vorneherein bloß defensive Haltung gegenüber dem erkennbaren Veränderungspotential, das die Informationstechnologie für die Gesellschaft und die Individuen darstellt. Er verfolgt ausdrücklich eine Vorwärtsstrategie, da er - wie schon gesagt - unter dem Eindruck der Prüfung neuer Möglichkeiten eine Reformulierung auch grundlegender anthropologischer Kategorien keineswegs ausschließt, ohne dabei in leichtfertiger und euphorischer Technologieakzeptanz Kritikfähigkeit preiszugeben und auf Korrekturforderungen zu verzichten.

4. Einsatzstellen einer anthropologisch interessierten Technikanalyse

Am Anfang dieser Vorgehensweise steht eine anthropologisch interessierte, intensive und grundlegende Technikanalyse. Auf welche Momente - geeignet zur Überprüfung anthropologischer Grundpositionen - diese beispielsweise stößt, sei an folgenden vier ausgewählten Charakteristika heutiger informationstechnischer Entwicklung verdeutlicht: den elektronischen Netzen und Verbundsystemen, den künftigen Rechnerarchitekturen, der wachsenden System-(Hardware/Software)-Komplexität und schließlich der Kommerzialisierung des Informationswesens.

Die Beispiele sind so gewählt, daß trotz des allgemeinen Ansatzes gerade auch die Datenschutzproblematik leicht erkennbar tangiert wird, ohne daß dies im einzelnen aber ausgeführt werden kann.

Beispiel 1: Elektronische Netze und Verbundsysteme

Neben Verkehrs- und Energieversorgungsnetzen bilden elektronische Netze auf lokaler, regionaler, überregionaler und globaler Ebene, auf terrestrischen Leitungswegen oder über Satelliten heute eine neuartige, weltweite Infrastruktur. Sie verbinden in beinahe beliebiger Komplexität Arbeitsplatzrechner untereinander oder mit Großrechnern - und selbstverständlich auch diese wieder miteinander. Die Netze ihrerseits sind oft zu Verbundsystemen zusammengeschaltet.

Das Spektrum der Anwendungen ist breit: Es reicht beispielsweise vom beliebigen Datentransfer zur Nutzung entfernter Rechnerkapazität, über den Zugriff auf ein weltweites Datenbankangebot, die Abwicklung von Bank- und Handelsgeschäften, die Abwicklung von Fernmeß- und Fernsteuerungsvorgängen bis hin zum Austausch elektronischer Postsendungen zwischen einzelnen Teilnehmern und Interessentengruppen.

Welches sind die Konsequenzen der Rechnervernetzung unter der uns besonders beschäftigenden Frage nach möglichen Veränderungen menschlicher Lebens- und Handlungsformen? Stichwortartig sei bloß einmal aufmerksam gemacht

- auf die weltweite Ausdehnung der Reichweite menschlichen Handelns und die unmittelbare Wirksamkeit dieses Handelns in Echtzeit (ohne Zeitverzögerung, wie bei herkömmlichen Medien und Methoden), was eine globale Aktions- und Reaktionskompetenz voraussetzt;

- auf Partizipationsmöglichkeiten an einem sich aufbauenden „Weltgedächtnis", was neue Dimensionen der Wissensorganisation erfordert und neue Qualifikationsmöglichkeiten eröffnet;

- auf das Erfordernis einer den Teilnehmer identifizierenden „Annabelung"; Partizipationsrecht erwirbt man nur durch Erfüllung von Pflichten, d. h. hier durch Offenlegung des eigenen Ressourcenpotentials und Interessenprofils.

Beispiel 2: Künftige Rechnerkonfigurationen

Das gigantische Anwachsen der Datenvolumina verlangt neben der Entwicklung immer kapazitätsstärkerer Massenspeicher (vgl. die Entwicklung elektro- bzw. magnetooptischer Plattenspeicher) auch immer höhere Verarbeitungsgeschwindigkeiten. Sie sind abhängig von immer kürzeren Impulswegen, die die unfaßbare Miniaturisierung elektronischer Bauteile bereitzustellen sucht. Da aber hier die prinzipiellen Grenzen absehbar sind, läßt sich die geforderte Rechenleistung nur durch das Konzept der Parallelverarbeitung erzielen, also durch die Parallelschaltung von simultan aktiven Mikroprozessoren. In der Erprobung sind bereits Anlagen Tausender solcher zusammengeschalteter leistungsstarker Zentraleinheiten. Der Einsatz dieser Maschinen setzt natürlich auch einen neuen Softwaretyp, nämlich ebenfalls parallelarbeitende Programmsysteme voraus und zugleich ein entsprechendes Betriebssystem mit einem den Parallelverarbeitungsprozeß steuernden und überwachenden Koordinierungsmechanismus.

Einsatzgebiete dieser Parallelrechner sind beispielsweise recherche- und vergleichsintensive Aufgaben medizinischer Diagnostik, Aufgaben der Meteorologie, Steuerungen komplexer Prozesse, ökologische und militärische Frühwarnsysteme, Simulationen biologischer, chemischer, physikalischer und ökonomischer Prozesse. (Man spricht in diesem Zusammenhang auch von Mikrokosmos-Maschinen.)

Auch hier fragen wir nach tiefergreifenden Auswirkungen. Parallelverarbeitende Systeme setzen die Zerlegung von Aufgabenstellungen in parallelverarbeitbare Module voraus und fordern damit das gewohnheitsmäßig eher linear und sequentiell-sukzessive Problemlösungsverhalten heraus. Denk- und Organisationsformen, die auf eine lange gewachsene Tradition zurückgehen und menschliches Handeln sehr tiefgreifend, wenn auch nicht immer bewußt wahrgenommen, beeinflussen, stehen möglicherweise vor radikalen Veränderungen. Mit Sicherheit sind als Folge dieser Parallelrechner-Entwicklungen auch Umstrukturierungen zahlreicher Arbeitsabläufe im Umfeld der betroffenen Einsatzbereiche zu erwarten.

Beispiel 3: Wachsende System- und Softwarekomplexität

Ein weiteres Charakteristikum der modernen Informationstechnologie ist die zunehmende Integration ehedem funktional selbständiger Techniken zu komplexen Systemen. Als Beispiel sei die Koppelung von Arbeitsplatzrechnern, (Fern-)Kopiersystemen (Telefax) und Übertragungstechniken genannt - oder zudem die Rechnerverbindung mit audiovisuellen Aufnahme- und Speichermedien über zugleich für Text-, (Bewegt-)Bild- und Tonübertragung geeignete integrierte Datenleitungen (ISDN). Nicht zuletzt ist natürlich aber auch eine Softwarekomplexität gemeint, wenn von wachsender Systemkomplexität die Rede ist. Zu denken ist hier einmal an vielfach verzweigte, über zahllose Variablen gesteuerte Verarbeitungsroutinen, dann an neuartige multidimensionale und multimediale Informationssysteme (z.B. Hypertextsysteme) oder an den Einsatz von Methoden der sogenannten Künstlichen-Intelligenz. Hoch ist schließlich noch das in diesen hard- und softwaretechnischen Entwicklungen steckende Veränderungspotential, das aus verschiedenen Gründen nicht unterschätzt werden darf:

- Der Mensch gerät in eine wachsende Abhängigkeit von der Funktionstüchtigkeit solcher Systeme, deren Ausfall er nicht durch konventionelle Aktionen ausgleichen kann. Bei Ausfall der Systeme dürfte nicht selten ein kaum noch kompensierbares Chaos drohen.

- Schwachpunkt der Systeme wird aber eher der menschliche Bediener sein, der dem von der geforderten Mensch-Maschinen-Interaktion ausgehenden Leistungsdruck nicht gewachsen ist.

- Die Konsequenz wird die Ersetzung von Menschen durch weitere Systeme sein mit der Folge der schrittweisen totalen Ausschaltung des Menschen durch System-System-Kommunikation.

- Die Undurchschaubarkeit der Softwarefunktionen entzieht die Verarbeitungsergebnisse häufig der Kontrolle durch den gesunden Menschenverstand und führt zu bedenklicher Computergläubigkeit.

- Datenwege lassen sich nur ungenügend und unvollständig verfolgen, Datenschutz ist damit aber vielfach illusorisch.

- Die Unüberschaubarkeit der Software macht sie aber auch änderungsfeindlich, was womöglich zu einer ungewollten Stabilisierung unerwünschter Verfahren und Strukturen führt.

Es wird zu untersuchen sein, in welchem Maße der Mensch unter dem Eindruck dieser Systeme seine Entscheidungsfähigkeit einbüßt bzw. sich die Qualität seiner Entscheidungen verändert.

Beispiel 4: Kommerzialisierung des Informationswesens

Die Vermarktung geistiger, kultureller Güter ist sicherlich kein neues Phänomen. Andererseits hat - wie die Frankfurter Buchmesse, bedeutende Kunstauktionen oder auch der globale Medieneinsatz zeigen - die Kommerzialisierung des Kulturbereichs ein nicht gekanntes Ausmaß erreicht. Seit dem weitgehenden Rückzug des Staates aus dem Fachinformationswesen (vgl. etwa die Entwicklung der Förderpolitik in der Bundesrepublik seit 1980) gilt diese Feststellung zudem für elektronische Informationen aller Typen und Inhalte. Die Konsequenzen lauten:

- Fachinformation gilt als Ware und wird folglich dem Marktmechanismus von Angebot und Nachfrage unterworfen; bei Marktversagen bedeutet dies Angebotsreduktion mit der Folge der Unterversorgung.

- Zugangsbarrieren entstehen möglicherweise über prohibitive Preise.

- Die für den Betrieb von Informationssystemen außerordentlich hohen Vorleistungen begünstigen nicht selten Monopolbildungen auf der Anbieterseite.

- Die hohen Einstiegskosten in das Geschäft mit elektronischen Informationen rechnen sich nur durch deren Mehrfachnutzung in zusätzlichen Dateien und Produkten, die unter Umständen die ursprüngliche Zweckbestimmung der Datenerhebung verletzen.
- Die Kommerzialisierung des Informationswesens leistet in jedem Fall einer quantifizierenden Betrachtung und Bewertung von Informationen Vorschub.

Der „Homo oeconomicus" als anthropologisches Leitbild von Kommunikation bedroht ganz sicher deren immer auch sozialisierende Funktion.

Soweit der knappe Einblick in ausgewählte Entwicklungsfelder des modernen Informationswesens, ohne daß wir uns auf eine genaue Analyse der angedeuteten Probleme und der möglichen Konfliktfelder einlassen konnten. Mit diesem Blick auf die Praxis der Technologieentwicklung soll lediglich für eine in Gang kommende Ethikdiskussion sensibilisiert werden, die mit der Notwendigkeit rechnet, unter dem Eindruck der sich abzeichnenden Folgen der Informatisierung für alle Lebensbereiche Daseinsqualitäten neu zu definieren (und nicht nur traditionelle zu verteidigen), bevor sie sich daran macht, Normen für ein verantwortliches Handeln in jenen Technologiewelten zu formulieren.

5. Problemfelder des „Menschseins" im Informationszeitalter

An zwei unterschiedlichen Problempunkten soll noch gezeigt werden, in welche Richtung unter dem Eindruck der sich abzeichnenden Veränderung die Suche nach möglicherweise neuen Konturen des Menschseins im Informationszeitalter weist.

So stellt sich zum einen allmählich die Frage, welche Rolle künftig der einzelne als einzelner unter den neuen kommunikativen Bedingungen, zumal am Arbeitsplatz, aber auch generell in einer informatisierten Lebenswelt, noch spielen kann und ob sich nicht das traditionelle, zumindest unter dem Einfluß christlich-abendländischen Denkens zugunsten des einzelnen definierte Verhältnis von Individuum und Gesellschaft nunmehr doch ziemlich deutlich zu einer künftig höher zu bewertenden Kollektivität hin verschiebt.

Partizipation an den weltweiten Informationssystemen, die letztlich Systeme auf Gegenseitigkeit sein werden, - Partizipation an weltweiter Wissensverarbeitung fordert womöglich den Preis der Einschränkung individueller Souveränität (vgl. auf politischer, europäischer Ebene ähnliche, die einzelnen Nationalstaaten betreffende Konsequenzen ihres Zusammenschlusses). Das für die Lösung der Menschheitsfragen immer dringlicher werdende Problem der gerechten Ressourcen-Verteilung schließt prinzipiell die allgemeine Verfügbarkeit individueller Erfahrungen und persönlicher Daten nicht aus. Wer seine persönlichen elektronischen „Gedächtnisbereiche" (d.h. seine privaten Informationssammlungen, deren es bereits heute unzählige gibt) nicht auch zur Deckung des Informationsbedarfs anderer öffnet, muß damit rechnen, künftig selbst keinen Anschluß mehr an Informationsströme zu erhalten. Wer seiner persönlichen Verdatung prinzipiell Widerstand entgegensetzt, fällt aus der wirtschaftlichen, sozialen, medizinischen oder kulturellen Versorgung weitgehend heraus. Dies sind sicher zunächst einmal überspitzte Formulierungen. Doch wer vom Staat oder auch vom Markt immer bessere Daseinsvorsorge erwartet, darf sich der Organisation einer entsprechenden Datenlage als Voraussetzung dieser Daseinsvorsorge nicht widersetzen, was dann etwa auch oder gerade auch die Diskussion um den Datenschutz auf eine neue Betrachtungsebene hebt.

Und noch an einem zweiten Fragenkomplex soll verdeutlicht werden, daß die Entwicklung einer Informationsethik nur aus einer anthropologisch interessierten und geleiteten Auswertung der informationstechnischen Erscheinungswelt resultieren kann. Gemeint ist das Thema „Macht".

Wenn es Ethik allgemein um Gerechtigkeit zu tun ist, dann muß der Frage der Macht unter den Bedingungen der Informatisierung besondere Aufmerksamkeit geschenkt werden. Es seien nur einige der vielfältigen Machtverhältnisse genannt, die das Informationszeitalter bestimmen werden und die eben ein hohes Maß an Problembewußtsein verlangen:

- die Macht der Chip-Hersteller, von denen alle Hardware-Hersteller abhängen. (Die außerordentlichen Investitionen für Weiterentwicklungen verstärken in diesem Bereich die Monopolisierungstendenzen);

- die Macht der Marktführer im Hard- und Softwarebereich (die über Kompatibilitäten und Inkompatibilitäten befinden);

- die Macht der Betreiber großer (Service-)Rechenzentren (die über Funktionstüchtigkeit oder Zusammenbruch von Unternehmen und Verwaltungen befinden);

- die Macht der Netzbetreiber und Anbieter von Telekommunikationsdiensten (ohne die der Informationsaustausch zum Erliegen kommt);

- die Macht der Wartungstechniker (ohne die bei Systemausfällen nichts mehr geht);
- die Macht der Datenbankhersteller, -anbieter und -vertreiber (die über die Speicherinhalte verfügen und die Zugangsbedingungen setzen);
- die Macht derjenigen, die über die Bedienungs- und Benutzungskompetenz der Systeme verfügen (und daher leicht Abhängigkeitsverhältnisse schaffen können).

Dies sind nur Beispiele für sich im Informationswesen abzeichnende neue Spielarten menschlicher Machtverhältnisse, die eine sehr genaue Beachtung erfordern. Es muß nämlich sicher nicht betont werden, welche globalen Dimensionen, welche globale Reichweite solche Macht im einzelnen annehmen kann (gerade auch die Macht einzelner) und wie endgültig Folgen eines Machtmißbrauchs oder auch nur des fahrlässigen Umgangs mit dieser Macht sind. Zu denken ist an alle Formen der Computerkriminalität, an unbefugtes Eindringen in Netze und Systeme und der „Infizierung" von Systemen mit der Folge der Datenlöschung, Ergebnisfälschung, Programmvernichtung usw. Zu denken ist auch an mögliche politische Probleme und Konsequenzen aus den genannten Machtverhältnissen. Tangiert sind Fragen nationaler Sicherheit und der Sicherheit von Bündnissen (Know-How-Ausverkauf, Geheimnisverrat). Erwähnt sei schließlich noch, daß sich aus der ungleich fortschreitenden Informatisierung das sogenannte Nord-Süd-Gefälle weiter verstärkt und sich daraus resultierende Konflikte künftig kaum werden vermeiden lassen können.

Bei der nicht überschaubaren Zahl der Beteiligten im Zeitalter der Masseninformatik ist eine Risikoabschätzung unmöglich. Ist die heutige Gesellschaft, die jeder einzelne, der involviert ist (ihre Zahl wächst täglich), vorbereitet auf den Umgang mit dieser Macht? Welche natürlichen oder elektronischen Kontrollmechanismen sind denkbar, und wer kontrolliert die Kontrolleure? Welche Rolle muß dabei das Bildungswesen spielen? Welche Aufgabe fällt dem demokratischen Rechtsstaat zu?

Die Liste der Fragen, die aus der Analyse der geschilderten Sachverhalte resultieren, läßt sich beinahe beliebig verlängern. Nicht zuletzt gilt auch für den Bereich der Informationsverarbeitung, was für eine Reihe von Feldern wissenschaftlicher Betätigung gilt, daß der Mensch offensichtlich schon mehr kann, als er zumindest derzeit versteht.

Wer vermag auf diese Fragen momentan bereits Antworten zu geben, die mehr sind als schöne Beschwichtigungen? Wer entwickelt den anthropologischen Bezugsrahmen, der der Herausforderung durch die Informationstechnologie standhält? Wer spricht mit wem? Welche Kompetenz ist dazu erforderlich? Welche Funktion hat die Wissenschaft, die Wirtschaft, der Staat?

Bevor Antworten gesucht werden, wird es erforderlich sein, für diese Fragestellung zuallererst ein Bewußtsein zu wecken, dafür zu sensibilisieren, daß nicht nur die Oberfläche unserer Alltage, sondern das Menschsein selbst durch die fortschreitende Informatisierung betroffen ist.

Zu Beginn war die Rede davon, daß die Informationswissenschaften sich auf dem Terrain dieser Problemstellungen noch sehr unsicher bewegen, wenn sie es dann überhaupt schon betreten haben. Doch selbst, wenn sie auf ihrem „Neuland" tatsächlich sicherer werden sollten, wird man sie nicht allein lassen dürfen - so wie von Medizinern und Biologen alleine auch keine allseits befriedigende Lösung der ethischen Probleme der Gentechnologie erwartet werden kann. Es sind daher die professionellen Ethiker um Hilfestellung gebeten und aufgefordert, miteinzutreten in die Auseinandersetzung um Analyse und Bewertung unserer informationstechnisch immer stärker geprägten Lebenswelt.

Medium und Verhalten

Vom Einfluß des Informationsträgers auf den Umgang mit der Information und das Verhalten des Menschen

von Klaus Wiegerling

Menschliche Personalität bildet sich nicht nur in unmittelbaren Erfahrungen aus, sondern wesentlich auch in einem symbolischen Austausch, der uns einen Teil der Fülle mittelbarer Erfahrungen unserer Mitmenschen und Vorfahren nahe bringt.

Der symbolische Austausch gründet in Zeichensystemen, die es ermöglichen nicht unmittelbar Zugängliches, nicht unmittelbar Einsichtiges und Präsentes verständlich und verfügbar zu machen: dies ist zuunterst die Sprache im Sinne der Rede als wesentliches Konstitutivum aller Sozialität und Geschichtlichkeit[1]. Gesellschaft wie Geschichte werden letztlich nicht unmittelbar erfahren, sondern in einer Reflexion auf konkrete intersubjektive Erfahrungen. Unmittelbar erfahren wir bestenfalls Geschichten und soziale Kleingruppen in konkreten sozialen Situationen. Beim Erfassen von Gesellschaft und Geschichte spielt das Begrifflich-Diskursive die zentrale Rolle. Vermittlungen von Abwesendem sind seit jeher auch bildhaft geleistet worden; die bildhafte Vermittlung des Abwesenden ersetzt allerdings nicht die begrifflich-diskursive. Freilich lassen sich Bilderfahrungen, Bildabfolgen- bzw. anordnungen durchaus in der Weise einer Grammatik erfassen, lassen sich Regularien benennen, die strukturelle Ähnlichkeiten zwischen Bildverstehen und Sprachverstehen aufweisen, dennoch werden wir hier über grundsätzliche Unterschiede zu sprechen haben. Das Begriffliche ist zuerst immer abstrakt, nur durch eine bestimmte Form der Kombination des Begrifflichen und durch die Imagination stellt sich eine Konkretisierung ein. Beim Bildhaften ist der Sachverhalt umgekehrt: Das Bildhafte ist selbst in seiner größten Abstraktheit noch konkret und kann nur durch einen ausdrücklichen Reflexionsakt in seiner Allgemeinheit erfaßt werden.

Es ist wesentlich für diese Untersuchung, daß man sich vor gewissen Trugschlüssen hütet, die durch Naivitäten einer rein technisch verstandenen Informationswissenschaft befördert werden. So wird zu zeigen sein, daß es den gleichen Inhalt in unterschiedlichen Informationsträgern nicht gibt, daß jede Transformation einer Information in einen anderen Informationsträger zugleich eine Veränderung der Information bzw. ihres Auffassungssinnes bedeutet.

Weiterhin wird zu zeigen sein, daß jedes Medium entscheidend von seinen Mitmedien, insbesondere dem jeweiligen Leitmedium, geprägt wird, daß der Stellenwert des Buches im Zeitalter elektronischer Medien ein anderer ist als zuvor, oder daß der Stellenwert des Bildes im Gutenberg-Zeitalter ein anderer war als zuvor.

Wenn hier von Verhalten gesprochen wird, so ist bewußt ein sehr weiter und neutraler Begriff gewählt worden, der ein Doppeltes einschließt: Verhalten als Tun und Lassen in Bezug auf andere Mitmenschen und Lebewesen als auch auf Sachen, wobei die beiden Seiten des Begriffes so organisch miteinander verwachsen sind, daß eine Scheidung ein künstliches, ja gewaltsames Unterfangen wäre. Praxis als gesellschaftliches und Poiesis als dingherstellendes Verhalten sind keine voneinander unabhängigen Kategorien. Die im engeren Sinne ungesellschaftlichen Sachverhältnisse sind von den mitmenschlichen Verhältnissen nicht zu trennen. Mitmenschliche Verhältnisse im Sinne des Ethos haben ursprünglich wenig mit unserem modernen Verständnis von ethisch zu schaffen. Wir verknüpfen den Begriff meistens mit einem individuellen Gewissen, mit einer subjektiven Disposition des Handelns, die sich den öffentlichen Ansprüchen eher verweigert als diese erfüllt. Gerade davon ist der ursprüngliche Sinn des Begriffes weit entfernt: ἔθος heißt Sitte, Brauch, bestimmt also das Überlieferte, durch Konventionen festgelegte und empirisch feststellbare Verhalten in einer Gesellschaft; ἦθος legt den Wert eher auf das Unsichtbare dieses Verhaltens, das in Gesittung und Charakter verinnerlicht ist. Charakter bildet sich durch Gewohnheit. Das heißt, es ist in Ethos ein Erziehungsauftrag mitformuliert. Der Charakter des einzelnen bildet sich in der Gemeinschaft durch Übung. Ethisch sein, heißt im Ursprung konform sein, heißt, um es mit Aristoteles zu sagen, die Fähigkeit des κοινωνεῖν, des Zusammenlebens zu besitzen.

Verhalten meint hier nun die Gesamtheit des gesellschaftlichen Agierens und Nichtagierens, inklusive sämtlicher Sachverhältnisse in seinen konkreten und somit empirisch verstehbaren Äußerungen.

Wenn es nun darum geht, das Verhältnis von Medium und Verhalten zu beleuchten, so sind folgende zentrale Fragen zu klären:

1. Was heißt Medium und was sind seine Charakteristika?

2. Was transportieren Medien?

3. Was heißt Informationsvermittlung?

4. Wie wird mit Medien und ihren Informationen umgegangen?
5. Wie bestimmt sich der Mensch gegenüber dem Medium?
6. Wie verändert sich die Information durch das Medium?
7. Wie beeinflußt das Medium das Verhalten des Menschen?

1. Was heißt Medium und was sind seine Charakteristika?

Alles Verstehen findet in spezifischen hermeneutischen Strukturen statt; dies sind Strukturen von Vormeinungen, geprägt von individual- und gruppengeschichtlichen Vorgaben, die sich allerdings nicht nur im verstehenden Individuum sedimentiert haben, sondern ebenso im Medium.

Der symbolische, mittelbare Austausch, der die räumliche und zeitliche Präsenz transzendiert und dadurch Öffentlichkeit im eigentlichen Sinne erst herstellt, ist stets an einen medialen Träger gebunden.

Als eines der frühesten räumliche und zeitliche Präsenz der Erfahrung transzendierenden und Öffentlichkeit herstellenden Medien muß das Theater gelten, das nicht zufällig dem religiöskultischen Bezirk als dem Urort medialer Vermittlung entwachsen ist. Schon dieser Bezirk ist durch die wesentlichen Charakteristika eines Mediums zu beschreiben: Er versammelt Menschen und bereitet somit Öffentlichkeit vor, und er transzendiert die örtliche und zeitliche Gebundenheit der Erfahrung, indem er auf Transzendentes verweist. Dies geschieht im kultischen Bezirk durch Weisen nichtalltäglichen, gebundenen, formel- und rätselhaften Sprechens, durch rituelle, für jedermann sichtbare Handlungen und auch durch im weitesten Sinne musikalische Pointierung und Ausgestaltung von Gesprochenem und ritueller Handlung, wobei die Distanz zum Vermittelten niemals aufgehoben wird. Informelles, Erbauliches und emotional Reizendes sind in diesem Bezirk vereinigt.

In den Anfängen des Theaters löste sich aus dem Chor ein einzelner ab, um mit dem Chor in einen Dialog zu treten. Mit dieser Abspaltung eines einzelnen aus dem Allgemeinen war der entscheidende Schritt zur Säkularisierung des Mediums getan, wiewohl das Theater noch lange unmittelbar im kultisch-religiösen Bezirk verblieb und sicherlich bis zum heutigen Tag diesem Bezirk nicht entraten ist und wohl nie ganz entraten kann.

Mit der Gegenrede des einzelnen gegenüber dem Chor findet eine erste Thematisierung des Verhältnisses vom einzelnen zum Medium, freilich noch im Medium selbst, statt. Der einzelne hat sich noch nicht selbst bestimmt, aber er hat erstmals in öffentlichem, medialem Rahmen Position bezogen. Es gibt von nun an in diesem Rahmen ein Identifikationsobjekt, zwar noch ohne ausgeprägte individuelle Züge, aber ein erster Schritt zur medialen Selbstfindung, zur Definition des Selbst über das Medium ist getan. Der einzelne, der sich dort gegen die und mit der Allgemeinheit artikuliert, ist mir nahe, weil er sich wie der Rezipient gegen und mit dem Allgemeinen behaupten muß. Diese Nähe überbrückt aber niemals die grundsätzliche Distanz zwischen dem medialen Bezirk (dem exponierten Platz, der Szene und dem Geschehen dort), und dem medial Angesprochenen.

Fassen wir damit zusammen, was die wesentlichen Momente eines Mediums sind, wobei Abstand genommen wird von der traditionellen Scheidung von ideellen und materiellen Momenten, da diese Scheidung bei genauerer Betrachtung mehr zur Verwirrung beiträgt, als sie Einsichten vermittelt. Die materielle Seite impliziert freilich schon Ideelles, die ideelle schon Materielles. Es gibt kein Medium ohne Materialität, ebensowenig eines ohne formende, d.h. ideelle Komponenten.Das Medium läßt sich also folgendermaßen charakterisieren:

a) es transzendiert die räumliche und zeitliche Gebundenheit des unmittelbaren Erfahrens;

b) es versammelt, stellt im medialen Ort eine Öffentlichkeit her; d.h. das Medium löst einerseits Örtlichkeit und Zeitlichkeit eines unmittelbar Gegebenen auf, stellt andererseits aber gerade Ort und Zeit für eine Öffentlichkeit her;

c) es vermittelt Abwesendes, allerdings nicht als es selbst; d.h. die Gegenwart des Abwesenden kann nur durch die Gegenwart eines Dritten gesichert werden. Wir können den Sachverhalt auch in logischen Termini ausdrücken. In medialen Verhältnissen wird der Identitätssatz an eine Bedingung geknüpft: A = A wenn B;

d) es schafft und bestätigt eine unüberwindbare Distanz zum Abwesenden, die unabhängig zur Nähe des Vermittelten bestehen bleibt; also auch das perfekteste Medium gibt uns nicht die Sache selbst[2]; wobei freilich das mediale Phänomen selbst zur Sache werden kann, beispielsweise bei der Betrachtung von Images;

e) es artikuliert eine Position zum Abwesenden und eine Position des Rezipienten zum Abwesenden; die Position wird im ersten Falle durch den konkreten Ort des Mediums zum Ausdruck gebracht, der die Präsentation des Abwesenden ermöglicht: Das Abwesende wird uns über eine konkrete Szene, ein konkretes Blatt, einen konkreten Bildschirm usw. vermittelt; im zweiten Fall wird die Position zum einen durch die leibliche Position und zum anderen durch die jeweilige soziale und historische Position des Rezipienten zum Medium in seiner Artikulation via Bildschirm, Lautsprecher, Textseite usw. bestimmt. D.h. mein Leib muß in irgendeiner Weise an das Medium „angeschlossen" sein.[3] Ich erfahre das Abwesende nur durch die relative Nähe eines Bildschirmes etc.;

f) es hält Abwesendes als Information verfügbar, speichert also, hält fest oder verzögert den Informationsfluß; dies geschieht durch unterschiedlichste Transformationen, durch Stilisierungen und besondere Einbettungen. Das Abwesende als Information zeichnet sich durch eine Art konservierende Präparation aus, wobei als die Urform der Konservierung die geformte Sprache gelten kann, die eine Mitteilung merk- und tradierbar macht;

g) es inszeniert das Vermittelte; d.h. das Vermittelte wird in eine Szene, ein Blickfeld gesetzt, es wird in einen bestimmten Brennpunkt gerückt, in welchem es erfaßt werden kann. Dieser Brennpunkt hängt von der Einrichtung des Mediums ab. Alles Vermittelte erscheint uns also in einem bestimmten szenischen Horizont in einer durch die „Szenerie" bestimmten Formierung;

h) es stellt eine besondere Weise der Nähe her; nicht im Sinne der natürlichen, alltäglichen Weltaneignung im Mesobereich, sondern eine Nähe, die bedingt ist durch Aufhebung von Raum- und Zeitdistanzen und weitgehender Aufhebung eigener kinästhetischer und lokomotorischer Weltaneignungstätigkeit;

i) es schafft Bedeutung. Bedeutungsverleihung ist eine verstehende, einordnende Leistung. Das Medium schafft Bedeutung, indem es einen Sachverhalt in einen bestimmten Verweisungszusammenhang setzt. Bedeutung wird durch Zuweisung und Einordnung hergestellt; dies gilt für die alltäglichen bedeutungsverleihenden Akte, die sich etwa in der Rede artikulieren, dies gilt ebenso in medialem Sinne: das Medium gibt bereits eine bestimmte Hierarchie vor, in der die vermittelte Sache überhaupt erst in Erscheinung tritt.

In dem so gespannten Koordinatennetz, aus dem Medien wie Engel und Propheten ebenso herausfallen wie Brillen und Fernrohre, erscheint ein Medium nie als neutrale Gegebenheit, sondern als aus einem konkreten historischen und kulturellen Bedürfnis heraus entstanden und in einer konkreten historischen und kulturellen Situation eingerichtet. Es richtet sich in seiner Entwicklung jeweils gegen ein Ungenügen an den bestehenden Medien: Die Schrift überwand die zeitliche und räumliche Gebundenheit der Rede, die elektronischen Medien überwanden die relative Trägheit der Druckmedien; die visuellen Medien überwanden das Ungenügen an der Abstraktheit der Schrift.[4]

Auch wenn ein neues Medium das alte nicht völlig verdrängt, so verändert es Sinn und Charakter des alten. Das alte Medium lebt oftmals nur noch in einer Nische weiter und erhält dort einen neuen auratischen Wert. So ist das klassische Druckhandwerk heute zum Kunsthandwerk geworden. Ungewöhnliche Drucke dienen heute kaum mehr der Informationsvermittlung im engeren Sinne, sondern rein ästhetischen Zwecken. Der Text hilft die künstlerische Intention des Druckers zu realisieren, er ist Mittel zum ästhetischen Zweck, nicht umgekehrt.

Mediale Veränderungen lassen sich tendenziell in folgenden Punkten fassen:

a) Verbesserung der Speicherkapazität;

b) Vermehrung der Breiten- bzw. Öffentlichkeitswirkung;

c) Erhöhung der Verbreitungs- bzw. Übertragungsgeschwindigkeit;

d) Verstärkung der Rezeptionsintensität;

e) Verbesserung der Steuerungsfunktionen, insbesondere durch Rückkoppelungs- und Interaktionstechniken.

Freilich müssen diese Tendenzen in einigen Punkten eingeschränkt werden. Eine Verstärkung der Rezeptionsintensität wird nicht uneingeschränkt angestrebt. Die Informationsquelle dient auch als Stimmungsmedium, d.h. Differenzierungen und Präzisierungen werden nicht generell angestrebt. Das Medium wird aus ökonomischen oder politischen Gründen so eingerichtet, daß es mehr das Unterbewußte als den Verstand anspricht, beispielsweise um bestimmte Bedürfnisse zu wecken oder assoziativ bestimmte Ressentiments aufzubauen. Den Verstand anzusprechen ist nicht unbedingt das primäre Ziel eines Mediums, ebensowenig wie der aufmerksame Rezipient die primäre Zielgruppe ist. Die Reduktion der begrifflichen Sprache zugunsten einer Bildersprache des Unbewußten ist eine deutliche Tendenz der Medienentwicklungen. Jochen Schulte-Sassen führt zu diesem Problem folgendes aus: „Medien bilden wie Diskurse Hierarchien, die nach hegemonialen Gesichtspunkten geordnet sind. Diese Medienhierarchie ordnet sich gegenwärtig um; das elektronische Medium ist dabei, das gedruckte Buch als hegemoniales abzulösen und die menschliche Subjektivität, die sich stets als vom hegemonialen

Medium abhängig gezeigt hat, umzustrukturieren. Konkret bedeutet das, daß die Elektronik die Rolle, die Images in öffentlicher Kommunikation spielen, neu bestimmt, und ihre marginale in eine zentrale Funktion transformiert. Deshalb werden nicht nur die Massenmedien und die Populärkunst, sondern auch die sogenannte hohe Kunst von den Images, die den öffentlichen Raum durchdringen und die menschliche Vorstellungskraft bestimmen, zutiefst betroffen. Die Images, die das menschliche Bewußtsein bestimmen, sind nach den Prinzipien einer Dramaturgie des Spektakels angeordnet, d.h. im Stil von emotional, sentimental und visuell aufgeladenen Vignetten, deren vager, fast austauschbarer *bewußter* Inhalt die ideologische Dimension solcher Vignetten verschleiert. Für die amerikanischen Fernsehnachrichten ist diese Dramaturgie weit konstitutiver als Analyse oder Information. Die Dramaturgie des Spektakels benutzt und vertraut kaum noch der Sprache um ihre Ziele zu erreichen. Dort wo sie vorherrscht, wird die Rolle der Wortsprache konstant auf eine untergeordnete Hilfsrolle reduziert - auf ein Medium, das für die Vermittlung bestimmter Minimalinformationen noch unabdingbar ist."[5]

2. Was transportieren Medien?

Die Antwort lautet: Information, was wenig besagt und so diffus bleibt, wie die Alltagsbegrifflichkeit nun einmal ist. Der gängige Gebrauch von Information schwankt zwischen dem inhaltlichen Verständnis von Nachricht und dem rein formalen Verständnis der Infomationstheorie, die Information als Maß für einen mittleren Informationsgehalt, also als quantifizierbare, statistische Größe, definiert.[6]

Informatio in der wörtlichsten Übersetzung als Einprägung erweist sich für unsere Fragestellung als sinnvollste Antwort. Medien sind Vermittlungsinstanzen. Zur Vermittlung benötigen sie nicht nur eine Öffentlichkeit, eine Präsentationsstätte für das Mitzuteilende und eine Transportkapazität, sondern freilich auch einen Inhalt. Was Medien transportieren, sind Bedeutungen, die auf eine Gegenständlichkeit oder einen Sachverhalt verweisen. Jenseits aller selbstbezüglichen Gegebenheiten verweist das Transportierte auf eine ursprünglichere außermediale Gegebenheit; dies häufig „aufgehalten" in einer medienintern vielfach gespiegelten Verweisungsstruktur. Der Film ist die Wirklichkeit selbst, aber er verweist selbst in der perfektesten Animation noch auf Schauspieler aus Fleisch und Blut, auf Örtlichkeiten und zeitliche Fixierungen, er verweist auf seine letztlich „handwerkliche" Realisation. Selbst die phantastischste Fiktion benötigt das authentisch Erfahrbare, wenn eine Vermittlung geleistet werden soll: Der Roboter redet wie Menschen reden, greift wie Menschen greifen und sieht wie Menschen sehen. Würden diese Vermittlungen vollkommen wegfallen, bewegten wir uns in einem Bereich des Unsinns oder des Unverständlichen.[7] Auch die phantastischste Fiktion lebt von der Analogie, vom Verweis auf konkret Erfahrbares. Ist dieser Verweis nicht mehr zu leisten, so gibt es nur noch die Möglichkeit, die Stanislav Lem in seiner Erzählung „Also sprach Golem" anbietet, nämlich das Schweigen.

Das Medium transportiert also etwas, was in es eingeprägt ist. Das ist bei der Schrift noch am ursprünglichsten zu verstehen, wenn wir an den Mythos vom Dekalog denken. Beim elektronischen Medium geschieht die Einprägung durch elektronische Kodierungen, beim klassischen Film durch einen chemischen Prozeß. Entscheidend aber ist, daß in jedem Medium durch „Einprägungen" Bedeutungen transportiert werden, die auf einen Gegenstand oder Sachverhalt verweisen, wobei Gegenstand bzw. Sachverhalt und seine Bedeutung nie identisch sind. Bedeutungen sind immer nur in einem Verweisungszusammenhang zu verstehen.[8] Das, was als Bedeutung transportiert wird, ist niemals neutral, und zwar in einem doppelten Sinne: Der Inhalt ist, bevor er medial transportiert wird, vorformiert, d.h. er ist nach bestimmten Kriterien gestaltet, nach narrativen etwa, nach Kriterien einer logischen Sondersprache oder musikalischer Gestaltung; d.h. weiterhin, jeder vermittelte Inhalt ist abgehoben von einem Nichtartikulierten. Um es im Sinne Derridas zu sagen: hinter der aktualisierten Schrift steht eine zweite Schrift, die niemals vollständig artikuliert werden kann. Das Gestaltete erscheint uns also als ein Ausgewähltes, nach Werthierarchien geordnetes, wobei auch Weisen der Unordnung, wie die Aleatorik, im Sinne eines Ordnungsprinzip aufgefaßt werden können.

Fassen wir zusammen: Alles, was Medien vermitteln, läßt sich durch folgende Momente charakterisieren:

a) das medial Vermittelte hat eine Bedeutung, die auf Außermediales verweist. Dies ist zu verstehen, einmal in dem Sinne, daß alle Vermittlung letztlich auf eine ursprünglichere Gegebenheit verweist; zum anderen in dem Sinne, daß alle Vermittlung auf etwas verweist, das aktuell im medial Gegebenen nicht völlig präsent ist. Das medial Gegebene ist also durch eine prinzipielle Inadäquatheit ausgezeichnet.

b) Das medial Vermittelte zeichnet sich durch eine vorausgehende Gestaltung aus, wobei diese Gestaltung bereits durch die Bedingungen des Mediums gefordert ist.

Jedes Medium hat seine eigene Transportkapazität. Wir können in einem Kleintransporter keinen Baukran transportieren, der Transport von Frischfleisch erfordert Kühlung, der von Eiern eine angemessene Federung. Kein Medium kann also das andere absolut ersetzen.

c) Das medial Vermittelte zeichnet sich durch eine besondere Bewertung aus.
D.h., es ist von technischen Erfordernissen, aber auch historisch-gesellschaftlich und subjektiv vorgeprägt. Der Filmbericht wird nach anderen Kriterien zusammengestellt als ein Zeitungsbericht; jeder Berichtstypus stößt auf unterschiedliche Rezeptionserwartungen. Hinzu treten innermediale Sonderkonzeptionen, die unterschiedliche Erwartungshaltungen erzeugen und bedienen. Die vorausgehende Bewertung des medial Vermittelten ist also nicht nur eine Bewertung nach Kriterien des Transports, sondern auch nach medialen Erwartungshaltungen oder Prägeabsichten.

d) Das medial Vermittelte zeichnet sich durch eine unauslöschliche Ferne aus.
Alles medial Gegebene kann von uns weder unmittelbar eingesehen, noch erzeugt werden. Das medial Vermittelte verweist letztlich auf eine unaufhebbare außermediale Ferne. Selbst die raffiniertesten Techniken, diese Ferne aufzuheben (Cyber-Space und seine pathologischen Derivate wie Cyber-Sex), stoßen an unüberwindbare Grenzen, nämlich, analog zum geträumten Raum, die Grenze einer unüberwindbaren Abgeschiedenheit des simulierten Raumes und die einer apperativen Abhängigkeit.

e) Das medial Vermittelte ist niemals das Zufällige, Kontingente.
Das Zufällige gibt es nur innerhalb eines medialen Arrangements. Indem es das Zufällige aus seiner konkreten Räumlichkeit und Zeitlichkeit löst, hat das Medium bereits eine Verdoppelung bzw. Wiederholung vorgenommen.

f) Das medial Vermittelte sind Informationen als Einprägungen in einem dreifachen Sinne:
I. Einprägung in den medialen Träger; II. Einprägung in Verstand, Unbewußtes oder Sinnlichkeit des Rezipienten, wobei nicht der intendierte Gegenstand oder Sachverhalt, sondern seine jeweilige Bedeutung eingeprägt wird; III. Einprägung auf den Informationsproduzenten selbst, denn er, sei er Journalist, Künstler oder Wissenschaftler, stößt immer schon auf bestehende mediale Bedingungen, die er selbst nicht geschaffen hat, steht in medialen Typologien und Rahmenbedingungen, die er zwar variieren, punktuell verändern, niemals aber in Gänze aufheben kann.

3. Was heißt Informationsvermittlung?

Anhand folgender Thesen soll die Frage erörtert werden:

a) Die Information über denselben Gegenstand bzw. Sachverhalt hat in verschiedenen Medien transportiert, auch verschiedene Bedeutung.

b) Jedes Medium liefert nicht nur die jeweilige Information, sondern auch einen bestimmten medialen Kontext, der auf die Rezeption der Information wirkt.

c) Das Medium vermittelt sich mit der Information immer auch selbst. Aus der Selbstvermittlung des Mediums ergibt sich, daß jedes Medium mit der Information auch eine Ideologie transportiert.

Jedes Medium hat seine eigenen Prämissen. So hat sich die Sprache des Fernsehens zu einer reduzierten Ergänzungssprache entwickelt. Das Bild soll sprechen und es spricht anders als das Wort. Es liefert im Gegensatz zum begrifflichen Medium etwas auf einen Schlag, appelliert zunächst an die Emotion. Wir kennen das berühmte Bild vom nackten Leichnam des amerikanischen Hubschrauberpiloten, der von einer rasenden Meute an einem Strick durch Mogadischu geschleift wird; und wir kennen die Wirkung dieses Bildes auf das öffentliche Bewußtsein. Als Lesende wissen wir aber auch, daß die Leiche nur dann durch die Straßen gezerrt wurde, wenn Kameras zugegen waren, daß also die Meute weit weniger raste als es vom Bild her den Anschein hat. Das entkontextualisierte, diskret gelieferte Bild ist ohne begriffliche Erläuterung nicht nur unverständlich, sondern ideal für jede Form des propagandistischen Mißbrauchs, denn es packt uns im Unterbewußten, ohne daß es den Sachverhalt erläutert. In Abwandlung von Kants berühmtem Wort, daß Anschauungen ohne Begriffe blind sind, kann man sagen, daß das entkontextualisierte Bild uns tatsächlich nichts „sehen" läßt.

Wir kennen zur Genüge propagandistische Absichten in der Bildberichterstattung: Ungeliebte Politiker werden in ungünstigen Situationen und Positionen abgelichtet. Was für das einzelne Bild gilt, gilt auch für den Film: daß die unterschiedliche Anordnung des Bildes, also die Bildmontage, unterschiedliche Wirkung erzielt, haben bereits die frühen Theoretiker der Montagetechnik dargelegt. Entscheidend ist, daß das einzelne Bild im visuellen Medium seinen Sinn durch den jeweiligen Kontext erhält. Dies gilt im Falle des Fernsehens auch für Programmstrukturen. Das Bild wirkt nicht nur in einem unmittelbaren Kontext. Die selben

Bilder in einer seriösen Nachrichtensendung bedeuten etwas völlig anderes als beim sogenannten Infotainment. Unterschiedliche Anordnungen der Nachrichten führen zu unterschiedlichen Einschätzungen ihrer Bedeutung. Jedes Medium ordnet seine Informationen nach eigenen Ordnungsprinzipien an. Das Schriftmedium erfordert eine gewisse Linearität und Diskursivität. Je komplexer der einzelne Texttypus ist, desto größer wird der Zwang zur Linearität der Anordnung. Beim visuellen Medium kann man, wie Schulte-Sasse ausführt, ein „Zerfallen logozentrierter narrativer Strukturen und neuartige Verschränkungen sprachlicher, visueller und musikalischer Elemente" feststellen, d.h. die Linearität des Schriftmediums ist zugunsten einer „nicht-narrativ fundierte(n) Assoziationslogik, die - wenn überhaupt - nur noch psychoanalytisch entwirrt werden kann", nahezu verschwunden.[9]

Es darf hier allerdings nicht vergessen werden, daß innermediale Ordnungsprinzipien gewaltig differieren und sich von Medium zu Medium stark annähren können. So stehen Boulevardkonzepte bei den Druckmedien gewissen Infotainment-Konzepten, die wir vom Fernsehen her kennen, näher als andere Konzeptionen innerhalb des eigenen Schriftmediums. Vor allem Text-Bild-Mischformen sprengen traditionelle mediale Ordnungsformen. Dennoch bleiben grundsätzliche Unterschiede zwischen den statischen und den bewegten medialen Formen, insofern bei letzteren die zeitliche Strukturierung des Mediums die entscheidende Rolle spielt.

Das Abwesende wird durch ein Medium in eine neue Ordnung gesetzt. In der Kunst ist das Herausnehmen von Einzelphänomenen aus seinem natürlichen Bewandtniszusammenhang, seine Einordnung in einen künstlichen Kontext ein wichtiges Gestaltungsmittel. Das Zitat, die Montage, das Arrangieren von bereits Gestaltetem, all das sind Methoden, durch Neukontextualisierung den Sinn eines Einzelphänomens zu verändern. Die „Schrift" ist selbst zur Botschaft in einem mythologischen Sinn geworden. Es geht nicht nur um die Bedeutung der schriftlichen Zeichen, sondern um das Medium selbst. Die Schrift verkörperte lange die entscheidende Wahrheitsmatrize und Orientierungsgröße für menschliches Verhalten. Das Fixierte als das Wiederholbare, Überprüfbare und Verweilende ist mehr als das flüchtig Dahingesprochene, mehr als das verklingende Wort. Darüber hinaus bindet die Schrift den Inhalt erst ein, legt ihn im Diskurs an, d.h., sie erläutert ihn, macht ihn verstehbar, macht Rätsel lösbar und legt die einzelne Bedeutung in einer Verweisung auf weitere schriftliche Äußerungen an.

Neil Postman versucht nachzuweisen, daß Medien eine bestimmte Epistemologie hervorbringen.[10] Jedes Medium liefert also auch die Wahrheitsmatrize, nach der Informationen zu beurteilen sind. Dies heißt für die Gegenwart, in der die visuellen Medien Leitmedium geworden sind, daß alle Wahrheit an die Oberfläche gerutscht ist. Die Kamera ist Auge Gottes geworden, dem nichts verborgen bleibt. Das Wort ist obsolet geworden. Photographische Darstellungen werden im allgemeinen Bewußtsein eher als Wirklichkeitsbeleg akzeptiert als begriffliche Analysen von Sachverhalten. Der ungläubige Thomas ist eine neue Variante des Gläubigen geworden.

Thomas J. Froehlich hat für computerbasierte Informationsmedien nachgewiesen, daß sie ihre eigene Unwahrheiten erzeugende Ideologie befördert: "Not only are such systems non-neutral, they support an ideology that has utilitarism at its roots. (...) The ideology also spreads some lies: that technology serves values but does not create them. Technology is always already an embodiment of a set of values both in its practice and in its nature, and further applications inculcate and foster these values."[11]

Die jüngsten welthistorischen Ereignisse des Zusammenbruchs der Länder des real existierenden Sozialismus konnte man auch als den Niedergang einer „anachronistischen" Ideologie des Schriftmediums begreifen. Die „Schrift", konkret die Marx-Engels Gesamtausgabe und ihre jeweiligen Exegesen, waren die zentrale Bezugsgröße der Kultur. Es bestand eine Nomenklatur, die durch die Semantik und Rhetorik des herrschenden Parteiapparates in der Auseinandersetzung mit der „Schrift" bestimmt wurde. So hohl diese Semantik und Rhetorik auch gewesen sein mag, sie ordnete tatsächlich die Gesellschaft, verlieh ihr eine gewisse Stabilität, eine Werthierarchie und dem einzelnen eine gewisse Sicherheit. Die alte Nomenklatur ist inzwischen verschwunden, aber es ist keine neue an die Stelle der alten getreten, denn die „Nomenklatur" der westlichen Welt ist keine der Semantik mehr, sondern eine der Matrizen und Phantome, der Hülsen und des Designs. Gerade weil sie nicht mehr semantisch ist, läßt sie den Menschen in Unsicherheit und weitgehender Orientierungslosigkeit zurück, denn es ist immer nur das träge Wort, das Sicherheit verleiht, wenn auch eine trügerische. Der Untergang der alten Kulturen des real existierenden Sozialismus kann auch - wenn freilich nicht ausschließlich - als eine medial bedingte kollektive Glaubenskrise interpretiert werden. Die Schrift, der herrschende begriffliche Diskurs, hatte als Wahrheitsmatrize endgültig an Geltung verloren.

4. Wie wird mit Medien und ihren Informationen umgegangen?

Der Umgang mit dem Informationsträger kreist zwischen zwei extremen Positionen:

A) Das Medium wird in seinem materiellen bzw. technischen Bestand als ästhetisches Objekt aufgefaßt. Das Buch gilt von seinen Anfängen an auch als Sammelobjekt. Ausstattung und Machart des Buches unterstreichen den ideellen Wert desselben. Auch bei modernen Informationsträgern spielt v.a. im außerberuflichen Gebrauch die Ästhetik eine immer bedeutendere Rolle. Fernsehgerät, HiFi-Anlage wie PC sollen sich dem Ambiente anpassen und individuellen Stil artikulieren.

B) Der Informationsträger verschwindet hinter seiner Funktion, das Medium bleibt unsichtbar, wird zum Nichtobjekt.

Zwischen diesen beiden Positionen liegen die tatsächlichen Umgangsmodi, die so charakterisiert werden können:

I) Das Moment des technischen Umgangs mit dem Medium. D.h., der materielle und intellektuelle Bestand des Mediums muß technisch beherrscht werden; genauer, es muß die jeweils notwendige Kulturtechnik, die den Umgang mit dem Medium ermöglicht, beherrscht werden.

II) Das Moment des nutzenden Umgangs mit dem Medium. Das Medium steht in einem alltagspraktischen Horizont: es wird für eine konkrete Problemlösung in Beruf oder Privatleben genutzt.

III) Das Moment des genießenden Umgangs mit dem Medium. Das Medium ist Regenarationshilfe im besten und Suchtmittel im übelsten Sinne.

In der Praxis lassen sich die beiden letzten Momente oft kaum mehr unterscheiden: Ich lese einen Roman, der in einem fremden Land spielt, nicht nur zur Unterhaltung, sondern auch, weil ich Geschäftsbeziehungen zu diesem Land aufbauen und dessen Sitten und Kultur kennenlernen möchte. Ich spiele ein Computerspiel, nicht weil es mich in besonderer Weise unterhält, sondern weil ich als Sozialpädagoge Einblicke in die Lebenswelt von Jugendlichen erhalten möchte. Auch bestimmte Sendekonzeptionen beim Fernsehen (Infotainment, Reality-TV etc.) versuchen diese Scheidung bewußt aufzuweichen.

Der Umgang mit Informationen ist niemals unabhängig vom Medium. Es geht nicht nur um die Frage, wie ich ein Medium nutze, sondern auch darum, wie sich ein Medium nutzen läßt. Eine Information ist nichts jenseits ihrer medialen Einbindung und hierarchischen Einordnung. Ihr Wert hängt von dieser Einordnung ab und steht in einem problematischen Verhältnis zur Menge der mit ihr angebotenen Informationen. Hans Sachsse schreibt: "Die Werte von Informationsmengen gehorchen keiner additiven Beziehung. Zusätzliche Information kann den Wert der bereits vorhandenen stark steigern, indem sie ihr erst „Bedeutung verleiht", aber sie kann die vorhandene auch entwerten. Bekanntlich gelingt der Informationstheorie die Definition einer Maßeinheit für den Informationsgehalt überhaupt nur dadurch, daß sie zuvor von der semantischen Seite der Information, d.h. von ihrer Bedeutung, ihrem Wert für Subjekte abstrahiert. (...) Der ständige Kritik- und Revisionsdruck eines Überangebots pluralistischer, sich widersprechender Informationen läßt es aber nicht mehr zur Bildung von Maßstäben kommen und zerstört die vorhandenen. Entscheidend ist, daß es für den einzelnen gar nicht auf die Menge der Information ankommt, sondern auf die Ordnung."[12]

Die Einbindung der Informationen in das jeweilige Medium hat unmittelbaren Einfluß auf die Umgangsweise mit ihm. Es gibt Medien, die eine höhere Rezeptionsintensität propagieren als andere, es gibt solche, die einen nutzenden und solche, die einen genießenden Umgang propagieren. Natürlich sind die genannten Momente in jedem Medium auszumachen, allerdings, durch die Ideologie des jeweiligen Mediums bedingt, in unterschiedlicher Gewichtung. Freilich ist das Lesen von stereotyp konzipierten Groschenromanen eine weit weniger anspruchsvolle Tätigkeit als das Sehen eines Bergman-Filmes, freilich läßt sich zwischen der Rezeption eines Boulevardblattes und der einer Infotainment-Sendung kein wesentlicher Unterschied ausmachen, aber dennoch ist die Behauptung, daß die unterschiedliche Bewertung von Medien letztlich nur in bildungsbürgerlichen Vorurteilen und konservativen Fortschrittsängsten liegt, nicht nur falsch, sondern selbst Produkt einer ideologischen Engsicht: Es ist eben nicht so, daß eine Information unabhängig von ihrem medialen Träger ist, daß man Informationen ohne Veränderung ihres Sinnes in ein anderes Medium übertragen kann und daß der mediale Fortschritt eine Verbesserung des gesellschaftlichen Informationsstandes und ein Mehr an informeller Freiheit bewirkten.

Zuletzt soll eine Umgangsweise erwähnt werden, die mit Informationsvermittlung eigentlich wenig zu tun hat, aber in der gegenwärtigen Diskussion eine wichtige Rolle spielt. Es geht um die Idee des *Hypermediums*, in dem die traditionellen Medien in einem elektronischen und digitalisierten Raum von an sich bedeutungslosen Informationen zusammengeschlossen sind, wobei die alten Medien als, wie Norbert Bolz sagt, „metaphorische Navigationshilfen"[13] benutzt werden. Einen Außenbezug dieses hypermedialen Raumes gibt es nicht mehr, alles was an Austausch noch bleibt, wird auf einer Benutzeroberfläche integriert, die Verweisungen nur innerhalb des medialen Raumes zuläßt. „Der Mensch", sagt Bolz, ist hier „nicht mehr Werkzeugbenutzer, sondern Schaltmoment im Medienverbund"[14] Das Medium ist also in dieser Konzeption nicht mehr um irgendeiner Vermittlung, irgendeiner Mitteilung willen da, der Mensch wird nur noch als ein Schaltmoment benötigt, das wahrscheinlich aus nostalgischen Gründen noch nicht substituiert worden ist. Der Begriff des Mediums müßte in diesem Schaltraum streng genommen revidiert werden. Bolz nimmt diese Revision in der Zuflucht in eine Paradoxie vor, die zwar die Sachlage nicht unbedingt erhellt, aber doch eine diskussionswürdige Beschreibung einer äußersten Möglichkeit des Umgangs mit dem Medium, sozusagen als „Nichtumgang", bietet:"Was heißt dann aber überhaupt „Medium" angesichts der nicht zielgerichteten, *intransitiven* Struktur der Massenkommunikation? Zugespitzt formuliert: Massenmedien vermitteln nicht; sie schließen Antwort und Reziprozität aus. So gilt der paradoxe Satz: Massenkommunikation fabriziert Nicht-Kommunikation. Daß innerhalb ihrer intransitiven Struktur Rituale von Scheinreziprozität inszeniert werden, scheint die Zuschauer heute nicht mehr zu beirren. Illusionslos konsumieren sie die Scheinkommunikation der Massenmedien als Chance der Bedeutungsverschonung.

Die virtuelle Realität der elektronischen Gemeinschaft tritt nun nicht einfach in Konkurrenz zur bürgerlichen Öffentlichkeit, sondern schließt sie aus. Der politische Raum schrumpft zum telematischen Netz. Wo Glasfaserkabel liegen, gibt es kein Forum mehr. Denn wer sich überhaupt informieren will, muß an den Kanalausgängen sitzen, also zu Hause. Wer statt dessen traditionelle Öffentlichkeit herstellen will, läuft Gefahr, die neuesten Nachrichten zu verpassen. Nicht mehr Textzeilen, Bücher und Gegenrede, sondern ausstrahlende Flächen, Bildschirme am „Ende" des Datenflusses bestimmen den gesellschaftlichen Diskurs. Mitteilungen der neuen Medien, vor allem der Massenmedien, sind nur Abfallprodukte ihrer Selbstorganisation. Wichtiger als das, was mitgeteilt wird, scheint das *Daß* der Kommunikation, in dem sich das Mediensystem selbst reproduziert. In diesem Zusammenhang kann man die technische Medialisierung als Verlust erfahren - daß wir kein Gespräch mehr sind. Aber sie steigert die Anschlußfähigkeit der Kommunikationen. Gerade die neuen Medien stellen sicher, daß Kommunikationen laufen, auch wenn man sich nichts zu sagen hat. Technisch medialisierte Kommunikation hat also eine Doppelfunktion:

– sie ist der Selbsterreger der Gesellschaft; und

– sie konstruiert deren Realität.[15]

Es muß nicht ausdrücklich darauf hingewiesen werden, daß bei Bolz' Ausführungen verschiedene Begriffe nur noch in einem metaphorischen Sinne verstanden werden können: von Nachricht, von Kommunikation, von Mitteilung kann in einem traditionellen Sinne keine Rede mehr sein. Dieser Einbruch des Metaphorischen scheint nicht grundlos ein wesentliches Charakteristikum der gegenwärtigen Diskussion von Medien zu sein.

5. Wie bestimmt sich der Mensch gegenüber dem Medium?

Der Mensch hat sich von seinen Anfängen an wesentlich über Medien bestimmt. Vermittelnde Instanzen waren Engel und Propheten; Jesus ist im christlichen Verständnis der mediator katexochen. Das durch sie Vermittelte schafft Distanz und eine besondere Wertbeziehung: das Abwesende ist das Eigentliche, Authentische, ist die Sache selbst. Immerhin hat das Vermittelte Anteil an diesem Absoluten. So galt das Geschriebene als das Wahrste des Diesseitigen.

Medien standen schon immer im Dienst sittlicher Prägung, von der erzieherischen und psychohygienischen Aufgabe des antiken Theaters bis zum bewußtseinsformierenden Einsatz des Filmes in der frühen Sowjetunion. In der Frühzeit des Fernsehens wurde angenommen, daß das Fernsehen zerfallende Familienstrukturen kitten oder einen wesentlichen Beitrag für die politische Bildung der Bürger leisten könnte. Als das Fenster zur Welt wurde das Fernsehen bezeichnet, sogar als Bollwerk gegen eine zunehmende Privatisierung, was uns heute geradezu absurd anmutet.[16]

Daß die Bestimmung des Verhältnisses gegenüber dem Medium zugleich eine Weise der menschlichen Selbstbestimmung ist, belegt Efraim Shmuelis Studie „Seven Jewish Cultures - A Reinterpretation of Jewish History and Thought"[17], in der aufgezeigt wird, wie sich die sieben wesentlichen jüdischen Kulturkreise, von der biblischen bis zur nationalisraelischen Kultur der Gegenwart, letztlich anhand der Auseinandersetzung mit und der Selbstbestimmung durch die Schrift bestimmen. Für Ernst Cassirer wird die Welt durch

Medienmetaphern erschlossen und gegliedert. Kultur wird insofern selbst zum Medium, kulturelle Äußerungen zu medialen Äußerungen, Kulturgeschichte zur Mediengeschichte. Nennen wir die wesentlichen Charakteristika der medialen Selbstbestimmung des Menschen. Der Mensch bestimmt sich:

a) als dem Medium unterstelltes Wesen.
Der Mensch ist der Schrift, aber auch den digitalen elektronischen Medien unterstellt; d.h., er ist den Medien Rechenschaft und Respekt schuldig, muß sich ihnen gegenüber verantworten, steht in ihrer Schuld. Medien verweisen auf Transzendentes, auf Allgegenwart und Gleichzeitigkeit, auf höheres, authentischeres Sein, ja haben wie Engel und Propheten sogar Anteil daran.

b) als dem Medium angeschlossenes Wesen.
Der Mensch ist an die mittelbare Welt angeschlossen. Jenseits dieses Anschlusses ist er außerhalb der Gemeinschaft; in gewisser Hinsicht sogar außer sich, insofern er unvermittelt ein geschichtsloses Wesen ist.

Über das Medium ist der Mensch an die Öffentlichkeit angeschlossen, d.h. erst über das Medium wird er zur öffentlichen Person. Das Medium darf aber nicht mit der Öffentlichkeit selbst verwechselt werden, denn letztere ist nur ein medialer Effekt. Aber die Öffentlichkeit unterstellt sich zunehmend dem Leitmedium und erfährt durch dieses eine bestimmte Strukturierung und Hierarchisierung.

c) als vom Medium abhängiges Wesen.
Abhängig ist der Mensch von Medien in informeller Hinsicht. Sogar die Funktionstüchtigkeit seines Leibes wird in der Medizin zunehmend von einer informellen Apparatur garantiert. Ohne massive mediale Unterstützung ist das Leben in einer hochkomplexen und hochtechnisierten Gesellschaft nicht zu bewältigen.

Als medial abhängig erweist sich der Mensch aber auch in sozialpsychologischer Hinsicht. Mitmenschlicher Austausch hat sich längst auf mediale Bedingtheiten eingelassen. Telephon und Fernsehgerät werden zum „Bollwerk" gegen Vereinsamung. Daß die mediale Inszenierung des menschlichen Miteinanders auch einen Verlust an Nähe anzeigt, muß nicht ausdrücklich betont werden. Mit einem gewissen Recht läßt sich behaupten, daß die mediale Selbstreflexion und Selbstdefinition zur Existentialontologie der Gegenwart geworden ist.

d) als informell defizitär bestimmtes Wesen.
Das Medium ist der Verweis auf das Ganze, es ist die Fülle des informell Zugänglichen. Der Mensch hat gegenüber dem Medium ein informelles Defizit. Der medialen Selbstbestimmung des Menschen geht aber eine andere Selbstbestimmung voraus. Das Medium bestimmt sich in einem historischen Prozeß auch selbst, d.h. es wird eingerichtet, wobei die Einrichtung den an sich offenen medialen Raum einschränkt. Jeder faktische Gebrauch eines Mediums ist zugleich seine Einschränkung. Das Medium wird zur selektiven Kraft, es transportiert, was seiner Transport- und Speicherkapazität angemessen ist. Dabei bleibt es an einen sozialen Ort gebunden. Dies ist einmal in einem ganz konkreten und ursprünglichen Sinne zu verstehen. Die Schriftgelehrten waren diejenigen, die über ein bestimmtes Medium verfügen konnten. Sie engten den Gebrauch des Mediums ein, wobei der Nutzen dieser Einschränkung nicht bestritten werden kann. Der Wert der Information hängt ja unmittelbar mit der Einschränkung ihres Gebrauchs zusammen. Diese Tatsache schränkt auch die Rede von hypermedialen Räumen oder virtuellen (Informations-) Welten ein, die einen vollkommen freien Datenaustausch und einen vollkommenen Anschluß an die Welt der Informationen suggerieren. Weder ist ein vollkommen freier Datenaustausch möglich, noch ein vollkommener Anschluß an die Welt der Information, es sei denn man meint damit den Anschluß an eine „bedeutungslose" Welt, denn Bedeutung wird erst durch Einschränkung gewonnen. Ähnlich wie die Arbeit der klassischen Schriftgelehrten ist auch die moderner Informationsfachleute einzuschätzen: Die Effizienz ihrer Tätigkeit hängt wesentlich von der Fähigkeit ab, den Gebrauch des jeweiligen Informationsmediums einzuschränken.

Doch auch in einem anderen Sinn kann vom Verbleiben des Mediums am sozialen Ort gesprochen werden: Massen- und Fachinformation klaffen heute wieder besonders weit auseinander, weil Fachinformationen zu einem ökonomisch lukrativen Gut geworden sind, die nur in eingeschränkter Weise öffentlich gemacht werden.

Zwar lassen sich moderne Massenmedien an jedem sozialen Ort finden, die Verfügbarkeit eines Fernsehgerätes in nahezu jedem Haushalt besagt aber keineswegs, daß dieses Medium von jeglicher sozialen Bindung unabhängig ist. Dieses Mißverständnis entsteht, wenn man die Verfügbarkeit der bloßen Materialität eines Mediums mit der Verfügungsgewalt über ein Medium verwechselt. Der Umgang mit schwierigen Texten muß in einer entsprechenden Sozialisation erlernt sein. Das Eindringen in bestimmte Bildwelten ist abhängig von der Schulung der Sehgewohnheiten.

Der Mensch bestimmt sich also gegenüber einem Medium, das sich bereits historisch bestimmt hat, d.h. die mediale Selbstbestimmung ist nicht absolut frei, sondern von der bereits vollzogenen Einrichtung des Mediums geprägt.

6. Wie verändert sich die Information durch das Medium?

Als Beispiel der Informationsveränderung soll die filmische Literaturadaption dienen. Der Film versinnlicht. Aus Begriffen werden Bilder. Die Bildanordnung löst den begrifflich-diskursiven Aufbau der Schrift zugunsten assoziativer Muster auf. Das assoziative Muster hölt die begriffliche Präzision aus, schafft aber neue Konnotationen. Wissenschaftlich können Sachverhalte nur begrifflich-diskursiv aufgearbeitet werden, denn Wissenschaft definiert sich wesentlich durch einen Exaktheits- und Allgemeingültigkeitsanspruch. Das Bild bleibt an das Kontingente gebunden, die Schrift entfernt sich davon. Dies ist das entscheidende Problem der filmischen Literaturadaption: Der Leser entwirft sich das Bild seines Protagonisten im Kopf, der Regisseur muß sich für einen Darsteller des Protagonisten entscheiden.

Die Hierarchien der Schrift und die des Bildes lassen sich grundsätzlich nicht zur Deckung bringen. Das Bild ist immer mehr als seine begriffliche Aufarbeitung, aber die begriffliche Aufarbeitung macht das Bild erst verständlich.

Beim Informationstransfer wird die Information in einen anderen Verstehensbezirk gesetzt. Der Informationsgehalt unterliegt so unterschiedlichen Einfärbungen: Die gleiche Geschichte, einmal im Gefängnis, einmal in einer Schulklasse und einmal im Kloster erzählt, ist nicht die gleiche Geschichte.

Aber nicht nur die örtliche, auch die zeitliche Positionierung führt zu Bedeutungsveränderungen. Dieselbe Geschichte am gleichen Ort denselben Menschen erzählt, ist nicht dieselbe, wenn sie zu verschiedenen Zeiten erzählt wird. Die Rezipienten haben sich in der Zwischenzeit verändert, erfahren manches intensiver, manches langweilt sie bei der Wiederholung, manches entdecken sie neu.

Jedes Medium hat in seiner Einrichtung konstante und variable Momente. Dabei sind nicht die materiellen Momente als die konstanten und die ideellen, inhaltlichen als die variablen anzusehen. Das Medium verändert sich tatsächlich mit einer bestimmten inhaltlichen Formierung auch materiell. Als Beispiel kann hier Peter Greenaways Shakespeare-Adaption „Prosperos Bücher" dienen, wo die inhaltliche Gestaltung des Filmes die Integration moderner Videotechniken in die filmische Konzeption erforderte.

Die konstanten Momente reduzieren sich zuletzt auf die Zugänge zum Medium. Die visuellen Medien benötigen immer eine Projektionsfläche bzw. einen Projektionsraum für das Bild. Gleich ob mir das Bild über eine Bildplatte, ein Videoband oder einen Film vermittelt wird, der Zugang zum Medium geschieht über die Projektionsfläche. Und selbst die unmittelbare Projektion des Bildes auf die Netzhaut würde letztere zur Projektionsfläche machen.

Variabel erscheinen dagegen die inhaltlichen Momente, sowie die jeweilige technische Realisierung der Mitteilung. Der einzelne Informationsgehalt scheint also austauschbar zu sein, ohne daß sich das Medium substantiell verändert. Bei genauerem Hinsehen stellt sich der Sachverhalt allerdings anders dar: Das Medium ist inhaltlich durch ein bestimmtes historisch und gesellschaftlich erwachsenes Kategoriensystem, durch eine bestimmte Nomenklatur formiert, die den jeweiligen Verständnishorizont des Mediums absteckt. Durch eine bestimmte Typologie der Informationsanordnung werden Sehweisen und visuelle Erwartungshaltungen habitualisiert. Wenn sich moderne Actionfilme durch eine besonders hohe Zahl von Schnitten auszeichnen, so wird jedes weitere Genreprodukt an diesen Vorgaben angemessen.

Jedes Medium verliert durch seinen historisch bedingten Gebrauch an Offenheit. Hinzu treten ökonomische Bedingungen, die eine Entfernung der medialen Strukturierung von allgemeinen Erwartungshaltungen nicht zulassen.

Die Information verändert sich allerdings nicht nur durch den Transfer vom einen Medium ins andere, sie ändert sich auch innerhalb des jeweiligen Mediums durch den Einfluß des Leitmediums.

So hat unter dem Einfluß des Fernsehens das Begrifflich-Diskursive in weiten Bevölkerungskreisen an Dignität verloren. Man glaubt dem Bild eher als der Schrift. Das Wahre ist die perspektivische Sicht einer Oberfläche, nicht das, was sie abschließt, und auch nicht das kontextuale Ganze. Beides kann letztlich nur begrifflich-diskursiv erfaßt werden. Das Wahre ist das Jetzt, nicht dessen historische Vermittlung, die nur begrifflich geleistet werden. Wir sind, um es mit Günther Anders zu sagen, unter dem Einfluß des Fernsehens Jetztgenossen, nicht Zeitgenossen geworden.

Die Einrichtung des Leitmediums prägt auch die Informationsvermittlung der anderen Medien. Von der graphischen Gestaltung bis zu Artikulationsweisen lassen sich Veränderungen in der Schriftkultur feststellen. Alle Medien gleichen sich dem Leitmedium im Design an, d.h. sie verändern ihre Inhalte so, daß sie der Standardrezeption nahe kommen. Dies freilich sind Tendenzen, die Ausnahmen in der Entwicklung gewisser medialer Einzeltypen zulassen. So bleiben bestimmte mediale Typen in einem exklusiveren historisch-soziologischen Umfeld relativ stabil, wie die Formen der wissenschaftlichen Publizistik belegen.

Alte Medien gehen zwar nicht zugrunde, wenn ein neues Medium Leitmedium wird, aber sie verändern ihren Sinn.

Halten wir also fest, daß sich mit der Veränderung des jeweiligen Leitmediums auch die anderen Medien ändern, und daß sich auch die scheinbar medienspezifischen Inhalte der prägenden Wirkung des Leitmediums nicht entziehen können. Das Leitmedium entscheidet letztlich über den Zugang zur Information, d.h. wie die Information zu verstehen ist, denn das Leitmedium ist die Basis aller medialer Erschließungsweisen.

7. Wie beeinflußt das Medium das Verhalten des Menschen

Jedes Medium formt sich seinen Rezipienten. Das Medium ist kein neutraler Vermittler, keine Brille, kein Mikroskop oder Fernrohr, sondern etwas, das selbst Wirklichkeit schafft. Und es zeigt sich, daß es eine immer schwerer entscheidbare Frage ist, ob das Medium primär Wirklichkeit abbildet oder schafft; ob die Wirklichkeit inzwischen schon in weiten Bereichen ein Abklatsch der medialen Wirklichkeit ist.

Realität muß unter medialen Bedingungen anders bestimmt werden. Sind Faktizität, Kontingenz, Objektivität als Sein für jedermann, Transzendenz in Bezug auf ein individuelles Bewußtsein, und, wie Husserl es ausdrückt, die Idee eines idealen Korrelates „einer intersubjektiven und ideell immerfort einstimmig durchzuführenden und durchgeführten Erfahrung"[18] die wesentlichen Charakteristika von Realität, so können unter medialen Bedingungen Kategorien des Scheins Seinskategorien ersetzen. Realität kann im medialen Raum unmittelbar nicht erfahren werden. D.h. zum einen, daß uns der mediale Raum im Gegensatz zur unmittelbaren Realität die Freiheit zur Distanzierung beläßt. Vom Medium können wir uns abwenden, wir können das Fernsehgerät abschalten, können uns einer anderen Erscheinungsebene zuwenden, was uns in der außermedialen Realität nur eingeschränkt bzw. in Zuständen geistiger Entrückung gelingt. Andererseits wird unser praktisches Verhältnis zur Welt im medialen Raum aufgehoben. Wir müssen zur vermittelten Welt keine Stellung beziehen; in der medialen Haltung sind wir aller Verpflichtung und Schuld enthoben. Der mediale Schein beläßt uns letztlich in einer Welt der Unbetroffenheit.

Auf Abbé Galiani Bezug nehmend stellt Blumenberg diesen Sachverhalt so dar: "Erst nachdem den Zuschauern ihre sicheren Plätze angewiesen sind, kann sich vor ihnen das Schauspiel der Gefährdung des Menschen entfalten. Diese Spannung, diese Distanz kann nicht groß genug sein: *Je sicherer der Zuschauer dasitzt und je größer die Gefahr ist, die er sieht, um so mehr wird er sich für das Schauspiel erwärmen.*"[19] Dies hat fatale Folgen. Grundbedingung für jedes ethische Verhalten ist die Bestimmung der jeweiligen Realität, denn wenn ich in die Welt einwirken will, muß ich deren Realitätsgehalt bestimmen. Dies kann keine vollständige Bestimmung sein, aber situationsbezogen und lebensweltlich-relativ muß Realität bestimmt sein, wenn ich in sie einwirken will. Wie oft ist auf der Bühne schon Anouihls Beckett ermordet worden, ohne daß ein Theaterbesucher eingegriffen hätte. Und dennoch behauptet niemand, diese Zuschauer hätten unmoralisch gehandelt. Dagegen ist es üblich geworden, Passanten als Feiglinge und Voyeure zu bezichtigen, die untätig an einer Stelle vorbeigingen, an der gerade eine Frau zusammengeschlagen wurde, obgleich sie Stein und Bein darauf schwören, daß sie glaubten, es handelte sich wieder einmal um eine Szene mit versteckter Kamera oder eine andere gestellte Provokation. Und auch die Realistik eines solchen Vorfalls ist kein Indiz für seine Realität. Erscheint nicht gerade die filmische Bearbeitung der Realität als besonders realistisch, eben das Zerfetzen eines Leibes durch die Kugel in Zeitlupe?

Die medial vermittelte Welt erschließt sich in anderer Weise als die natürliche, die sich in räumliche Nähe und Ferne, und darauf aufbauend in Sinnähen und -fernen oder in Bewandtniszusammenhänge gliedert. Diese traditionelle Gliederung der Alltagswelt läßt sich in einer vernetzten Welt nicht mehr aufrecht erhalten. Ein Minister, der eine alte Frau via Bildschirm täglich im Altersheim besucht, steht ihr oft näher als ihr Sohn, den sie nur noch zu Ostern und Weihnachten sieht. Die Realitätsauffassung wird mit der zunehmenden „Programmvielfalt" subjektiver und uneinheitlicher. Verschiedene Sendeanstalten verbreiten verschiedene Weltbilder. Schwierig bis unmöglich wird auch die Scheidung von Original und Reproduktion. Nicht selten wurden wir mit Archivbildern über Ereignisse, die gerade stattgefunden haben sollen, getäuscht. Sind nun die medial erfahrenen Bilder Realität oder eben doch nur eine bestimmte Deutung derselben, oder sind sie gar eine eigene Weise der Realität, die unter Umständen auch die Täuschung real macht; ist es tatsächlich so, daß durch die Wiederholung, wie Anders meint, die Lüge wahr wird? Was man mit Sicherheit behaupten kann, ist eine eigenartige Durchmischung der Wirklichkeit, wobei der Bildschirm zunehmend die maßgebliche Wahrheitsmatritze wird. Es ist längst analog zu Canettis Kien ein Mensch vorstellbar, der die Realität dessen, was er draußen in der Welt erlebt, erst dann für belegt hält, wenn er sie am Bildschirm bestätigt findet.

Die Welt, die wir erfahren, ist eine medial durchmischte, in der Sekundärerfahrungen ins existenzielle Zentrum rücken. Medial inszenierte Betroffenheit wirkt nicht selten nachhaltiger als authentisch Erfahrenes. Die Welt wird mittelbarer und abstrakter trotz zunehmender bildlicher Konkretisierung; sie wird also medialer, verliert an Authentizität, gewinnt jedoch an Inszenierungsqualität.

Leider werden heute viele Diskussionen, ja sogar „wissenschaftliche" Studien über die Wirkung der Medien auf den Menschen aus durchsichtigen politischen oder ökonomischen Interessen, durch die Behauptung in ihrem Ergebnis unbrauchbar gemacht, daß sich kausale Zusammenhänge nicht feststellen ließen. Es wird so getan, als wenn sich in personalen Beziehungen je hätten Kausalitäten feststellen lassen. Der Begriff der Kausalität gehört jedoch allein in den Bereich naturwissenschaftlicher Betrachtung. In personalen Verhältnissen waltet niemals kausale Notwendigkeit, sehr wohl allerdings lassen sich Motivationsverhältnisse ausmachen, die ein Moment der Freiheit oder Unbestimmtheit implizieren. Wenn die Mutter eine drogenabhängige Prostituierte und der Vater ein gewalttätiger Zuhälter ist, dann ist die Wahrscheinlichkeit, daß das Kind auf die schiefe Bahn gerät, hoch, aber es liegt keineswegs eine kausale Notwendigkeit vor. Es geht also bei der Bestimmung der Wirkung von Medien auf den Menschen um Motivationsverhältnisse. Und diese zu bestreiten, würde im übrigen ganze Disziplinen wie die Soziologie und die Psychologie infrage stellen. Es mutet schon seltsam an, wenn Fernsehleute bestreiten, daß ihre Sendungen das Verhalten der Menschen beeinflussen, gleichzeitig aber um Werbepartner buhlen mit dem Hinweis, daß ein Werbespot in guter Positionierung das Kaufverhalten der Zuschauer enorm beeinflussen kann.

Jedes Medium ist in einem bestimmten Wertkontext gegeben. Es ist gesellschaftlich geformt und seinerseits formgebend für die Gesellschaft. Über den Wert eines Mediums ist, bevor es öffentlich genutzt wird, schon entschieden worden. Ob der dem Medium zugemessene Wert allgemein angenommen wird, ist eine andere Frage. Es muß nicht ausdrücklich betont werden, daß es immer die ökonomischen und politischen Nutznießer sind, die die Einführung eines Mediums propagieren.

Beschränken wir uns auf den Einfluß der dominierenden visuellen Medien auf das Verhalten des Menschen, wobei auch der Einfluß anderer Medien in abgrenzender Weise thematisiert wird. Es sollen in pointierter Weise Tendenzen aufgewiesen werden, die mitunter in unterschiedliche Richtung weisen. Doch Motivationsverhältnisse sind komplexer Art, die zwar nicht beliebig wirken, jedoch unterschiedliche Wirkrichtungen zulassen. Dabei darf nicht übersehen werden, daß das dargestellte Medium die benannte Wirkung nicht ohne außermediale Komponenten entfalten kann. Daß der kindliche und jugendliche Dauerfernseh- und -videokonsument an einer sozialen Vernachlässigung durch Eltern bzw. Erzieher leidet, daß Alte, deren Welterleben wesentlich in medialen Erlebnissen gründet, an Vereinsamung leiden, ist eine selbstverständliche Voraussetzung für bestimmte Prägungen. Natürlich sind Bildungsmängel, ökonomische Zwänge oder unbewältigte Lebenskrisen eine wesentliche Voraussetzung für einen drogenartigen Umgang mit Medien; und selbstverständlich trifft jede mediale Prägewirkung auf eine bestimmte gesellschaftliche Disposition des Rezipienten.

Andererseits muß auch gesagt werden, daß mediale Prägewirkungen durch soziale Komponenten zwar begünstigt werden, daß soziale Defizite aber nicht der alleinige Grund für mediale Prägungen sind. Medien wirken auch da, wo von sozialen Defiziten nichts Wesentliches auszumachen ist.

Bei der Frage, ob die Gesellschaft mehr das Medium prägt oder das Medium mehr die Gesellschaft, bewegen wir uns an der Grenze aporetischer Fragestellungen. Auch wenn die Einrichtung des Mediums durch Personen ökonomischer Potenz und technischer, publizistischer und künstlerischer Intelligenz erfolgt, so darf nicht übersehen werden, daß die mediale Apparatur eine Eigendynamik und u.U. eine eigene mythische Verselbständigung erfährt. Das einmal in die Welt gesetzte Medium erweitert zwar in bestimmter Hinsicht die Möglichkeiten des Nutzers, schränkt aber zugleich, wie alles Hergestellte, Möglichkeiten auch ein. Ist eine Gesellschaft erst einmal medial erschlossen, führt kein Weg der gesellschaftlichen Gestaltung und Selbstfindung mehr am Medium vorbei.

Die Standardisierung der Trivialliteratur erfordert den einfältigen Leser und bestärkt ihn in seiner Einfalt. Eine Angebotsverengung und Standardisierung von Programmstrukturen verengt auch die Typologien der Rezipienten. Das Medium schafft sich seinen Kunden. Unter keinem Umstand darf der Rezipient auf einen Geschmack gebracht werden, der die Programmstruktur und damit den ökonomischen oder politischen Zweck infrage stellt. Günther Anders spricht hier von einer Prägung der bereits Geprägten:"Immer ist der Konsument bereits vorvorbildet, immer schon vorbildbereit, immer schon matrizenreif; mehr oder minder entspricht er immer schon der Form, die ihm aufgeprägt werden wird. Jede einzelne Seele liegt der Matrize passend auf, gewissermaßen wie ein Tiefrelief einem ihm korrespondierenden Hochrelief; und so wenig der Matrizenstempel die Seele noch eigens „beeindruckt" oder gar in diese einschneidet, weil die Seele auf ihn bereits zugeschnitten ist; so wenig hinterläßt die Seele in der Matrize Spuren, da diese eben bereits gespurt ist. - Das Hin und Her zwischen Mensch und Welt vollzieht sich also als ein zwischen zwei Prägungen sich abspielendes Geschehen, als Bewegung zwischen der matrizengeprägten Wirklichkeit und dem matrizengeprägten Konsumenten."[20]

Diskussionen über Volksbildung oder Volksaufklärung durch das Leitmedium werden naserümpfend und unter dem allseits bekannten Zensurvorwurf gerade von denen abgetan, die maßgeblich das Volk „gebildet" und am rigorosesten erzogen haben. Aus der durchaus wünschenswerten Abklärung als Aufklärung über die Aufklärung ist eine Gegenaufklärung zur Sicherung bestimmter Ideologien und Machtansprüche geworden. Wenn aus Nachrichten Action News und aus Dokumentationen Reality-TV-Shows zur Befriedigung von Gaffbedürfnissen werden, hat sicherlich nicht die Freiheit des einzelnen gewonnen. Nachdem man dem Rezipienten systematisch jegliches intellektuelle Bedürfnis aberzogen hat, nachdem man ihn auf ein gaffendes Reizklümpchen reduziert hat, kann man ihn optimal mit dem bedienen, was im Interesse der die Anstalten unterhaltenden Geldgeber liegt. Wer Bildungs- und Erziehungsansprüche ablehnt, ist kein neutraler Befriediger des Publikumsgeschmacks, sondern ein bedingungsloser Befürworter kommerzieller Formierungen des Rezipienten. Eine Beförderung der Kritikfähigkeit liegt nicht im Interesse der Werbepartner, die längst nicht mehr auf Produktinformation setzen, sondern auf Stimmungserzeugung und Vernebelung des Gemüts. Der Kunde soll beim Gefühl gepackt werden, nicht beim Verstand, was ihm gut täte.

Kommen wir zu einigen Wirkungsaspekten des Leitmediums Fernsehen in seiner gegenwärtig dominierenden Gestaltung[21] und fragen im Anschluß, welche ethischen Konsequenzen sich daraus ergeben:

a) Zerstreutheit

Studien belegen, daß Kinder und Jugendliche, deren Fernseh- und Videokonsum überdurchschnittlich hoch ist, besonders stark zur Unkonzentriertheit neigen. Selbst die Zunahmen von Legasthenie als Scheinlegasthenie, insofern die eigentliche Krankheit nur selten vorkommt, wird in einen Zusammenhang mit extremem Fernsehkonsum gebracht. So taucht Legasthenie als extreme Konzentrationsschwäche besonders häufig bei Kindern von Alleinerziehenden oder aus sozialschwachen Familien auf, die einen hohen Fernsehkonsum haben. An Grundschulen laufen bereits Versuche, eine bestimmte Art von „Montagspädagogik" für fernsehgeschädigte Kinder einzurichten. D.h., daß die ersten beiden Stunden am Montag völlig der Aufarbeitung des Fernsehkonsums vom Wochenende dienen, zumal ein konzentriertes Arbeiten in diesen Stunden ohnehin nicht möglich ist. Die Gründe, warum die Zerstreutheit durch Fernsehen befördert wird, liegen wesentlich in bestimmten Gestaltungen des Mediums. Die sogenannte Diktatur der Geschwindigkeit[22], die Tatsache, daß sich die Form der Fernsehdramaturgie in den letzten Jahren in Richtung Temposteigerung verändert hat, befördert eine neue Form der Unduldsamkeit. Sendungen werden immer häufiger mit einer Fülle von Kurzbeiträgen aufgefüllt. Wie im Film haben sich auch in der Fernsehdramaturgie die Schnittfolgen erhöht, was zu einer schnelleren, aber auch oberflächlicheren Verarbeitung der Bilder zwingt. Eine reflexive Einholung des Geschehens ist kaum mehr möglich und seitens der Hersteller auch nicht angestrebt. Filmanalysen gewisser Actionfilme ergeben zuweilen einen unlogischen Aufbau der Filmhandlung und widersinnige Details, die wiederum nicht ins Gewicht fallen, weil das Detail ohnehin nicht mehr wahrgenommen wird und der Handlungsaufbau mehr oder weniger gleichgültig ist. Peter Sloterdijk sieht in seiner Betrachtung des modernen Actionfilms einen „Rückschritt vom Drama zur Aktion". Er schreibt: "Wer ins Kino geht, riskiert immer eine anthropologische Lektion, und wer Aktions-Kino liebt, ist eo ipso der Paläoanthropologie nahe, weil action (...) den lange vermißten Schlüssel zum Affe-Mensch-Übergangsfeld liefert. Ich gehe von der Beobachtung aus, daß die heutige Populärkultur einen Rückschritt vom Drama zur Aktion inszeniert: An die Stelle von interpersonalen Konflikten des hochkulturellen Dramentyps treten nun auf breiter Front interbestialische oder intermaschinelle action-Sequenzen. (...) Ich werde (...) zeigen, inwiefern auch solchen action-Szenen ein gewisser Bildungssinn zukommt - allerdings nicht im Sinne von Humanisierung, sondern von Hominisation. (...) Der moderne action-Film ist eine Gattung experimenteller Vor- und Frühgeschichtsschreibung, die mit den Mitteln avancierter Film-Technik die archäologischen Geheimnisse der Menschheit bearbeitet. Im action-Kino kommt ein Aspekt der Wahrheit über das menschheitsbildende Inaugural-Ereignis an den Tag, das man summarisch überschreiben könnte: die Sezession der Menschenhorden von der Alten Natur."[23] Man kann Sloterdijks Analysen für den Rezipienten durchaus im Sinne eines intellektuellen Regressionsprozesses interpretieren, denn der Paläanthropologie nahe sein und Paläanthropologie zu betreiben sind durchaus verschiedene Dinge. Das Aktionskino führt uns - und das bringen Sloterdijks weitere Ausführungen zu Tage - auf eine Stufe, in der der Mensch in gewisser Hinsicht auf Urinstinkte reduziert ist. Der Intellekt spielt in diesem „Affe-Mensch-Übergangsfeld" bestenfalls die Rolle eines Funkens, der die Möglichkeit des Redens von Menschsein zuläßt, aber noch lange nichts mit einer qualitativen Bestimmung des Menschseins zu schaffen hat. So benennt Sloterdijk Laufen und Schießen als Universalien des Aktions-Kinos und gleichzeitig als anthropologische Grundkategorien[24]. Ohne auf seine Analyse im einzelnen eingehen zu wollen, läßt sich festhalten, daß der Action-Film, der neben dem Videoclip für die entscheidenden Neuerungen in der visuellen Kultur gesorgt hat, in gewisser Hinsicht die visuelle Wahrnehmung im Sinne einer reinen Oberflächenwahrnehmung verändert hat. Bilder sind Lebensbeschleuniger geworden. Laufen, Ducken, Werfen sind ihre primäre Botschaft. Am Ende siegt die Geschwindigkeit: „Ich bin einsam, aber schneller", heißt das Motto des klassischen Westernhelden. Das Erfassen von weiten Spannungsbögen, von verwobenen Handlungsstrukturen und Wirkungen des Bildaufbaus, all das erfordert Kontemplation und Verstand, und all das läßt sich hier nicht finden.

Der zerstreute Mensch als Fernsehmensch springt zwischen diversen Weltorten hin und her, er ist nie bei sich selbst, insofern er keine Zeit hat, seinen Ort zum Mitgeteilten zu bestimmen. Er ist außer sich in jeder Beziehung. Ein Zu-sich-kommen würde einen horror vacui auslösen, weshalb eine möglichst andauernde Verstopfung der Sinne notwendig ist, nur sie garantiert seine Vermeidung. Günter Anders drückt dies so aus:"Wenn von „Subjekt" oder „Subjekten" hier überhaupt noch gesprochen werden kann, so bestehen diese lediglich in seinen Organen: in seinen Augen, die sich bei ihren Bildern; seinen Ohren, die sich bei ihrem Sportsmatch; seinen Kiefern, die sich bei ihrem gum aufhalten - kurz: seine Identität ist so gründlich desorganisiert, daß die Suche nach „ihm selbst" die Suche nach etwas Nichtexistentem wäre. Zerstreut ist er also nicht nur (...) über eine Vielzahl von Weltstellen; sondern in eine Pluralität von Einzelfunktionen."[25]

b) Passivität

Aus dem Unangenehmen, Nichtunterhaltenden blendet sich der Fernsehmensch per Knopfdruck aus. Nichts nötigt ihn in einer als Spiel inszenierten Welt zum Handeln. Er steht unter keiner öffentlichen Observation und hat keine öffentlichen Sanktionen zu fürchten. Mit der Außenwelt ist er mittels Bildröhre verbunden. Die Welt betrifft ihn nur in ihrem Unterhaltungswert, wobei Krieg, Mord und Totschlag längst zu Unterhaltungsangeboten geworden sind. Er verfügt über diese Welt durch Knopfdruck, nicht durch tätige Aneignung.

Dies gilt freilich auch für den Menschen, der in der Welt seiner Bücher lebt. Canettis Kien lebt in seinem eigenen Kosmos. Erst ein existenzieller Zusammenbruch setzt ihn der Welt aus. Natürlich gerät diese Aussetzung zur Groteske. Dies gilt ebenso für Don Quichotte, der allerdings im Gegensatz zu Kien die Begegnung mit der Welt sucht, also aus eigenen Stücken in die Welt drängt. Er tut dies jedoch so, daß er dabei niemals die Welt seiner Träume und Sehnsüchte verläßt. Das Medium organisiert also auch bei diesen extremen Vertretern der Gutenberg-Welt die Weltauffassung, so daß aus Windmühlen Riesen werden.

Es zeigt sich aber ein entscheidender Unterschied in den Weisen der Passivität: Die extremen Vertreter der Gutenberg-Welt formen immer noch die Welt selbst, zwar mit dem Medium, aber sie tun dies mit außergewöhnlichen Imaginations- und Übertragungsleistungen, die die begriffliche Welt realisieren. Die Art der Passivität muß also, was die Rezeptionsweise anbetrifft, unterschieden werden. Von einer Passivität im Sinne reiner Affizierung der Sinne kann hier nicht die Rede sein.

Die Weltaneignung via Bildschirm erhöht die Akzeptanz des vermittelten Weltbildes. Mediale Angebote, die eigene Imaginations- und Transformationsleistungen erfordern, erweisen sich als widerständiger und weniger eingängig; d.h. ihre suggestive Wirkung ist geringer, ebenso die Akzeptanz des vermittelten Weltbildes. So zeigt sich, daß Jugendliche mit hohem Fernsehkonsum tendenziell Gewaltanwendung bei sozialen Konflikten eher akzeptieren als Jugendliche mit niedrigem Konsum.

c) Voyeurismus

Die Bildröhre wird zum Schlüsselloch. Die Anonymität der Wohnstube schützt den Zuschauer vor böser Nachrede und öffentlicher Kontrolle. Mit den gesteigerten voyeuristischen Möglichkeiten stellt sich ein Schamverlust ein. Scham als Gewißheit gefehlt zu haben, als ein Bewußtsein in seiner Person auf den Fehlenden reduziert zu werden, erfordert die Präsenz des anderen, nicht unbedingt als Kontrolleur, aber als Aufforderung zur Rechtfertigung oder zum Schuldeingeständnis.

Und noch in einer anderen Hinsicht ist ein Schamverlust zu konstatieren. Wenn das Fernsehen die Tendenz hat, Privates, ja Intimstes öffentlich zu machen, und wenn das Private und Intime durch seine Veröffentlichung einen allgemeingültigen Charakter erhält, dann ist diese eine Form der Legitimierung.

So stellen sich optische Verzerrungen ein: Ein ultrarechter Hinrichtungsspezialist stellt sich als treusorgender Familienvater dar, ein Kinderpornohändler als Briefmarkensammler und Hobbysamariter. Das so veröffentlichte Private verschleiert die Wahrheit. Aus Problemen kleinster Minderheiten werden die Gesellschaft bewegende Dinge; umgekehrt werden gewaltigste öffentliche Gaunereien zu familiären Verfehlungen umgewidmet. Durch die tendenzielle Zunahme der Gleichordnung von Öffentlichem und Privatem verzerrt das Medium Sachverhalte wohl am nachhaltigsten.

Die Lust von sicherer Distanz aus, das Intimste und Geheimste quasi durchs Schlüsselloch zu erfahren, ohne das Risiko des Ertapptwerdens und ohne eigene Aktivität, erfährt medial allgemeine Verbreitung. Was einmal gelangweilten Potentaten vorbehalten war, ist heute Allgemeingut geworden. Caligula und Nero mußten noch größte Maßnahmen veranlassen, um zu ihrem voyeuristischen Vergnügen Schlachten schlagen und Welten brennen zu lassen; dies besorgt für uns kleine Voyeure längst CNN und RTL, ohne daß die Geschichte je übel von uns berichten wird. Ein demokratischer Fortschritt, könnte man zynischerweise sagen.

d) Selbstinszenierung und Weltinszenierung

Möchte ich in der Politik etwas werden, muß ich mich gut ins Bild setzen. D.h., ich muß mich medialen Erfordernissen anpassen. Der „Fernsehmensch" ist nicht am Austausch von Argumenten interessiert, sondern an guten Inszenierungen. Nicht um Wahrheit oder die bessere Sache wird gestritten, sondern um ein Plebiszit für den erfolgreichsten Blender oder Schreihals. Es geht um rhetorische Gags und die gute Inszenierung der Rede, keineswegs jedoch um Argumente. Und das Primat des Inszenitorischen hat neue Formen gesellschaftlichen Drucks geschaffen. Nicht was du sagst ist wichtig, sondern wie du es sagst. Das Gesagte soll sensationell und provokativ vorgetragen, es muß aber nicht begründet sein. Die Behauptung kommt ohne Begründung aus, wie Rosa von Praunheims Coming-Out-Kampagne belegte.

Inszenierung als Schlüsselmoment des Öffentlichmachens, des Verständlichmachens, des Sichgehörverschaffens und der Emphase sind keine Erfindung der visuellen Kulturen unseres Jahrhunderts. Der antike Priester beherrschte diese inszenitorische Kunst ebenso, wie der antike Dichter. Inszenierungen haben im Milieu der Herrschenden immer eine Rolle gespielt. Die neue Qualität in unserer Zeit ist die Erweiterung des Inszenitorischen auf Lebensbereiche, die bisweilen davon weitgehend unberührt geblieben sind.

Welche Rolle das Inszenitorische auf der politischen Makroebene spielt, läßt sich am Bosnienkrieg ersehen. Immer wieder versteht es ein Karadzic, die mediale Abhängigkeit der Welt für seine Zwecke zu nutzen. Und immer noch findet durch eine Proportionen verschleiernde „objektive" Medienarbeit in den westlichen Gesellschaften die Mär Verbreitung, daß in Bosnien alle „Kriegsparteien" gleich seien. Zudem wissen die Völkermörder sehr genau, daß ab einer bestimmten Quantität der Berichterstattung selbst das Ungeheuerliche an Reiz verliert und aus den Schlagzeilen verschwindet. Kein Mensch redet heute mehr von den serbischen KZs, die noch vor Jahren die Öffentlichkeit bewegten.

e) Nachahmung

Die Darstellung neuer Gewaltmöglichkeiten motiviert das Nachahmeverhalten insbesondere bei Jugendlichen in bestimmten Entwicklungsphasen, sowie bei Kindern im Vorschul- und frühen Schulalter. Die Gewaltfähigkeit ist ein wesentlicher Aspekt der Selbstbestimmung und Identitätsstiftung bei männlichen Jugendlichen. In bestimmten Lebensphasen läßt sich ein Rambo besser inszenieren als ein Einstein. Man kann anhand von Statistiken zur Jugendkriminalität feststellen, daß Gewaltbereitschaft und Gewaltdelikte bei Jugendlichen in außerordentlicher Weise zugenommen haben, und daß die Gewaltarten, wie die Erfahrungen der Jugendgerichte belegen, in ungewöhnlichem Maße von Film-, Video-, und Fernsehdarstellungen inspiriert sind.[26] In einem Gespräch der *Süddeutschen Zeitung* vom 1.2.1992, das mit Schülern geführt wurde, die täglich Horrorfilme sehen, heißt es am Ende des Artikels:" *Aggressiv kann ich auch ohne solch einen Film sein,* sagt Tom. Sinkt dadurch die Hemmschwelle? *Nicht während des Anschauens oder danach,* sagt er. *Aber als Summe schon.* Wenn es zu einer Auseinandersetzung komme, würde man sich nicht damit begnügen, *einen nur zusammenfallen zu lassen. Da möcht man denn schon, daß was bricht."*

Nachahmung ist aber keineswegs nur bei jüngeren Rezipienten auszumachen. Man erinnere sich nur an die filmerfahrenen Auftritte der Gladbecker Geiselnehmer vor der Kamera, beispielsweise, wenn sie die Möglichkeit ihrer Selbsttötung andeuteten, indem sie sich den Lauf ihrer Waffe in den Mund schoben. Filmunerfahrene hätten sich ohne Frage auf „altdeutsch" die Waffe an die Schläfe gehalten. Tendenziell steht die stärkere Festgelegtheit älterer Rezipienten einem allzu raschen Nachahmeverhalten entgegen. Dies ist auch der Grund, warum die Werbeindustrie stärker auf die jüngeren Generationen fixiert ist, obwohl vom Altersaufbau unserer Gesellschaft die älteren Generationen eigentlich die umworbenere sein müßte, zumal sie auch die ökonomisch potentere ist.

f) Verantwortungsverlagerung

Eine vermeintlich positive Auswirkung auf das gesellschaftliche Ethos ist die Möglichkeit, durch Massenmedien Einsichten in fremde Welten zu erlangen und somit die eigene Verantwortungsbereitschaft zu mehren. Ohne Frage konnte ein bestimmtes Verständnis für ökologische und ökonomische Zusammenhänge und damit eine allgemeine Verbreitung eines Weltgewissens in der ersten Welt nur mit der zunehmenden medialen Vernetzung erreicht werden. Es ist unbestreitbar, daß das Leitmedium moralischen Druck auf politische Entscheidungen ausüben kann - selbst dann, wenn es eine unmittelbare Betroffenheit nicht gibt; ebenso unbestreitbar ist aber auch das Gegenteil, wenn man an seine propagandistischen und desinformierenden Möglichkeiten denkt.

Der „Fernsehmensch" nutzt das mediale Angebot, um seine Verantwortlichkeit ins Nirgendwo zu verlagern. Er bevorzugt die Fernstenliebe, denn sie erfordert bestenfalls seinen Geldbeutel. Verantwortung wird durch das Massenmedium also eher relativiert oder verlagert als angenommen. Alle Verantwortlichkeit gründet letztlich in der Autonomie des Individuums, gerade die aber muß das Leitmedium Fernsehen zur Erhöhung seiner Wirksamkeit ausschalten. Es kann seine ökonomische und propagandistische Wirkung erst dann voll entfalten, wenn der Rezipient eigene reflexive Aneignungsaktivitäten weitgehend einschränkt und sich der medialen Prägewirkung sozusagen widerstandslos aussetzt.

g) Wahrheitsveräußerlichung

Der Mensch trifft seine Entscheidung zunehmend aufgrund der Wahrnehmung von Oberflächenphänomenen, nicht durch begriffliches Erfassen struktureller Zusammenhänge. Er glaubt nur, was er sieht, verschanzt sich in seinen Bildwelten wie hinter Festungsmauern. Interessanterweise hat dieser moderne Typus des ungläubigen Thomas noch eine esoterische

Seite. Er kennt noch einen zweiten Glauben, nämlich den, daß er kraft seines Bewußtseins Einfluß auf die Welt nehmen könne. Dieser monadische Typus bleibt so oder so in seinen Bildwelten und inneren Bewegungen gefangen. Er kennt nur zwei Bereiche, die absolute Äußerlichkeit und die absolute Innerlichkeit, nicht aber den Bereich begrifflicher Durchdringung der Wirklichkeit bzw. eines vermittelbaren Verstehens, denn der könnte seine „gläubige" Existenz in Frage stellen.

Fassen wir damit zusammen und fragen nach den ethischen Konsequenzen aus dem Dargelegten:
Die wohl alles entscheidende Konsequenz aus den medialen Veränderungen der letzten Dekade ist die immer problematischer werdende Verankerung unmittelbarer Verantwortlichkeit. Der mediale Mensch ist ein vernetztes Wesen, seine Verantwortlichkeit ist teilbar. Er lebt zerstreut und flüchtig, als ein Divisum, das nur schwer zu fixieren und für sein Verhalten zur Verantwortung zu ziehen ist. Wo die Zwischenschaltung regiert, ist direkte Verantwortlichkeit nicht mehr zu benennen. Das Handeln des Menschen wird stärker denn je von visuellen Eindrücken bestimmt, die den Anspruch auf Objektivität und Wahrheit erheben. Die Reizbestimmtheit des Verhaltens dieses Menschen sprengt die Verinnerlichung der vergangenen nachreformatorischen und schriftorientierten Jahrhunderte. Das moderne Ethos entfernt sich damit von einem Ethos, das Triebbeherrschung und Autonomie einfordert. Der vielpropagierte Individualismus ist ein Titel der Werbewelt geworden, der mit Selbstbestimmung im Sinne kritischer Selbsteinschätzung und Autonomie nichts zu tun hat.

Der nach inszenitorischen Gesichtspunkten handelnde postmoderne Mensch, der nicht selten das Erregen von Aufmerksamkeit mit Persönlichkeit verwechselt, lebt nach der Devise: Es ist gleich, was du tust, aber es ist nicht gleich, wie du es tust; oder anders: Ästhetik geht vor Ethik.

Der postmoderne Mensch richtet sich in der Mittelbarkeit seiner Vernetzung ein, verharrt in Trägheit, verändert nicht, sondern läßt Veränderung geschehen. Wenn er Verantwortung übernimmt, dann solche, die ihn nur mittelbar fordert. Was er trägt, trägt er in vernetzter Weise.

Vielleicht ist Benny aus Michael Hanekes Film „Bennys Video" der extremste, aber „deutlichste" Typus dieses postmodernen medialen Menschen: Er hält Kontakt mit der Welt draußen über die Videokamera, die die befahrene Straße vor seinem Fester auf einen Bildschirm bannt. Alles, was er erfährt, wird in die Mittelbarkeit gebannt, selbst der Mord, den er an einem

Mädchen begeht, existiert letztlich nur noch am Rande eines Videofilms. Durch die Mediatisierung des Geschehens verliert sich jeglicher unmittelbare Verantwortungsbezug. Als er gegen Ende des Filmes gefragt wird, was er sich dabei gedacht habe, fragt er zurück: Wobei? Das ungeheuerliche Geschehen ist aus seinem Bewußtsein verschwunden und hat sich irgendwo in eine gleichwertig mediatisierte Welt eingeordnet. Diese entropische Welt kennt keine Hierarchien mehr, nichts steht im Hintergrund, nichts im Vordergrund. Der Verlust von Werthierarchien verläuft parallel zu Strukturentwicklungen im Leitmedium. Alles ist dort gleichgeordnet: Unterrichtung ist Unterhaltung. Das Grauenvolle und das Niedliche stehen unvermittelt nebeneinander. Alles geht, gleich ob ich mich zum Kinderschänden oder zu einer Religion bekenne, Hauptsache ich bekenne öffentlich. Privatheit ist bestenfalls noch als zu enthüllender Rätselbezirk zugelassen. Ob die Enttabuisierung aller Lebensbereiche allerdings, wie Hans Peter Duerr optimistischerweise meint, ihre Grenzen hat, muß insofern dahingestellt bleiben, als weniger das Ergebnis der Enttabuisierung für die Macher entscheidend ist, als vielmehr der Prozeß. Und um den am Laufen zu halten, ist die gelegentliche Errichtung von Tabuzonen durchaus förderlich und in der Strategie enthalten.[27]

Alles erfährt bei der Einrichtung des Leitmediums die gleiche Bewertung, alles hat den gleichen Rang. Die Wirkung dieser Gleichordnung auf das Verhalten der Menschen ist wohl die fatalste. In den diskursiv-begrifflichen Medien ist Gleichordnung nicht zu realisieren, weil der mediale Transport ohne Hierarchie nicht zu bewerkstelligen ist.

Wir haben mit diesem Phänomen der Gleichordnung noch vergleichsweise geringe Erfahrung, aber uns klingt alle noch der Satz von Wim Wenders im Ohr, als er in Bezug auf die europäisch-amerikanische Auseinandersetzung um den freien Zugang zum Filmmarkt sagte: „Wer im Jahr 2000 die Bilder beherrscht, beherrscht die Welt!"

Anmerkungen

1) Vgl. Ernst Cassirer, Was ist der Mensch? Versuch einer Philosophie der menschlichen Kultur, Stuttgart 1960, S.39: "Die unberührte Wirklichkeit scheint in dem Maße, in dem das Symbol-Denken und -Handeln des Menschen reifer wird, sich ihm zu entziehen. Statt mit den Dingen selbst umzugehen, unterhält sich der Mensch in gewissem Sinne dauernd mit sich selbst. Er lebt so sehr in sprachlichen Formen, in Kunstwerken, in mythischen Symbolen oder religiösen Riten, daß er nichts erfahren oder erblicken kann, außer durch Zwischenschaltung dieser künstlichen Medien."

2) Vgl. Günther Anders: Die Antiquiertheit des Menschen, München 1956; Die Welt als Phantom und Matrize. Philosophische Betrachtungen über Rundfunk und Fernsehen § 17, § 18, § 19. Anders stellt dort fest, daß die Nachricht als vom Gegenstand abgelöstes Prädikat, d.h. als Vor-Urteil zu begreifen ist. U.a. heißt es in § 17:" Jede Nachricht ist also als Teil-Lieferung schon ein Vor-Urteil, das wahr, aber auch falsch sein kann: jedes Prädikat schon ein Präjudiz; und durch jeden Inhalt der Nachricht wird der Gegenstand selbst, da er hinter dem alleingelieferten Prädikat im Dunkel zurückbleibt, dem Adressaten vorenthalten. Dieser wird also, da er in eine bestimmte Perspektive (in die des Prädikats) hineingezwungen ist, und da ihm der Gegenstand, den das Urteil angeblich enthält, vorenthalten wird, unselbständig gemacht." (Lizenzausgabe DBG, S. 158f.) In § 19 heißt es am Ende: "Da kein Urteil so unverdächtig, so unscheinbar, so verführerisch ist wie dasjenige, das angeblich nichts ist als die Sache selbst, liegt in ihrem Verzicht auf das ausgebildete „S ist p-Schema" ihre betrügerische Kraft. Was wir vor dem Radio oder dem Bildschirm sitzend, konsumieren, ist statt der Szene deren Präparierung, statt der angeblichen Sache S deren Prädikat p, kurz: ein in Bildform auftretendes Vorurteil, das, wie jedes Vorurteil, seinen Urteilscharakter versteckt; aber, da es heimlicherweise eben doch eines ist, den Konsumenten davon abhält, seinerseits noch einmal die Mühe des Urteilens auf sich zu nehmen."(Lizenzausgabe DBG, S.163)

3) Jean Baudrillard behauptet in „Videowelt und fraktales Subjekt" (in: Ars Elektronica (Hg.): Philosophien der neuen Technologie, Berlin 1986), daß der Mensch selbst Teil einer televisuellen, kommunikationstechnologischen Welt ist. Er sei subjektiv noch ein Mensch, virtuell und praktisch aber schon eine Maschine. Baudrillard kehrt die Frage nach der Anbindung der medialen Techniken also um. Er sieht den Menschen an die mediale Apparatur wie an Prothesen und künstliche Organe angeschlossen und gebraucht für die Bezeichnung dieses Sachverhaltes den englischen Ausdruck „connected". Das Entscheidende an Baudrillards provokativen Überlegungen ist die Einsicht, daß der Mensch nicht einfach der medialen Struktur gegenübersteht, sondern selbst Teil von ihr, an sie angeschlossen ist, wie an einen Herzschrittmacher; und von diesem Anschluß her leitet er zusehends die Bedeutung seiner Existenz ab.

4) Einen gegenwärtig in der Film- bzw. Bildtheorie enorm wirksamen Entwurf des Verhältnisses von Bild und Begriff bietet Ludwig Klages in „Der Geist als Widersacher der Seele" (Leipzig, 1929-32, 3 Bände) an. Er weist Bildern einen größeren Wirklichkeitsgehalt als gegenständlichen Begriffen zu. Das begriffliche Denken ist für ihn nichts anderes als eine steigerungsfähige Gegebenheit, die sich nach der Intensität des Bilderlebens richtet. Aus der ursprünglichen Wirklichkeit der Bilder schafft das Denken erst die Dinge. Das Bild ist allein wirklich und wirksam, und das vollkommene Gegenteil des Begriffs.
In der Psychoanalyse bzw. Psychotherapie wird das Bildhafte dem Unbewußten als authentischer Bezirk zugewiesen, was Hanscarl Leuner in seiner Studie „Katathymes Bilderleben. Ergebnisse in Theorie und Praxis" (Bern/Stuttgart/Wien 1983) dazu veranlaßt, dem Patienten während der Therapie Möglichkeiten vorzuschlagen, wie die Bildgeschichten des menschlichen Unbewußten reorganisiert werden könnten. Ziel der Therapie ist es, durch bestimmte Bildanordnungen die Psyche zu stabilisieren ohne den Umweg über eine Begriffsarbeit, die zu leisten vielen Patienten nicht möglich ist. In den USA werden Leuners Theorien inzwischen schon bei der Filmgestaltung bzw. Programmgestaltung angewandt; man darf freilich davon ausgehen, daß diese Nutzung eher ökonomischen, denn therapeutischen oder psychohygienischen Zwecken dient.

5) Jochen Schulte-Sasse: Von der schriftlichen zur elektronischen Kultur: Über neuere Wechselbeziehungen zwischen Mediengeschichte und Kulturgeschichte; in: Gumbrecht/Pfeiffer (Hg.): Materialität der Kommunikation; Frankfurt/M. 1988, S.438f.
6) Vgl. Rafael Capurro: Information. Ein Beitrag zur etymologischen und ideengeschichtlichen Begründung des Informationsbegriffs, München 1978; Rafael Capurro: Was ist Information? Hinweise zum Wort- und Begriffsfeld eines umstrittenen Begriffs, HMD 133, 1987.
7) Vgl. dazu Klaus Wiegerling: Literaturkritik und das Problem der Zeitadäquatheit; in: DalbergerHofBerichte 2. Eine literarisch-kritische Nachlese (Hg. Literaturbüro Rheinland-Pfalz), Mainz 1990. S.74 - 80.
8) Vgl. Edmund Husserls Ausführungen im § 12. Fortsetzung: Die ausgedrückte Gegenständlichkeit, aus „Logische Untersuchungen Bd.II/1" (1901 ff.), Tübingen 1968 ff. "Die Notwendigkeit der Unterscheidung zwischen Bedeutung (Inhalt) und Gegenstand wird klar, wenn wir uns durch Vergleichung von Beispielen überzeugen, daß mehrere Ausdrücke dieselbe Bedeutung, aber verschiedene Gegenstände, und wieder daß sie verschiedene Bedeutungen, aber denselben Gegenstand haben können. Daneben bestehen selbstverständlich auch die Möglichkeiten, daß sie nach beiden Richtungen differieren, und wieder daß sie in beiden übereinstimmen. Das letztere ist der Fall der tautologischen Ausdrücke, z.B. der in verschiedenen Sprachen miteinander korrespondierenden Ausdrücke gleicher Bedeutung und Nennung (London, Londres; zwei, deux, duo usw.).
Die klarsten Beispiele für die Sonderung von Bedeutung und gegenständlicher Beziehung bieten uns die Namen. Bei ihnen ist in der letzteren Hinsicht die Rede von der „Nennung" gebräuchlich. Zwei Namen können Verschiedenes bedeuten, aber dasselbe nennen. So z.B. der Sieger von Jena - der Besiegte von Waterloo; das gleichseitige Dreieck - das gleichwinklige Dreieck. Die ausgedrückte Bedeutung ist in den Paaren eine offenbar verschiedene, obwohl beiderseits derselbe Gegenstand gemeint ist. Ebenso verhält es sich bei Namen, die vermöge ihrer Unbestimmtheit einen „Umfang" haben. Die Ausdrücke ein gleichseitiges Dreieck und ein gleichwinkliges Dreieck haben dieselbe gegenständliche Beziehung, denselben Umfang möglicher Anwendung."(S.47)
9) Vgl. Jochen Schulte-Sasse: Von der schriftlichen zur elektronischen Kultur. (a.a.O) S.433/434.
10) Neil Postman: Wir amüsieren uns zu Tode - Urteilsbildung im Zeitalter der Unterhaltungsindustrie, Frankfurt/M. 1988 (Original 1985). Dort heißt es auf S.34:"daß Wahrheitsbegriffe jeweils sehr eng mit den Perspektiven bestimmter Ausdrucksformen verknüpft sind. Die Wahrheit kommt nicht ungeschminkt daher und ist niemals so dahergekommen. Sie muß in der ihr angemessenen Kleidung auftreten, sonst wird sie nicht anerkannt, mit anderen Worten:"Wahrheit" ist so etwas wie ein kulturelles Vorurteil. Jede Kultur beruht auf dem Grundsatz, daß sich die Wahrheit in bestimmten symbolischen Formen besonders glaubwürdig ausdrücken läßt, in Formen, die einer anderen Kultur möglicherweise trivial oder belanglos erscheinen.
11) Thomas J.Froehlich: Ethics, Ideologies, and Practices of Information Technology and Systems; in: Information in the Year 2000: From Research to Applications, Proceedings of the 53rd Annual Meeting of the American Society for Information Science, Volume 27, Medford, NJ, 1990. S. 251.
12) Hans Sachsse: Ethische Probleme des ethischen Fortschritts. Überarbeitete Fassung des gleichnamigen Originals aus: H.S.: Technik und Verantwortung, Freiburg i.Br. 1972; in: Lenk/Ropohl(Hg.) Technik und Ethik, Stuttgart 1987, S.64 - 68.
13) Norbert Bolz: Neue Medien; in: Information Philosophie 1, 1994; S.49.
14) Norbert Bolz: Neue Medien (a.a.O.), S.50.
15) Norbert Bolz: Neue Medien (a.a.O.), S.53 f.
16) Vgl. Monika Elsner/Thomas Müller: Der angewachsene Fernseher; in: Gumbrecht/Pfeiffer (Hg.) Materialität der Kommunikation (a.a.O.).

17) Efraim Shmueli: Seven Jewish Cultures - A Reinterpretation of Jewish History and Thought; Cambridge 1990 (Hebräisches Original Tel-Aviv 1980).

18) Edmund Husserl: Cartesianische Meditationen, Den Haag 1950, S.138.

19) Hans Blumenberg: Schiffbruch mit Zuschauer - Paradigma einer Daseinsmetapher, Frankfurt/M. 1979, S.39.

20) Günther Anders: Die Antiquiertheit des Menschen, München 1956; S. 195 (Lizenz-ausgabe)

21) Die gegenwärtig dominierende Gestaltung ist die Prägung des Mediums von kommerziellen Interessen, sowie seine Veränderung durch neue technische Möglichkeiten, die ebenfalls durch kommerzielle Interessen befördert werden. Als ein Beispiel wäre hier die zunehmende Trivialisierung der Hauptprogramme und Hauptsendezeiten zu nennen, desweiteren eine zunehmende Sektorialisierung der Angebotsstrukturen (ganze Fernsehanstalten konzentrieren sich auf eine spezielle Rezipientengruppe: Junge, Sport- oder Kunstinteressierte).

22) Vgl. Hertha Sturm: Fernsehdiktate: Die Veränderung von Gedanken und Gefühlen. Ergebnisse und Folgerungen für eine rezipientenorientierte Mediendramaturgie, Gütersloh 1991.

23) Peter Sloterdijk: Sendboten der Gewalt - Zur Metaphysik des Aktions-Kinos; in: P.S.: Medien-Zeit - Drei gegenwartsdiagnostische Versuche, Stuttgart 1993, S.17 - 19.

24) Vgl. Peter Sloterdijk: Sendboten der Gewalt. (a.a.O.), S.20 f.

25) Günther Anders: Die Antiquiertheit des Menschen (a.a.O.), S.140 f.

26) Als einer der außergewöhnlichsten Belege muß wohl der englische Fall des zweijährigen James Bulger gelten, der von zwei elfjährigen Schülern erst entführt und dann auf grausamste Weise gefoltert und schließlich getötet wurde. Die beiden Schüler „spielten" tatsächlich weitgehend nach, was sie in dem Horror-Video „Child's Play 3" gesehen hatten.

27) Hans Peter Duerr:"Die Spirale der medialen Reize ist nicht endlos. Vorerst aber bleibt es dabei, daß die fortschreitende Enttabuisierung der Gesellschaft mit der Erschließung und Ausbeutung neuer Märkte gekoppelt ist. Ein aktuelles Beispiel ist die Entdeckung der Alten als sexuelle Leistungsträger. Das kann ja einerseits eine begrüßenswerte, enthemmende Nachricht für die Senioren sein. Auf der anderen Seite scheint es mir, daß hier den Jugendkult ergebene Sozialpädagogen den Veteranen sexuelle Wünsche aufschwatzen, sie in Wahrheit nur unter Leistungsstreß und Vollzugszwänge setzen, anstatt sie in Würde impotent werden zu lassen (...) Steigerbar ist nicht so sehr die Darbietung von entblößtem Fleisch, sondern die von Brutalität. Auch Kriege dienen voyeuristischen Interessen, das ist unübertreffbares Reality-TV. Möglicherweise aber wächst die Erkenntnis, daß der Hedonismus nicht das Glück, sondern in sehr dürftigem Maße nur die Lust einlöst. Sogar obsessive Lustgewinnler könnten eines Tages einsehen, daß sie nur durch Beschränkung an ihr Ziel kommen. Vielleicht werden deshalb die Hedonisten der Zukunft die schärfsten Verfechter der Prüderie sein." („Das Gewissen hat versagt", Interview mit Hans Peter Duerr, in DER SPIEGEL Nr.2, 1993, S.173)

Qui a peur de l'information?

von Daniel Bougnoux

L'information n'est pas une valeur comme les autres. A l'heure où nos principaux médias, victimes de dérapages mémorables, font leur examen de conscience, il peut être utile de verser au dossier quelques réflexions de base sur cette notion étrange, et si aisément pervertie.

1. Il n'y a pas d'information en soi. Toute information est étroitement relative au sujet connaissant, à la sensibilité de ses capteurs, à sa culture, à ses curiosités. „On ne lit pas tous le même journal" (chante Alain Souchon), ni dans celui-ci les mêmes rubriques, ni dans un article les mêmes choses. Un homme et son chien prélèvent sur le même territoire des informations incommensurables. Et l'individu selon les circonstances réagira autrement aux mêmes informations: un chat affamé, ou gavé de croquettes, traitera différemment la vision d'un moineau. Dans chaque cas nous nous montrons sensibles aux seuls signaux que filtre notre clôture informationnelle; et cette clôture dépend étroitement de l'état de notre organisme et de nos aptitudes cognitives, qui engendrent un monde propre fortement cloisonné. La chauve-souris ou le dauphin habitent des „mondes propres" dont nous n'avons guère idée; mais cela peut se dire des animaux qui vivent imbriqués à notre territoire, voire de nos voisins ou de nos enfants. En bref: à l'immense variété des informations potentielles qui nous assaillent à tout moment, nous opposons une ouverture extrêmement sélective, et nous rejetons tous les signaux non traités dans le bruit. Mais dans ce bruit d'autres organismes puisent leur information pertinente. Chacun traite le monde à ses propres conditions, et appelle information la forme capable d'épouser ou de compléter celle de son organisme. Très peu d'informations sont donc désintéressées ou „objectives"; étape finale de l'organisation vivante, la connaissance est une ruse de notre vie, qu'elle vise d'abord à organiser et à défendre. Et les informations sélectionnées ne font qu'exprimer la façon dont chacun renouvelle, étend ou protège son monde propre ou sa vie, c'est-à-dire le voyage de sa forme mortelle à travers le bruit.

2. Qu'est-ce qui fait qu'un message circule ? Personne n'attend notre information, à moins que celle-ci ne concerne son monde propre ou une communauté de relations déjà instituée. La pertinence d'une information se limite en effet aux milieux et aux réseaux où elle se diffuse, hors desquels s'étend pour chacun l'empire du bruit. Le premier canal ou medium d'une

information, c'est donc la mise en contact ou la relation, qui par définition relèvent moins de la connaissance que de la reconnaissance: pour contacter quelqu'un, il faut lui proposer non un écart mais une continuité ou une redondance, une confirmation qui renforce ce qu'il sait (aime, désire ou recherche) déjà. En rhétorique cela s'appelait captatio benevolentiae („caresser dans le sens du poil"). Pas de communication sans cette résonance cognitive, premier degré de communauté entre l'émetteur et le récepteur. Le message qui circule le mieux est celui qui flatte nos stéréotypes (comme la musique d'aéroport ou la philosophie de BHL, partout diffusées), celui qu'un récepteur peut facilement reprendre à son compte et co-produire. Pour voyager à travers le bruit, la moindre de nos informations doit se capitonner de redondance, de cautions et de séduction. D'où l'antagonisme de l'information et de la communication, néanmoins contraintes de cohabiter dès lors que celle-ci (la communauté, la connivence participative ou la chaleur du massage) est la condition et le préalable obligé de celle-là (le message qui ouvre, qui complique ou éventuellement contredit nos mondes propres). Si „communiquer c'est entrer dans l'orchestre" (Bateson), il est clair que l'euphorie communautaire, l'harmonie ou la redondance sont la basse continue ou la partition déjà écrite sur lesquelles nos informations nous parviennent. Toujours la (bonne) relation soutient, cadre et pilote le contenu du message: cela s'appelle faire sens. C'est une loi de l'apprentissage que nous ne pouvons acquérir de nouvelles connaissances qu'en les intercalant finement entre de larges plages de redondance. Pour son acheminement, son traitement et sa survie, l'information proprement dite est partout fondée, qu'il s'agisse d'une conversation, d'un progamme scolaire ou de celui d'une chaîne de télévision, sur l'écosystème nourricier d'une communication qui entretient le sens mais peut aussi l'étouffer (quand l'entretien déchoit en bavardage, le professeur en animateur ou le présentateur en disc-jockey). Une information qui pour mieux se pousser tombe au niveau de la relation pure, flatteuse et narcissisante, s'annule en tant que telle.

3. Une variation qui arrive à une forme. Sans reprendre ici la théorie mathématique développée par Shannon et Weaver en 1948, on vient de voir qu'on peut définir l'information par la réduction d'incertitude qu'apporte un message; et que la communication en revanche, fondée sur la recherche du plus large contact (redondance relationnelle ou édredon communautaire), est très pauvre en information véritable. Vue sous cet angle l'information a deux façons de mourir: par le bruit pur, quand on ne peut la raccorder à aucun réseau, attente ni disposition préalable - à aucun code ; et dans la répétition ou la prévisibilité totale, quand le message dit ce

que tout le monde sait déjà, ou peut se déduire d'un message antérieur. Pour qu'une information nous parvienne, il faut donc que notre „forme" (notre culture ou système cognitif) soit déformable. Une pensée rigide ou cristallisée n'admet plus d'information; mais une pensée trop amorphe ou fumeuse non plus. L'information meurt par excès de fermeture autant que d'ouverture, et vit d'un compromis entre ces deux écueils du cristal et de la fumée. La redondance d'une tautologie ou la facile prévisibilité d'une vérité de La Palice sont fatales à l'information (quoique essentielles à la communication); mais l'émission de hasard pur, ou une excessive distorsion infligée aux codes de reconnaissance (poèmes dadaïstes et autres „incolores idées vertes furieusement endormies"...) ne le serait pas moins. L'imprévisibilité totale rejoint la totale redondance dans l'insignifiance du bruit. Pour être reçue et faire sens, il faut qu'une information soit perçue comme variation ou écart à une forme, à un contexte ou à un code préalables, et eux-mêmes invariants.

4. L'information n'est pas l'énergie. Une information peut avoir de grandes conséquences énergétiques (le commutateur qui met à feu la fusée, le communiqué qui annonce une déclaration de guerre, etc.), mais elle-même ne contient qu'une énergie minuscule, et cette différence d'échelle de la cause à l'effet caractérise justement un phénomène informationnel: énergie et information ne sont pas du même ordre. Plus précisément, il conviendra de toujours bien distinguer une relation d'information d'une relation de type stimulus-réponse (à laquelle se limite notre exemple de la fusée). Nous dirons qu'une relation d'information, ou sémiotique au sens strict, se remarque à ceci que le récepteur peut ne pas y répondre, ou y répond à ses propres conditions. Ce point important découle directement de la clôture informationnelle envisagée supra. Dans le montage d'un arc réflexe, on ne peut pas ne pas répondre au stimulus: la chaîne énergétique d'action-réaction court-circuite l'interprétation ou à la mentalisation. De même on ne peut pas ne pas communiquer (= se comporter), et cette forte remarque de Watzlawick est une raison supplémentaire de bien distinguer communication et information. Car l'usage de cette dernière est beaucoup plus libre: on réservera le concept d'information à ce qu'on a toujours le droit d'ignorer, de retenir, d'interpréter ou de trahir, au lieu de le restituer tel quel... Avec l'information on a le choix de la réponse, élaborée selon notre monde propre ou à nos propres conditions. Nous appellerons „triviale" avec Von Foerster la relation stimulus-réponse ou de cause à effet (chaque fois que la réponse est contrainte), alors que la relation informationnelle ou sémiotique en général insère entre l'émetteur et le récepteur un troisième terme ou un espace intermédiaire, qu'on nommera de la

différance (Derrida), de l'interprétant (Peirce), ou plus généralement de la computation. Ce qui distingue un ballon d'un petit chien n'est pas la trajectoire que l'un et l'autre sont bien forcés de parcourir au stimulus „coup de pied", mais le fait qu'aussitôt immobilisé, l'animal computera ses options: mordre son agresseur, s'inhiber sur place ou choisir la fuite. Tant qu'il y a de la „vie", il y a de l'interprétation, qui toujours mesure notre degré de liberté. Un vivant qui ne traiterait les sollicitations extérieures que par stimulus-réponses serait au bord de la tombe. Certes la mort, le réel ou la force des choses ne manqueront pas un jour d'écraser „trivialement" tous nos choix. Nous n'y couperons pas, mais nous les tenons (provisoirement) à distance par la très soutenable légèreté des lettres, des chiffres ou des images. Le monde symbolique nous sert à contenir le réel. L'information c'est ce qu'on zappe, ou ce qu'on peut toujours ignorer.

5. La carte ne se confond pas avec le territoire. Le signe n'est pas la chose, et s'en sépare par la coupure sémiotique: le mot „chien" n'aboie pas. En effet. Faut-il en conclure que les descriptions politiques ou les sondages ne font pas de politique, que les images de la guerre du Golfe et les communiqués n'ont pas eux-mêmes fait la guerre, ou que l'informateur se garde de jouer à l'acteur enrôlé dans le phénomène...? On a beaucoup dit que la première victime d'une guerre était la vérité ou l'information. Il est rare que celle-ci conserve son niveau de surplomb, son recul et son espace tiers d'interprétation: l'actualité dès qu'elle devient un peu forte écrase la carte sur le territoire, la relation symbolique sur la contagion indicielle et les infos sur l'arc stimulus-réponse... Ce court-circuit d'une communication plus directe est la tentation presque irrésistible des journalistes. Lequel, dans l'urgence et la chaleur participative, n'a rêvé de faire l'événement, de voir sa description devenir prescriptive, et l'annonce précipiter l'état du monde? La désinformation qui fit partie de la guerre du Golfe ou les images du vrai/faux charnier de Timisoara, pour citer des exemples ressassés, mais aussi l'annonce d'un scandale („affaire des fausses factures" ou profanation de Carpentras), ou d'un krach boursier (octobre 1987)..., tous ces „constats" dont il serait aisé d'allonger la liste ont en commun d'avoir hâté ou co-produit le cours d'événements qu'ils ne semblaient que décrire. Ces effets de performatif ou d'annonce en général (chaque fois que dire, c'est faire) ont été bien débrouillés par la pragmatique des actes de langage. Or le fantôme du performatif, soit du prophétisme et de la magie (= agir par des mots sur les choses), hante un appareil d'information étroitement enchevêtré au monde politique ou des affaires en général. Le rêve de les séparer semble bien chimérique. Gouverner en effet, une entreprise ou un état, est-ce autre chose que faire croire,

et diriger l'opinion ? L'information n'est pas l'énergie mais la pragmatique étudie la force des mots, ou l'efficacité symbolique en général. Certains mots créent poétiquement ou performativement tel phénomène par la simple alchimie d'en parler. Et d'autres faits inversement demeurent sous-développés faute d'accéder à l'appareil médiatique: le silence exterminateur de ces performatifs négatifs m'effraie ! Quels actes (de langage) entrent dans l'actualité ? Comment les principaux médias tiennent-ils l'agenda (annonce des choses-à-faire)? Question de (bonnes) relations toujours, d'autorité, de connivences ou de réseaux. Les contenus qui en découlent (l'information proprement dite) peuvent aussi en périr: l'oblitération de la coupure sémiotique tue l'info.

6. L'information est une grandeur ordinale. Et non pas simplement cardinale: informer c'est hiérarchiser, ou évaluer; et ce jugement est la part irréductiblement performative de l'appareil (qu'on voudrait sobrement constatif) des médias. Ceci découle de la structure obligatoirement qualitative de l'espace et du temps d'un message (due elle-même à la clôture informationnelle). Parce que nous ne pouvons recevoir toutes les informations, celles qui viennent en tête (de manchette ou de temps d'antenne) sont nécessairement ressenties comme les plus importantes. Et taire inversement, ou publier telle info en queue de journal ou en petits caractères, c'est l'enterrer. Combien de faits demeurent sous-developpés faute d'accéder à l'appareil médiatique, ou d'y figurer assez longtemps ? Jamais on ne le saura (par définition); et il n'existe pas d'instance d'appel, ni d'alternative médiatique, à ce défaut de visibilité.

7. Des nouvelles toujours plus fraîches. Nous disions que l'information a l'étrange propriété de n'exister qu'entre l'ordre et le désordre purs, entre la clôture du cristal et l'ouverture de la fumée, et qu'elle exige un zeste de communication ou de relation tout en pouvant périr par elles. Il faut ajouter au tableau de ces comportements bizarres l'oscillation de sa valeur entre direct et différé. Car l'info est une marchandise, qui atteint des prix fort élevés (dans le cas d'un renseignement „confidentiel défense", d'un secret industriel ou d'un tuyau boursier...). Or l'un des paramètres de cette valeur marchande, à côté de la véracité intrinsèque du renseignement, est évidemment sa fraîcheur: dans les trois exemples cités, le temps déclasse l'information (en la rendant plus accessible). Si je paye chaque matin cinq francs mon journal, celui d'avant-hier ne sert plus qu'aux usages domestiques du papier. Les médias se livrent à une permanente course de vitesse dans l'accès, le traitement et la diffusion des infos, et à cette course la radio et la télévision, qui accèdent de mieux en mieux au temps réel du direct, battront toujours l'imprimé nécessairement en différé. Or que voit-on au moment où

l'information s'installe dans le direct ? La „couverture" de la guerre du Golfe n'a pas peu servi à révéler ce paradoxe désormais bien établi: le direct produit de la sensation, de la relation excitée et un notable dégagement de chaleur, mais assez peu d'information. Au cours des haletantes journées de cette guerre rythmée par les communiqués de CNN et des états-majors dont nous, zappeurs fous, étions aussi les otages, nous aurons beaucoup participé et peu appris. Comme les salades, les nouvelles se consomment toujours plus fraîches, mais l'information qui accède au direct (stade ultime de la fraîcheur et triomphe de l'appareil médiatique) se renverse en sensation, en stimulus-réponse (on ne peut pas ne pas répondre), bref en communication, dont le suspect consensus qui l'entoure montre assez la fonction communautaire.

Avec le direct qui propulse dans le temps même du phénomène, notre participation ou contagion indicielle oblitère la coupure sémiotique, notre carte redevient „territoire". Deux types se dégagent, une presse à sensations que les techniques audio-visuelles du direct alimentent chaque jour davantage, et une autre qu'on dira d'opinion ou d'information, qui repose sur le différé ou la re-présentation plus que sur la présence. Ce différé ménage aussi le temps du recoupement ou l'espace de vérification des trop immédiates nouvelles, donc le recul critique, une intériorité aussi ou rumination constructive liée à la culture typographique, et quelques vieilleries encore, au nombre desquelles la démocratie (dont l'exercice en direct abolirait l'essence même, fondée sur la représentation).

8. Aimez-vous les informations? La question se pose dans la mesure où ce qui casse la redondance ou le rêve communautaire n'a pas toujours bon visage. Qui voulait savoir ce qui se passait réellement en Chine au moment de la Grande Révolution Culturelle ? On préférait lire Pékin-Information ou La Cause du Peuple, qui alimentaient le délire sectaire; un vrai reportage aurait désespéré Vincennes. Ces journaux d'idéologues rêveurs qui déguisaient leur haine de l'information en chantage moral sont certes devenus illisibles, mais la désinformation connaît aujourd'hui d'autres ruses. Qui veut savoir la cause des conflits „absurdes" qui agitent les pays limitrophes à notre périmètre de sécurité? Un exposé un peu fouillé des motifs déborderait les plages audio-visuelles, lasserait notre patience et notre bonne conscience. Nous préférons en général le spectacle, fût-il horrible (surtout s'il est horrible), d'une guerre à un cours d'histoire-géo ou d'économie: un petit Soudanais squelettique effraye - mais dérange moins tout de même que d'expliquer l'échange inégal et l'intérêt des grandes puissances. L'image télé zoome sur les effets sans s'attarder au travelling ou au panoramique sur les causes, qui demeurent

hors champ. On a vite fait de conclure, en bonne logique cathodique, de cet invisible hors champ à „Je ne veux pas le savoir", d'où s'enchaîne „Ça n'existe pas"; un cours de matières premières ne fait pas sens (sensation) à l'écran.

Plus généralement il est permis de douter qu'on plonge dans les infos au retour du travail pour augmenter ses connaissances ou sa conscience critique. Dans le tumulte de la maisonnée, la lecture tranquille du Monde offre un rempart salutaire; et le Journal Télévisé où les présentateurs rivalisent d'aménité, de petites phrases et d'enchaînements zappés ne laisse pas le temps de s'ennuyer. Nous n'aimerions pas qu'on nous prive de cette „messe du 20 heures", où l'information épouse en douceur la communication; où nous jouissons d'abord, au spectacle des désordres extérieurs, de notre monade domestique à la fois ouverte sur le vaste monde et si délicieusement close... Vivre ensemble séparément: selon un compromis typiquement imaginaire, l'écran nous façonne une conscience concernée-blasée, attentive-picoreuse, ouverte-douillette ou vigile- crépusculaire (très peu de spectateurs savent énumérer sans oublis les rubriques d'un JT d'une demi-heure, dont le texte total tient pourtant en moins de trois feuillets). Ce flot du JT ne relève ni du Vrai ni du Bien, mais peut-être du Beau selon Kant, c'est-à-dire d'une vision désintéressée. Pour trouver belle la tempête, argumente Kant, il ne faut pas être en mer. De même nous prêtons un intérêt de distraction, plus esthétique que pratique, aux infos que nous observons du rivage. Ces événements traités en spectacle arrivent ailleurs, dans l'espace-temps imaginaire ou primaire du rêve selon Freud. Certes quelques séquences nous bouleversent, et provoquent à réfléchir; mais le dispositif même du flot favorise la dissipation et l'envie de dormir. Les pires catastrophes peuvent arriver, c'est nouveau et intéressant. Le monde (des autres) peut s'écrouler, „Emile s'en fout" (chante Guy Béart). Où passe à la TV la frontière entre l'information et la communication, et que préférez-vous ? D'un côté le Journal, les magazines de reportage et les débats, de l'autre les divertissements, la pub, le sport, les fictions et les jeux. Partage en voie d'effacement: la prouesse communicationnelle de la TV, c'est qu'on peut toujours y traiter l'information comme un jeu. Déjà Les Inconnus préfigurent le JT de l'an 2000, où le présentateur est flanqué de deux joueurs qui devinent les nouvelles du jour en appuyant sur des sonnettes !

9. L'information contre l'information. Notre clôture informationnelle dépend de notre constitution organique, mais aussi de nos informations antérieures sédimentées en doctrines, en systèmes, théories ou idéologies. Nos premières connaissances s'agglutinent, cristallisent, et désormais solidaires et solides s'opposent efficacement aux informations concurrentes ou

nouvelles. Tout se passe comme si chaque organisme ne pouvait tolérer qu'une dose limitée d'information ou d'ouverture, au-delà de laquelle il se referme comme une huître. Combien de gens sur les grands sujets philosophiques, moraux ou politiques, ont „fait leur religion"? On ne les fera plus sortir de là. La forme de nos informations durcit au fil du temps, comme nos cartilages ou nos artères, et nous sommes tous menacés de ne détenir qu'une culture périmée, obsolète: nos chères connaissances, si difficiles à acquérir, font désormais obstacle aux autres.

On voit par ces brèves remarques combien il est difficile d'extraire ou d'acheminer une véritable information, dont plusieurs dragons nous séparent:

– le processus primaire ou, sous diverses formes, l'envie de dormir;

– la communauté et ses réseaux de communications, de relations, de connivence;

– la course au direct, la concurrence née de l'urgence du flot et ses effets de stimulus-réponse (qui nous transforment en chiens de Pavlov);

– l'interaction de l'informateur et de l'acteur ou le désir de s'engager, de participer...;

– la clôture informationnelle (organique, psychique, culturelle).

Nous aurions dû ajouter la censure, si elle ne découlait largement des facteurs que nous venons d'énumérer. Tous nous rappellent le prix de l'info, cette „valeur pas comme les autres", et finalement si rare: quel chemin il aura fallu faire, dans certains contextes, pour extraire, vérifier et réussir à imposer des mots aussi lourds de sens que Goulag ou Tazmamart !... Mais notre société de communication, si ouverte et si tolérante, n'admet-elle pas l'info à doses également homéopathiques? La bataille de l'information est toujours à reprendre, contre les autres et contre nous.

A côté de la censure deux domaines resteraient à examiner, celui des oeuvres d'art, si riches en informations mais qui échappent au flot, et celui des énoncés scientifiques qui recherchent, accumulent et périment l'information par définition même. Pour conclure sur la bande moyenne des phénomènes (à laquelle nous nous sommes bornés), il faut souligner combien l'information est par nature éparse, évasive, capricieuse ou intempestive: à chacun ses infos, feux-follets sur le chemin de sa vie. On aimerait la prescrire mais elle échappe à la ligne droite, ou à l'orthodoxie. Par où passe notre information? Comment avons-nous appris ce qui compte vraiment? Certains voudraient canaliser l'information comme on dirige l'énergie dans les conduites forcées de l'école, de la caserne, des usines, des bureaux... Des instituteurs à la règle de fer ont voulu nous faire croire aux Idées platoniciennes et au même soleil pour tous (ou au même journal: en ce temps-là il n'y avait à la TV qu'une seule chaîne). Que le savoir était un édifice, et les intellectuels des intercesseurs obligés. Mais notre lumière naturelle se brise et scintille, notre République s'effrite en démocratie et les réseaux ramifient une raison qui ressemble au rhizome plus qu'à la pyramide. Qui sera juge de la pertinence des infos? A l'audimat devenu notre règle, qu'avons-nous à opposer? Il n'y a pas d'instance centrale de distribution ni de rectification, et il n'est pas souhaitable qu'il y en ait une. L'information, cette grandeur impalpable, ne réside ni dans les choses ni en nous, mais au milieu ou transversalement à nos médias, mot ironique dont l'étymologie rappelle que la relation de communication est première, et que la bataille de l'info se livre toujours entre nous.

3. Ethische Fragen in der Informationpraxis

3.1 Ethische Fragen auf Makroebene

Moral issues in information science[*]

von Rafael Capurro

Introduction

The following ideas on moral issues in information science have two sources: the article by *Kostrewski* and Oppenheim „*Ethics in information science*" [1], and some observations by *Schwarz* (Royal Institute of Technology Library, Sweden) on paper „*Ethical problems in the field of specialized information and communication*" [2]. First I will refer to this background which can provide, I think, a general approach to the moral issues in this field. In the second part, I present some of the latest discussions on these matters as recorded in information science literature. I pay particular attention to the questions raised by the production, storage, dissemination, and use of specialized information through electronic devices ('reference databases' as well as 'source databases') [3]. Nevertheless, this does not exclude more general aspects concerning, for example, the broad social implications of computer technology. These broad aspects of information science ethics can be discussed, I suggest, within the framework of 'communicative ethics', to which I shall refer in the conclusion.

1. Background
1.1. The paper by Kostrewski and Oppenheim

In the editorial introducing the publication of „Ethics in Information Science", Gilchrist expresses the hope of promoting „*some debate on whether information scientists can afford morals and, if so, whether they can translate such ideas into a practical code which can avoid pious sentiment on the one hand, and unenforceable dogma on the other*" [4]. This clear distinction between the debate of ethical problems, and the elaboration of a professional code of ethics could quite profitably be emphasized. It will occupy us later on in this paper. Concerning the content of the Kostrewski-Oppenheim paper, the editor critically remarks that it is difficult to identify its aim, since the argument goes off in all directions. This dispersion should come as no great suprise if one considers that the authors, as they themselves at the very beginning remark, are discussing questions which until then, i.e. until 1980, were not

---

[*] Previously published by the Royal Institute of Technology Library, Stockholm 1985 as Report TRITA-LIB-6024. Reprint from North Holland Publishing Company; Journal of Information Science 11(1985) 113-123.

found on the front pages of the current information science literature. This situation has, in my opinion, only slightly changed since then. By contrast, the authors point to the evolution of American codes of practice in the field of librarianship. The following topics are considered:

a) Ethics in research

Intellectual dishonesty (or 'cheating') in information science research is not a main ethical issue to be discussed, due mainly to the nature of research findings in this science, which still lacks its own theoretical foundation and whose empirical findings are (still) relatively few in comparison with other sciences.Giving credit to colleagues: this issue concerns questions of co-authorship as well as questions of the right to publication. Areas of research that should not be attempted: The issue, raised by Belkin and Robertson [5], refers to the possible use of research results for manipulating recipients of information in the case of sender-oriented (in contrast to user-oriented) systems.

I agree with Kostrewski and Oppenheim that this point should not be underestimated, as information science is essentially concerned not only with information (or knowledge content) but also with its use, and so empirical observations of social behavior must be carried out.

b) Ethics in the teaching of information science

Questions concerning the influence of teaching presented in a biased manner apply, as the authors remark, to all subjects. Information science, being a discipline in its infancy, may be particularly affected by these problems.

c) Ethics in information work

This third field of investigation raises the largest and, I think, also the most specific questions. They are:

- Use (or more acurately: abuse) of work facilities (databases, for instance) by information scientists for private purposes.

- Confidentiality of information: this point concerns the confidential treatment of enquirers' data and their requests by information officers. It implies also the question of advantageous accessibility to information on the part of information officers with respect to the layman, and the possible conflicts (also with regard to third parties) which can derive from this situation.

- Bias of information presented: this means for instance, filtering the search results for particular purposes.

- Problems of information brokers, i.e. of online searchers; for instance if two clients ask for the same information and one of them wishes the exclusion of supply to third parties of his search results. Also pricing policies play a role here in (ethical) decisions.

- Ethical problems for online vendors: who must face up to problems of confidentiality regarding the correctness of the distribution of printed search results, as well as other kinds of interrelations between both parties.

- Information as power: the authors point to the broad social (and socio-political) implications of online information retrieval and mainly to the possibility of restriction of distortion of the information flow. They argue in favour of a wide availability of the new information techniques, while at the same time they admit that printed material, being less difficult to control, is more democratic. The possibilites of abuse or distortion make the argument clearer, that information technology (and technology in general as well as science) is not neutral or, in other words, that it always implies an ethical dimension. Within this context the authors discuss the problem of developing countries as one particular set of underprivileged information users [6]. In conclusion, information scientists, researchers as well as practitioners, have specific ethical responsibilities within their own professional fields of research and their own working institutions as well as with regard to society in general. Concerning the question of a code of ethics, the authors want it to be prepared by a controlling professional body, something which does not exist in our profession. The article provoked a number of reactions which is indeed a sign that it addressed an important issue [7]. My own paper, to which I will now briefly refer, was inspired by it.

1.2. My own views

In my paper in the *Ethical problems in the field of specialized information and communication* I conceived the concept of „specialized information" as including all kinds of scientific, technical, economic, and societal knowledge. I described as a main characteristic of our field what Diemer [8] has called the „Copernican revolution" in information. This means that instead of viewing knowledge as something 'absolute', i.e. separated from its producers and users, information science is confronted with the relativizing situation of a plurality of views and goals from which knowledge can be regarded and searched. As Henrichs remarked [9], this relativity remains tacit when we use the concept of 'objective knowledge', which can then be considered as 'potential information'.Taking into account these two ideas, I first raised the question of the general ground of information science ethics.The basic principle of any ethical reflection is human freedom. This principle is related to the information and communication field for instance in the UN Chart of Human Rights (Art. 19), as well as in the 'Basic Law' (Grundgesetz") of the Federal Republic of Germany (Art. 5, I, p.1). The principle of human freedom can be philosophically interpreted as the openness of human beings to each other as well as to the world which they share, as the radical possibility of talking to and hearing from each other. In this sense, freedom is something we are responsible for because our being together in a common world can, as we all know, be completely distorted, for instance in totalitarian regimes. As ethical questions raised by research and teaching of information science are already being considered through educational theory as well as by scientific research ethics, I concentrated my exposition on the problems of information work.

1.2.1. Ethical principles in the field of information production

As already mentioned, the ethical questions in this field are closely related to those of the ethics of scientific research. I found that in considering the results of research produced by specialists from the point of view of their communication, authors are ethically responsible for the truthfulness and objectivity of their statements. Truthfulness means on the one hand the honest search for truth and, on the other, openness to criticism. Objectivity points to the degree of informativeness, which should be more qualitative than quantitative, as opposed to the point of view of the information disseminator. To achieve this goal it is necessary to use the best available (information) means. This can lead to different kinds of ethical conflicts if, for instance, such means are monopolized by a person or a group of persons, or they are practically not accessible, or they are explicitly eluded in order to achieve premeditated goals.

1.2.2. Ethical principles in the field of information dissemination

In the field of information dissemination practical work one is confronted with the following ethical issues:

a) Principle of accessibility

Specialized information should be available to everyone, while taking note of political, economical or other kinds of restrictions. This is a matter of high ethical importance, if we think for instance of ethnic minorities, race discrimination, conflicts between 'information rich' and 'information poor' nations ('information colonialism'), information conflicts between developed nations, questions of monopolies and democratic controls etc. Can a 'paperless society' (or, more modestly, 'paperless communication of specialized information') guarantee the 'democracy' of printed media? How shall we achieve the ethical balance between oral, printed, and electronic communication?

b) Principle of confidentiality

This ethical field comprises all kinds of questions concerning the responsibility of information disseminators with the information itself as well as with the protection of personal data about producers and users including research results and modifications, etc. This principle also concerns all kinds of intrusion into the private sphere of users from the side of the database producer.

c) Principle of completeness

In the case of a database producer, for instance, this principle points to the possibility of information discrimination or of biased selectivity, through which users would be misled. This question concerns also the process of abstracting and indexing. At the same time it should be remembered that a database producer is not responsible for the truth content but only for the correctness (or correct reproduction) of data. Limitations of this principle concern the problem of selectivity and evaluation of knowledge contents, and the problem of what can be called 'information pollution', i.e. the inflationary character of information to be coped with. Completeness is furthermore an ideal representation which can turn into ideology if one 'forgets' the radical incompleteness and processibility of human knowledge as well as the many different channels through which it is being distributed.

1.2.3. Ethical principles in the field of information use

Considering the plurality of goals that users can have when they look for specialized information, the ethical questions concerning its use are very diversified indeed. In my paper, I pointed to the principles of objectivity, (qualitative) completeness, and the search for truth. As we are accustomed to think of truth in the sense of scientific validity, I remarked on the broader sense that this term must have, in order to include theoretical as well as practical goals for handling information. Kostrewski and Oppenheim pointed to different possible ethical conflicts in the field of information use, as for instance, the filtering of search results, the misuse of information (and of information facilities) for different purposes. In conclusion, and quoting Aristotle's *Nichomachean Ethics* (1094b), I remarked that ethics should not aim at the same kind of precision as other sciences. The ethical discourse can only give hints for personal and socially responsible action. Its two basic dangers are to fall into casuistry on the one hand, or to consider itself, in a fundamentalist manner, as a dogmatic guideline for action or as its theoretical substitute. With this latter remark I would like to discuss the criticisms by Schwarz, to which I shall now turn.

1.3. The criticisms by Stephan Schwarz

When I discussed these matters with Mr. Schwarz during a meeting some time ago, he made two basic comments on my ideas: one concerning the problem of the interrelation between general ethical statements and their practical codification, and the other regarding the nature of ethical 'oughts'. With regard to the first point, he stressed the intrinsic weakness of ethical codes which do not capture the essence of ethical aspects, just because ethics cannot be codified. As a commentary to his views, he mentioned an article by Ladd: *The Quest for a Code of Professional Ethics. An Intellectual and Moral Confusion* presented at a workshop of the American Association for the Advancement of Science, and which has been recently published in a book edited by Johnson and Snapper on *Ethical Issues in the Use of Computers* [10]. In his paper, Ladd argues that due to its essentially problematic character ethics cannot be codified. Ethical principles are the (temporary) result of argumentation, and are not established by consensus or decision-making. To speak about a 'code of ethics' is therefore a misleading formulation. Such codes have pros and cons: they inspire 'ethical' conduct in professionals, advise and alert them, but they can also have negative side-effects, giving professionals a sense of complacency, even covering up 'irresponsible' conduct, and, what is more important, they can act as a defence mechanism diverting attention from the real 'macro-' and 'micro-ethical' problems of the profession. With these two concepts, Ladd points to the problems that a group confronts in its relation to society, and to the problem within the group itself (including clients, colleagues, and employers). The key question for a professional society concerning ethics is not to establish a code, but to promote the discussion on ethical issues connected with its activities. Following this argument, Schwarz stressed the doubts he has, on whether ethical codes may cause more harm than good, since good people in the profession will not need them, and the 'bad guys' will not adhere to them anyway. I agree with Ladd's arguments concerning the difference between ethical arguments and codes. I also think that the discussion on ethical problems should be the key issue. This discussion should lead to consideration of „the inherent incompatibilities and limitations" (Schwarz) of ethical principles. The concept of 'principle', having metaphysical connotations, could, indeed, be misleading if it were taken as a dogmatic ground to establishing a 'code of ethics' in the sense criticized by Ladd. If principles are the result of argument, and therefore always open to further discussion, then they are, as the word itself expresses, not an 'end' but a 'beginning'... They are not absolute grounds imposed as rules or laws. In this sense, and with regard to the nature of 'oughts', I considered the ground on which ethical problems arise in our field, namely human freedom, as openness to each other and to the world. To talk about the 'oughts' can indeed be subversive. In his paper „Research, integrity and privacy" [11] Schwarz cites the following passage from J. Weizenbaum's Computer power and human reason": „Some scientists, though by no means all, maintain that the domain of science is universal, that there can be nothing which, as a consequence of some 'higher' principle, ought not to be studied. And from this premise the conclusion is usually drawn that any talk of ethical 'oughts' which apply to science is inherently subversive and antiscientific, even anti-intellectual." [12]

The concepts of integrity and privacy discussed by Schwarz concern the protection of personal data I referred to under the principle of confidentiality. Reflections on integrity presuppose, as Schwarz remarks, a reflection on 'personality', 'liberty', 'confidence' and 'respect'. Privacy, as defined by Schwarz: „concerns the individual's right and ability to decide for himself what information may be communicated to, from, or about him, and the obligation of others to respect such right." Integrity „has to do with the individual's right and ability to decide and act autonomously, perhaps in particular matters of developing and adhering to a personal morality (functioning as a 'moral agent'), and the obligation of others to respect this freedom" [13]. These concepts lead to ethical problems, for instance when the information freely communicated by authors is unduly manipulated by storage and retrieval processes. To quote Schwarz again: „Even in representing and communicating purely technical or scientific data one has to be extremely careful to avoid any interpretation or application of data that is incompatible with their true significance." [14] Taking into consideration that something like 'absolute objectivity' is unattainable, the significance of this ethical issue is manifest.With regard to 'ethical codes' Schwarz concludes that ethical problems are too complex to be formalized. Codes entail generalizations and have to ignore the question of application by the individual agent „which is after all the essential part of morality" [15]. The discussion of the concept of 'freedom of research' carried out by Schwarz has, I think, a similar significance and is also intrinsically related to the question of 'freedom of information' and to the special problems raised by the electronic storage and dissemination of specialized information. Ethics need to be specified in an argumentative manner in our field, if we want to deal with its problems which lack, also in this respect, empiricial studies and theoretical foundations. Given the complexity of ethical matters which is distorted if reduced to generalized codes as well as to a rigid canon of apparently unequivocal and dogmatic principles, ethical discourse must be above all, and this is also underlined by Schwarz, a prudential" discourse. Prudence is a virtue, i.e. a source of action which characterizes the situation of someone who is conscious of his or her limitations. It delimits the anti-criterion 'Everything is allowed', as it makes us aware of an ambivalent situation which does not allow the schizoid unification of opposites, or the simplistic 'solution' of giving one of them up. We just do not know in advance what is absolutely 'good' or 'bad'. A prudential ethical discourse has the function of preserving ethical sensitivity, and is therefore the condition for becoming responsible, i.e. moral within an unforseeable future [16].

2. Moral issues in information science literature

I shall base the following exposition on the distinction made by Ladd between 'macro-' and 'micro-ethical' problems. The former concern, as I have already mentioned, the problems that a group confronts in its relation to society. In our case it has to do with the general social implications of information technology and, in particular, of information retrieval. The topics discussed here include: post-industrial society, the relationship between 'information poor' and 'information rich' countries, free flow of information, privacy and media etc. 'Micro-ethical' problems are those problems arising within the group itself. The group of information workers includes users, producers, and disseminators of specialized information. Some of the ethical problems being discussed are for instance: the question of accessibility, data security, professional ethics, (ethics of research, teaching, and information work), copyright issues, etc.

2.1. Macro-ethical problems

Two state-of-the-art reviews on the broad subject 'Information and Society' have been published in the Annual Review of Information Science and Technology"; one by Parker in 1973, and the other by Kochen in 1983 [17]. In the introduction Kochen states that the term 'information', which in the 1950's, under the influence of mathematical communication theory, was expected (unrealistically, as Kochen remarks) to be distinguished from 'meaning', has now (in the 1980's) come to mean 'decision-relevant data'. With regard to the concept of 'society', it was Bell who characterized the post-industrial stage as information-based, i.e. as a society based on high technology which facilitates well-informed rational decision-making. Of course, as Kochen remarks, other less technocratic alternatives are possible, but it seems that no matter what, the production and communication of knowledge, and not so much the technology itself, would play the significant role in the future society. „The central theme of the discussion", says Kochen, „is that information and knowledge can help us cope with these dilemmas but only if it is balanced by human values and judgement. It will not suffice for information professionals to have only specialized technical or professional skills [17]. They must also be humanistically enlightened generalists if they are to help bring knowledge to bear on these vital issues." [18] Kochen discusses the following six dilemmas:

2.1.1. Security and information

Two ethical dilemmas are considered. One concerns the gap between expert knowledge and the informedness of the public in matters concerning defence and security. The other point concerns the dilemma between openness or freedom of information and the constraints of national (and, as I would like to add, international!) security. The discussion on this subject has been recently critically examined in a book by Demac [19]. According to Russell Pipe, „a formidable challenge in the 1980s is how to reconcile the traditional principle of an open and largely unrestricted flow of information across borders with legitimate protective measures and outright protectionism." [20].

2.1.2. Employment and information

This is a broad and (indeed) important field. In the narrow field of specialized information Kochen foresees a further developemt of the general trend towards end-user searching, while information specialists will take care of the design and maintenance of user-friendly systems and languages. The ethical discussion concerning the dilemma between technological change and the organization of work is of vital societal relevance.

2.1.3. Business, industry, and information

Under this heading Kochen discusses the political and economical conflicts involved in the shaping of the 'information society' on the one hand, and the problem of informed decision-making in the business world on the other.

2.1.4. Planning

Here the dilemma arises when one considers the complexity of computer-based systems, and the questions of their control. In the field of specialized information, we see the problem of having adequate knowledge relevant to planning, which is not communicated to and used by decision-makers. We have only to remember the ecological crises, institutional changes, problems of social health, etc.

2.1.5. Decentralization

In the field of information retrieval we have been observing the tendency of computing centres towards an ever increasing degree of centralization. The fusion of computer through international networks is also one more step in this direction. This enables collective work to be conducted and supports the internationalization of information. Parallel to these developments, we are confronted with the growing presence of microcomputers, and advances in the field of expert systems. At a recent conference on the application of microcomputers in information, Kochen formulated the ethical dimension of the problem with the following words: „What, then, are the benefits of the new technologies? Will microcomputers and associated communication media, as has the car and TV, change our lifestyles and, in retrospect, make us aware of as many negative as positive benefits? Will they restrict or expand the options for our individual choice and will they help us make more or less informed choices? On balance, will they help us become a more informed society and if so, will that help us become more human in our evolution toward a wiser and better species? That is the key question." [21] At the same conference Henrichs [22] in his welcoming address pointed to the dilemma of an increasing decentralization which would bring about an irresponsible fragmentation of the world's knowledge, limiting efforts at cooperation, and creating mini-monopolies which are, in the final analysis, nothing but the reverse of the coin of large scale monopolies. The problem is complicated even more if we consider that systems transparence should not mean giving up privacy and integrity, and the confidential character of certain types of information; especially when this confidentiality is desired by the producer and/or user of the information.

2.1.6. Information overload and mismach

This dilemma came at the beginning of the modern information revolution, and in particular, of information retrieval with bibliographic databases. Complex issues require complex interdisciplinary, as well as integrated approaches to information. New forms of knowledge representation and processing challenge our self appraisal. The epistemological and ethical discussions concerning the implications of research and development in the field of Artificial Intelligence are an expression of this challenge. The internationality of information raises cultural questions, concerning, for instance, the problem of information barriers [23], on the one hand, whereas on the other it poses new problems (for instance to developing countries) concerning their legitimate national rights and interests, the problems of information colonialism (or even imperialism), the threat of cultural traditions (as underlined by Rosenberg [24]. The question of privacy and integrity pervades all these dilemmas [25]. Auerbach [26] has recently stressed the urgent need for ethical reflection if professional respsonsibility towards society is to become, as it should, a topic of major concern in a society based and threatened by information.

2.2. Micro-ethical problems

Codes of ethics, or, *pace* Ladd, codes of practice, should not by any means be identified, as we have already seen, with the argument and open discussion of ethical problems within a profession. Nevertheless, they are, I think, an expression of such discussions or, in other words, they are among others one kind of response to the ethical problems with which the professionals are confronted. As a result of such inner-professional discussions the American Society for Information Science identified the following issues in 1984, where professional values or ethics play a significant role:

- Downloading,
- Privacy (deliberate or inadvertent disclosure of files/data),
- Copyright (software privacy, intellectual property, etc.),

- Pricing (competition),
- Computer Crime (felonious actions),
- Security (protection of passwords, IDs, etc.),
- Intellectual/Academic Freedom,
- Career Paths/Job Security/Tenure,
- Transborder Data Flow,
- Public/Private Sector (fee paid, free goods, subsidy, etc.),
- Client Relationships,
- Employer/Employee Relationships,
- Concealing or Falsifying Information [27].

The discussion of each one of these points, as well as of others not explicitly mentioned as, for instance, ethical responsibilities for indexers [28], or ethics in database searching [29], goes beyond the scope of this review. I will, however, mention in some detail, the codes of practice issued by EUSIDIC. Three have been published up to now. They deal respectively with:

(1) Database and databank producers,
(2) Host services,
(3) Telecommunications for publicly available information services. Two more on 'Brokers and End Users', and 'Downloading' are at the draft stage.

I should like to mention some of the points discussed by EUSIDIC members previous to the publication of the codes. In the 1982 issue of *Newsidic*, the EUSIDIC newsletter, [30] Aitchison drew attention to the interrelations between the database producer and author/publisher, host/online service, and user. While, for instance, the database producer should reproduce documents (or their surrogates) accurately (I mentioned this point in my ethics paper under the principle of completeness), publishers should supply their journals regularly. Database producers should provide databases to selected hosts under openly-stated arrangements or, if provided generally, under the same conditions to all hosts on the one hand; while hosts should maintain a satisfactory service providing continuous and reliable access to the database on the other hand. With regard to the use of data, they should be treated confidentially by the database producer and, correspondingly, they should be provided by the host to the producer.

Information brokers should be permitted to make temporary storage on machine-readable form of copies of search outputs for display, but they should not distribute generally or sell copies of outputs from the database without the permission of the database producer.

Finally, with regard to the user, the database producer should make every effort to ensure that the user can obtain the documents referred to on the database, and should provide training opportunities; while the user should make full use of them, providing feedback on problems and errors encountered in the database or in its implementation.

In the same Newsidic issue, Popper underlined the question of a code of conduct from the point of view of what a user can expect from online systems. He accentuates, for instance, reliable access to those databases the user requires. There should be no interference by the telecommunication element, or by other reasons not stipulated in the contract. Users should have access to commercially offered information sources. Their data should remain confidential. Fees and dues should not be discriminatory. Their obligations concern the contract stipulations, especially with regard to exploiting (without permission) copies of databases or duplication of search output for profit. Finally, Citroen made some remarks to promote discussion of a code of conduct for information intermediaries: they should inform clients about the principles of the techniques employed, they should only accept professional assignments for which they are qualified, they should guarantee the confidentiality of information entrusted to them, they should not use passwords for other purposes than for those they were allocated, they should treat personal data confidentially, and charges should be reasonable. The EUSIDIC code of practice for database and databank producers comprises eight points of which a selection follows:

(1) There should be a clearly stated policy with respect to the selection of material for inclusion in the database (points 1.1 and 1.2) (cf. my 'principle of completeness').

(2) The information in the database should be correct. Users and vendors should be made aware of significant errors. The responsibility for corrections lies with the producer (points 1.3, 1.4, 1.5) (cf. my 'principle of completeness').

(3) The principles used in creating specialised indexes should be clearly stated. Online vendors should make clear how a database is implemented, and they should give notice to the users, when a database is withdrawn either totally or from a particular service (points 1.6, 1.7, 1.8) (cf. my 'principle of accessibility').

With regard to host services EUSIDIC proposes eight rules (cf. my 'principle of accessibility') including:

(1) Free availability of services to all potential users (points 2.1, 2.2).

(2) Personal data may be collected by hosts for different purposes (for instance on behalf of a database producer or for legal and/or accounting purposes). It should be treated confidentially, including the data concerning end-user search strategy. All parties concerned should have full details of what information is being collected, for what purposes, who has access to it, and for how long it is retained (points 2.3, 2.4, 2.5, 2.6).

(3) The host should ensure that the documentation necessary to use the system is made available to all users. If the system is internationally available, the services (user support, documentation, and training) should be offered in different geographical locations (points 2.7, 2.8).

Finally, EUSIDIC proposes ten rules concerning telecommunications for publicly-available information services which include:

(1) It considers that the fairest basis for the calculation of telecommunication charges for a given services provided by public administrations is on the basis of the cost of providing that service, plus a reasonable profit margin (point 3.1).

(2) If a database network required cannot for any reason be provided by public administration, physical or legal obstacles should not be placed in the way of other bodies offering to provide the required services (point 3.2).

(3) Administrations have a duty to ensure that what is connected to public networks will not harm the network or maintenance personnel. No political, geographic or economic discrimination for or against equipment should be made (point 3.3).

(4) Administrations should recognise that continental and intercontinental data networks are vital for many new and future information services. They should be efficient and economic. Leased circuits are an important option which should not be impeded by administrations (points 3.4, 3.5, 3.6, 3.7).

(5) The communication authority should not normally be concerned with the content of what is being carried (3.8).

(6) New publicly-available data services will require the maximum of flexibility in terms of charging and access (point 3.9).

(7) Administrations have the duty to attempt to satisfy many different sectors, both nationally and internationally (point 3.10). To sum up, then, we can say that all these rules aim to preserve the openness of information flow, taking into account at the same time the protection of personal data as well as the legitimate interests of all parties involved in the process of producing, storing, distributing and use of information. Openness, confidentiality, accuracy, and fairness can be considered as essential ethical cornerstones in our field. But, as Ladd remarked, they should not be used to give us a sense of complacency or, what is worse, to cover 'irresponsible' conduct. Professional ethics is not a 'special' ethics, basically separated from 'macro-' or 'communicative ethics', as I suggest in the last part of this paper.

3. The paradigm of communicative ethics

Until now, I have used the term 'morality' and 'ethics' as if they were synonyms. This is partly correct, if we consider that Latin thinkers, such as Cicero, translated the Greek concept of ethics as „philosophia moralis" [31]. In both cases the meaning originated in connection with the designation of customs, practices, and traditions (ethe, mores). Since Cicero, philosophy has often been subdivided into „philosophia rationalis" or logic, „philosophia naturalis" or physics, and „philosophia moralis" or ethics. Within the domain of ethics, which was established as a science by Aristotle, a distinction is usually made between ethics and morality. Bertrand Russell for example, defines ethics as consisting of „general principles which help to determine rules of conduct", whereas „it is not the business of ethics to arrive at actual rules of conduct, such as 'Thou shalt not steal'. This is the province of morals. Ethics is expected to provide a basis from which such rules can be deduced" [32]. This expectation is, I believe, a misinterpretation, if one hopes to deduce the concrete historical forms of morality from their ethical foundations. If we are not to commit the 'naturalistic fallacy' (G.E. Moore) of deducing moral categories from empirical (or metaphysical) concepts, then we have to presuppose that concepts such as 'responsibility', 'duty' etc. are to be founded on human freedom „Ought" does not follow from is", as philosophers say. Ethics is then the search by argument for a (non-naturalistic as well as non-subjectivistic) foundation of morality [33]. In what sense do we speak of ethics as a science, or, in other terms, how well (or mis-) founded can ethical reasoning be? In his introduction to Aristotle's Analytics Ross remarks that Aristotle's attitude to logic is not unlike his attitude to ethics. In his study of each there is much that is pure theory, but in both cases the theory is thought of as ancillary to practice - to right living in the one case, to right thinking in the other [34]. In both cases, according to Aristotle, we start by intuitive knowledge of first principles, and combine them with (scientific) knowledge got (by induction) from sense-perception. In the field of ethics this combination is called „sophia". This Aristotelian approach fails in two respects:

(1) sense-perception is not of 'pure facts' but it is (as it would be called in hermeneutics) interpreted perception.

(2) first principles are not really so self-evident, i.e. we cannot rely ultimately on them.

If there is no absolute ground for ethical reasoning, and if the perception of ethical problems is influenced by our ethical (and non-ethical) views, then all ethical discourse is necessarily hermeneutical, i.e. open to criticism, and it never substitutes the moral option itself that cannot be definitely deduced from it. According to Gadamer [35] (in implicit opposition to Ross) this was clearly seen by Aristotle, whose ethics do not rest on an absolute ground (as do Plato's and Kant's) but, as I have already quoted (Eth. Nic. 1094b) it does not aim at the same kind of certainty as other scientific disciplines. It is also in this sense, I think, that Schwarz criticizes the role of 'ethical codes' as preconceived patterns, where 'prospective responsibility' is restricted in terms of correspondence with foreseen performance. Such a view tends to simplify and generalize real life situations to fit them into a too narrow framework of norms and values... it tends to transform a dynamic morality into a static one" [36]. Schwarz suggests, as a possible remedy, a 'cybernetic approach' to moral questions, within which the whole complexity of moral and non-moral components as well as prospective and retrospective aspects should be analyzed, comparing the alternatives, and stressing the role of personal responsibility, which is not just the mechanical application of anonymous rules. As the Belgian philosopher Hottois recently remarked [37], prudence" is the cardinal virtue of ethical reasoning, if we are to avoid the fallacies of metaphysical, technocratic, and positivistic theories which overvalue man's knowledge or power, or just aim to leave aside the perspective of enigma, and openness which characterizes not only human existence but also the technical, and, of course, the cosmic process. In the field of information science (and technology) we need, I think, such a prudent ethics which is a communicative, and an evolutionary one. It is a communicative ethics not only because it deals with the field of (specialized) information and communication, but also because it considers communication as the medium through which the complexity of retrospective and prospective aspects in this field can be discussed. It is an evolutionary or, as we could also say, a hermeneutical ethics because it does not presuppose the clarity and validity of first principles, but it questions and criticizes them, taking into account the complexity and limitations of concrete situations. The paradigm of a communicative ethics has been further developed by the German philosophers Apel [38] and Habermas [39], and it has been recently put into explicit relation to our field by the sociologist Vowe [40]. A key feature of this paradigm is the conception of an open community in which argumentation and mutual respect are the basic results. Ideally, a 'universal audience' is concerned from which the actual or real communication communities are distinguished. Without going now into the details of this (transcendental) argumentation, I would like to comment that such an 'ideal' could become an ideology, if a real community aiming at its performance closes itself by becoming what the French philosophers Lávinas [41] calls a 'totality', i.e. a structure which can no longer be questioned by all those communities which are excluded de facto. The ethical relation is founded, as Lávinas rightly stresses, on a 'face to face' basis, and not on the primacy of anonymous rules. It is, I think, this specific ethical interrelation between human beings which we want to protect, when we talk about privacy, be preserving at the same time its openness. It would be an illusion to believe that because we have 'better' communication media, we are communicating better. We would be reducing means to ends... and at the end, we could even be dominated by the communication power itself. But there is no reason for passivity or resignation, I think, if we aim at a constant and tentative clarification of the process of communication. Such a clarification should take seriously the 'finite' or conjectural nature of human knowledge, which could be ethically used for promoting survival [42]. The ethics of knowing, the information science ethics, is (or should be) an ethics of individual and collective responsibility towards knowledge, its production, communication, and use. A community that takes for granted a vacuum in these matters is probably oriented towards dissolution.

References and notes

[1] Kostrewski and C. Oppenheim, Ethics in information science, Journal of Information Science 1 (1980) 227-283.

[2] Capurro, Zur Frage der Ethik in Fachinformation und -kommunikation, Nachrichten für Dokumentation 32 (1) (1981) 9-12.

[3] C. Cuadra, Ed.: Directory of Online Databases, Vol. 5 (Santa Monica, CA, 1983). Gilchrist, Editorial, Journal of Information Science 1 (1980) 247.

[4] A. Gilchrist, Editorial, Journal of Information Science 1 (1980) 247.

[5] N.J. Belkin and S.E. Robertson, Some ethical and political implications of theoretical research in information science, paper presented at the ASIS Annual Meeting 1976.

[6] Together with the article by Kostrewski and Oppenheim, two other contributions in the same issue of the Journal of Information Science deal with problems of information in the third world: A.M. Woodward, Future information requirements of the third world, pp. 259-265, and, B.V. Tell, The awakening information needs of the developing countries, pp. 285-289.
A. Gilchrist commented on the interrelations between the three papers with the following words: „A journalist writing recently remarked that 'Information is wealth; rapid and wide access to information is power', and this is perhaps one of the more interesting and more intractable problems underlying the ethical aspects for the Information Society, and those engaged in peddling information. This is highlighted particularly in connection with the 'information gap' between the industrial countries and the Third World which is touched on in the paper by Kostrewski and Oppenheim, and which underlies the papers by Woodward and by Tell, also in this issue. At this level, it is difficult to distinguish between ethics as a way of life and ethics as a professional code - and yet the two are obviously related" [4].
L.F. Lunin, B.K. Eres, Eds., Perspectives on international information issues, J. ASIS (May 1985) 143-199; and J. Conquy Beer-Gabel, Information du Tiers Monde et Coopération Internationale (Paris, La oc. Francaise 1984).

[7] M.E.D. Koenig, Ethics in information science, Journal of Information Science 3 (1981) 45-48.

[8] A. Diemer, Klassifikation, Thesaurus und was dann? Nachrichten für Dokumentation 23 (2) (1972) 52-57.

[9] N. Henrichs, Informationswissenschaft und Wissensorganisation. in W. Kunz, Ed., Informationswissenschaft (Oldenbourg, München, 1978) 150-169.

[10] J. Ladd, The quest for a code of professional ethics: an intellectual and moral confusion, in Deborah G. Johnson and J.W. Snapper, Eds., Ethical Issues in the use of Computers (Wadsworth, Belmont, 1985) 8-13.

[11] Stephan Schwarz, Research, integrity and privacy. Notes on a conceptual complex, *Social Science Information* 18 (1) (1979) 103-136.

[12] J. Weizenbaum, Computer Power and Human Reason (Freeman, SF, CA, 1976).

[13] S. Schwarz [11, pp. 104-105].

[14] Op.cit., p. 106.

[15] Op.cit., p. 109. [16]

[16] R. Capurro, Technics, Ethics, and the Question of Phenomenology, paper presented at the XVIIth International Phenomenology Conference (Theme: „Morality within the Life World") Frankfurt, 21-26 June, 1985. Proceedings to be published in: *Analecta Husserliana* (Reidel, Dordrecht/ Boston). My paper is based on an analysis of: Gilbert Hottois, *Le Signe et la Technique* (Paris, 1984).

Dordrecht/Boston). My paper is based on an analysis of: Gilbert Hottois, Le Signe et la Technique" (Paris, 1984).

[17] Manfred Kochen, Information and society, in: Martha E. Williams, Annual Rev.Sci.Techn 18 (1983) 277-304.

[18] For further issues see: Bruce Williams, The information society - how different? Aslib Proceedings" 37 (1985); Michael Marien, Some questions for the information society, The Information Society" 3 (1984) 181-197; Susan Artandi: Computerized information systems implications for society, in: K.R. Brown, ed., The Challenge of Information Technology", FID Congress, 1982, (North-Holland, Amsterdam, 1983) 93-97; Jack Meadows, Social limitations on the use of new information technology, Journal of Information Science" 6 (1983) 11-20; James D. Halloran, Information and communication: information is the answer, but what is the question? Journal of Information Science" 7 (1983) 159-167.

[18] Op.cit. p. 281.

[19] Donna A. Demac, Keeping America Uninformed. Government Secrecy in the 1980s" (The Pilgrim Press, New York, 1984). For a review of the literature on this subject see my report: „Schützt die Einschränkung des wissenschaftlich-technischen Informationstransfers die US-'National Security'? (FIZ-KA-3, 1982).

[20] G. Russel Pipe, Transborder data flow: main issues, trends and impacts on international business, in: Juan F. Radanad G. Russel Pipe, Eds., „Communication Regulation and International Business", Proceedings of a Workshop held at the International Management Institute (IMI), Geneva, Switzerland, April 1983 (North-Holland, Amsterdam, 1984) 49.

[21] Manfred Kochen, Impacts of microcomputers on information use patterns, in, Carl Keren and Linda Perlmutter, Eds., The Application of Mini- and Micro-Computers in Information, Documentation and Libraries", Proceedings Tel-Aviv, Israel, March 13-18, 1983 (North-Holland, Amsterdam, 1983) 470.

[22] Henrichs, Welcoming address, in: Carl Keren et al. [21, pp. 5-7].

[23] J. Michel, Linguistic and political barriers in the international transfer of information in science and technology, Journal of Information Science" 5 (4) (1982) 131-135; and the discussion of the arguments by Jim Davies, Linguistic and political barriers in the international transfer of information in science and technology: A reinterpretation, Journal of Information Science 6 (1983) 179-181.

[24] Victor Rosenberg, Cultural and political traditions and their impact on the transfer and use of scientific information, Information Services & Use" 1 (1981) 75-80.

[25] Cf. [6]

[26] Isaac L. Auerbach, Professional responsibility for information privacy, Information Systems Management 2 (1985) 77-81: „The price that concerns me, and should concern you, is the forfeiture of individual freedom through the loss of privacy... I am increasingly concerned about the totalitarian potential of centralized data banks. As information management professionals, you are the experts in computer security, and with this knowledge you must act as if the private rights of individuals throughout the world depend on you - because they do. A professional ethic that directly concerns the safety and well-being of the public applies here." (p. 81). Cf., G. Salton, A progress report on information privacy and data security, J. Amer. Soc.Inf. Science" (March, 1980) 75-83; cf., David H. Flaherty, ed., Privacy and Data Protection - An International Bibliography" (Mansell, 1984).

[27] Julia C. Blixurd and Edmond J. Sawyer, A code of ethics for ASIS. The challenge before us, ASIS Bulletin" (October, 1984) 8-10.

[28] Harold Borko and Charles L. Bernier, Indexing Concepts and Methods" (Academic Press, New York, 1978) 223-226.

[29] Childress, Ethics in Database Searching, Online '83 Conference Proceedings, Chicago, IL. 10-12 October, 1983, pp. 11-14.

[30] Newsidic 52 (March, 1982).

[31] Cicero, De fato

[32] Bertrand Russell, Outline of Philosophy" (Unwin, London, 1979) 180.

[33] Stephen E. Toulmin, An Examination of the Place of Reason in Ethics (Cambridge, 1968).

[34] Aristotle's Prior and Posterior analytics, a revised text with introduction and commentary by W.D. Ross (Clarendon Press, Oxford, 1949) 25.

[35] Hans-Georg Gadamer, Über die Möglichkeit einer philosophischen Ethik, in: Kleine Schriften I (Mohr, Tübingen, 1967) 179-191.

[36] Stephan Schwarz, On responsibility in planning and decisionmaking, report TRITA-LIB-6006, May 1977, p. 275.

[37] Cf. [16]

[38] K.O. Apel, Die Kommunikationsgemeinschaft als transzendentale Voraussetzung der Sozialwissenschaften, in: Transformation der Philosophie" (Suhrkamp, Frankfurt, 1976).

[39] J. Habermas, Theorie des kommunikativen Handelns" (Suhrkamp, Frankfurt, 1981).

[40] Vowe, Information und Kommunikation" (Westdeutscher Verlag, Opladen, 1984).

[41] E. Lávinas, Totalitá et Infini" (Martinus Nijhoff, The Hague, 1969).

[42] Charles L. Bernier, Ethics of knowing, J. Amer. Soc. Inf. Science" (May 1985) 211-212.

Ethical Considerations in Technology Transfer[*]

Von Thomas J. Froehlich

Abstract

Issues in technology transfer are examined from the perspectives of Kantianism and utilitarianism and in terms of the factors that must be considered in moral deliberation: i.e., factors of social responsibility; social utility; and individual, professional and institutional survival. In current practice, utilitarianism operates under the guise of technology needs assessment. The article advances the argument that ethical deliberation in technology transfer is biased toward the utilitarian view, that utilitarianism has inherent difficulties in projecting the consequences of technology transfer, that utilitarian principles are often sabotaged by political or self-serving goals and ideologies, and that the perspectives offered by Kant and feminism are important aspects in establishing what should be a dialectical process about determining which technologies are appropriate and how they should be transferred.

Introduction

Wales seems an unusual place for an American to reflect on ethical considerations in technology transfer, particularly the transfer of information technology, and the role of information professionals in the process. Yet it is the experiences of teaching several summers at the International Graduate Summer School in Aberystwyth that invoked these reflections. Students, faculty, and professionals from as many as forty different countries gathered for this cross-cultural educational experience, now under the auspices of the Department of Library and Information Studies of the University College of Wales. (Before its merger with the University College of Wales, the school was known as the College of Librarianship Wales. The summer program has been renamed the International Graduate Information Summer School.) The summer school was designed, in part, precisely for the purpose of facilitating transfer of information technologies from developed countries to less developed countries (LDCs). Information technologies are an integral part of successful technology transfer, and contribute to an LDC's ability to develop and sustain scientific and technological activities. During these summer programs, information professionals from various countries discovered many shared needs and concerns, but the diversity of needs, the plurality of problems, and cultural differences also became apparent. This heterogeneity made the issues of technology transfer and ethical considerations all the more difficult.

---

[*] Reprinted with permission from *Library Trends*, Volume 40, Number 2, pp. 275-302.
Copyright © 1991 The Board of Trustees of the University of Illinois.

Transfer of technology touches on such issues as global economics, balance of trade deficits, political and social beliefs, balances of power, allocation of world resources and environmental issues. Its rise to prominence as a geopolitical issue stems from imbalances between advanced or developed countries and under-developed or lesser developed countries. Graham (1982) reports that northern or developed countries account for 95 percent of all the world's research and development while southern countries, representing 70 percent of the world's population, generate only 4 percent (p. 45). Technology transfer is important for economic development, but much of the available technology is invested with proprietary rights so that it cannot be freely transferred.

Approaches to Technology

There are many ways in which technology can be understood. For this article we will distinguish among three levels: (1) technology in general; (2) technological practices and (3) technological packages. In general, technology can be characterized as a group of techniques, either intellectual or embodied, orchestrated as a totality for solving a particular problem or set of interrelated problems. The technologies with which information professionals are familiar can be divided into two kinds: (1) „intellectual technologies" (Taylor, 1986) such as classification, cataloging, indexing and abstracting, technologies that perform „value-added processes in information systems" and (2) technologies as embodied systems of tools or procedures, such as computer systems and their use in online public access catalogs. In practice, this distinction is difficult to maintain, because intellectual technologies, manifest in the mental activities of theoreticians or experienced professionals, lead to forms of embodiment: e.g., theories of classification lead to systems such as Dewey Decimal, thesauri, authority lists, etc. These embodiments, taken up by professionals, may in turn influence perceptions and intellectual organization.

The intellectual technologies are like Kant's schemas, structures by which experience is organized and which make experience possible. For example, information professionals acquire classification schemes through courses, lectures, exercises and reading; but once the schemas are acquired, they become devices through which classifiers and catalogers structure their experience of intellectual works, which thereby transform their experience of those works. This may not always be appropriate. Sanford Berman (1981) noted that the 1979 *Dewey Decimal Classification* had inadequate coverage of popular music and gay issues and had ambiguous treatment of North American Indians. Classification schemes and subject headings tend to reflect the biases of the general population. These biases may inhibit the easy applications of such classifications to local issues in a developing country.

In addition to characterizing the technology and associated with information work, one should also distinguish, as Pacey does (1983), between technology and technology practices. Technology practices are individual or generic applications of technologies in a specific context of people and organizations: „...technology-practice is thus the *application of scientific and other knowledge to practical tasks by ordered systems that involve people and organizations, living things and machines*" (Pacey's emphasis, p. 6). Technology practice is geared to specific contexts, which entail cultural and organizational constraints. For example, a Dewey Decimal classification used in a special library may be adapted to meet local needs and objectives. Recommendations for appropriate classification embodied in the Dewey rules may be overridden to suit organizational requirements.

Thus intellectual technologies lead to forms of embodiment (classification schemes) which in turn, through the activities of trained or experienced professionals, lead to specific practices (e.g., classification of a particular text for a particular information-seeking environment). But it should be a dialectical process: problems in particular classifications should lead to reflection on the forms of embodiment and the grounding intellectual technologies. Unfortunately, there are three reasons why this may not occur: (1) practices may pose insoluble problems: e.g., in hierarchical classification schemes, it is often difficult to expand the vocabulary, modify the meaning of a term, or describe complex concepts (Meadow, 1967, p. 26); (2) practitioners may not communicate difficulties to classification rule makers; and (3) classification schemes have historical inertia and tend to be inflexible.

A technological package, a third approach to technology, can be seen as an uprooted technological practice. A given technology is developed for a particular cultural and historical environment. Upon its success, the developers often attempt to generalize the technology by disengaging it from its original application. Examples include many library automation systems, such as NOTIS, which have been „home grown" - that is, built for a particular university setting; they then become a technological package marketed to other universities and applications. This deracination process lies at the core of the notion of a technological package, which has been adapted from Crowther's (1986) characterization of information technologies:

closely inter-related sets of hardware, software, ... human resource (and skill) requirements and guidelines, ... which 'work' or 'function' together in a strictly technical sense (e.g., reducible to a highly controlled laboratory situation), apart from contextual considerations, in order to produce or transform a good, service or standard. The technology becomes a technological package when it is labelled by a policy symbol and subjected to a series of technological utility and economic efficiency decisions. (p. 1)

For Crowther, a technological package is the mechanism by which technology is transferred and therefore is the unit around which assessment occurs. It is an important notion because it describes actual phenomena, and understanding its character leads one to understand the complexity, as well as occasional failures, of some transfers. The technological package is „a classic case of a technological solution looking for a problem to solve" (Rogers and Larsen, 1984, p. 269) without regard to the appropriateness of the problem or the context.

Ethical Frameworks

With these distinctions in mind, two familiar philosophical positions can be introduced as frameworks for ethical considerations - i.e., Kantianism and utilitarianism. These positions do not of course exhaust the pluralism that exists in current ethical inquiry. Part of the difficulty in discussing applied ethics lies in developing some shared standards, difficult enough in the diversity of American culture and even more problematic in an intercultural context. Yet the positions of Kant and utilitarianism were chosen because, according to Kohlberg (1976), they are dominant and commonly held across cultures.(Kohlberg has claimed that these two positions are stages in a process of moral development that is shared across cultures. He argued that there were six definable stages in the moral development of persons. The stages were divided into three levels: preconventional, conventional, and post-conventional morality. In the latter two levels, the ones characteristic of mature morality, each stage reflects the utilitarian and Kantian position respectively, but the later level has a deeper appropriation based on a personal commitment to a sense of justice rather than social determination (conventional morality is based on shared norms and values that sustain groups and societies). People who progress through these levels or positions do not necessarily know their philosophical names, originators or advocates. Nevertheless, if Kohlberg is correct, they come to live according to these positions as their ethical development matures. Although there are some difficulties and challenges to Kohlberg's position, for the utilitarian and Kantian aspects of conventional morality (level

2), since they seem to be the guiding ethical views of many cases of technology transfer.) Even if people, transferrers and transferees alike, do not know their names, they practice behavior that can be described in Kantian or utilitarian terms.

The Kantian Approach

The Kantian position of the 'categorical imperative' appears to be a rationalization for the golden rule: do unto others as you would have them do unto you. One of Kant's (1959) formulations of the categorical imperative is: „Act so that you treat humanity, whether in your own person or in that of another, always as an end and never merely as a means" (p. 47). Kant admonishes us to treat ourselves and other people as ends worthy of respect, and never merely as means.

Kant's position was formulated as a personal ethics; in fact ethics for Kant was anthropocentric, dealing with man's relation with himself or other men. The stakeholders, however, in technology transfer can be persons, groups, or institutions of various sorts - i.e., governments, corporations, foundations, nonprofit agencies, scientific committees, or countries. In this article, „institution" will be used as a generic term to cover these various collectivities. To extend the value of the categorical imperative, one must include these institutions as actors, because they are entities with some degree of autonomy, with their own status and rights. Given the view in the United States that corporations have legal status as individual entities, one could simultaneously argue, as we for the moment will assume, that any institution can be accorded the status of moral agent. Philosophically, it is not easy to justify this assumption (especially for Kant where moral worth is traceable to a rational will), for collectivities, like governments and other institutions, exist only in and through individuals, and yet it is clear that governments and institutions make choices. Their actions and directions represent a will for the institution as a whole. In this sense, institutions have an autonomous life. Assuming the moral agency of institutions, Kant's categorical imperative can be restated: treat all institutions not merely as means, but at the same time as ends in themselves. Just as an information professional, from this Kantian perspective, has no right to regard his employing institution as a mere means to his livelihood, organizations in both developed and developing countries in Kant's eyes must avoid being mere users of each other.

With these views in mind, one could argue that Kant's categorical imperative gives rise to three factors for ethical considerations in technology transfer: promotion of organization survival, preservation of individuality, and presence of good will. These can be compared to the four factors isolated by Rubin (1990) in a paper on „Ethical Issues in Library Personnel Management"-- organizational survival, individuality, social utility and social responsibility. (The notion of principle implies settled rules of action. But these considerations are less rules than constituent elements that contribute to the moral deliberation that lead to a choice and/or action, upon an appeal to some ethical principles, like fairness or justice. Ethical principles imply sets of values or rules that are invoked in the process of weighing these diverse factors.) The factor of organizational survival, derived from Thompson's Organizations in Action (1967), originates in the view that a fundamental function of an organization is to perpetuate itself, so that the organization survives and prospers. While Thompson derives this consideration by analogy to the moral self-interest of individuals found in the work of Locke and Hobbes, it appears to be associated with the Kantian notion of the autonomy of the will from the version of the categorical imperative quoted earlier: „Act so that you treat humanity, whether in your own person or in that of another, always as an end and never merely as a means" (my emphasis, p. 47). If institutions have moral agency, they also are ends, never to be treated merely as means. This implies, as Rubin suggests, that those who run or serve institutions have an obligation to make the organization as efficient as possible to serve organizational ends (otherwise they would be treating organizations as mere means in themselves).

But in the world of information professionals, there is a related consideration - survival of the profession. Each profession is also never merely a means but an end and must be granted rights of survival. One of the origins of ethical conflict is precisely the clash between organizational and professional survival: on occasion, obligations to the profession may override organizational survival or vice versa. For example, if an information professional is asked to pad the account of a client with inappropriate online searches, such activity may promote institutional survival but at the expense of professional survival. Since this factor applies to organizations and professions, it might be better called the principle of institutional survival.

There is another dimension of survival that must be included in contemporary ethical discussions, that of planetary survival. The advent of technologies with large-scale impacts have changed the character of the ethical arena. These changes have led Jonas (1984) to create new formulations of Kant's categorical imperative: „Do not compromise the conditions for an indefinite continuation of humanity on earth," or „Act so that the effects of your action are compatible with the permanence of genuine human life" (p. 11). Paradoxically, these versions of the imperative move away from Kant's focus on intentional states and move toward the utilitarian mode of thinking, as they necessarily focus on the consequences of an action, and so these versions will be taken up during the discussion of utilitarianism.

Like the factor of institutional survival, the factors related to individuality are founded on the original versions of categorical imperative. People are individuals in an organization and ends in themselves. Their individuality must be respected, and Rubin argues that they should have as much freedom in the marketplace as practicable. Rubin adds: „Restrictions on employee conduct and expression require a valid rationale. In other words, the Principle of Individuality implies that all rules, regulations and punishments should have a clear rationale, i.e. 'just cause'" (p. 8). This principle can be applied to organizations as well. Organizations should have as much freedom as possible, and restrictions on organizational behavior in the marketplace should have 'just cause.' For this reason, the principle might be better called the principle of autonomy, since it affirms the autonomy of individuals and organizations in pursuing their goals subject only to constraints based on just cause (e.g., the prevention of environmental pollution).

Some further clarifications of Kant's position can be productive here. At the center of Kant's moral philosophy is the notion of a good will. A good will is an unqualified good, unlike other kinds of goods - for example, wealth, power, or information technologies - which can be abused. A good will is a will that acts for the sake of duty. It is because of this intention that an action accrues moral worth for the person: i.e., when an action is performed because of the belief that it is right, it accrues moral worth for the person acting. In Kant's view, it is not because good consequences are achieved that an action is good; rather, an action is good when it was attempted because it was the right thing to do (e.g., the action of providing agricultural information to a developing country with problems of starvation is good, despite the fact that a drought destroyed the crops). Somewhat problematically, Kant disassociates a good will from inclination: Kant believes that an action is hardly moral if we are inclined to do it anyway - e.g., a corporation that gives away computers to universities or developing countries because of tax write-offs or obsolescence of models is performing actions that have no moral worth even if the consequences are good. The reason, according to Kant, is that, although its actions were in accord with moral duty, they were not done for the sake of that duty.

Kant seems to imply that there must be a certain level of consciousness in moral action - i.e., one must be aware that what one is doing is in accord with one's duty. This notion seems to run contrary to the Aristotelian view that moral worth is related to properly acquired moral habits. For example, if a person or institution is in the habit of donating obsolescent models of computers to charitable causes, such actions are morally praiseworthy because they are in accord with good character formation and not because the institutions are conscious of their duty. They are the kind of actions a good person of good character would perform. One would think that Kant would agree, but he seems to insist on a certain level of awareness of duty.

Given that this motivation is the element that supplies moral worth, Kant must determine some objective content for the moral law. He reasons that you should „act only according to that maxim by which you can at the same time will that it should becomes a universal law" (p. 39). In this version of the categorical imperative, Kant is suggesting that an action is morally acceptable if doer of that action could wish that the principle that guides it become a universal law. For example, one could not wish that lying becomes a universal law; if it did, communication of fact would become impossible since not everyone would make the same assumptions on the basis of what they were told.

Kant does not imply that concrete laws of conduct can be deduced directly from the categorical imperative; rather it operates as a criterion for judging the morality of subjective principles of conduct which Kant calls maxims. Suppose that I choose to supply agricultural information for use in a poor rural area where there are no proprietary rights on the information or its use. The maxim of this action is: I will provide technological and scientific information to needy countries or people, where the supply of that information will not infringe on copyright, misuse of employer's resources (e.g., duplicating costs), etc. I ask myself whether I could will that this maxim become a universal law, namely that anybody in a position such as mine would do the same, and decide that I can so will it. Hence the maxim is morally justified. Interestingly, in terms of this example, there may be some who would feel justified in the misuse of employer's resources and/or in the infringement of copyright, for example, if they deemed that a higher good would be served, namely, the alleviation of famine, disease, or poverty. Kant would have difficulty in endorsing such actions as acceptable moral law, precisely because he sees justice and universality tied together. For him, it is still is a matter of stealing, albeit from the rich to the poor, and to wish that it become a universal law would be to advocate actions inconsistent with fundamental notions of morality, namely, justice, fairness, and contracts.

Through the criterion of universalizability, one can determine the admissibility of certain maxims into proper ethical code. So the maxim, „steal information from vendors or employers, everyone else does," is inconsistent when universalized - i.e., vendors and employers would cease to exist if everyone stole from them. Kant's position is often called a formalism since it only determines the form of the moral law (universalizability) and not its content.

In the context of technology transfer, whether considering a technology, a technology practice, or a technological package, the Kantian approach is embodied by those for whom good will is a valuable and moral asset, supplying a proper motivation for the distribution of scientific and technological information and experience for the promotion of economic development. Although tangible results are hoped for in the transfer process, their failure to occur does not detract from the basic morality of the situation - i.e., that individuals and institutions of whatever variety should operate with good will and treat each other as ends and not merely as means. On the other hand, Kant's view also accords with one's intuitive feeling that if a technological package is foisted on a developing country sheerly on the basis of a profit motive for the developer, such actions are morally questionable despite beneficial results.

The Utilitarian Perspective

John Stuart Mill (1957) explains the utilitarian principle:

„The creed which accepts as the foundation of morals, Utility, or the Greatest Happiness Principle, holds that actions are right in proportion as they promote happiness, wrong as they promote the reverse of happiness. By happiness is intended pleasure, and the absence of pain; by unhappiness, pain and the privation of pleasure." (p. 10)

The utilitarian position focuses on results or consequences, striving, as it does, for the maximum amount of happiness for the most number of people. Mill's position is a modified hedonism; he believes that most people seek happiness or pleasure as an end, but he attempts to apply this to the entire social setting. The slogan of the utilitarians, „the greatest happiness of the greatest number" is directed toward both a wide and a just distribution of pleasure and its maximization.

It is because the distribution was supposed to be both broad and just that Mill's views have had wide impact. One interpretation of Mill argues that it implies that people should enjoy rights to the basic necessities of life - i.e., adequate food, housing, a job, and favorable working conditions. In fact, politicians, social activists, judges and decision makers of all varieties have all adopted his beliefs in the creation of social programs, legislation and plans for economic development. The attempt to bring about the general happiness represents their method of implementing utilitarian principles. Smart sees behind utilitarianism the „motive of generalized benevolence" (in DeMarco, 1986, p. 26), and one can see this motive behind the use of technology transfer for economic development and for supporting the „modernization cycle," a process in which developing countries undertake technologies to improve the general conditions of their societies.

One may understand the dynamics, benefits, and difficulties of utilitarianism by employing an example. Take the case where the personnel of an agricultural library in a developing country are deciding whether to automate its library system. Such a system would supply many benefits - e.g., improved agricultural production through the availability of knowledge of crops, techniques for enhancing crop culture, and avoiding or inhibiting crop diseases and pests; increased income for farmers; and increased prosperity and health because of adequate or increased harvests. But not only would it supply benefits, but also the benefits would be superior - i.e., the easy availability of agricultural information, increased speed of access to such information, the elimination of much irrelevant information, and elimination of work required to duplicate research results of the information. From these benefits, certain deficits must be subtracted - i.e., reliance on externally created technologies, depletion of financial resources and increased indebtedness to developed countries, difficulty in getting skilled human resources to run and maintain the operation, increased educational requirements for creating such human resources with reliance on developed countries or companies for training, increased educational requirements for users needed to overcome language and technophobic barriers, higher unemployment due to technological replacement of the large numbers of personnel typically employed in a manual system, difficulties in fostering the need for information on the part of the end-users, difficulties in enhancing the literacy standards so that end-users can use the information, the consequences of misused or misapplied technologies (e.g., use of incorrect pesticides or incorrect dosages), the consequences of inappropriate technologies (e.g., use of dangerous pesticides), increased „brain drain" by loss of bright students who emigrate to developed countries. These benefits and deficits must be added up within individuals and across individuals to arrive at a general sum. This sum is to include those consequences that are associated not only with the present, but also those associated with the immediate and remote future. A long-range ecological disaster would ultimately devalue a high level of current general happiness. Furthermore, the availability of the information and its use for increased agricultural production should not unduly favor one segment of the population (e.g., rich landowners) at the expense of another (e.g., poor local farmers). For a utilitarian and other consequentialists, an action is moral if it promotes the long-range general happiness for the most people and/or if it inhibits the general amount of displeasure.

This example illustrates a number of critical features of utilitarianism. These include: (1) a distinction among pleasures in terms of quality; (2) the additive nature of benefits and deficits; (3) that there is a temporal factor that must be considered in calculating the general happiness; (4) that the general happiness is a good to every individual; and (5) that there should be a just distribution of the benefits. Let us move on to a delineation of the problems associated with such a view.

Not all forms of utilitarianism (e.g., the theories of Bentham) have argued for qualitative distinctions among pleasures, but it was a view that Mill (1957) supported and demonstrated in his famous assertion that it „is better to be a human being dissatisfied than a pig satisfied" (p. 14). In certain areas it seems to be justified: increased agricultural production due to increased knowledge and experience is superior to local agricultural production bound to sheer „grunt work" because of inappropriate technologies (e.g., failure to rotate crops). In other contexts, it can be hazardous to associate labels of inferiority or superiority with physical or mental pleasures (e.g., is sex inferior to book reading?), because these pleasures are variously good at diverse times and are not a matter of inferiority or superiority. Inferiority as a label is often employed only to indicate abuse or fixation on certain kinds of pleasure, typically physical.

Not all „grunt work" farming may be bad. Given some good information about appropriate techniques, such production may be environmentally safer and instill large amounts of self-esteem for the farmers. Part of the problem for Mill is that he wants to make qualitative distinctions based on pleasure. If one makes qualitative distinctions among pleasures, it is not the basis of some difference in pleasure that these are made, but according to other values. The superiority of informed agricultural production versus grunt work production is not simply a matter of pleasure (it is true that less physical effort may be involved and there may be increased production, but these are quantitative measures) but of other values - i.e., freedom from ignorance, increased knowledge, better control of and relationship to nature, more leisure time.

Mill attempts to establish these differences in quality on the basis of a competent judge. He argues that if one of two pleasures is preferred by people who are competently acquainted with both, „even though knowing it to be attended with a greater amount of discontent, and [who] would not resign it for any quantity of the other pleasure," the preferred pleasure is superior in quality (p. 12). Mill's description has to do with weighing quantitative and qualitative pleasures within the individual, but our example generalizes to social dimensions. Determining and weighing qualitative and quantitative pleasures in the aggregate has always been a difficult problem, especially in matters bearing upon the public sector. In matters of the public interest, who are to be regarded as the competent judges: politicians, scientists, or pollsters (reflecting a consensus of the general population)? In matters of technology transfer it is more difficult to decide since the experts presumably must be competent to assess a technology from the viewpoints of both the donor and receiving cultures. The problem is aggravated if the technology is newly applied, because there is little knowledge of the potential or actual consequences. Even the methods of technology assessments are geared to the donor culture, and they may be inappropriate for the receiving culture. If the experts are attached to the donor culture, they may have a serious lack of understanding of the receiving culture - i.e., its needs and traditions. If they are in the receiving culture, they may not be able to fully assess the effects of the technology in itself and more so in its application to their own culture.

As an alternative judge, one might resort to appealing to a consensus by major players or the public in a sort of „participatory technology" - e.g., if the public is given sufficient information, it will come to a consensus about what technology it will need or reject. Brooks (1973) indicates the problems with this view:

This seems an unrealistic hope. What is more likely to happen with greater participation, as traditionally visualized, is that any adversely affected group or interest can exercise a veto power over a technological enterprise, almost regardless of other affected interests or values. Unfortunately, all policy, including that relative to technology, requires a measure of both consistency and continuity among objectives, which is difficult to reconcile with participatory democracy in the decision process. (p. 255)

Nonetheless, this is precisely the strategy recommended by Noar (1982) with respect to the social responsibility of multinational corporations which should operate in a „socially desirable manner." What is socially desirable is to be determined on the basis of whether activities will be seen to bring about welfare improvements in the countries in which the companies exist. „Periodic public opinion polls, or more informal methods in the less developed countries, are seen to provide the necessary inputs for the overall corporate guidelines for action, which in turn will influence strategic corporate decisions" (p. 219). To reiterate Brooks, this seems naive since it is not clear that those polled could really understand or predict the consequences or non-consequences of a corporate course of action.

Implied in the discussion so far is that pleasures (whether qualitative or quantitative) are additive in some way, and that these pleasures and pains can be computed into a sort of aggregate happiness. But this calculus of pleasures must be examined. In some instances, two pleasures can enhance the individual pleasures. Using the example of the agricultural library, there would be greater happiness if both the citations were available online and the source documents were immediately available than if there were source documents alone (with few or faulty access points in a manual system) or online references alone, with months to obtain the source documents, if they were at all available. In other instances, two pleasures may be in conflict, as, for example, trying to promote full employment while simultaneously trying to automate the agricultural library in a country with a large population and little local technological resources or expertise. On other occasions, a pleasure may be enhanced with the addition of a pain, as when the successful implementation of an automated system is enhanced by the number and degree of difficulties overcome, such as low availability of capital, language barriers, unstable governments, low prestige of information professionals, lack of available trained personnel, and poor existing information infrastructures (Eres, 1981, p. 99). In simple comparisons, one often can make a judgment, but when one combines all these factors, it is difficult to estimate overall results. For example, in the plans to automate the agricultural library, one would have to take into account the unhappinesses of all those who remained unemployed and their offspring - i.e., the unhappiness of the government in reduced tax revenues because of reduced unemployment; all the happiness of the patrons due to the quick easy efficient access to the materials of the library; their unhappiness when the equipment breaks down; and the unhappiness caused by reliance on external suppliers and the cost of acquiring, maintaining and repairing the equipment. There is also a temporal element in the computation, since the consequences to be considered are not simply the current ones, but those in the future as well. At the extreme, one must take into account the effects of a technology transfer on the survival and quality of life on planet earth in the distant future. As noted earlier, Jonas (1984) believes that Kant's ethics are inadequate to deal with contemporary situations. Previously, man's actions had little effect on the self-sustaining character of nature or on the ability of the planet to sustain life. Now actions undertaken by whatever individual or institution, be it corporation, government, or social agency, can have grave consequences for life on the planet. In the new ethics, increased knowledge is vital to proper moral decision making, especially where actions involve or promote these serious consequences. Hence, Jonas reformulates Kant's imperative: „Act so that the effects of your action are compatible with the permanence of genuine human life"; or „Act so that the effects of your action are not destructive of the future possibility of such life" (p. 11). Although these formulations remind us to avoid ecological disaster, they make two shifts from the original Kantian perspective. First, they heighten the role of knowledge. For Kant, the knowledge required for ethical decision making was not that of a scientist or expert, but of a knowledge „of a kind readily available to a man of good will" (p. 5), a man of common sense. The impact of one's actions did not have consequences except for the foreseeable future. Current moral action requires „predictive knowledge," but paradoxically, as Jonas points out, such knowledge is unavailable since man lacks experience in the long-range effects of certain actions upon the life of the planet. So a dilemma appears: on the one hand, the need for knowledge of consequences as a prerequisite for performing utilitarian calculation, and on the other, the inadequacy of predictive knowledge. This is especially perplexing for developing countries for two reasons: (1) they are more vulnerable to a lack of knowledge of consequences (both in terms of the technology and of its application to their environment); and (2) technologies, such as the use of certain pesticides that are no longer tolerated in developed countries, are often foisted on them by unscrupulous businessmen. Even though these technologies may be recognized as harmful, they are often tolerated because they are cheap and they offset other large scale problems, such as severe shortages in food supply.

Thus the utilitarian computation of the consequences of technology transfer is complicated by many additive and temporal factors. When a decision maker opts for the importation of a technology such as computer hardware and software for automation, he must consider the current and future benefits of all affected persons - e.g., the benefits to be derived from the avoidance of hunger, poverty, disease, and ignorance; economic growth and development; stimulation of research and productivity; increased stature in the international community. From this aggregate he must subtract the cost of the technology and the resultant dependency it fosters; those adverse consequences resulting from misapplied technology as in the improper use of pesticides; environmental costs including the depletion of natural resources, pollution and long-range (and often unknown) adverse consequences including those that may affect life on the planet; costs of science policy development and implementation; costs of the failure of anticipated results; the erosion of cultural identity. If the moral quality of a choice for a transfer of technology depends on its consequences (as the teleological dimension of utilitarianism suggests), there will be a long wait to determine the verdict of such a choice.

Furthermore, there is an uneasy relation between the individual's happiness and general happiness in utilitarianism. Mill suggests that since each person's happiness is a good to that person, the general happiness is a good to everybody. Taken at face value, this is the fallacy of division, arguing that a property associated with the whole must be associated with the parts. One could imagine that with our agricultural library, some individuals may very well be unhappy, despite an increase in the general well-being of the society. Farmers who were excluded from use of the library because of economic, educational, or other barriers, and thus excluded from implementing the information contained therein through appropriate technologies, would discover the falling value of their current production efforts, making them unable to make a living and to sustain a family. On a positive side, economic growth in a country as a general good does tend to facilitate economic growth throughout a society. But such growth may disproportionately favor some constituents at the expense of others.

This suggests another problem: utilitarianism aims for a just distribution of those goods. Given the greatest happiness principle, a corresponding principle of justice to which utilitarians should appeal is that the allocation of resources should be such that there will be the most happiness for the most number of people. In the case of a developing country, funding decisions for technology transfers would address the more fundamental problems of a society - i.e., poverty, starvation, disease. Funds might go to a medical facility first before they would go to the agricultural library. Or would they? Which are the more fundamental problems? Would a best maximization principle imply a single obvious, well-defined course of action or set of priorities, where there are conflicting goods or conflicting competing avenues for combating sundry evils?

For example, in the agricultural library, conflicts are bound to arise between organizational demands and social responsibilities. As noted earlier, Rubin (1990) has suggested difficulties in balancing the factors of social responsibility, social utility, and institutional survival (p. 6). In the context of library personnel management, factors related to social utility are concerned with promoting the greater good of society within the context of the organization's goals. Personnel managers must maximize resources to promote the public good. For our agricultural library, the budget would have to be allocated so that it would best fulfill its mission - i.e., to provide agricultural information to those sectors of the society most in need of it. In this manner, it would fulfill both the goals of social utility and institutional survival.

But social responsibility is concerned with advancing the larger goals of a developing country. In this respect, the library may be inclined to hire more staff than it needs (to enhance national full employment demands) and to hire less qualified but native citizens (to inhibit economic dependence on external countries); it may concern itself more closely with the problems of the impoverished and ignorant through such things as literacy and outreach programs (as opposed to serving the needs of the wealthy and privileged); may acquiesce in cutting budgets (so that other critical problems in other areas of the economy may be addressed); may defer from automation (to increase employment and to avoid dependence on external technologies). These choices would aim for a harmonious society in which all or most people would enjoy basic rights to food, shelter, clothing, education, etc.

Such a concern for social responsibility, however, would often stand in tension with institutional survival since losses entailed by actions promoting social responsibility would infringe on a library's economic well-being. Promotion of organizational survival fosters an organization that is efficient and economical. The agricultural library fulfills its goals by minimizing staff requirements, by hiring only the best educated and most highly skilled workers, by purchasing the only most reliable technology, and so on. In this respect, the unhappiness of some individuals (e.g., those fail to gain employment or other benefits from the system) would be overridden in favor of the greater social good. In addition, poor personnel practices would also deflate the profession's standing, a matter of special concern in developing countries where the value and prestige of trained professionals is not well established. Thus professional survival would also be threatened. And the promotion of the library's social utility function - to provide agricultural information - may also be impaired by expending resources on programs or actions promoting social responsibility. The choice of a technology, including information technology, is to many competing demands and many uncertain results. Yet the utilitarian calculus demands - whatever or however the choices - a projection of results.

Reinterpreting Mill in Contemporary Terms

Such choices based on calculations of the general happiness have been undertaken. The apparatus of utilitarianism has taken on several guises in contemporary life. In the context of technology transfer, it is actualized under the rubric of technology needs assessment, a preliminary analysis of an LDC's needs and capabilities, so that appropriate technologies can be imported for economic development, and a trajectory for successful technology transfer may be established. Hetman (1973) reformulates the utilitarian principle in contemporary economic terms: „a mass society devoted to maximizing economic growth and the average expectancy of material well-being" (p. 258), accomplished by a technology that „has to be put at the service of the economy" (p. 257). Such technology incorporation is part of the „modernization cycle" for developing countries so that they can effectively deal with their local problems and can learn to compete in the world market or to participate in the „New International Economic Order." Hetman's assessment entails three parts: technological utility, social relevance, and political acceptability. With respect to the first part, a reason for introducing a technology is to gain some sizable advantage with respect to existing technologies. In order to determine this, the available technologies and their variants must be explored as a set of options. With respect to the second issue, each option must be subjected to a test of social relevance that includes assessment of direct economic costs and benefits and all other identifiable effects and impacts (on the environment, society, individuals and values). Following an assessment of social relevance with each option, political acceptability must be determined - e.g., it might be the case that the preferred options, though socially relevant or technologically useful, may not be politically acceptable. This acceptability must be ascertained through a multi-constituency procedure where impacts on affected parties are examined and evaluated in terms commensurate with those expressing overall social relevance. Depending on the importance given to values of various social and political groups, several socio-political alternatives can be formulated. The final step is the choice of an acceptable alternative which appears most suitable in a given socio-political contest. (Hetman, 1973, p. 268-269)

In terms of information technologies, this process is further complicated because traditional cost benefit analysis may not apply to the ultimate product of such technologies - i.e., information or knowledge. Even though one hears of the „economics of information," the phrase is misleading since traditional economics, based on supply and demand, cannot be readily applied to information. As Eres (1981) notes: „Knowledge is cumulative and generally unquantifiable. The process of acquiring knowledge is complex. An article read today might trigger research in 20 years" (p. 98). One cannot predict the long-range effects of the acquisition of information. Although there is a commodity sense to information, it is derived from the containers of information - i.e., a specific physical unit such as document, book, microfiche, online citation or text. But information is not properly quantifiable, and one could argue that the commodity sense is incidental to the real meaning of the term. Information, as Fox (1982) points out, is not a count noun, but is related to the „propositional content" of a text or texts, what the texts affirm or deny. If information is a unit in this sense, it is elusive since any unitization occurs ultimately through the meaning that the information creates in the information seeker's mind, where different parts, sources, and elements of texts are bound. For example, an information seeker's understanding of technology may have been acquired through a variety of texts, references, and sources, and the unit of comprehension must be traced back to all these sources. Even when we associate information with a particular text or journal, one cannot readily determine the effects of its absence from a collection (Kent, 1974, p. 303). How can we estimate how the absence of a text or the absence of online or on-disc searching prolonged or wasted the work of other researchers? Although we do know that such absences have important effects, calculating the consequences of their absence is close to impossible. Brooks (1973) claims the same is true of technology: „The problems of assessing the absence of a technology can be much more difficult than assessing any particular proposed technology" (p. 249).

Setting apart for the moment the difficulties of quantitatively assessing the consequences of information or information technologies, the iterative process suggested by Hetman earlier is only to determine whether to undertake a certain technology, but utilitarian principles demand some computation through the whole process, including actual consequences. Unfortunately, a technology chosen for transfer is not necessarily created, implemented, maintained, or used in harmony with the objectives for which, it was originally assessed. And the secondary effects may have more impact than the original direct intended effects. Dede (1981) asserts:

Research in the field of technology assessment has shown that the unintended, second order effects of a technological innovation on society are frequently more influential, long-term than its direct and deliberate effects. For example, in many crowded areas one can travel by car no faster than by horse - the greater speed of the automobile has been lost through congestion - but automotive pollution and petroleum availability remain as major societal concerns. (p. 204)

According to Crowther (1986), technology transfer is constructive when the following conditions are supported: the capacity to determine a country's major socioeconomic problems and to translate them into a coherent set of technological requirements; the marshalling of the population to innovate, implement and deal with the effects of the innovation; simplified presentation and ample diffusion of information regarding the technological options; an analysis of hardware and software requirements and costing of these items; and an awareness of the ideological or social value content to technologies and technical decisions (p. 2). Unfortunately, Crowther's experience with information services in Latin American countries indicates that these conditions are countervailed, and the information technologies adopted by the services „enhances the personal value and not necessarily the national development value of the information" (p. 3).

Not only are intended consequences often sabotaged, the long-range general happiness in the form of basic developmental needs is sacrificed for immediate goods. For example, Akin M. Makinde (in Murphy et al., 1986) explains the imbalance of happinesses caused by the oil found in Nigeria:

As long as the oil revenues lasted, Nigerians lavished their foreign exchange on innovations that were completely unrelated to their basic developmental needs. In fact, agriculture, the major source of foreign exchange, was abandoned as the population gravitated to big cities to enjoy the products of technology.... The desire to enjoy foreign technological products has led to a wide gulf between the rich and the poor, with contractors of technological products and government officials becoming millionaires overnight. In fact, it is now estimated that a few individuals in Nigeria have more money that the national treasury!" (pp. 182-183)

The considerations that we have looked at so far are concerned with technological practices and consequences and with technology transfers in the form of technological packages, inappropriately uprooted, applied or implemented practices. But leaving the discussion at this point would seem to imply that the problem lies only in the practice or in the package or in its implementation but not in the technology itself or in the marketplace of the available technologies.

Consider that there is an information problem in an LDC looking for a technological solution. Given this kind of problem, there is a belief in a free marketplace of available information technologies, similar to the notion of the free marketplace of ideas. There exists a marketplace of goods and services of all available information technologies. From this marketplace any developing country can freely choose any technology in terms of the problem under consideration. Given that the technologies adequately address the needs or problem of the developing country, these technologies are supposedly of equal value. But just as in the free marketplace of ideas, one cannot assume that competition has pruned the market to the best or the most appropriate: some technologies may dominate, occlude or exclude more efficient ones. One merely has to think of the domination of IBM in setting standards for the computer market, especially in the personal computer market, even in the face of its confused strategies and some poorly conceived products. In information technologies, Library of Congress and Dewey classifications have commanded the classification market, and the commercial bibliographic retrieval systems have established Boolean, deductive systems as the standard. In cataloging, OCLC has dominated the market, and although it has not captured the market, it sets standards with which other catalogers must contend.

There are many reasons for this uneven marketplace - e.g., historical events, economics, and consequences of past choices. Given the need for economies of scale, the range of economically feasible designs for a technology is limited. With respect to the use of information technology in an educational setting, Dede (1981) remarks: „In brief the educational quality of the device (or instructional unit) and the profit margin of the manufacturer will be inversely related" (p. 206). Furthermore, he asserts: „Market forces, if the sole criterion..., will dictate that the educational hardware and software produced be designed for the needs of the largest and richest body of consumers: the middle and upper class majority culture" (p. 211). Given the availability of such software and hardware, it is not hard to understand the emergence of technological packages (e.g., computer hardware and software), that are then foisted into inappropriate settings or used for inappropriate problems.

And it is easy to foresee the motives of information technology salespersons in their assessing and addressing the needs of developing countries. If one were to adopt a more cynical attitude, one could argue that these motives are suspect. Mowshowitz (1984) calls computer literacy a

„euphemism for consumer training. It should take only a moment's reflection to realize who stands to gain the most by promoting computer literacy. Is it the free choice of a neutral technology that is bringing computers into the schools?" In view of the developing countries' drive to enter the modernization cycle, can one really speak of the free choice of neutral, equally available technologies? That is to say, not only are the available technologies unequal, the prevailing belief that technologies are neutral is mistaken (Mowshowitz, 1984; Froehlich, 1990). Every technology is undertaken with a technological practice in mind and is bound to a set of values for which it was undertaken. Technological packaging attempts to hide the value-laden roots, but proper needs assessment must uncover these values to insure their appropriateness and utility for the problems to be solved.

Crowther (1986) remarks that technological development opposes the modernization cycle, since the cycle focuses on the technology rather than the context and purpose for its use:
The modernization cycle is inherently contradictory to technological development. It is the proper function of the technology itself rather than human or natural environmental stress, that is monitored and corrected; technology assessment in this cycle explicitly emphasizes technological utility and economic efficiency rather than social relevance or political consequences, and commercial criteria override the consideration of basic needs. (p. 8)

The choices from the marketplace are uneven and so put constraints on the fulfilling of objectives. And decision makers, in facing the available choices, are not necessarily guided by utilitarian principles and needs assessment.

In the context of technology transfer, there are necessary unhappy choices - e.g., when budgets and resources are limited, some members will be serviced before others. Mechanisms to develop and facilitate agricultural or medical information transfer may be given higher priority than educational information or vice versa. As noted earlier, the content of the greater good or the maximized happiness or minimized displeasure is not achieved through utilitarian principles or through an abstract notion of justice, but by setting priorities and solving problems in turn. Taylor (1985), in an essay on „The Diversity of Goods", suggests that this is precisely an area where utilitarianism founders - that it assumes homogeneity of goods where actually only conflicting heterogeneity exists (p. 244). Each stakeholder comes to the deliberation process of determining the greater good with different traditions and different priorities. Such differences are often amplified by the differences between developed countries and LDCs and within LDCs by competing segments of the society with diverse cultural backgrounds. Thus, there is a diversity of competing goods (not clear goods opposing clear evils) or, more often, a diversity of competing evils (which area of the economy to address first - poverty, ignorance, disease?) for which utilitarianism supplies no governing principles for choices. Although it can be agreed that there is a greater good or a greater happiness, what the greater good is and how it should be actualized is fraught with difficult choices, that are ultimately political.

According to Brooks (1973): Although the consequences of various technological choices may be clarified by analysis, there is no objective or scientific basis on which final choices can be made. The choices themselves are political, depending on a complex interplay or bargaining process among conflicting economic, political and ideological interests and values. The chips in this bargaining game involve not only immediate choices at issue, but also unrelated perceptions and interests. For example, many people who opposed supersonic transport in the United States did so because it was a convenient symbol for uncontrolled technology, rather than because of its specific environmental impact or economic viability. (p. 251)

Similarly, in addition to such good reasons for technology transfer as increasing the general welfare, there may be a series of reasons based on less desirable motives - e.g., prestige value of owning computer technology, centralization of power at the expense of democratic values, vested interests. In the case of information technologies in particular, Katz (1988) sees politics as the driver of the diffusion of such technologies (pp. 47-78).

The ideals of utilitarianism - i.e., its „generalized benevolence" - tend to be vulnerable to corruption because of the number and variety of stakeholders in the decision-making and implementation process and their diverse interpretations of what the general happiness is and how to best realize it, interpretations often colored by simple self-serving interests. Again the problematic relation of individual and collective happiness and the importance of motivations based on good will is seen here. The ethical can be confounded or clarified by the political, but the former seems to be more often the case since stakeholders, whether experts or members of a participatory technology, have such diverse perceptions and motivations.

In sum, if we look at the application of utilitarian principles to issues of technology transfer in developing countries, we find that technology needs assessment is confounded on many fronts- - e.g., in lack of predictive knowledge for determining a set of effects; in difficulties in ensuring that the intended effects are achieved; in establishing priorities on reasonable grounds (either by experts or participants); in balancing competing demands of various factors or from differing interpretations of the greatest good and how it may be achieved; in creating a fair distribution of goods; in uncovering the implicit values of technological packages; and in the constraints of available technologies.

Dialectic of the Kantian and utilitarian themes

The difficulties surrounding the actualization of utilitarian principles, and the confusion surrounding the determination of results, do not invalidate utilitarianism as a moral perspective or obviate the need for some mechanism of needs assessment (however flawed). It only underscores the difficulties of making choices among conflicting or competing goods and evils, ensuring intended effects, and making overall assessments. Attempts to define moral choices pale in the face of poverty, starvation, disease and ignorance: how can citizens of an LDC hope to enjoy an ethical life if their basic needs are severely compromised? The Mother Theresas and social activists of the world have long recognized the fundamental necessity of providing for basic needs.

Part of the problem of contemporary culture, as suggested by Jonas (1984), is that we are forced to endorse the utilitarian view, and the calculus of happiness takes the upper hand. Ellul (1980) asserts that technological morality has two characteristics: „(1) It is behavioral (in other words, only correct practice, not intentions or motivations, counts), and (2) it rules out the problematics of traditional morality (the morality of ambiguity is unacceptable in a technological world)" (p. 244). For Ellul, all moral evaluation, including that required in technology transfer, is forced into the utilitarian framework. Utilitarianism is, of course, not wrong per se, but its domination as a sole moral perspective and its sacrifice of the ethical to the political is problematic. It offends the intuitive notion that morality should be related to good intentions and good will.

One could argue the other side of the case as well: proper motivation and good will are not the only basis for moral evaluation. Good motivations that fail to produce beneficial results will not serve the severe problems that confront LDCs. Although the calculus of utilitarianism or needs assessment is difficult to perform, so too are Kant's motives elusive: proper motivation and good will can be faked, they are not readily discernible, and our perceptions may be unreliable. This invisibility of real motives is probably the source, at least in part, of the ambiguity of „traditional morality," the ground of its unacceptability to „technological morality." Motives are neither verifiable or quantifiable. Furthermore, technology transfer that promotes a genuine good cannot be morally dismissed because the motivation is not pure. The point is that each perspective offers a partial truth, and both perspectives can be engaged as two poles of a dialectical clarification process that can be used to evaluate the moral dimensions of technology transfer.

This article has examined only two ethical perspectives based, in part, on the work of Kohlberg (1976); there are other perspectives and other variations of Kant's and Mill's views that are not represented here. In addition, one must acknowledge that Kohlberg's work has been criticized, and if the dialectical reasoning that we are advocating is based on problematic research, one should recognize these difficulties and the alternatives they raise. An alternative perspective is offered by Gilligan (1982). She suggests that the moral development of women is different than that of men. In her view, Kant and Mill advocate an „ethic of rights," Kant in terms of the rights and autonomy of moral agencies, and utilitarianism in terms of a complex dialectic balancing of the rights of all parties in a transfer process. Women, in Gilligan's view, are more concerned with preserving human relationships and hence are advocates of an „ethic of care," or an „ethic of responsibility." Those attached to an ethic of rights are concerned with the abstract rules of justice (whether Kantian or utilitarian), notions of social contract, and the rights of moral agents, whether individual or institutional (Held, 1988, p. 12). A feminist approach calls for a reasoning that is more narrative and contextual, noncontractual and focused on others, so that caring relationships become the basis for ethical behavior. Gilligan's (1987, p. 25) work indicates that both such methods of moral reasoning occur among men and women, that reasoning in the manner of an ethic of care occurs more frequently in women (and less frequently in men), and that, among men and women who are socially similar, there are fewer differences. What accounts for these differences is unclear, but Gilligan and others have argued that it is tied to differing ego development in men and women. For men, masculine ego development is based on individuation and separation from the mother; for women, feminine ego development is based on attachment (Chodorow, 1978; Gilligan, 1982). Most feminists do not wish to propose that a different basis for morality be constructed on these observations. They are only concerned that the feminist view not be discredited, that any male-gender bias not be perpetuated in moral theory, that concerns traditionally characteristic of women (e.g., concern for children) not be dismissed from moral reflection, and that the feminist view be integrated into a more comprehensive moral theory (Held, 1988, p. 13).

If one grants the legitimacy of this critique, does it significantly change the dialectical perspective proposed earlier for matters of technology transfer? It is not clear that the feminist perspective prescribes any different set of moral principles; what it may call for is a different approach to problems of technology transfer, a different weighing of factors and elements (derived from context) and a recognition of the legitimacy of certain topics that have been omitted from many discussions of ethical theory - e.g., care for each and every country and care for those as yet unable to frame their needs.

If one integrates the feminist viewpoint, one must balance an ethic of rights with an ethic of care. In the ethic of rights, one must balance competing claims and rights of stakeholders in a complex dialectical process, weighing contrasting factors and the competing claims of individuals and institutions, recognizing the factors of social utility and social responsibility, and respecting the autonomy of individuals and institutions, including organizations and countries. On the other side, an ethic of care underscores a common history and a sense of an advancing smallness of the planet. Paradoxically, it may accentuate certain features of both Kant and Mill. It extends the Kantian motive of good will beyond the rights and autonomy of individuals to care for the human family and planet as such, and to the unconditional acceptance of the rights of all persons and institutions. It also extends the utilitarian emphasis on generalized benevolence to a sense that the whole planet and the human family is a system of interconnected parts so that any exploitation of individuals, groups, societies, or countries will have an impact on the whole and return to haunt both the exploiters and the exploited. It does not change the nature of the problems of technology transfer nor the nature of principles to which one might appeal (e.g., fairness to all parties); it only changes the perspective from one of separation (balancing rights and principles) to one of connection and contextualization. An ethic of care could not be blind to specific individuals and context, and therefore it would advocate a view of fairness in contrast to that suggested by Rawls' (1957) technique of a „veil of ignorance." In his method, stakeholders could decide on the fairest allocation of resources or rights if each of the stakeholders could assume, for the duration of the decision-making process, that none of them could know what their post-decision status was to be until after the decision was reached and a course of action was implemented. For example, in the case of the agricultural library and its decision to automate, the stakeholders would assume that they would make choices not knowing whether, after the choice was made and implemented, they were the minister of agriculture from the developed country, the head librarian, the vendor from the developed country, a wealthy farmer, an illiterate farmer, a user, a consumer, or a staff member. In this way, Rawls thinks that stakeholders would be more inclined to make rulings that were fairer to each party since each stakeholder, under the veil of ignorance, would not know where he or she would be at the end of the process. But the feminist position would argue that the veil of ignorance may be itself a problem because the context cannot be ignored, and a genuine fairness may acknowledge differences among the specific stakeholders. For example, fairness may mean that one ignore the demands of the wealthy farmers (perhaps even penalizing those who previously abused the available systems) or the administrators and heed more fully the demands of those who suffered more past inequities (illiterate farmers, those members who have the most barriers to technology usage). In general, feminists do not demand that this perspective dominate, only that this voice be respected in the deliberation process.

Even if Kohlberg's theory is incomplete and feminism adds new principles (and not just perspectives), one can still regard moral deliberation in technology transfer as enhanced through a dialectical process in which the coexisting poles of Kantianism, and utilitarianism, „masculinism" (if that is how one may characterize the history of philosophy, as having been dominated by male thinkers) and feminism, are useful for framing ethical issues and coming to closure on them.

In conclusion, issues in technology transfer are not simple, and, although ethical considerations may amplify their complexity, such considerations are essential for evaluating the appropriateness and consequences of certain technologies and their transfer, since they can clarify issues and raise important challenges. There is an implicit ideology bound to the information age, an ideology that is selfserving and full of dubious values and that may work against the quality of life in LDCs and on the planet. Part of this ideology is the belief that all problems can be solved through some form of technology, that technologies are morally neutral, and that technology is an unqualified good. One of the functions of ethics is to critique this prevailing ideology. Dahlgren (in Slack, 1987, p. 27) calls for a conscious ideology to counter this tacit yet dominant ideology. Ellul (1980) observes that one option is the practice of an ethic of non-power as a resistance to the domination of technology in our culture. This option, infrequently recognized, but often necessary, states that appropriate technology may mean the absence or the minimization of technology, the refusal to implement technology or the simplification of technology, even those information technologies that at first blush may seem to solve a myriad of problems. Could it be suggested, as Dosa (1985) does, that many authors „overestimate the role of information technology and present it as a panacea to all project-related problems..." (p. 146) in providing technical assistance for development? Sometimes appropriate technology may mean engaging one's own resources and simplifying and refusing high-tech solutions to problems. Only by doing so might we inhibit the spread of ill effects of technology to LDCs and preserve a viable planet for all countries, both developed and developing.

References

Aristotle (1952). Nichomachean ethics, tr. W. D. Ross. New York: Bobbs-Merrill Company, Inc.

Berman, S. (1981). DDC: 19 An Indictment. In The joy of cataloging: Essays, letters, reviews, and other explosions. Phoenix, AZ: Orxy Press.

Brooks, H. (1973). The state of the art: technology assessment as a process. International Social Science Journal, XXV (3), 247-255.

Chodorow, N. (1978). The reproduction of mothering: psychoanalysis and the sociology of gender. Berkeley, CA: University of California Press.

Crowther, W. W. (1986). The education and training of information specialists to facilitate constructive technology transfer to and among developing countries. In M. L. Dosa & T. J. Froehlich (Eds.), Education and training for technology workshop, Montreal, 1-11 September 1986 (pp. 200-13). The Hague: International Federation for Information and Documentation.

Dede, C. (1981). Educational, social and ethical implications of technological innovation. Programmed Learning and Educational Technology, 18 (4), 204-213.

DeMarco, J., & Fox, R. M. (1986). New directions in ethics: the challenges of applied ethics. New York and London: Routledge & Kegan Paul.

Dosa, M. L. (1985). Information transfer as technical assistance for development. JASIS 36 (3), 146-152.

Ellul, J. (1980). The power of technique and the ethics of non-power. In Woodward, Kathleen, ed. (1980). The myths of information: technology and postindustrial culture. Madison, WI: Coda Press.

Eres, B. K. (1981). Transfer of information technology to less developed countries: a systems approach. JASIS, (March), 97-101.

Fox, C. J. (1982). Information and misinformation: an inquiry into information and misinformation, informing and misinforming. Westport, CT: Greenwood Press.

Froehlich, T. J. (1990). Ethics, ideologies, and practices of information technology and systems. In D. Henderson (ed.), Information in the year 2000: From research to applications (Proceedings of the 53rd annual meeting of the American Society for Information Science, 4-8 November 1990, Toronto, Canada). Medford, NJ: Learned Information, Inc.

Gilligan, C. (1983). In a different voice: psychological theory and women's development. Cambridge, MA: Harvard University Press.

Gilligan, C. (1987). Moral orientation and moral development. In Kittay, Eva & Meyers, Diana T., eds. (1987). Women and moral theory. Totowa, NJ: Rowman and Littlefield.

Graham, E. M. (1982). The terms of transfer of technology to the developing nations: a survey of major issues. North/south technology transfer: the adjustment ahead. Paris: OECD.

Held, V. (1988). Report on feminist moral theory. Newsletter on Feminism and Philosophy, ed. Nancy Tuana. Newark, Delaware: American Philosophical Association (April), 11-13.

Hetman, F. (1973). Steps in technology assessment. International Social Science Journal, XXV (3), 257-272.

Jonas, H. (1984). The imperative of responsibility: in search of an ethics for the technological age. Chicago: The University of Chicago Press.

Kant, I. (1959). Foundations of the metaphysics of morals, tr. Lewis Beck White. New York: The Liberal Arts Press.

Katz, R. L. (1988). The information society: an international perspective. New York: Praeger.

Kent, A. (1974). Unsolvable problems. In Debons, Anthony, ed. (1974). Information science: search for identity. New York: Marcel Dekker, Inc.

Kohlberg, L. (1976). Moral stages and moralization: the cognitive-developmental approach. In T. Lickona, ed., Moral development and behavior: theory, research and social issues. New York: Holt, Rinehart and Winston.

Meadow, C. (1967). An analysis of information systems: an introduction to information retrieval. New York: John Wiley and Sons.

Mill, J. S. (1957). Utilitarianism, ed. Oskar Priest. New York: The Liberal Arts Press, Inc.

Mowshowitz, A. (1984). Computers and the myth of neutrality, SIGCSE Bulletin, 16, 1, Appendix C.

Mowshowitz, A. (1976). The conquest of will: information processing in human affairs. Reading, MA: Addison-Wesley.

Murphy, J. W.; Mickunas, A.; & Pilotta, J.J. (1986). The underside of high-tech: technology and the deformation of human sensibilities. Westport, CT: Greenwood Press.

Noar, J. (1982). A new approach to multinational social responsibility. Journal of Business Ethics 1, 219-225.

Pacey, A. (1983). The culture of technology. Cambridge, MA: The MIT Press.

Rawls, J. (1957). Justice as fairness. Journal of Philosophy, LIV, 653-662

Rogers, E., & Larsen, J. (1984). Silicon valley fever. New York: Basic Books.

Rubin, R. (1990). Ethical issues in library personnel management. Paper submitted for publication.

Slack, J. D., & Fejes, F. (Eds). (1987). The ideology of the information age. Norwood, NJ: Ablex Publishing Corporation.

Taylor, C. (1985). Philosophy and the human sciences: philosophical papers 2. Cambridge: Cambridge University Press.

Taylor, R. (1986). Value-added processes in information systems. Norwood, NJ: Ablex Publishing Corp.

Thompson, J. D. (1967). Organizations in action: social science bases of administrative theory. New York: McGraw-Hill.

Woodward, K. (1980). The myths of information: technology and postindustrial culture. Madison, WI: Coda Press.

Information Technologies and Social Equity: Confronting the Revolution*

von Ronald D. Doctor

The applications of the computer have developed to such an extent that the economic and social organization of our society and our way of life may well be transformed as a result. Our society should therefore be in a position both to foster this development and to control it so that it can be made to serve the cause of democracy and human growth.

Valery Giscard d'Estaing, President, Republic of France. From a letter to Simon Nora, Inspecteur General des Finances, December 20, 1976(79)

Abstract

Under prevailing policies, serious social equity issues are arising as we move further into the Information Age. Recent surveys indicate that there is a significant gap between the 'information rich' and 'information poor', but there is little up-to-date research on the magnitude, nature and consequences of this gap. As a society we are giving inadequate attention to ensuring that as new computer and telecommunications technologies become more pervasive, their benefits are distributed in ways that don't exacerbate existing disparities between the rich and poor. The underlying issue is one of social empowerment. If 'knowledge is power', then a dominant element of our society for the rest of the century is likely to be a struggle for control of information resources and the power associated with that control.

We can begin to deal with these issues by creating a system of National and Regional Institutes for Information Democracy. The Institutes would explore the nature of information-related empowerment issues, the character and causes of the 'information gap', and would develop and implement means for mitigating associated equity problems. They would serve as a development and support structure for state and community-based Experimental Mass Information Utilities, a concept developed by Harold Sackman and his co-workers in the early 1970s. The Institutes system would provide a focus for research and implementation activities designed to mitigate equity problems, and in the process, would expand information industry markets.

I. Introduction and Preview

How can we ensure that the benefits of information age technologies are distributed equitably to all people? That is one of the pressing questions we must deal with as we move deeper into the 'Information Age'. It is a question involving power and control in society, a question of

---

*
Reprinted from JASIS Vol. 42, No. 3, April 1991, pp. 216-228. © by John Wiley & Sons, Inc.

how technology, vested interests and people interact. Explorations of this question range from utopian to Luddite, from Wells' (1938) dream of the Universal Encyclopedia[1] and Bush's (1945) vision of the Memex[2] to Webster and Robins' (1986) fear that the Panopticon Principle is in operation today[3].

Current policies tend to place control of information resources in the hands of an affluent oligopoly, effectively denying their benefits to many of our citizens. Such an approach threatens the very roots of our democratic society. Before we proceed too far along this path, we need to examine where we are today, consider where we want to be tomorrow, and plot a course that will get us there at the least cost, with the least disruption and with greatest benefit to all.

To explore the character and causes of the gap between the 'information rich' and the 'information poor' and to develop and implement means for reducing it, I propose creation of a system of National and Regional Institutes for Information Democracy. The Institutes would serve as a development and support structure for state and community based Experimental Mass Information Utilities, a concept developed by Harold Sackman and his co-workers in the early 1970s. The Utilities would be designed to bring the benefits of Information Age technologies to *all* the people, no matter what their economic circumstances. In the process, vast new markets would be opened for the information industry, markets that otherwise would be inaccessible. The system, if it works, would produce a 'win-win' situation.

This article examines these issues and options in four major sections. The remainder of Section I reviews some of the social characteristics of the Information Age. The second section explores some of the basis for social equity concerns by focusing on the distribution of microcomputer ownership and use across socioeconomic groups. The third section describes the Institutes approach for dealing with information related equity issues. The concept of a system of National and Regional Institutes for Information Democracy, coupled with locally-based Experimental Mass Information Utilities also may be helpful for integrating the various research activities that make up the field of information science. The final section offers concluding remarks.

---

[1] Wells, H.G. (1938). World Brain. Garden City, N.Y.: Doubleday.
[2] Bush, Vannevar (1945, July). As we may think. Atlantic Monthly, 1:101-108.
[3] Webster, F. and Robins, K. (1986). *Information technology: A Luddite analysis.* Melvin J. Voigt, ed. Communications and Information Science series. Norwood, N.J.: Ablex Publishing. See pp. 343-346 for a lucid description of Jeremy Bentham's conception of the Panopticon.

Ronald D. Doctor: Information Technologies and Social Equity

Technology As A Social Phenomenon - Forces of Change Colin Cherry (1985) and others (Kranzberg, 1985; Cleveland, 1985; Mayo, 1985; Zuboff, 1988; Brand, 1987; Beniger, 1986)[4][5][6][7][8][9] have noted that technology and its societal context are inseparable; that technology is, above all, a social phenomenon that shapes, and is shaped by its host society. An understanding of this central concept is essential if we are to deal effectively with the equity effects of information technologies.

Cherry[10] wrote about the great Ages of Society and the forces of change that drive societal development. He considered telecommunications and computer technologies as the major components of an Information Age, an Age of Access.

Melvin Kranzberg also considered the Information Age as one of the great revolutionary ages of society. Like Cherry, he observed that a technological revolution results from numerous technical, political, economic, cultural and social changes throughout society.

One of the characteristics of a true technological revolution is that a great many innovations take place at about the same time. Their coming together creates a synergistic, indeed, explosive, impact upon the production of goods and services.(Kranzberg, 1985)[11] Kranzberg concluded that the necessary elements for an 'Information Revolution' are present today. We are facing a social revolution driven by rapid evolutionary changes in computer, communications

---

[4] Kranzberg, M. (1985). The information age: Evolution or revolution. In *Information technologies and social transformation*. Guile, B.R. ed. Series on Technology and Social Priorities. National Academy of Engineering. Washington, D.C.: National Academy Press.

[5] Cleveland, H. (1985). The twilight of hierarchy: Speculations on the global information society. In *Information technologies and social transformation*. Guile, B.R. ed. Series on Technol. and Social Priorities. Natl. Acad. of Engineering. Washington, D.C.: Natl. Acad. Press.

[6] Mayo, J.S. (1985). The evolution of Information technologies. In *Information technologies and social transformation*. Guile, B.R. ed. Series on Technology and Social Priorities. National Academy of Engineering. Washington, D.C.: National Academy Press.

[7] Zuboff, S. (1988). *In the age of the smart machine: the future of work and power*. N.Y.: Basic Books.

[8] Brand, Stewart (1987). *The Media Lab: Inventing the future at M.I.T.* New York: Penquin Books.

[9] Beniger, James R. (1986). *The control revolution: Technological and economic origins of the information society*. Cambridge MA: Harvard University Press.

[10] Cherry, *Age of access*, op cit.

[11] Kranzberg, Information Age, op. cit., p.37.

and information technologies and by the interaction of those technologies with our social institutions.

This revolution, evolving from the convergence of a constellation of new technologies, involves the entire fabric of society. It changes where and how people work, live, play and pray. It brings new social patterns and cultural values. It changes and weakens traditional institutions (Kranzberg, 1967, Vol 1, Ch. 13)[12].

The technologies change society, and society resists some changes and modifies the direction of technological development. New social patterns, changing cultural values, disarray in existing institutions, all these produce resistance to the technological progenitors of change, slowing the social dislocations inherent in revolutionary activity. In this way, society gains the time needed to adapt to, or change, the technological forces acting on it. This societal interaction with changing technology is what Ogburn (1964) called cultural lag[13]. Cultural lag, in Kranzberg's view, is evidence that society imposes its will, however unconscious and disorganized, on technology.

Power and Control

Most commentators on the Information Age agree that societal changes will be formidable. But, there is little consensus as to *how* our political and economic systems will change as we move deeper into this new Information Age. The extremes are represented by technological optimism on the one hand and neo-Luddite reaction on the other.

Frank Webster and Kevin Robins[14] have presented a powerful Luddite analysis. They argue that we are witnessing an intensified centralization of the tools of control; that increased power is being vested in an oligopoly; that there is a growing disparity between the affluent, who are able to access the new technologies, and the economically disadvantaged, who effectively are

---

[12] Kranzberg, M. (1967). Prerequisites for industrialization. In, *Technology in western civilization.* Kranzberg, M. and Pursell, C.W. ed. New York: Oxford University Press. Vol 1, Chapter 13.
[13] Ogburn, W.F. (1964) *On culture and social change: Selected papers.* Duncan, O.D., ed. Chicago: University of Chicago Press.
[14] Webster, F. and Robins, K. *Information technology*, op cit.

denied access. They note that there is little in our history to make us sanguine about closing this growing gap between the 'haves' and 'have-nots'.

Stewart Brand[15], somewhat less 'Luddite' in outlook, tends to agree. Although impressed with the promise of new technologies, he cautions about the instability of the socio-political system as we move into the Information Age. Brand warns of the growing inability of our political institutions to guide and control the new technological developments. He argues that information is the dominant wealth-creating process, and the principle information technologies are computing and telecommunications. As these technologies develop, economic and political power will tend to become more highly concentrated.

Considering the powerful economic and political forces at work, Brand foresees the need for a new principle as fundamental as freedom of speech and press: The right of access. „You may not choose to reach everyone, or be reachable by everyone, but the connection should be possible". This requires „universal connectivity, directory information, agreed standards and a legal right to interconnect".[16]

Brand's call for a new 'right to access' is critically important, but perhaps the concept needs to be expanded. A simple right to access very likely will be insufficient to remedy the equity problems with which we are concerned. Access will be of little benefit to large portions of the population, unless it is accompanied by equipment and training that allow effective *use* of that access. What we need then is a 'right to access' in the broader sense of a 'right to *benefit* from access'. The Institutes system proposed in this paper offers one way to achieve this fundamental right.

Colin Cherry[17] and Harlan Cleveland[18] offer a different perspective. They argue that the new information technologies distribute and disperse information capabilities, tending to decentralize control of information and its concomitant power. If carried through, this would be a major reversal of the centralization of power brought on by the Industrial Revolution.

---

[15] Brand, *The Media Lab*, op cit.
[16] Brand, *The Media Lab*, op cit. p.219
[17] Cherry, *Age of access*, op. cit.
[18] Cleveland, Twilight of hierarchy, op cit.

Cleveland, particularly, expresses the optimistic view with great clarity. He believes the inherent properties of computer and telecommunications technologies will lead to greater diffusion of knowledge, and therefore greater democratization in society. He foresees dramatic changes in the five major hierarchies[19]:

- Hierarchies of power based on control
- Hierarchies of influence based on secrecy
- Hierarchies of class based on ownership
- Hierarchies of privilege based on early access (structural unfairness)
- Hierarchies of politics based on geography

If knowledge is power[20], then „the wider the spread of knowledge, the more power gets diffused"[21]. Cleveland believes openness and participatory democracy will spread. This vision demands attention. The political and economic implications of the societal changes that Cleveland predicts are staggering. If the hypothesis that great power is associated with information, is valid, then I foresee increased contention for control of information and knowledge resources. This struggle for control is likely to be a dominant element of our society for the rest of this century.

Predicting the Future

Prediction, of course, is a tricky business. The diverse social settings and myriad forces that characterize the interactions between technology and society generate such uncertainty that it is very difficult to predict with confidence what forms future societal issues will take.

---

[19] Cleveland, Twilight of hierarchy, op. cit., p.60

[20] This widely quoted aphorism is attributable to Francis Bacon who said „knowledge and human power are synonymous",
Bacon, F. (1561-1626). *Bacon's Novuum Organum* (Aphorism i). Th. Fowler (Ed.), 2nd ed. Oxford: Clarendon Press, 1889.
Bacon also said, "Knowledge itself is power" (Nam et ipsa scientia potestas est) in *Religious meditations: Of heresies*.
Bacon, F. (1561-1626). Essayes, religious meditations, places of perswasion & *disswasion*. From the first edition of 1597. London: F. Etchells and H. Macdonald, 1924.

[21] Cleveland, H. (1985). *The knowledge executive: Leadership in an information society.* N.Y.: Truman Talley Books.

Cherry showed that „a technological artefact has no specific meaning outside a social context. ... it is the social situation that gives it a particular significance"[22]. As a consequence,

> [I]t is also difficult, if not well-nigh impossible, to guess what will be the future uses, significance, and values of radically new inventions of our own day ... [because] we do not know what will be the social conditions of the future, what will be the new customs and habits, the new institutions, the political and economic changes.[23]

Kranzberg agreed, noting that „the same technology can have quite different results when introduced into a different cultural setting".[24]

Perhaps Cherry and Kranzberg are correct. We cannot foresee what impacts the 'Information Age' will have on society. But we know from history that the impacts will be significant, unevenly distributed and diffused, assimilated and modified at uneven rates. The fact of change is clear. The direction is not.

As a democratic society, our choices are finite, and few. We can move in the direction of *laissez faire* policies; or we can take a pro-active position, recognizing that some directions of change are more desirable than others. We can try to shape policies that will move us toward a more equitable and democratic future.

---

[22] Cherry, *Age of access*, op. cit., p.58
[23] Cherry, *Age of access*, op. cit., p.59
[24] Kranzberg, Information Age, op. cit., p.50

II. Social Equity Issues: Recent Studies

Should public policy be designed to ensure some form of universal access to computers and computerized information-bases? Should special training in how to use these systems be provided as a public right, or should we simply trust that existing institutions gradually will achieve the necessary levels of training? Are there other ways to resolve the equity issues that arise as parts of our society reap the benefits of advanced technologies while others fall farther and farther out of the mainstream? These are issues we are failing to deal with today, issues, nevertheless, which we can not afford to ignore.

A Rationale for Social Equity Concerns

As our society shifts more toward a market orientation regarding new computer and telecommunications technologies, there is a danger that existing patterns of inequality will be reinforced. Some people will have access to information (and its associated power) more readily and quickly than others. The risk, according to Webster and Robins[25], is that we will create a new basis of inequality as the gap widens between the information rich and the information poor.

The Congressional Office of Technology Assessment has noted that the advent of electronic dissemination of information raises new equity concerns. If electronic formats provide competitive advantages, those without electronic access are disadvantaged, and will be increasingly disadvantaged, unless overt action is taken to cure this problem.[26]

In 1989, the Executive Office of Management and Budget (OMB) forecasted that by the year 2000, almost two-thirds of American households will own personal computers; and 6-8 million businesses and 40-50 million households will have electronic access to databases containing information on available products and services from private and public organizations.[27]

---

[25] Webster and Robins, op. cit., p.255-256.
[26] *Informing the nation: Federal information dissemination in an electronic age* (1988). US Congress, Office of Technology Assessment. OTA-BP-CIT-396. Washington DC: US GPO.
[27] *Management of the U.S. Gov., Fiscal Year 1989. Office of the President and OMB*. This ref. app. in „National policy and the national agenda: US competitiveness and inform. technol." D. Maynard and B. C. Carroll, *Bulletin of the ASIS*, 15(3):17, 1989. Maynard and Carroll also note that the federal budget for information technology in 1988 was about $17.4 billion.

The OMB report is silent about what happens to the other one-third of US households that do not have computers, are unlikely to obtain them, and, presently, wouldn't know what to do with one if they had it.

Critics[28,29,30,31] of current information policy note that current trends exacerbate equity problems. Their concerns center on the following observations:

- There is increasing concentration, in fewer and fewer companies, of information resources and the means to deliver information. This trend is exacerbated by current efforts to rely on private sector activity to disseminate data and information gathered by the federal government.
- Concentration of information resources in commercial firms, whose primary motivation is profitability means that information technology will be available only to those with plentiful resources. Eventually this consolidation of power will work to the detriment of the individual, rich or poor.
- Rural areas will be slower to benefit from new information technologies than urban areas. Rural communities are less densely populated and are a poor investment for cable TV and telecommunications operators in comparison to wealthy urban locales. Information technology vendors have demonstrated a pronounced bias toward affluent, urban clients.
- Large numbers of low income people (including old, sick, unemployed and low skilled workers) can not afford information technology equipment or information company fees for services. They are effectively excluded from participation in the electronic grid that will provide a cluster of information services to more affluent homes. Yet these people, perhaps more than any other segment of society, are most in need of specialized electronic services to resolve everyday problems.

Recent surveys of computer ownership and use by age, race, economic and sociocultural status tend to confirm these concerns.

---

[28] Webster and Robins, op. cit.
[29] Mosco, V. (1989). *The pay-per society: Computers and communication in the information age. Essays in critical theory and public policy.* Norwood, N.J.: Ablex.
[30] Mosco, V. (1989, July 1). Deja vu all over again? *Society* 26(5):31.
[31] Mosco, V. (1988). Introduction: Information in the pay-per society. In V. Mosco and J. Wasko, (Eds.), *The political economy of information.* Madison: Univ. of Wisconsin Press.

Recent Socioeconomic Research

Various surveys since 1981 are remarkably consistent in the picture they paint regarding the *distribution* of computer ownership and use across socioeconomic groups:

1. Dutton, Rogers and Jun in a 1987 review of 11 earlier surveys[32] (ranging from 1970 to 1985) found that microcomputers provide a significant educational advantage to children. They also found that these advantages are unevenly distributed across economic, ethnic and gender categories[33 34 35]. The 11 surveys indicated that social status (including education and income) is a consistent predictor of adoption and use of personal computers. „The strength of the association between socioeconomic status and the adoption of personal computers leads to policy concerns about inequity as a social impact."[36]

2. Kominski's 1988 report of a 1984 Census Bureau survey indicated lack of access to computers by school age children was correlated to family income and linked to race and education[37].

   - 37% of children in families with incomes of more than $50,000 have computers in their homes.
   - Only 3.4% of children in households with income less than $10,000 have computers at home. 17% of all white children, 6% of blacks and less than 5% of Hispanics use a computer at home. But, given the opportunity, black children use

---

[32] Dutton, W., Rogers, E., Jun, S., (1987). Diff. and soc. impacts of PC's. *Comm. Res.*, 14(2): 219ff.
[33] *The road after 1984: The impact of technology on society,* (1983). L. Harris & Assoc. Paper presented at the Eighth International Smithsonian Symposium, 1983. Also see, Highlights of the road after 1984: Study of the impact of technology on society. L. Harris & Assoc., Inc. In *Privacy and 1984: Public opinions on privacy issues. Hearing before the Gov. Inform., Justice, and Agricult. Subcommittee of the House Committee on Gov. Operations*, 98th Congress, April 4, 1984. Washington, D.C.: U.S. GPO, 1984. (Y4.G 74/7 P93\12.)
[34] Lautenberg, F.R. (1984, April). Equity in computer education. *Computing Teacher*, p.13-14.
[35] Tichenor, P.J., Donohue, G.A., and Olien, C.N. (1970). Mass media flow and differential growth and knowledge. *Public Opinion Quarterly,* 34:159-170.
[36] Dutton, Rogers and Jun, op cit., p. 231, April 1987.
[37] Kominski, R. (1988). Computer use in the U. S.: 1984. *Current Population Reports, Special Studies,* Series P-23 No. 155, Iss. Mar. 1988. US Dept. of Commerce, Bureau of the Census. Washington DC: US GPO.

computers at home more than their white counterparts. White children used home computers on average 2.8 days/week; black children averaged 3.8 days/week.

The Census Bureau noted that „for children at the lower end of the economic spectrum, lack of access to computers during their school years may further limit their employment opportunities as adults."[38]

3. A 1988 report by the Educational Testing Service (ETS) found that computer ownership and use divides along income and ethnic lines[39].

They found clear ethnic differences in computer competence, favoring White students over Black and Hispanic youngsters. Much of the difference derived from different levels of access to computers in school and availability of machines at home.

4. The ETS study also found that student competence with computers correlates strongly with the level of parental education, and with attendance at nonpublic schools.

The higher the parents' education level, the more likely the children were to be currently studying computers in school and to have a computer at home. Parents who graduated from college were about twice as likely to own a computer as high school graduates, and 3 times as likely as those who didn't finish high school.

Families whose children went to non-public schools were more likely to have a computer in the home, and to demonstrate superior competence.

5. Unequal access also results in a structural gap between rural and urban environments in the US, according to Dillman's 1985 study[40][41].

---

[38] Who uses a computer? (1988). *Statistical Brief from the Current Population Survey*, US Dept of Commerce, Bureau of the Census. SB-2-88.

[39] Martinez, M. E. and Mead, N. A (1988, April). *The nation's report card. Computer competence: The first national assessment*. Princeton NJ: Educational Testing Service.

[40] Dillman, D. (1985). The social impacts of information technologies in rural North America. *Rural Sociology*, 50:1-26.

[41] LaRose, R. and Mettler, J. (1989). Who uses information technologies in rural America. *J. of Communication 39*(3):48-60.

The ETS study confirmed that students from advantaged metropolitan areas were the most computer competent. Students from rural and disadvantaged metropolitan areas were the least competent.

The most important factor affecting computer competence across communities and regions was family ownership of a computer. About half of 7th graders in advantaged metropolitan areas own computers. But only one in five of their *rural* peers have home access to a machine.

These and other data point to computer ownership and availability of school-based instruction as primary determinants of competence. And these in turn are strongly correlated to income and affluence.

Developing a Research Taxonomy

James Danziger[42] observes that „the impacts of computer technology on society are an extraordinarily important area for rigorous social scientific research. However to this point there is only a modest amount of empirical research and a dearth of cumulative findings on this subject." He notes that before discussing the impacts of computing, we should develop a taxonomy that encourages systematic study and evaluation.

Danziger offers such a taxonomy as a conceptual framework for research. He focuses on two broad 'object units of analysis', individuals and collectivities[43]. Each object unit would be evaluated in terms of four classes of impacts:

1. Orientations (e.g. computing increases reliance on quantifiable criteria)
2. Interactions (e.g. effects on centralization or decentralization of authority and control)
3. Capabilities (e.g. creation or use of knowledge, mastery of environmental conditions)
4. Value Distribution (e.g. ways in which technology might alter the distribution of wealth, power, welfare, privacy, autonomy and survival)

---

[42] Danziger, J. N. (1985, March). Social science and the social impacts of computer technology. *Social Science Quarterly*, 66(1):3-21.

[43] Danziger's 'collectivities' are further divided into five components: organizational, institutional, societal subsystems, societal systems and international systems.

Two modifications would improve Danziger's taxonomy. First, it needs a time element, an impact category that is sensitive to the rapid rate at which new computer and telecommunications technologies are introduced and adopted. Lacking this element, social science research on the impacts of information technologies runs the risk of being outdated by the time the research is completed and published.

The second modification is more significant for our purposes. The framework needs greater differentiation of the individual as an 'object unit of analysis'. To be useful for socioeconomic purposes, the taxonomy should provide income, gender and socio-cultural differentiation as well as differentiation between urban, suburban and rural environments.

Still, the problem of anticipating technology and evaluating socioeconomic impacts in a rapidly changing environment has not been solved. One way to implement a cohesive research program based on Danziger's taxonomy is to develop large scale, adaptive pilot programs that would explore new delivery mechanisms for information technologies. Such programs could intermix research with implementation in real and diverse operating environments.

The next section describes how creating an integrated system of National and Regional Institutes for Information Democracy and Experimental Mass Information Utilities might fill these research needs. Through prototype programs, enhanced research, and innovative financing for community based programs and equipment acquisition, the Institute system also would provide the primary mechanisms for mitigating information age equity issues.

III. Creating an institutional framework

In the first section, we observed that some social analysts see the new computer and telecommunications technologies as a democratizing force. Others note that these technologies may only widen the gap between the 'haves' and 'have-nots'. The fact is technology *alone* will do neither. It is how we *use* technology and how we *promulgate* it that determines the good or ill we derive from it.

In our system of government, diffuse economic and social forces determine access to knowledge. The power associated with possession of knowledge is limited to those who have the economic resources to acquire access to the new technologies and are in a social environment that enables them to use that access effectively.

If a socioeconomic group does not possess the *training* to use computer and telecommunications technologies *effectively*, then the power of those technologies is denied to them. The ability to use a technology includes not only individual skill and intelligence but social organization as well. If the social organization of the user (or user group) does not facilitate effective and timely use, much of the power of the technology may be dissipated.

So, we see that whether the 'gap' indicated by recent surveys will grow or narrow over time depends on our educational and social policies and programs. But developing new technology-based social programs in a time of rapid technological change is difficult at best. Attempts to deal with various aspects of this problem have been sporadic over the past 25 years.The 1960s and '70s were innovative times for the library and information professions. Under the impetus of federal funding, libraries experimented with community outreach programs[44]; information and referral (I&R) services were developed[45]; and a host of community information centers were created[46], many designed to serve special populations.

---

[44] Kochen, M. and Donohue, J. (Eds.) (1976). *Inform. for the community*. Chicago: ALA.
Benson, Ch. S. and Lund, P. B. (1969). *Neighborhood distribution of local public services*. Berkeley, CA: Univ. of California, Instit. of Gov. Studies.

[45] Long, N. (1976). Information and referral services: A short history and some recommendations. In Kochen and Donohue (Eds.) op cit. p.55-73.

[46] Forsman, C. (1976). Crisis inform. services to youth. In Kochen & Donohue (Eds.), p.133-143.
Hess, C. (1979). *Community Technology*. NY: Harper & Row.

Many of these activities died when federal funding expired, but some continued and others evolved into more narrowly-scoped reference services, specialty I&R services, and highly focused research activities.

Today, we're beginning to see a rebirth of these activities. Computerization of traditional library functions is accelerating. Within the past ten years library automation has progressed from computerized word processing to automation of library circulation systems, and more recently, to computerization of the library catalog. The current trend is to make these computerized catalogs available to the general public.

In an Online Public Access Catalog (OPAC), patrons use computer terminals located within the library or on a university campus to search the catalog for items they need[47].
In a *Remote* OPAC (ROPAC), the library allows telephone access to its catalog through modem-equipped home or business computers. Some ROPACs are implemented through individual libraries, but most of those reported in the literature involve large academic libraries or consortia of public and academic libraries. Over 100 online library catalogs and databases are available remotely through the Bitnet/Internet E-mail system[48,49].

In a Remote OPAC *Community Information System* (ROPAC-CIS), the library computer system provides a variety of information services relevant and important to its patrons and locale. Currently, only a relatively few libraries provide remote access to their catalogs. Even fewer take full advantage of the computer's ability to make the library an effective community information center. Still, significant ROPAC-CIS activities are underway in Colorado[50,51] and Santa Monica, California[52] and are planned in Cleveland[53]. In addition, by November 1990,

---

[47] Lancaster, F.W. (1982). *Libraries and librarians in an age of electronics.* Arlington, VA: IRP.
[48] Updegrove, D. A., Muffo, J. A., and Dunn, J. A. Jr. (1990). Electronic mail and networks: New tools for institutional research and university planning. *CAUSE/EFFECT,* 13: 41-48.
[49] St. George, A. and Larsen, R. (1990). Internet-accessible library catalogs and databases. (Electronic file available from stgeorge@unmb.bitnet, or stgeorge@bootes.unm.edu (Internet))
[50] Nelson, N. M., (1989, May). Library technology: Uncover, OPACs, NeXT, Kids, and More. *Information Today,* 6(5):37-38.
[51] Magrath, L. L. (1989, Spring). The public and the computer: Reactions to a second generation online catalog. *Library Trends* 37(4):532-537.
[52] „Phone-first" fever spreads as libraries add dial-up access (1989, October). News Fronts section. *American Libraries* 20(9):839.
[53] PC access to Cleveland PL: A 'large, urban PL first', (1989, Jan). *American Libraries,* 20(1): 17.

about 15 university libraries were operating computerized campus-wide information systems (CWIS). This transition from OPAC to ROPAC to ROPAC-CIS portends significant changes in the way libraries operate and in the way information is delivered at the community level[54][55][56]. Two other activities with roots in the early 1970s also are important to this discussion.

First, research on information needs and uses gathered momentum. The emphasis of this research gradually shifted from describing how people behaved in libraries to determining the underlying needs of different populations and the context in which those needs exist[57]. Brenda Dervin carried this work a step further by focusing on how people *use* information to solve problems in their everyday lives, an approach she calls 'sense-making'[58][59]. More recently Elfreda Chatman's research has stepped beyond the bounds of the library to examine the information needs and sources of low income populations[60]. What is still lacking however, are effective means for delivering the needed information to these groups.

The second noteworthy activity came in the early 1970s when Harold Sackman and his co-workers[61][62], building on ideas expressed almost 40 years earlier by Supreme Court Justice Louis D. Brandeis, developed and explored the concept of Experimental Mass Information Utilities (EMIU). They saw these utilities as a way to deal with the societal impacts of a rapidly changing computer and telecommunications environment.

---

[54] Dowlin, K.E. (1984). *The electronic library: The promise and the process*. Neal-Schuman.
[55] Edelman, H. (1986). *Libraries and information science in the electronic age*. Phil.: ISI Press.
[56] *Rethinking the library in the information age. Volume II. Issues in library research: proposals for the 1990s.* Library Development Staff, Library Programs, Office of Educational research and Improvement (OERI), U.S. Dep. of Education. Washington D.C.: U.S GPO, 1989.
[57] Katzer, J. (1987). User studies, information science, and communication. *The Canadian Journal of Information Science 12*(3/4):15-30.
[58] Dervin, B. and Fraser, B. (1985). *How libraries help*. Sacramento: Cal. State Library. This report is a good summary of Dervin's 'sense-making' approach to determination of information needs.
[59] Dervin, B. (1989). Users as research inventions: How research categories perpetuate inequities. *J. of Communication 39*(3):216. This issue is titled, *The information gap: How computers and other new communication technologies affect the social distribution of power.*
[60] Chatman, E. A. (1990, Spring). Alienation theory: Application of a conceptual framework to a study of information among janitors. *RQ 29*(3):355.
[61] Sackman, H. (1971). *Mass information utilities and social excellence*. Princeton: Auerbach.
[62] Sackman H.; Boehm, B. (eds.) (1972). *Planning community inform. utilities.*, NJ: AFIPS Press.

The Experimental Mass Information Utility (EMIU)

The key word here is experimental. These utilities would have flexible operating agendas and would tailor their activities to the communities in which they operate. They would experiment with alternative services and delivery mechanisms, continuously seeking optimization for their clientele. These experiments would evaluate alternative utility designs, testing and developing public information services to best serve the *local* public interest.

The EMIU would be a significant change in public utility philosophy, „from [emphasizing] narrow economic interests to broader social values, where those values themselves are continually subject to social experiment under evolving democratic forms".[63]

The EMIU concept focuses on the usefulness of „pooled social information". The object, according to Sackman, is „to make a significant portion of the cultural store of useful information available to all citizens through computer utilities". The experimental concept would include „prototype centers for collecting, pooling, analyzing and disseminating user experience with computer utilities". To go along with this, Sackman also proposed „a national census of information services ... to determine whether equitable distribution of information services is being attained, within reasonable bounds, throughout the country".[64] Using the EMIUs as a focusing device, Sackman proposed a dynamic taxonomy for social science research on the effects of telecommunications technologies[65]. The EMIUs would deal with four classes of problems:

Social Effectiveness Problems	*Normative Problems*
User quality assurance	Classification
Pooled social information	Individual differences
	Performance norms
Methodological Problems	*Behavioral Problems*
Conceptual	Learning
Performance measures	Individual differences
Experimental techniques	Real-time dynamics
	Problem-solving

---

[63] Sackman, *Mass information utilities*, op. cit., p.27.
[64] Sackman, *Mass information utilities*, op. cit., p.141.
[65] Sackman, *Mass information utilities*, op. cit., p.136-156.

It is testimony to Sackman's foresight that after almost 20 years of extraordinary technological advances, his proposal and taxonomy are still viable. What is needed now is to merge the methods of Dervin and Chatman and the research frameworks suggested by Danziger and Sackman into a unified whole. The system of Institutes proposed in this paper would be a focal point for the needed integration.

Structure and Roles of the National and Regional Institutes

The National and Regional Institutes for Information Democracy would tie together into a cohesive, multidisciplinary structure the diverse threads that we call library and information studies. They would focus on research *applications*, particularly those useful for solving information-related equity issues, and would provide an institutional home for the EMIUs.

The goals of the system, the nature of the problems to be solved, the constituencies that are targeted patrons of the system all suggest an institutional form. That form should serve local needs and integrate with existing institutions (particularly local educational and library systems), be responsive to local and state interests, and be sensitive to a national agenda.

In structuring the Institutes, we can draw on lessons learned from the operations of the Agricultural Extension Services, the National Institutes of Health, the regional solar energy centers that existed briefly in the late 1970s and early 1980s, and from past and current operations of I&R services and library-based community information centers.

We also can learn from past and current private sector activities. The videotex failures of the last decade will be instructive; So will the teletex successes like Compuserve and Minitel. The mass marketing activities of Prodigy and the burgeoning activity of the Regional Bell Operating Companies also can serve as models.

Both the public and private sectors have sensed unmet markets and are moving forward to fill them. At present though, these efforts are fragmented. What is missing is a conceptual framework to tie them together, an institutional system that would pick the best aspects of each, and ensure that these services would be available, effective, usable and low cost for all people. That's where the Institutes come in.

The National Institute for Information Democracy (NIID) would be responsible for creating the basic research taxonomy, securing core-level funding, coordinating with related federal institutions such as the Library of Congress and the National Library of Medicine and overseeing the research activities of the Regional Institutes (RIIDs). It would seek, and contract for assistance from the state-based RIIDs.

The National Institute would be located in Washington, D.C. as part of an existing cabinet level agency. Its presence in Washington would help the system be more sensitive and responsive to federal requirements and queries than would otherwise be the case. The Regional Institutes would serve a mediating function between federal and state/local governments and would administer and help develop the operational programs.

Each of four Regional Institutes for Information Democracy (RIIDs) would have a Board of Directors, whose members would be appointed by the Governors of participating States. They would be funded by the National Institute but also would be free to seek independent funding. The RIIDs would be responsible for creating and carrying out information equity research programs and prototype implementation programs and for implementing Mass Information Utilities (EMIUs) within their states.

To work effectively the RIID system must produce a sense of ownership in the organization. Consequently its programs would be coordinated through field representatives in each State, keeping operational personnel close to the people they serve. Regional administration, with frequent meetings of state representatives, would produce a synergism and pooling of experience that would meld the diversity and common interests of the states into a unified program. This type of structure tends to build effective programs with both a regional *esprit de corps* and separate state and local identities.

In addition to the EMIUs, other RIID programs would deal with acquisition of information products and equipment, create innovative financing mechanisms, help develop and coordinate library and public school programs and ensure cooperative relationships with the information industry. Each EMIU would focus on different clientele: urban, suburban, rural and small business. Particular emphasis would be given to developing information skills among the economically disadvantaged, but would not be limited to this area. In a matrix structure, the people-oriented activities would be supplemented by programs involving the public library and public school systems, training for adults as well as school-age children, and equipment distribution, sales and leasing programs.

The National and Regional Institutes would have three initial tasks[66]:

1. Perform systems analyses of proposed computer utility prototypes in sufficient detail so that the basic working structure would be spelled out. The results would lead to working system cost-effectiveness estimates. This task requires an appropriate interdisciplinary team.

2. Try the leading concepts for an experimental utility on a small and easily managed scale in a live setting. The objective would be to examine the hypotheses and questions raised in the research framework and to develop pilot program methodologies. These then would be applied to larger scale prototypes.

3. Cultivate the interest and cooperation of other parties essential for successful social experimentation with prototype utilities in each user community. The goal would be to develop a pre-agreed charter as a basis for developing and evaluating the utility prototype.

Implementing such a system of information utilities could profoundly change the nature of social and political interactions in our nation.

Operations of the NIID/RIID/EMIU System

Initially, each EMIU would focus on helping individual citizens and small businesses acquire and learn to use information and information technologies to deal with their everyday problems. Although each EMIU's agenda should be tailored to its community, with participation of community leaders and citizens, it is useful to identify a sample EMIU program. Here are some of the things EMIUs might do:

1. Experiment with alternative organizational, ownership and regulatory forms in different parts of the country.

    These could include full public ownership (municipal information utility), full private ownership under a franchise arrangement (subject to regulation) and public-private joint development (municipal information utility, with and without regulation).

---

[66] These tasks are paraphrased from Sackman, *Mass information utilities*, op. cit., p.155-156.

The EMIUs, in cooperation with NIID/RIID, would develop innovative public-private financing arrangements to ensure low cost availability of equipment and services to participating households. These arrangements might include cost-reducing tax incentive programs that enable cooperating private sector firms to lease or otherwise offer computer and telecommunications equipment, services and training to public and school libraries at an affordable, low cost. The object would be to ensure that public libraries and schools in all areas of the nation have sufficient equipment and skills to offer computer training and online services to their patrons and students.

2. Provide entry-level microcomputer systems with 'user-friendly' interfaces, especially designed for mass audiences, to households and small businesses for low monthly lease fees.

This universal acquisition program is analogous to current utility water heater leasing and telephone leasing programs. Some customers might be eligible for 'lifeline' rates, similar to electric and gas utility special rates for low income and elderly customers. Others might choose to purchase systems, at low cost, or with favorable financing. The purchase and leasing program could operate as a joint public-private endeavor, like current home weatherization programs.

3. Develop and introduce EMIU based educational programs to enhance the learning process at all levels.

These could operate under cooperative agreements with local school systems. Equipment and training, including 'train-the trainer' programs could be provided by the EMIU, supported by its regional institute. The program would focus on practical aspects of telecommunication information systems: how to get information and how to use it for everyday endeavors. Programs would be tailored to each community's specific needs. There would be a special focus on economically disadvantaged areas.

4. Help local public school systems develop special education and training programs targeted to different classes of users, different socioeconomic groups.

Telecommunication linkages between school and home could significantly enhance the educational process. Educational programs, homework assignments, adult education programs could be tailored to individual needs. They would be available at times convenient to the student, providing greater flexibility and motivation for use.

5. Help local library systems develop telecommunications service packages, including online gateway services.

   The EMIU might contract with library systems for delivery of those services to participating households and small businesses. All necessary equipment, software and training could be provided to the libraries by the EMIU.

6. Make information acquired and developed by the government and marketed by private vendors available to public and school libraries. Availability would be at low regulated prices, with unlimited license to the libraries and schools to provide this information through the EMIUs.

7. Enter joint public-private development agreements with local telephone companies for online services and with local computer firms for maintenance, training, and additional equipment purchases.

8. With NIID/RIID, develop and participate in research into the sociology, economics and legal aspects of 'shared' information resources.

9. Help develop a national information inventory of information resources and applications for different socioeconomic groups of citizens. The inventory would focus on resources and requirements needed and available for computerizing the public libraries and schools of the nation.

Developing motivational and educational programs and offering equipment and useful services will be the key to EMIU success. Flexibility and adaptability will be required.

Current, Related Activities

There is ample evidence in the operations of the National Institutes of Health and the Agricultural Extension Services to indicate that this is an institutional model that can work. In addition, some aspects of the system I propose already are being tried, with apparent success, through France Telecom's Minitel-based Teletel system, which was first proposed in 1978 by Nora and Minc[67] and recently was introduced in the US[68].

By mid-1990, France's Teletel system, with its Minitel terminals and 14,000 services was serving more than 5.5 million customers, increasing by 800,000 per year, and expanding into other European countries[69] (Conhaim, Nov/Dec 1990b). MinitelNet, a France Telecom operation of its Intelmatique, S.A. subsidiary, began operations in New York in early 1988. It serves as a gateway to Teletel in France. Like its French counterpart, the service offers low cost terminals and „kiosk" type billing (no subscription fees). Intelmatique has enterd into cooperative agreements with a number of Regional Bell Operating Companies (RBOCs).

The telephone companies of Canada and the US have begun to offer gateway services[70]. Bell Canada is implementing its 'Alex' system in Toronto and Montreal. Alex is a large scale consumer videotex effort that is a superset (and competitor) of Minitel[71]. There also is burgeoning activity among the Regional Bell Operating Companies (RBOCs)[72]:

---

[67] Nora, S. and Minc, A. (1980). *The computerization of society: report to the Presid. of France.* Cambridge: The MIT Press. Originally published as *L'Informatisation de la societe*, c1978.

[68] *MinitelNet directory of services* (1988). New York: Intelmatique S.A. MinitelNet, an operation of Intelmatique S.A., began operations in New York in early 1988. It serves as a gateway to more than 1,500 French information services. Like its French counterpart, the service offers low cost terminals and 'kiosk' type billing (no subscription fee). Intelmatique has entered into cooperative agreements with a number of Regional Bell Operating Companies. Currently, Minitel serves 4 million customers in France and recently expanded into Belgium.

[69] Conhaim, W. W. (1990b). RBOC update: The opening gateways. Link-Up, 7(6): 18-19, 34-35.

[70] On March 7, 1988, Judge Harold Greene granted the Regional Bell Operating Companies permission to provide gateway access to information services produced by outside organizations. Fourteen months later, 4 RBOCs had gateways in 7 locations.

[71] Conhaim, W. W. (1989, February). Focus on Videotex. *Information Today* 6(2):33.

[72] Conhaim, W. W. (1989, May). Focus on Videotex: Local services begin to develop on RBOC Gateways. *Information Today* 6(5): 43-45.

1. Bell Atlantic is trying low cost gateway services for consumers in Washington D.C. and Philadelphia. By November 1990, Bell Atlantic was offering 60 services in Washington and 100 in Philadelphia.[73][74] (Conhaim, 1990b).

2. Southwestern Bell ran a year-long market trial of SourceLine in Houston. It included low-cost monthly terminal rental[75]. In March 1990, at completion of the one-year, $10 million trial, Southwestern Bell shut down their service pending further study of the reasons for not meeting the company's profitability objectives. U.S. Videotel, Southwestern Bell's system operator, took over the system, implemented a flat-rate fee structure and expanded to Dallas[76].

3. BellSouth is trying its Transtext Universal Gateway in Atlanta, with an emphasis on local services. The planned objective of 300 initial users was quickly exceeded. By November, 1990, BellSouth had more than 3,500 customers (Conhaim, 1990b).

4. NYNEX operates Info-Look in New York (190 services, Boston (150 services) and Burlington, Vermont (35 services). Bell Canada and NYNEX have agreed to provide mutual access to each other's services (Conhaim, 1990b).

5. US West introduced and aggressively marketed gateway services in Omaha in October 1989 with Minitel-type terminals. Customers could lease the terminals for $7.95 per month, or buy them for $200 to $300[77]. Customer signups exceeded expectations, reaching 2% penetration by October, 1990. By November 1990, US West had more than 700 services online, about 40% of them locally produced. With its success in Omaha, US West has announced that service will be expanded to Minneapolis and St. Paul by the end of 1991. (Conhaim, 1990b).

---

[73] Bell Atlantic Starts Gateway Service (1989, March/April). *Link-Up* 6(2): 1.
[74] Bell access to catalog a „first" (1989, June). News Fronts, *American Libraries* 20(6):492.
[75] Conhaim, Wallys W. (1989, September). Videotex leaders call for cooperation and consistency. Information Today 6(8):32-34.
[76] Smith, R. B. (1990, March 15). Future Shock: People got hooked but then abandoned telephone 'gateways'. *Wall Street Journal*, v.CXXII (52):1,A6.
[77] Smith, R. B. *Wall Street Journal*, March 15, 1990, op cit.

As the RBOCs move cautiously, but deliberately into mass market teletex and videotex services, their major competition will come from Prodigy, the Sears-IBM joint videotex effort. Prodigy's sponsors have spent around a half billion dollars and several years exploring and preparing for their entry into this market. By February 1990, Prodigy offered services in more than 26 cities, had 160,000 accounts[78] and more than 200 national advertisers[79].

In the public sector, public libraries around the country are beginning to provide dial-up access to online community information systems linked to their online public access catalogs[80]. In December 1988, the Colorado Alliance of Research Libraries (CARL) began operating one of the most advanced and widespread ROPAC-CIS systems in the nation[81]. CARL supports more than 1,700 dedicated terminals[82], includes more than 4.2 million bibliographic records and offers an online database of more than 600,000 articles from over 10,000 journals available in their member libraries. The system is accessible to individual microcomputer users via telephone for a low fee. Users have access to databases of current facts and information of local and state interest in addition to traditional library services. The system supports more than 2 million transactions per day. In addition to its core system in Colorado, CARL has interconnected sites or affiliates in 7 other states (Arizona, Hawaii, Iowa, Maryland, Massachusetts, Washington and Wyoming).

Northwestern University's Center for Urban Affairs and Policy Research developed, with the City of Chicago, one of the more innovative community oriented information systems in 1983[83]. The Chicago Alternative Neighborhood Information Project collects, packages and disseminates city-held information to more than 200 community organizations (but not to individuals)[84]. The project was endorsed by the City of Chicago and is maintained by them.

---

[78] Guenther, R. (1990). Citicorp skips comp. in new home-banking plan. *Wall St. J. v.122* (4):B1,B8.
[79] Conhaim, W. W. (1990). Developing videotex as a consumer medium. *Inform. Today,* 7(3): 31.
[80] *Bulletin of the ASIS,* 15(5), 1989. This issue focuses on online library services.
[81] Nelson, N. M. (1989). Library technology: Uncover, OPACs, NeXT, Kids, and More. *Information Today* 6(5):37-38.
[82] CARL offers document delivery online (1990, March). *Information Today,* 7(3):40.
[83] De Zutter, H. (1983, December 23). *Sharing the data: city opens files to neighborhood groups.* Chicago: Neighborhood News Reader 13(13). Quoting Andrew Gordon.
[84] *Affirm. Neighborhood Info, Chicago* (1984). NW Univ. Center for Urban Aff. and Policy Res.

These various programs are impressive. Each contains one or more elements of the Institutes system. However, the programs are fragmented and uncoordinated, and *none* are dedicated to bringing the benefits of new information technology to individuals who can not now afford it. The Institutes system can help focus these activities on a set of coordinated equity-based objectives, and in the process, create multiple 'win-win' strategies for all of the key interest groups.

Implementation Issues

The primary purposes of this paper have been to identify social equity problems associated with the rapid spread of information age technologies and to suggest an approach for dealing with those problems. This paper has presented the Institutes concept as one way to approach information equity issues. It is important to recognize, however, that the Institutes are only one of many potential approaches. No one approach, whether a new Institutes system or existing systems like library networks can be assumed to be the delivery mechanism of choice at this point. Comparative evaluation of the Institutes and other approaches is needed and will require extensive multidisciplinary research.

Two key implementation issues need attention:

1) Identification and analysis of alternatives to the Institutes, and
2) Identification of initial and long term funding sources for the Institutes (or their alternatives). Previous parts of this Section have touched on both topics. Although detailed examination of them is beyond the scope of this paper, some discussion of each is warranted here.

A multi-level institutional system like the Institutes is one way to deal with the complexity and pervasiveness of information equity problems. Readers of this Journal undoubtedly will be able to suggest other approaches. Some alternatives will be based on existing systems like the telecommunications-based Regional Bell Operating Company gateways. Others may involve extensions of existing libraries or library networks like CARL.

A strength of the Institutes system as proposed in this paper is that it can include *and coordinate* such diverse activities. In this sense then, the Institutes are a flexible focusing and coordinating mechanism. They are inclusive and integrative. With the EMIUs, they offer a way to experiment with local solutions to information equity problems while maintaining a national perspective.

Developing initial and sustained funding for major societal programs is an extremely complex and lengthy endeavor that usually involves consensus politics. The Institutes would be no exception. Given that their work would involve activities vital to both private and public sector organizations, it is likely that both sectors would play a role in their structure and funding, and indeed, may compete for funding. In any case, the normal process of research, debate, planning and consensus building (in this instance, through prototype EMIUs based initially on existing organizations like library networks) is prerequisite to funding decisions.

Both implementation topics, exploration of alternatives and consideration of funding mechanisms are appropriate subjects for follow-on research and concept development activities.

IV. concluding remarks

Colin Cherry pondered the interactions between technology, society and the individuals within society. He noted that technology is „a *social* fact, created and perpetuated by the society" and that „such social facts react back upon the individual and help make him a member of that society."[85]

Technology is an *active* social phenomenon, something more than the material artefacts we usually envision when we speak of *technology*.

The specific technological environment in which any of us live does not decide precisely what our activities shall be. Rather it offers us what might be termed specific 'liberties of action'. ... Thus when any new invention appears there is no way of telling exactly how it will be used within a given community, but only the general types of action that it offers.[86]

... [The powers of invention] for change lie in the hands of those who have the imagination and insight to see that the new invention has offered them new liberties of action, that old constraints have been removed, that their political will, or their sheer greed, are no longer

---

[85] Cherry, *Age of access*, op. cit., p.25.
[86] Cherry, *Age of access*, op. cit., p.59.

frustrated, and that they can act in new ways. New social behavior patterns and new social institutions are created which in turn become the commonplace experience of future generations.

Such realization does not come easily, quickly, or even 'naturally', for the new invention can first be seen by society only in terms of the liberties of action it currently possesses. We say society is 'not ready', meaning that it is bound by its present customs and habits to think in terms of its existing institutions. Realization of new liberties, and creation of new institutions means social change, new thought, and new feelings. The invention alters the society, and eventually is used in ways that were at first quite unthinkable.[87]

This is a message of hope for those who might otherwise see technology as overpowering and with inevitable consequences. *How* we are to achieve these 'liberties of action' is a question the Institutes are designed to answer.

It is up to all of us to seize the opportunity these new telecommunications technologies offer. Our choices, collectively, will determine our path to the future. Through *laissez faire* policies, we can leave these technologies to be developed for the sake of short term profitability, or we can take steps now to ensure that the new technologies develop, and are implemented in ways that benefit *all* of our people. By moving toward a system of National and Regional Institutes and Experimental Mass Information Utilities, we can take the first step toward achieving Information Democracy.

---

[87] Cherry, *Age of access*, op. cit., p.51.

THE INSTITUTES FOR INFORMATION DEMOCRACY

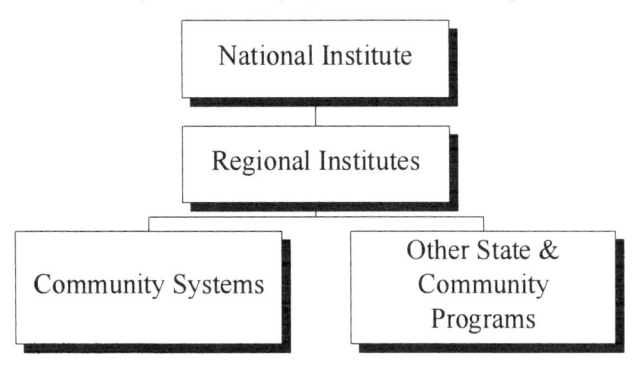

```
                National Institute
                        |
                Regional Institutes
                   /          \
        Community Systems    Other State &
                             Community
                             Programs
```

Ronald D. Doctor, The University of Alabama

THE NATIONAL & REGIONAL INSTITUTES FOR INFORMATION DEMOCRACY

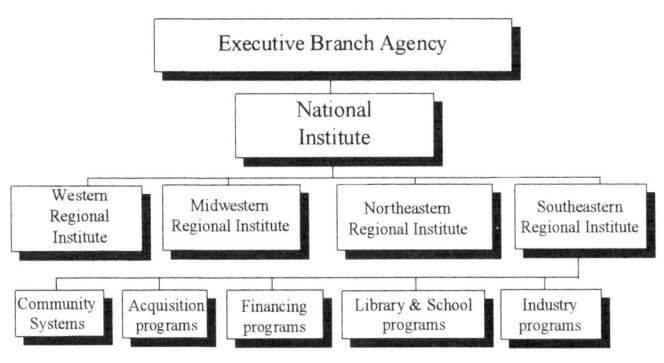

```
              Executive Branch Agency
                      |
               National Institute
          /        |        |        \
    Western   Midwestern  Northeastern  Southeastern
    Regional  Regional    Regional      Regional
    Institute Institute   Institute     Institute
       |
  Community  Acquisition  Financing  Library & School  Industry
  Systems    programs     programs   programs          programs
```

Ronald D. Doctor, The University of Alabama

THE NATIONAL AND REGIONAL INSTITUTES FOR INFORMATION DEMOCRACY

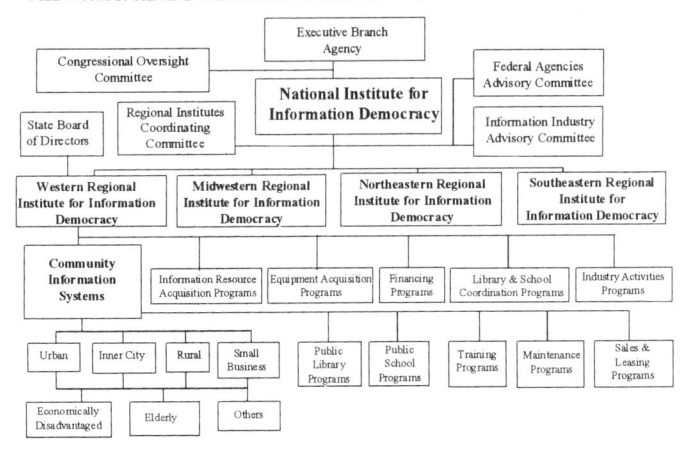

```
                              Executive Branch
                                   Agency
   Congressional Oversight            |                    Federal Agencies
        Committee                     |                   Advisory Committee
         |          Regional Institutes   National Institute for
   State Board      Coordinating          Information Democracy    Information Industry
   of Directors     Committee                                      Advisory Committee
         |_____|_____|_____|
         |                |               |               |
   Western Regional   Midwestern Regional  Northeastern Regional  Southeastern Regional
   Institute for      Institute for        Institute for          Institute for
   Information        Information          Information            Information Democracy
   Democracy          Democracy            Democracy

   Community      Information Resource  Equipment Acquisition  Financing   Library & School      Industry Activities
   Information    Acquisition Programs  Programs               Programs    Coordination Programs Programs
   Systems

   Urban    Inner City    Rural    Small       Public      Public     Training    Maintenance    Sales &
                                   Business    Library     School     Programs    Programs       Leasing
                                               Programs    Programs                              Programs

   Economically     Elderly    Others
   Disadvantaged
```

Ronald D. Doctor, The University of Alabama

3. Ethische Fragen in der Informationpraxis

3.2 Ethische Fragen auf Meso- und Mikroebene

Ethical and Legal Issues Raised by Information Technology: The Professional-Producer-Product Mix[*]

von Robert F. Barnes

I suppose that at some time in most of our childhoods, we have laughed in great glee when we saw Bugs Bunny, Daffy Duck, or another rascally character running off a cliff and continuing to run until he looked down to see nothing underneath. I don't wish to suggest that information professionals are likely to be in quite the same position, but at least the analogy bears pursuing a bit. The work of an information professional often requires substantial technical and technological support. If that ground is removed, disaster can ensue! Of course, one great difference is that Bugs, Daffy, or whoever, was quite all right until he discovered his predicament. In today's world, innocence and ignorance provide no such defense; what you don't know *can* hurt you. When you lose your technological infrastructure, you have a problem, whether you realize it or not!

Perhaps a slightly better analogy is from a cartoon I think I remember - but then I remember many things that never happened. At any rate, this one should have. In this scenario, from a boat in the center of a pond, Donald Duck (I think it was) was busily conducting a „marshland symphony" of frogs, insects, and all sorts of creatures. All went well until, of course, the boat began to leak. Not realizing it, Donald continued to conduct with verve and gusto, until finally with a great „blurp," the boat went down. It requires no very great imagination to envision an information professional in a similar situation - busily running searches, providing references, answering questions - while the leaky „boat," a defective technological infrastructure on which all this activity depends, is slowly sinking.

I'm not suggesting that all the activities of an information professional rest that heavily on technology. The trend, however, is clear, and is probably irresistible. Today, of course, what happens most often when something goes wrong with the technology is that the system simply goes „down." In such a case, though nobody likes it, everybody knows it, so no one is misled. To be sure, with emergency information systems, all sorts of unpleasant consequences might

---

[*] From Information Ethics: concerns for Librarianship and the Information Industry. Ed. by Anne P. Mintz. © 1990 Rutgers Graduate School of Library and Information Studies Alumni Association by permission of McFarland & Co., Inc., Jefferson NC 28640.

ensue in certain critical situations. But these are fairly special sorts of circumstances. The analogy to Donald's situation is the one in which the system just isn't working properly, and nobody knows it until it's too late. The symptom is entered into a diagnostic matrix improperly, the legal reference is misread, the address for the fire department's run is misprinted, etc.

The point is that increasingly, the information professional's activity rests on a technological infrastructure, and failure of this infrastructure can result in damage as fully as much as can failure of the professional's own activities. Without trespassing (too much) on my colleague's topic of „information malpractice," let me refer to a classic case in which, due to inexperience of an observer at a court hearing, the wrong information was reported and published, and the observer's employer was successfully sued for damages. Think how easy it would be, in a computer program of thousands of lines, for a crucial cross-reference to be omitted, with essentially the same result. In the cited case, it was reasonably clear just who was at fault and how. But when the infrastructure falls, where does the blame lie?

In my class on „Computers and Society," we consider a number of such possibilities of Computer failure. For several reasons, we often focus on medical diagnosis systems. Particularly with the introduction of „expert systems" techniques into medical diagnosis, it is easy to imagine a case where a physician consults a computer-based diagnosis system that, under a rare combination of circumstances, encounters a „glitch." A misdiagnosis results, and prescribed treatment is ineffective, and the patient dies. My students have a pat answer for this: the machine's answers cannot supersede the doctor's judgement; the doctor, as the professional, retains the responsibility. Ultimately, this may indeed be the case, but it's not as simple as all that. This open-and-shut view overlooks the extent to which we are all dependent on the information we are provided. If the doctor is not an expert in tropic diseases, say, and his expert human consultant is, it would be a rare person who would disregard the consultant's recommendations. Similarly, if the system's expertise is in an area that the doctor's is not, and the system is apparently a well tested and widely accepted one, it doesn't seem immediately clear that the doctor is defenseless against a liability claim.

The analogy to the information professional's situation seems fairly clear. I think we may expect to see information systems in which special area expertise is represented that is far beyond the expertise of the average information professional. Moreover, even in general knowledge systems, the information professional may well not know how the system „works." In fact, if some of the stronger predictions about the applicability of „neural net" computing techniques are born out, we might have information systems of which it could be said that in a sense, nobody knows how they work. If all this is correct, the question of potential liability for the producer/product may be as important as the question of potential liability for the professional. (I'll say in a bit why I include the product here, as well as the producer.)

What might the liability be for a producer who supplies a faulty product? In general, it depends on what sort of thing the product is and the circumstances under which the product was supplied. Liability may be classified as of two sorts: *strict liability* and *negligence*.[1] Again, without wishing to poach on my colleague's turf, I'll say a little about both. (I suspect that she'll be dealing mostly with negligence, while I'll be dealing with strict liability, but I want to begin by contrasting the two.) Negligence, by its very nature, implies fault. If negligence is demonstrated, both *consequential* damages and *punitive* damages can be assessed. The one seeks to repair the damage due to the negligence; the other, as its name suggests, seeks to penalize the negligent person. In contrast, strict liability has been called „no-fault" liability. Although punitive damages are not assessed, consequential damages for strict liability can be assessed *although the defendant is at no fault whatever*. How remarkable! Why do we admit such an obviously unfair principle into the law?

Granted that the doctrine of strict liability is controversial (in fact, a National Endowment for the Humanities seminar on the philosophy behind strict liability is to be held at Yale this summer), it has at least some grounds. In general, strict liability is assessed only against the maker of a faulty product - it is often referred to as „product liability." In this form it says that the maker of a defective product is liable for damages caused by the defect, even without any negligence in its design or manufacture.[2] Three reasons are given:

1. *The stream of commerce rationale.* The maker of a product initiates its entry into the stream of commerce, and does so to earn a profit. The maker should therefore be the one to bear the loss if the product is defective.

2. *The control of risk rationale.* The maker of a product is in a better position than the buyer to know the risks involved in the use of the product. The maker should therefore be the one to bear the loss if the product is unsafe.

3. *The cost-spreading rationale.* The maker is in a better position than the user to bear costs by spreading them over a larger user population. The maker should therefore be the one who is assessed the cost of damages arising from the product.

These are necessarily brief accounts of the grounds for strict liability. The relevance is that if these conditions hold, assuming no negligence on the part of the information professional using a system, there may be a good case for assigning liability to the maker of the system, even in the absence of negligence there.

A note in passing. Although the notion of strict liability is an old one, it has only relatively recently become as strong as it is. There is in fact an interesting sequence of cases, ranging over a period of about eighty years, in which the first and the last cases are remarkably similar, except that the verdicts are oppositely directed. In the first case (Winterbottom v. Wright), a driver of an English mail coach was injured due to faulty repair on the coach. His suit was dismissed on the grounds that the driver himself did not have a contract with the man who repaired the coach. This doctrine, of „*privity of contract*" limits the liability of a product's manufacturer only to those who have purchased the product from him, thus forbidding recovery by third parties. In the series of cases I've mentioned, the scope of liability is gradually enlarged until in the last case (MacPherson v. Buick), although the plain-tiff bought the car from the dealer, not the Company, and the fault was due to a wheel made by another firm, Buick was held liable. Under current doctrine, therefore, liability for damage incurred by an information client, when the fault lies in the information system rather than the professional, liability could presumably be deflected to the maker of the system.

One further point, however. Law is not entirely resistant to social conditions and pressures. Although much of the cry about a „liability crisis" has died down in the last few years it is clear that there is a widespread liability problem. If professionals restrict their practices and municipalities restrict their services rather than face inordinate insurance premiums no one's good is being served. The possibility of either legislative or judicial relief cannot be ruled out. What might be done? Although the view is controversial, some have argued that product liability is at root not quite as „no-fault" as it might seem. That is to say, in order to sue for negligence, one must first demonstrate that negligence has occurred - presumably by pointing out just what action or in action was negligent. With respect to product liability, it makes sense to understand the defectiveness of a product as evidence that some sort of negligence was present, although the particular negligent action or in action might not be identifiable. By following this line of thought, the burden of proof in a strict liability case might be increased somewhat by requiring the plaintiff to prove that the faultiness of the product does indicate negligence, still without having to identify just where the negligence lies. Alternatively, the burden of the defense might be lightened somewhat by allowing a defendant to show the absence of negligence, though this itself might be difficult. All this supposes that the information system used by the information professional is indeed a product. Clearly, if it includes hardware, and the fault lies in the hardware, no problem arises. With software, this is not quite so clear. The problem here is not what one might suppose - that software is an intangible and therefore does not constitute a product. It is well established that products need not be tangible. The problem is that software is written and sold in such a wide variety of ways, it is not clear that it will always qualify as a „product" according to the rationale behind strict liability. If you commission me to write a software package to run an information system on your machines, in quite a reasonable sense, it is you, not I who has brought it into the stream of commerce. Similarly, it is more likely you than I who knows the details and risks of use. And finally, if the package is entirely yours, I cannot spread the liability cost by selling it elsewhere. Thus, in such a case, it is entirely possible that such a package might not be held to fall within the meaning of the term „product."

In fact, this is exactly the proposal of Jim Prince.[3] He compares software to clothing. One may: (1) order a suit to be custom-tailored; (2) purchase an already made suit to be modified or altered to one's needs; or (3) buy an off-the-rack suit „as is." Clearly, in case (3), the suit is a product; but in case (1), says Prince, the suit should not be considered a product within the legal sense of the term. Instead, the suit is the result of a service, and services have not traditionally been subject to strict liability, as they do not meet the underlying rationale. (Case (2) is a hybrid, he says, and should be treated differently, depending on whether the fault lies in the suit itself or in the tailoring.) Thus, depending on similar factors, your information system software might be considered either a product or the result of a service, and as such; either would or would not be subject to product liability, should it prove faulty.

Of course, this supposes that there is no apparent negligence on the part of the maker of the system. In cases of negligence, punitive damages can be assessed, as well as consequential damages. Thus, in cases where negligence is apparent, a negligence suit tends to be more attractive to the plaintiff. On the other hand, as noted above, negligence is harder to prove, since fault must be demonstrated. Thus, where the exact nature of the fault is not apparent, a strict liability suit is more attractive.

Whether for negligence or strict liability, the above discussion deals with the assessment of liability against the producer. As an alternative, John Snapper, from the Center for the Study of Ethics in the Profession at Illinois Institute of Technology, has quite a different suggestion.[4] In a discussion of a failure in a medical diagnostic system Snapper suggest that the machine itself be held liable. At first, this seems absurd, for how can one hold a mere machine liable for anything? Snapper's argument goes as follows. First of all, we must get clear as to what liability involves. Strict liability shows that an assessment of liability does not necessarily imply fault or blame. Liability merely provides an answer to the question: „Who pays?" Now ask, when a physician is held liable for malpractice, who pays? The insurance company, initially. (but then, of course, it spreads its costs!) In the same way, insurance on the system would protect against liability assessed against it. Ah, one may respond, but the physician pays the insurance premiums - the computer can't! But, observes Snapper, the physician often doesn't pay the premiums - a hospital or medical group does in the same way, the hospital or medical group could insure both its computer systems and its physicians. This is just the bare bones of Snapper's argument, and I'm not convinced even by the complete version, but it does show that fresh thinking on such issues is both needed and possible.

All this applies to the role of the information professional as the supplier of information. There's another problem involved with the information professional as the custodian of information. We are all aware of the importance of security and confidentiality in handling information. Presumably, in our professional roles, we ourselves all show due regard and care for these principles. Here, however, is another area of potential producer/product failure. Stories of viruses have shown us all that computer systems are often much more vulnerable than we expect. Stories of hacker penetration of supposedly secure systems show that even well-protected systems can be entered illicitly.[5] Here is an entirely new way in which systems can fail. A breach of security can lead to lost data, spurious data, or compromised data. It is entirely possible that a security weakness in the design of a system could be the basis for lawsuits.

I've said a great deal about legal issues, and nothing (except by implication) about ethical issues. But I think that legal issues, in part and at heart, are ethical issues. We tend to think of ethics as governing our relations with other people, but this is too restricted a view, I believe. Ethics more broadly governs our relations with our profession and our society and more narrowly, our relations with ourselves and with one another. When dangers such as those I've discussed exist, our unawareness of them is itself unethical, for awareness of our responsibilities is a precondition for our acting on them. Furthermore, enlightening others and encouraging them to take on appropriate ethical responsibilities is itself an ethical good. Insisting, to the limits of our ability and authority, on good information technology - good producers and good products is thus a part of our ethical responsibilities as professionals. And finally a profession is not merely the set of its individual members; it requires interaction among them and joint effort by them. Thus, in providing a forum for discussion of ethical issues, a meeting such as this itself contributes to the ethical level of the profession. I'm delighted to have had a chance to participate, and I hope you have found food for ethical thought.

References

1. An excellent article comparing negligence and strict liability with respect to faulty computer programs is „Liability for Malfunction of a Computer Program," by Susan Nycum, which appears in the *Rutgers Journal of Computers, Technology, and the Law* 7 (1979): 1-22

2. The standard analysis of strict liability is found in the *Restatement of Torts:* „One who sells any product in a defective condition unreasonably dangerous to the user or consumer or to his property is subject to liability ... although the seller has exercised all possible care in the preparation and sale of his product."

3. „Negligence: Liability for Defective Software." *Oklahoma Law Review* 33 (1980): 848-855.

4. *Metaphilosophy* 16 (1985): 289-295.

5. A fascinating article in the latest Communications of the ACM, „Stalking the Wily Hacker," tells of a case in which the computer systems of Lawrence Laboratory of Berkeley, and some 30 other Institutions, were penetrated by persons apparently from Germany.

Ethics, Ideologies, and Practices of Information Technology and Systems*

von Thomas J. Froehlich

Abstract

There is an increasing preoccupation with technology in America and our professional association, the American Society for Information Science (ASIS). ASIS's desire to establish and adopt a code of ethics acknowledges the possible abuses and misuses by information professionals of information technologies (both intellectual and computer), systems and services, and their users. Focusing on the element of technology and technological practices in information systems and engaging the perspective of recent continental philosophers and others (e.g., Heidegger, Habermas, Dreyfus, Ellul, Pacey and Mowshowitz) this paper argues, contrary to the commonly held view, that information technology itself and information technological practices are not value or morally neutral, and that any moral deliberation involving information systems and services must grapple with this view. The intrinsic, accidental and cultural features of information technology and systems are discussed as they give rise to ethical considerations for information professionals and as they endorse an implicit ideology of the so-called information society. Dimensions of this ideology are then examined in terms of its implications for the profession.

Our age is preoccupied with technology. In like manner, so is the American Society for Information Science. The theme of many conferences focuses on information technologies and their applications: e.g., the 1990 Mid-Year Conference on „Microcomputing in the 1990s: Unlocking the Power" and the 1988 Mid-Year conference on the „New Technologies (Laser Optical Disk and Video-Based Information Systems)." Presumably we are encouraged to believe that these technologies will make our work more fruitful and efficient. Thereby they will promote a better life for our sponsors, clients or the world, with less ignorance, poverty, disease, hunger, environmental pollution, or any other of the evils that beset man.

Unfortunately, very few (notable exceptions are Heidegger [1], Habermas [2], Dreyfus [3], Ellul [4], Mowshowitz [5]) are asking where these technologies are leading us -down a primrose path to the everlasting nuclear bonfire or to a genuine improvement of the human condition, at least for our sponsors or patrons. Even with the thawing of the cold war, the United States sustains a course of developing a technology to save us from technology. Is this not the

---

* Reprinted with permission from Information in the Year 2000: From Research to Applications, Proceedings of the 53rd Annual Meeting of the American Society for Information Science, Volume 27, pp. 245-255. Copyright © 1990 Learned Information, Inc., Medford, New Jersey.

rationale for SDI, the Strategic Defense Initiative, a counter technology to the technology of sophisticated nuclear weaponry? We must also wonder whether the SDI with which we are familiar, the Selective Dissemination of Information, is a case of and contributing cause to the former. Is there something in these technologies that promotes a certain understanding of the world and human information-seeking problems and of how they are to be solved? With a little reflection, one can assert that there is an ideology behind these technologies and their use for information seeking problems, but are we aware of and should we endorse the values that such technologies foster?

It is often asserted that information specialists should be neutral with respect to the information they provide. As Foskett [6] notes the librarian should have no creed, no morals, no politics. This seems fair enough: the specialist should subscribe to no party's viewpoint and should avoid bias in difficult matters, by providing a wide range of materials on such matters [7]. But such a view of neutrality is naive, because the provision only occurs *from that which is only and already available in the system and within the context of the information technologies and technological practices that constitute the system, including the specialist.* These dimensions have already severely compromised any simple sense of neutrality. This does not mean that non-neutrality implies the existence of an independent will in technology itself [5]. However, I would argue, with Ihde [8], Heidegger [1] and others, that a given technology inclines the ways to which it is put to use and achieves a relative autonomy when it is institutionalized in a particular context; it also embodies a set of values that come with the establishment and use of that technology.

Distinctions should be drawn among technique, technology and technology-practice. Technique is any structure or device to manipulate or reality for some purpose. A technology is a technique or organized group of techniques that are institutionalized as a totality for a specific purpose or objective. In the field of information science there are two common kinds of technologies: (1) „intellectual technologies" [9], technologies used to organize, store and access available „information resources," [10] technologies that perform „value-added processes in information systems" [9] and (2) technologies as embodied systems of tools or procedures that transform our experience in undertaking information-seeking behaviors, for example, in the use of computers and software for online public access systems. In practice this distinction gets blurred, since intellectual technologies lead to forms of embodiment, e.g., dictionaries, thesauri, authority lists, but these are the result of a process which itself is intellectual [11]. In addition, following Pacey, there are technology practices, which are individual or generic applications of technologies for a specific context of people and organizations: „...technology-practice is thus the application of scientific and other knowledge to practical tasks by ordered systems that involve people and organizations, living things and machines." [12] While it is obvious that technology practice in the third sense has organizational and cultural aspects, technology *per se* also disposes itself to certain cultural and organizational constraints.

My thesis is that technology, in particular information technology, is non-neutral, that it is value-laden, despite the standard naive view that technologies are indifferent tools, whose value dimensions emerge when they are put into use, i.e., in technology practices. While one acknowledges that technology practices are embodiments of values at least insofar as they fulfill in the organizational setting the functions for which the system was built, one tends to think of a technology *per se* as value neutral. Abbe Mowshowitz [5] in his rejection of such a view calls this approach „the grab-bag theory": computers are simple tools which can be arbitrarily applied to any number of potential applications. One merely has to put one's hand into the bag of potential applications and pull out the one she prefers. Such a view does not take into account that there are a variety of social and cultural constraints which mediate the realization of some applications and bars others. For example, the use of computer-based online public access catalogs (OPACs) in Malaysia or Indonesia as replacements of manual systems may entail multiple, high costs, because in those and other developing countries, computer technology is expensive to purchase and maintain, manual labor is cheap, and full employment is a national objective.

Computer Technologies

Computers are not simple, self-contained technologies, but are the product of society and the limitations to their employment derive from the social relations with it. In Heidegger's terms, a given technology exists within a referential totality wherein that instrument or technology establishes and deploys its meaning [1, 3]. So, an OPAC implies the existence of a complex variety of interconnected structures (libraries, journals, thesauri, controlled vocabularies, databases, library users, etc.) and projects (e.g., information seeking behaviors, the use of information in problem solving, etc).

For Mowshowitz, such systems imply social relations which form a matrix that act as a „selection-mechanism that maps potential applications to actual applications." [5] Mowshowitz argues that these relations can be partitioned into three components: (1) intrinsic features which include (a) the properties of hardware, software and systems and (b) the requirements for the production of computer technology; (2) accidental features and (3) techno-cultural paradigms. After explaining what these dimensions mean for Mowshowitz, the same model will be applied to information technologies.

Intrinsic Features

Intrinsic features determine the bounds of what is currently possible. There are limitations about what can be done with the technology. Speed of computations, transfer rates, storage capacity all restrict the potential applications, and hence compromise neutrality. A given computer system or technology practice also constrains its uses. For example, there are large differences between the uses of a mainframe bibliographic database system and a personal computer. The characteristics of the technology, its manufacture and consequent applications set further limits on its use. Before the advent of the personal computer and its speed and power, most software was developed for mainframe environments. It was technological breakthroughs such as the 286 and 386 processors that made possible cheap, reliable, powerful and fast PCs. In addition, the possible applications of the computer are a function of the skill of the user or the available software: word-processing, game-playing, spreadsheets, and database management programs tend to dominate the market. In bibliographic applications, we are still limited by the inability of computer hardware and software to handle bibliographic data efficiently and effectively, and with the inability of computers to effectively handle open-ended queries. Most bibliographic systems demand variable length records, requiring complex delimiting structures, directories and keys to decipher those structures and layers of inverted indexes to locate records. Such structures inhibit easy storage, retrieval or modification. Even the control of the production of technology can be considered part of the intrinsic features: the cost of starting up and manufacturing integrated circuits is so exorbitant that the field is dominated by a small group of producers. IBM, for example, as a producer of technology has had enormous impact, by its architectural designs, on what the market will produce and with what it will be compatible.

Accidental Features

Accidental features are concerned with the context within which computers are used. There is an interaction among social, economic and political factors and the technology which affect the development and dissemination of computer technology and which it affects. Users and developers of technology, e.g., scientists, engineers and inventors are affected by social forces, such as the strategic and tactical objectives of an organization (e.g., IBM). Similarly, privacy has been a concern of individuals in the United States. The advent of computer technology, with its capacity for networking, record matching and file searching in various systems, did not create the problem of privacy, but it has aggravated its scope and character. The magnitude of possible invasion by individuals, groups and agencies and the methods of security have grown considerably.

Computer technology, affecting and affected by such organization and social forces is far from neutral: power can increase with increased access to computing and levels of data that a system may contain. Economic forces also shape how technology is used. For example, with regard to „computer literacy," Mowshowitz calls it „basically a euphemism for consumer training. It should only take a moment's reflection to realize who stands to gain the most by promoting computer literacy. Is it the free choice of a neutral technology that is bringing computers into the schools?" [5]

Mowshowitz ridicules any notion of neutrality with regard to computers:

> All of the foregoing examples reveal the influence of concrete historical circumstances on the use that is made of computer technology. In some cases choices are influenced by customary practices and norms; in other cases, they are dictated by the special interests of stakeholders and other pressure groups. The latter form of influence is especially apparent in the growth of computer-communications... Is the technology neutral for the average American citizen, rich or poor, employed or unemployed? Are the actions of the proverbial man in the street determining the development of automated banking, electronic mail and computer-aided instruction? ... The idea of the computer as a neutral instrument in the face of the existence of such stakeholders as IBM, AT&T, and CBS would be laughable if it were not held by so many. [5]

Techno-cultural Paradigms

This component addresses cultural constraints. „In general, cultural constraints are defined by the way we think, the way we view the world, the way we deal with experience and the basic values that guide our conduct." [5] Prevailing paradigms reflect deeply set cultural values and orientations which change very slowly. Mowshowitz sees the divide and conquer method so dear to American culture amplified through computer technologies. For example, the division of labor and reduction of complex tasks to a series of simple ones are characteristic of factory manufacture, whose output has been enhanced through the use of industrial robots, computer-driven machines that speed up the rate of the simple tasks and often combine these tasks into a more complex production.

Information Technologies

When applying the grab-bag theory of computer technology suggested by Mowshowitz to information technologies, one can see reflected in it a „free market" paradigm, not unlike the notion of the free marketplace of ideas. That is, there exists a marketplace of all available goods and services, including information technologies. From this marketplace one can freely choose any technology in terms of the application under consideration. Given that the technologies adequately address the needs of the client, these technologies are supposedly of equal value. But just as in the free marketplace of ideas, we cannot assume that competition has only facilitated the best: some technologies may dominate, occlude or exclude more efficient ones. One merely has to think of the domination of IBM in setting standards for the computer market, especially in the PC market, where despite the demise of some of their widely-touted products, they continue to set industry standards. In information technologies, Library of Congress and Dewey classifications have commanded the classification market; and the commercial bibliographic retrieval systems have established Boolean, deductive systems as the standard. In cataloging, OCLC has dominated the market, and while it has not captured the market, it sets standards with which other catalogers must contend.

Information retrieval systems often require computer technology, and so all the compromises that erode the neutrality of computer technology generally also apply to information technology, including bibliographic retrieval systems. To information technology, we must add the intellectual technologies that characterize so much of the work of information specialists: e.g., knowledge organization, classification, indexing, abstracting. The intellectual technologies that are the foundation of information storage and retrieval are the product of society, and the limitations on their use derive from their history and the social relations with these technologies. The social relations form a matrix that act as a selection-mechanism which maps potential uses of knowledge organizations to their actual uses and implementations. Again, following the work of Mowshowitz, but expanding his third category to include an ethical and ideological dimension, these relations can be divided into three components: (1) intrinsic features which include (a) properties of the knowledge organization structures or Boolean retrieval systems and (b) the requirements for the production of such technologies; (2) accidental features and (3) techno-cultural paradigms derived from the ontological position of Western culture.

Intrinsic Features

With regard to intrinsic features, we can separately discuss intellectual technologies and those technologies embedded in online bibliographic systems. The properties of a classification scheme (e.g., Dewey Decimal or Library of Congress), the rules for classification and cataloging, and the free-text and controlled vocabulary will affect an information system and the uses to which it may be put. For example, there are intrinsic difficulties with hierarchical classification schemes. One can expand the vocabulary of such a system, but modifying the meaning of a term can be quite difficult. Furthermore, it is often difficult to describe complex concepts. Charles Meadow uses a good example of trying to accommodate „artificial earth satellites" in Dewey classification. In trying to achieve descriptors that are mutually exclusive (one of the goals of such classification, so as to develop a tidy universe of mutually exclusive sets), we run into difficulties trying to develop descriptors that will have reconnaissance satellites, both manned and unmanned; and space and earth. As he notes, in this class of languages, „there are some concepts which either are not able to be stated with a single descriptor, or are not able to be separated from another concept." [13]

Classification schemes and subject headings tend to reflect the biases of the general population, such as racism, sexism, and nationalism [14]. For example, Sanford Berman [15] complained of the 1979 *Dewey Decimal Classification* that it had inadequate coverage of popular music, gay issues, and ambiguous treatment of material for North American Indians. Furthermore, the major classifications are based on Western culture. While this has been a natural consequence of an historical evolution, that process only validates the fact that Western approaches to reality are embedded in such systems at the expense of other traditions. Third world cultures, in particular, if they want to join the „information society" must learn English and Western classification, even if they are not appropriate to their own needs and cultures: hence, there is a rise in cultural, particularly American English, imperialism in the construction, maintenance and use of bibliographic database retrieval systems.

According to Ihde [16], all technology entails an „amplification-reduction structure." What he means is that while certain features of an phenomenon are amplified through a technology, others get reduced, eclipsed or obscured at the same time. So, for example, in abstracting and indexing, access points to documents and document surrogates are created. Certain features of a journal article are amplified, namely those concepts or ideas with which the article mainly deals. At the same time, there is information loss, because at a certain point, a descriptor will no longer be assigned to a document, or aspects of the subject matter will not be detailed in the abstract. What aggravates this issue further is that, given a certain „propositional content" to an article (Fox [17], i.e., what the document affirms or denies about a phenomenon) the assignment of a descriptor or a set of descriptors is a function of the specificity of the indexing language and specificity of individual indexer in choosing a descriptor. All these dimensions alter retrieval effectiveness and the possible uses (with degrees of success and failure) to which a particular system may be put.

If we move from the intrinsic properties of classification to the intrinsic properties of online retrieval systems, another set of values come into play that mitigate against any sense of neutrality. First of all, such systems presuppose database producers, who make decisions about the journals which are to be indexed and abstracted. Granted while neutrality has improved insofar as the selection of journals is broader than it has been in the past (e.g., due to budgetary constraints, physical access, etc.), there is still a restriction of the universe of available information, typically entailing judgment against information provision by non-Western, non-industrialized societies. Furthermore, if we look at the gamut of vendors and the available databases, the majority of them are oriented toward information in business, science and technology. This sets boundaries on available information and it sets agendas for what constitutes the „more important problems" to be solved by society.

Most commercial systems are Boolean, deductive systems: i.e., they permit searching by one or more terms or phrases in Boolean relations. A document or citation will be retrieved if and only if it has those terms and those relations stated in the query on an exact match basis. According to Gerrie [18] the following assertions can be made about the limitations of such systems. Such systems cannot accommodate open-ended or incomplete queries, partial matching, or probabilistic models. With respect to the retrieved set of citations, there is no order of preference, except those that the system can develop by sort order, and these sort orders are hardly qualitative measures (e.g., currency or the most recent articles are no guarantee of better quality). From the system's delivery point of view, every citation is equally valuable as any other, and there is no ordering of citations based on the degree of relevance to the query, let alone based upon degree of relevance to the information need. Boolean systems tend to demand a binary judgment: relevant/not-relevant. Again, given the nature of such systems based upon inverted file structures, indexing terms and phrases cannot be changed readily, since such a procedure would entail tracking terms and phrases across diverse and scattered index files. This means that online systems are constrained in a variety of ways: what sorts of questions can be asked, whether, how and in what manner they can be answered, and how satisfactorily they may be answered. The vagaries of commercial systems are such that they often demand the use of information intermediaries to fully exploit them. Such intermediaries act as gatekeepers to the system, and if they are incompetent or biased (not only in the ordinary sense but also with respect to searching skills already acquired or the use of systems with which they are already familiar), the gates to available information may be shut or open on the wrong pasture [19].

If we look at the requirements for the production for such technologies, either intellectual or embodied, large scale expenditures are involved. Even the earliest database producers required outside funding. For example, DIALOG, founded in 1963, had a contract with NASA for the Lockheed Information System, and SDC developed ORBIT in the mid-60s under contract from the Department of Defense. For a database producer or vendor huge capital investments are required for journal collection, personnel for abstracting and indexing, and computer technology for enabling and facilitating such activities. Such capital investments make it unlikely that the major information utilities (DIALOG, SDC, OCLC, etc.) and classification schemes will be displaced in the marketplace or that their standards of practice will be ignored by up-and-coming producers of databases. In addition, competition is rapidly being reduced to only a few major competitors, especially as the competitors swallow smaller companies: e.g., Maxwell Online's assimilation of BRS.

Furthermore, despite the rapid growth and expansion of power of computer technologies, it is unlikely that Boolean systems will be replaced by probabilistic ones. The latter systems would be able to handle open-ended queries, genuine browsing capabilities (rather than merely providing alphabetically related terms, they would enable the patron to look at documents or citations in the region of his query), best match of query to documents, etc. However, such capabilities require magnitudes of increase in computational power and storage and retrieval, more complex indexing, major reindexing of already indexed materials, and major restructuring of current systems. Such activities and technologies are unlikely to occur.

Accidental Features

The accidental features of information technologies include the concrete historical circumstances within which these technologies arise and are used. We have already noted that some major vendors have emerged through funding by governmental research projects, basically oriented toward defense. A survey of DIALOG databases indicates that the majority of them are oriented toward business, science and technology. In fact, in the online market DIALOG claimed a 58% share of the information specialist market in 1987. Business use accounted for 85% of all online database revenues in 1987 [20]. Given the law of supply and demand, it is not surprising that the business, scientific and technical database costs can run from $100 to $250 per connect hour.

Such observations mitigate against the view that information databases are socially and morally neutral instruments whose good or bad results depend on the choices of end-users or information specialists who use them. In the naive view, information needs „just happen" in the marketplace or in the scholar's den, and it behooves the information specialist to provide the „relevant" information and to avoid the „irrelevant" information. But the choices can only be those made available through the database producers and vendors and those which can be addressed through the mechanisms and contents of the various information retrieval systems, each of which is shaped by historical, social, economic, and political objectives. Furthermore, it is unlikely that most information needs are generated autonomously, but by market demands (even the scholar's research agenda) and by what the current technologies can fulfill.

Techno-cultural Paradigms

Techno-cultural paradigms for information technology can be illustrated by the new visions of knowledge production in the information society, those promoted by the mongers of high tech information technology. If we listen to such prognosticators as Daniel Bell [21], John Naisbett [22] and others, postindustrial culture will be characterized by a knowledge class, governed by a meritocracy, where those who produce best will be amply rewarded by society. The preeminent mode of knowledge production, science, will continue through the application of the scientific method, and those who master segments of that production will be the experts who will solve those problems appropriate to their expertise. In this „culture of expertise" [23], one of the major tools will be the scholar's workstation: a high tech access to the world's knowledge. The scholar need never leave her desk to have the breadth and width of human knowledge at her fingertips. No one need mention that the variety of technologies used to create such a system may be ineptly designed, executed, coordinated or used that most of the relevant information is hidden from view by these very technologies. A prerequisite for doing any responsible research is to do a „literature search" to insure that the problem for investigation had not been addressed previously or to determine what methods had already been applied. Unfortunately, such searches (assuming that they succeed, and that they manage to make connections among diverse literatures) may not reveal the quality of the previous work (without reenacting that work), and they may inhibit duplicate efforts that may invalidate the published results, or that may open vitally new and different approaches. With technology at the fingertips, it is easy to defer to the work of others, assume that it is done well, and one may waste time making sure that one's work is original and creative. Furthermore, this version of science production is another example of the divide and conquer method, and an amplification of it. While such a method engenders the increasing specialization of the sciences, it is unclear that it will enable easier connections among the specializations or an understanding of the totality of a science. It is also unclear what sophisticated use (apart from bibliographic retrieval, communication and wordprocessing) humanities scholars or artists will have for these workstations or how these workstations and their access to the world's knowledge will solve the value questions about the quality of life we want this technology to serve.

According to Ihde [24], the use of such technologies reshapes our understanding of how to approach problems. Not only does the technology extend our senses, but it modifies our experience. Just as a car extends our ability to walk, so too it transforms our perception of the world, just as our visual appropriation of the world is different in a car than when walking. When something gets amplified in the technology, other features get reduced and go unnoticed; there is information loss in the current indexing, but as new information arises and our perception of problems change, the old information will grow in information loss, because of the inability of systems to reflect new approaches to old texts. All this is due, of course, to value-neutral information technologies. Pacey [25], following a thought of Lewis Thomas, argues that such technologies may be 'halfway technologies.' Such technologies as the result of half-understood problems are expensive and elaborate. Better solutions require more research, especially as regards the nature of the problem to be solved. It is not hard to believe that the scholar's workstation may be a 'halfway' technology, and that we are substituting quantities of information for the more precious commodity of qualitative information.

It would be impossible to sketch all the dimensions of techno-cultural paradigms of information technologies. What may be useful is to draw out a few implications that these technologies have, in terms of ethics and underlying ideologies.

Ethical and Ideological Implications

As one implication that provides the basis for ethical and ideological considerations, it may be argued that the use of computer-based information technologies enhances those dimensions of human thought that Kant calls 'calculative reason', that part of the continuum of rationality that analyzes, deduces, computes, quantifies, etc. What gets displaced or reduced is 'intuitive reason,' that dimension of human thinking that makes *gestalt* assessments as in our various everyday activities such as complimenting someone on how well they look or interpreting the meaning of a dance or a painting. Furthermore, the growth of such technologies and their increased use suggests an increasing domination of calculative reasoning. One can note the early inculcation of computer literacy in children and fascination with the computer games. While we may agree with Mowshowitz that computer literacy is a euphemism for consumer training, it may also be the case that the same phenomenon is occurring under the rubric of „information literacy." While information literacy does seek to broaden an information seeker's view of available resources, there simultaneously occurs a socialization process about how information problems are be addressed. This trend and other evidence also suggests the growth of calculative reasoning at the expense of intuitive reasoning. It socializes one from thinking through problems on one's own and replaces self-analysis with literature searching. It facilitates a deference to authorities where it may not be warranted: in many disciplines authority is a function of fashion and taste [26].

Current information systems tend to be combinations of two technologies - the intellectual and computer technologies. They are built with certain assumptions and for certain results. Not only are such systems non-neutral, they support an ideology that has utilitarianism at its roots. An ideology here is to be not understood as a self-conscious social and political mechanism, as used by strident Marxist rhetoricians, but as a semi-conscious, semi-articulate process that marshals political, economic and social forces. If it has an articulate form, it is usually provided by the visionaries of high tech alluded to above and by those who are most likely to benefit from such a vision. It is not a vision of a necessary future, but a vision promoted as if it were a necessary future, a vision that occludes other possibilities and that conceals the values that such a vision fosters. Jacques Ellul in „Technique and Non-Power," asserts that technological morality has two characteristics. „(1) It is behavioral (in other words, only correct practice, not intentions or motivations, counts), and (2) it rules out the problematics of traditional morality (the morality of ambiguity is unacceptable in a technological world)." [27] It is clear that he sees the utilitarian view in the ideology behind technology, and this applies to information technology. The core of this ideology is not that utilitarianism is right as *a* perspective, but that it is the *only* approach, and that other approaches are too full of ambiguity to be tolerated or useful. This approach fosters power and growth by consensus, and is attuned to quantity and consequences; it ignores motivation and denigrates the unique and individual. The ideology also spreads some lies: that technology serves values but does not create them. Technology is always already an embodiment of a set of values both in its practice and in its nature, and further applications inculcate and foster these values.

The utilitarianism fostered by this ideology requires clarification. The utilitarian view, popularized by Jeremy Bentham and John Stuart Mill [28], endorses „greatest happiness principle," that the objective of morality is to achieve the greatest amount of happiness of the greatest number of people. In fairness to Mill, while he popularized utilitarianism, there exists a current popular version (the one to which I allude) that runs contrary to his respect for individuals, as documented in his essay, *On Liberty*. The popular version is oriented towards consequences and quantity, often at the expense of individuals. It promotes a sense of democracy that equalizes the value of every individual in inappropriate ways. Yet while everyone is entitled to an opinion, not all opinions are equal; and the happiness of the many should not systematically sacrifice the happiness of the few. One of the ongoing problems of democracy is that a consensus of shabby opinions may override more rational approaches to problem resolution, and yet this flaw is tolerated so as to avoid possible abuses of rule by „experts" who may also be misguided on other grounds. At any event, the popular utilitarianism espouses the collective at the expense of the individual.

Information technology espouses the same view and thereby fosters the utilitarian approach. The utilitarian approach in information technologies entails the following aspects:

(1) Since it is difficult, if not impossible, to develop qualitative measures, all elements of data in an information system (whether payroll statistics or bibliographic citations) are of equal value. If qualitative distinctions are to be made, they must be based on computational techniques. A simple instance of this view is the algorithm that drives the information retrieval system called SIRE, also called Personal Librarian, which ranks document surrogates in terms of word frequency occurrence in the document or document surrogate: the higher the occurrence of a word in a document, it assumes the more likely the document has to do with that word, and by implication the subject that the word names or with which it is associated. While such systems are often very effective in obtaining relevant hits, it is clear that this measure as a qualitative measure is quite inadequate. In some sense the levelling of information that occurs in information retrieval systems has also occurred to the word, „information," itself. Theodore Roszak in *The Cult of Information* has argued that the word has become so overworked and applied to so many phenomena that „the *meaning* of things communicated comes to be leveled, and so too, the value." [29]

(2) The utilitarian approach to systems fosters the view that more data produce better understanding. Data glut, the uncritical placement of data into information systems, massive literature searches, a pathological need for statistics (and the invalidation or dismissal of non-empirical approaches) all seem to be manifestations of this posture. Yet, as Roszak points out, data or facts bear an uneasy relation to ideas. It is through the latter as integrating patterns that the mind seeks to dominate the former. He asserts that „Ideas create information, not the other way around." [30] This is not quite right, as there is a dialectical process between facts and ideas, but the point is the contemporary systems exaggerate the flow in one direction alone - from data to idea.

(3) With utilitarianism as the overriding principle, selectivity both in terms of system inputs and outputs appears to be simply a function of knowledge organization, indexing and abstracting policies and practices, all of which are accepted as „givens" and the problem is mainly to apply these givens to the queries or documents at hand. While this selectivity has some qualitative measures (e.g., in terms of choice of descriptors and, in some databases, whether they are major or minor), it employs little other qualitative methods, such as ranking documents in terms of peer evaluation or in order of likely relevance to the query. Furthermore, whatever selectivity there is is very much a function of the paradigm of a field with its conscious and unconscious dimensions. Selection is thus not neutral in terms of choice of relevant problems, acceptable methodologies, proper research agendas, indexing structure and depth, nature, number and diversity of journals indexed, etc. These tacit and explicit standards and agendas are couched in value-ridden judgments of the current experts or focus groups of the field or discipline, especially those who control funding. These standards and measures filter down to information professionals who work in those fields. It would interesting to see how the Religion Index might appear if Taoists (only if they could allow themselves to be prey to the illusions of knowledge, especially cumulative knowledge) were in charge of selection of journals, descriptors and abstracts or how Medline might appear if selection were at the hands of holistic health practitioners.

(4) Utilitarian systems tend to be built around a profile of the average user or group of average users. Such systems tend to ignore the unique, the eccentric, and the extraordinary, and thus dissuade the very creative and original.

An alternative system might be called the Kantian system and it would preserve the following values:

(1) There are qualitative differences of data in the system. Such differences, even for different users, should be integrated into the system.

(2) Less data and/or better data may produce better understanding. Such systems should have the facility of identifying the adequacy or value of its resources. There should be stronger filtering mechanisms in systems, filters that would inhibit data from entering the system and/or exiting the system or would provide methods for ranking and blocking output in terms of likely relevance to query or likely authority or qualitative superiority (based upon criteria of whatever nature chosen by the user).

(3) Under this view, selectivity is not merely a matter of the application of given knowledge organization, abstracting, indexing, etc., but requires explicit evaluation of the material available through the collection and rapid modification of systems to accommodate the extraordinary and unique. Such an evaluation is at a minimum the result of peer evaluation -- evaluation labels should be attached to system documents (given whatever orientation) and invoked at the user's request according to the user's criteria.

(4) All users are equal but not of equal value -- each human being should be accorded the proper information at the right time to the right extent to the right degree with the right amount under the right circumstances (to echo Aristotle's qualifications for the context of a good moral act). The Kantian system, respecting the dignity and autonomy of individuals, must accommodate the diversity and variety of users, and this means accommodating the uniqueness of some users and their needs.

Creating and maintaining such a system is an expensive proposition, and pragmatic, utilitarian claims inveigh against it. No current information retrieval system (commercial or experimental) can accommodate these measures of quality and this diversity. Could one be invented? Or is such a system inherently anti-technological? That is, given the parameters that make technology possible and able to work, such as uniformity of structures and homogeneity of cogs so as to achieve system interaction, etc., those very parameters become devices that block a system's ability to handle uniqueness, just in the same way that choices of certain descriptors for a bibliographic citation provide access to information and also block access because they prevent other descriptors from being used, descriptors which precisely would match the odd request with the right document. Furthermore, the levelling by the systems (by homogenization of inputs) creates a levelling in the use of the system, a levelling in the outputs and perhaps in the long run a levelling of the users. Uniformity facilitates conformity.

Despite this unresolved, perhaps unresolvable, speculation about the impossibility of Kantian systems, one can see that an ideology lurks in the so-called information age, an ideology that supports a certain view of the world, scholarship, knowledge, and information professionals that may work against the quality of life. Peter Dahlgren in „Ideology and Information in the Public Sphere" [31] calls for a conscious ideology to come to counter this dominating ideology, by critiquing and making conscious this ideology. Jacques Ellul suggests that an option to confront this ideology is to practice an ethic of non-power as a resistance to the domination of technology in our culture. One of the more insidious dimensions of the dominating ideology is that it masks the politics that directs technological development under the guise of inevitable, autonomous, technological progress. But, as David Noble notes in *The Forces of Production*:

> For when technological development is seen as politics, as it should be, then the very notion of progress becomes ambiguous: what kind of progress? progress for whom? progress for what? And the awareness of this ambiguity, this indeterminacy, reduces the powerful hold that technology has had upon our consciousness and imagination, and it reduces also the hold upon our lives enjoyed by those whose social power has been long concealed and dignified by seemingly technological agendas. Such awareness awakens us not only to the full range of technical possibilities and political potential but also to a broader and older notion of progress, in which a struggle for human fulfillment and social equality replaces a simple faith in technological deliverance, and in which people, with their confidence restored, resume their proper role as subject of the story called history [32].

Should one not suggest that in ASIS and in society that information professionals consciously examine the values that they serve through technology, systems, practices and services, both in their overt and covert agendas, so as to facilitate a genuine progress? Such progress may call for a resistance to the lures of the information technology mongers. While ASIS and its members like to see themselves in the noble role of helping to solve world problems, may it not also be the case that ASIS is part of the problem by endorsing willy-nilly a technological agenda, the negative dimensions of which it conveniently ignores?

Part of this technological agenda is to see information professionals as neutral information providers, as well-oiled gears (if they are competent) of the information retrieval system. In this agenda information professionals are *mere* information providers (non-interpreting, indifferent, with no politics, no morals and no religion), with no biases or evaluating interpretations of the information they provide and certainly with no responsibility for the ways in which the information is used. Such a view, while it promotes certain half-truths (that professionals are not psychoanalysts for their clients and that their values should not arbitrarily override the values of the information-seekers), does a disservice to professionals and the profession: to have professionals regard themselves as *mere* information providers is to have them treat themselves as mere cogs in a technological machine, and to denigrate their value as human beings. Such a view is wholly at odds with Kant's categorical imperative to „Act so that you treat humanity, *whether in your own person* or in that of another, always as an end and never merely as a means." [33]

Treating oneself merely as a means also occurs when the values that a professional espouses are blind adherence to rules, regulations and codes of ethics (e.g., the code of ethics of the American Library Association). Yet as Lawson Crowe and Susan Anthes point out:

> Unquestioned conformity to rules and regulations is neither a necessary nor sufficient condition to make an action ethical. We must ask *why* we accept the rules we do, what interests they serve, and what values they protect. In short, only when we make our values explicit are we in a position to make ethical choices [34].

It is precisely the ability to evaluate that makes professionals valuable and in fact professional; the refusal to evaluate or shallowness of evaluation makes professionals poor. The values that attracted students to the profession often provide them for a basis of making value-assessments of what is good and valuable for themselves, the system and users (and to understand those occasions where their values must be deferred to the patrons'). Their morals, politics and religion (be it atheism), not the abeyance of such, form the foundation for ethical deliberation. And as for the non-neutrality of systems, it is just those same values that prompt the professional to expose to the client the limitations, capabilities, biases, frameworks and intrinsic, accidental and cultural aspects of the systems of which they are a part, just as a good answer to a reference question exposes the sources and their frameworks from which the answer was obtained. Only in such a way can information professionals compensate for the lack of neutrality of systems and technologies. The value (or the lack of value) of systems primarily derives from professionals that front-end or found the system as intermediaries of the intellectual and embodied technologies.

Will the code of ethics of ASIS make professionals better parts of the technology and system or better interfaces to the technologies and systems? Will it support real progress by encouraging moral deliberation and by providing moral support when it is appropriate or necessary? Will it expose dubious agendas and support alternate ones? Will it stand for better professionals in a genuinely better world? One hopes so, so as to confront the vagaries of non-neutral technologies and systems.

Notes

[1] **Martin Heidegger**, *Being and Time*, tr. by John Macquarrie and Edward Robinson (New York: Harper & Row, 1982); *The Question Concerning Technology and Other Essays*, tr. by William Lovitt (New York, NY: Harper and Row, Publishers, 1977).

[2] **Jürgen Habermas**, *Knowledge and Human Interests*, tr. Jeremy J. Shapiro (Boston, MA: Beacon Press, 1971).

[3] **Hubert Dreyfus**, *Being-in-the-World: A Commentary on Heidegger's Being and Time. Division I* (Cambridge, MA: MIT Press, 1990); *What Computers Can't Do: The Limits of Artificial Intelligence* (New York: Harper & Row, 1979).

[4] **Jacques Ellul**, „The Power of Technique and the Ethics of Non-Power." In *The Myths of Information: Technology and Postindustrial Culture*, ed. by Kathleen Woodward (Madison, WI: Coda Press, 1980).

[5] **Abbe Mowshowitz**, „Computers and the Myth of Neutrality," *SIGCSE Bulletin*, 16, 1 (1984) Appendix C. There are no page references to this article.

[6] **D. J. Foskett**, *The Creed of a Librarian: No Politics, No Religion, No Morals* (London: Library Association, 1962).

[7] **Noel Peattie**, „Truth, Libraries and Revolution." In John Swan and Noel Peattie, *The Freedom to Lie: A Debate About Democracy* (Jefferson, NC: McFarland & Co., Inc., 1989) 35-105.

[8] **Don Ihde**, *Technics and Praxis* (Dordrecht, Holland: D. Reidel Publishing Co., 1979).

[9] **Robert Taylor**, *Value-Added Processes in Information Systems* (Norwood, NJ: Ablex Publishing Corp., 1986).

[10] I deliberately wish to avoid the use of the term, „knowledge" in information retrieval work. The use of „information resources" emphasizes merely the availability of opinions, knowledge or whatever, without inferring any judgment about the quality of those resources.

[11] Intellectual technologies are like schemas of Kant or cognitive psychologists. Information professionals acquire classifications through lectures, classes, exercises, and reading, but once they are acquired they become devices through which catalogers structure their experience of intellectual works. Furthermore, it transforms their experience of the works.

[12] **Arnold Pacey**, *The Culture of Technology* (Cambridge, MA: The MIT Press, 1983) 6.

[13] **Charles Meadow**, *An Analysis of Information Systems: An Introduction to Information Retrieval* (New York: John Wiley and Sons, 1976) 26.

[14] **Robert Hauptman**, *Ethical Challenges in Librarianship* (Phoenix, AZ: Oryx Press, 1988) 26.

[15] **Sanford Berman** „DDC 19: An Indictment." In his *Joy of Cataloging: Essays, Letters, Reviews and other Explosions* (Phoenix, AZ: Oryx Press, 1981) 177-185.

[16] **Ihde**.

[17] **Christopher Fox**, *Information and Misinformation: an Inquiry into Information and Misinformation, Informing and Misinforming* (Westport, CT: Greenwood Press, 1982).

[18] **Brenda Gerrie**, *On Line Information Systems: Use and Operating Characteristics, Limitations and Design Alternatives* (Arlington, VA: Information Resources Press, 1983) 45.

[19] **Donna A. Shaver, Nancy S. Hewison,** and **Leslie W. Wykoff**, „Ethics for Online Intermediaries," *Special Libraries*, (Fall, 1983): 238-245.

[20] **Randy Hartley** of Predicasts, Cleveland, Ohio, supplied the data, originally given in a presentation for NORASIS in November, 1988.

[21] **Daniel Bell**, *The Coming of post-Industrial Society: A Venture in Social Forecasting* (New York: Basic Books, 1973).

[22] **John Naisbett**, „The Major National and International Societal Problems and Issues Whose Resolutions Require Information Service in the Year 2000." In *Strategies for Meeting the Information Needs of Society in the Year 2000*, ed. by Martha Boaz (Littleton, CO: Libraries Unlimited, Inc., 1981) 56-64.

[23] **Pacey**, 35-54.

[24] **Ihde**.

[25] **Pacey**, 35.

[26] **Patrick Wilson**, *Second-Hand Knowledge: An Inquiry into Cognitive Authority* (Westport, CT: Greenwood Press, 1983).

[27] **Ellul**, 244.

[28] **John Stuart Mill**, *Utilitarianism*, (New York: The Liberal Arts Press, Inc., 1957).

[29] **Theodore Roszak**, *The Cult of Information: The Folklore of Computers and the True Art of Thinking* (New York: Pantheon, 1986) 14.

[30] **Ibid.**, 105.

[31] **Peter Dahlgren**, „Ideology and Information in the Public Sphere." In *The Ideology of the Information Age*, ed. Jennifer Daryl Slack and Fred Fejes (Norwood, NJ: Ablex Publishing Corporation, 1987) 27.

[32] **David F. Noble**, *Forces of Production* (New York: Alfred A. Knopf, 1984), xv.

[33] **Immanuel Kant**, *Foundations of the Metaphysics of Morals*, tr. Lewis Beck White (New York: The Liberal Arts Press, 1959) 47 (my emphasis).

[34] **Lawson Crowe** and **Susan H. Anthes**, „The Academic Librarian and Information Technology: Ethical Issues," *College and Research Libraries* (March, 1988) 127.

Ethics in Librarianship: A Management Model[*]

von Rosemary Ruhig Du Mont

Abstract

A management model of ethical decision making is presented. The model combines individual variables with situational variables and shows why policymakers must exercise moral judgement in performing their duties. This article also examines the notion of social responsibility as an ethical issue.

Introduction

The study of ethics in the information professions is a subset of the study of ethics in general. Thus, a definition of *ethics* may be helpful in clarifying this concept. There is no agreement on the exact definition of the term ethics. Some use it to refer to the art of determining what is right or good. It is also used in three different but related ways signifying: (1) a general pattern or „way of life," (2) a set of rules of conduct or „moral code," and (3) inquiry about ways of life and rules of conduct (Dwivedi, 1987, p. 22). As a concept, the purpose of ethics is to establish principles of behavior that help people make choices among alternative modes of action. Making such choices often involves ethical dilemmas, because these are marked by multiple and noncomparable dimensions. The dimensions are the results - both benefits and harms - that are going to affect the organization, the society, and the individual as a result of a decision or action (Hosmer, 1988, p. 10). In essence, *ethical behavior* is what is accepted as „good" and „right" as opposed to „bad" or „wrong" in the context of the governing moral code (Schermerhorn, 1989, p. 604).

The determination of what is right rather than what is wrong has been generally codified in the form of law, although not all situations have been, and can be, covered by any such codification. Laws are rationalized for the welfare of society; thus, any behavior considered ethical should also be legal in a just and fair society. This does *not* mean, however, that simply because an action is not illegal it is necessarily ethical. In other words, just living up to the „letter of the law" is not sufficient to guarantee that one's actions can be or should be considered ethical (Schermerhorn, 1989). The following examples of ethical questions can be considered in this context:

---

[*] Reprinted from Library Trends (Fall 1991) 40(2), 199-375. ©1991 by the Board of Trustees of The University of Illinois.

- Is it ethical to take longer than necessary to do a task?
- Is it ethical to do personal business on the employer's time?
- Is it ethical to call in sick to take a day off to catch up on chores at home?
- Is it ethical to fail to report rule violations by a co-worker?

None of these examples is illegal. But many individuals would consider one or more of them to be unethical.

The values held by an individual, group, or society are the basic components of an ethical system. Yet uncertainty is a fact of complex dynamic organizational life. The interests and values of another individual, group, or society and laws regarding both are unclear. Ethical standards, therefore, are not universally accepted, but rather they are the end product of discretionary decision-making behavior affecting the lives and well-being of others (Pearce & Robinson, 1989, pp. 148-49).

Ethics in the information professions is concerned with the application of moral standards to the conduct of librarians and other individuals involved in information dissemination. It is a type of applied ethics concerned with clarifying the obligations and dilemmas of librarians and other information professionals who make decisions regarding the acquisition, processing, and dissemination of information to individuals, groups, and society at large.

Evolution of Ethical Concerns in Information Professions

Tracing the development of ethics as an area of concern for information professionals will help in identifying the factors that are responsible for and that influenced the evolution of ethical behavior. Although ethical issues in librarianship were of some concern prior to the 1960s (see Table 1), it was the rise of the social responsibility debate in the decade of the 1960s that caused ethical concerns to become of major importance to librarians and other information professionals.

The concept of social responsibility is fundamentally an ethical concept. It involves changing notions of how human needs should be met and emphasizes a concern with the social dimensions of information service that has to do with improving the quality of life. Social responsibility provides a way for the information profession to concern itself with the social dimensions of service and be aware of the social impact of that service.

Table 1: Stages of ethical orientation

	Stage 1	Stage 2	Stage 3
Ethical attitudes	Traditional (before 1930s)	Stakeholders (1930-1950s) i.e., staff, patrons	Affirmative action (1960s - present)
Orientation	Institutional self-interest	Institutional interest, stakeholder interest	Enlightened self-interest, stakeholder interest, societal interest
Social values	Personal and user problems must be left at home	Employees have needs beyond economic needs and users have needs beyond information needs	Societal interest and participation is fundamental to our success
Political	No government involvement desired	Government support is a necessary evil	Government information agencies must cooperate to deal with societal problems

Historically, librarians saw that their major responsibility was to the collection; caring for the materials within the library building was their primary concern (Du Mont, 1977, p. 24). Many modern information professionals now acknowledge that they are responsible to any individual or group (i.e., stakeholder) with an information need. These stakeholders can be any constituency in the library's environment-users, nonusers, employees, suppliers, government agencies, public interest groups, and host communities.

Table 2 illustrates a four-stage model of a social responsibility continuum. Stage one encompasses responsibility for the library collection. Stage two adds responsibility for employees. Stage three includes responsibility to library users - those individuals who have made a conscious decision to use the library's information resources. Stage four expands responsibility furthest by proposing that information professionals are responsible to society in general and includes users and nonusers alike.

Table 2: Social responsibility continuum of an information professional

Stage 1	Stage 2	Stage 3	Stage 4
Collection development and maintenance	+ Employees only	+ Information users	+ Society as a whole

What information professionals do in terms of pursuing social goals depends on to what or to whom they believe they are responsible. A stage one information professional promotes collection development and maintenance. At stage two, information professionals accept responsibility for the employees in their organization and focus on human resource concerns. Because they will want to get, keep, and motivate good employees, they are concerned with appropriate education and training, improved working conditions, expanded employee rights, increased job security, and the like. A stage three professional expands goals to include high quality service, an excellent collection, good relations with the public, and the like. A stage four professional aligns with an active interpretation of social responsibility. At this stage, professionals see their responsibility to society as a whole. Their service is defined in terms of advancing the public good. The acceptance of such responsibility means that such information professionals actively promote social justice, support social and cultural goals, and take political positions even if such actions are perceived negatively by some.

Each stage carries with it an increasing level of discretion. As professionals move to the right along the continuum, they have to make more decisions based upon situational variables not of their own making. By the time professionals reach stage four, they are required to think about ethical dilemmas not necessarily solely within the context of their organizations but to decide what is right and what is wrong from a societal perspective. They may follow self-chosen ethical principles, upholding values and rights regardless of majority opinion (Trevino, 1986). Obviously, not all professionals perceive reaching stage four as an appropriate goal. Some stay in stage one, which emphasizes responsibility for collection maintenance and development, or stage two, which emphasizes appropriate behavior for a librarian as a professional, or stage three, which emphasizes fulfilling the duties and obligations of a professional librarian through high quality service to users.

There never has been established any simple right - wrong dichotomy to help information professionals make decisions regarding their appropriate domain for ethically responsible action. The social responsibility movement of the 1960s did provide fuel for debate. The concept of intellectual freedom, called the profession's „central ethic", was used to frame issues as diverse as civil rights, the war in Vietnam, women's rights, and the war on poverty (Bundy & Stielow, 1987). On one side, there were those who were in stage four on the social responsibility continuum, defining intellectual freedom as a genes of value judgments supporting a radically pluralistic egalitarian society. On the other side were those who viewed social responsibility from stages one and two of the continuum, defending intellectual freedom from a position of collective and individual neutrality (Peattie, 1987, pp. 43-57).

As the debate waned in the 1970s, it was obvious to many proponents and opponents of the social responsibility movement that there were several key issues in the debate that had not been, and perhaps cannot yet be, settled. One key issue concerns the operational definition of social responsibility. How shall a library's resources be allocated to help solve social problems? With what specific problems shall a given library concern itself? What priorities shall be established? What goals or standards of performance shall be established? What measures shall be employed to determine if a library is socially responsible or socially irresponsible?

In the past, the traditional library environment provided little or no information to the decision maker that was useful in answering the above questions. The concept of social responsibility itself provided no clear guidelines for ethical behavior. Given this lack of clarity, librarians who wanted to be socially responsible were left to follow their own devices or relied on some rather vague generalizations about social values and public expectations.

Another problem with the concept of social responsibility is that it has not always taken into account the environment in which the library functions. In the past, many advocates of social responsibility treated the library as an isolated entity that had the ability to engage in unilateral social action. Eventually, it came to be recognized that libraries are severely limited in their ability to respond adequately to social problems. There are physical, organizational and attitudinal barriers that have to be overcome (Martin, 1989).

The last issue that remains unresolved in the debate about social responsibility concerns the moral basis of the notion. The term *responsibility* is fundamentally a moral one that implies an obligation to someone or something. It is clear to most people that librarians have professional responsibilities to acquire, process, and disseminate information products and services efficiently to users of libraries. These responsibilities constitute the reason for the existence of libraries. But why do librarians have social responsibilities and to whom? What are the moral foundations for a concern with the social impact of information services?

The proponents of social responsibility, though well intentioned, have produced no clear and generally accepted moral principle that would impose on the information professions an obligation to work for social change. Various arguments have been made to try to link moral behavior of the profession to the performance of libraries. Little has been accomplished, however, by way of developing a solid and acceptable moral argument for the notion of social responsibility. Thus, although those promoting social responsibility are very moralistic in many of their statements, in debate with others, they do not articulate a philosophical basis for the social responsibilities discussed (Bundy, 1980).

The emotionally laden nature of the discussion on social responsibility presents the possibility that debate on the subject will continue indefinitely with little prospect of agreement being reached on the scope of the issues involved or their solution. Beginning in the late 1970s and continuing through the 1980s, a theoretical and conceptual reorientation has begun to take place regarding the information profession's obligations to its various constituencies. The new approach can be labeled „social responsiveness" (Pearce & Robinson, 1989, pp. 147-148) and it has become clear that the shift from responsibility to responsiveness reflects a significant change of focus. This new focus has shifted the discussion from moral imperatives related to social responsibility to a more technical and neutral approach that includes social responsiveness.

The Public Library Association's guidelines for identifying roles for public libraries reflects this shift (McClure et al., 1987). The process described in the guidelines includes identification of both internal and external mechanisms, procedures, arrangements, and behavioral patterns of the library's constituent groups taken collectively. It establishes mechanisms to judge the capability of libraries to fulfill certain roles. Attempts are made to identify key variables within the library that relate to its responsiveness and discover structural changes that will enable the library to respond adequately to social demands. The important questions are not moral, related to whether a library should respond to a social problem out of a sense of social responsibility, but more pragmatic and action oriented, dealing with the library's ability to respond and the changes necessary to enable it to respond more effectively.

One of the advantages of this approach is its managerial orientation. The concept ignores the philosophical debate about responsibility and obligation and focuses on the problems and prospects of making libraries more socially responsive. The process lends itself to analytical techniques in utilizing specific methods, such as data collection and analysis and numerical interpretation of results. The utilisation of data through this process can help decision makers determine how best to institutionalize social policy throughout the library. Organizational structures can be evaluated; the roles of information professionals can be delineated; personnel policies can be structured to reward appropriate „socially responsive" behavior; and goal statements can be formulated that reflect the roles identified.

Even though this approach seems to answer many of the questions faced by those concerned with the social responsibility debate, social responsiveness does not offer answers to all questions. The concept of social responsiveness does not provide guidance on how resources should be allocated to fulfill the various library roles. Libraries respond to the same problems in different ways and to varying degrees. And there is no clear data as to what pattern of responsiveness will be the most successful. The philosophy of responsiveness does not help a library to decide what roles it should have or what priorities should be established. In the final analysis, social responsiveness provides no better guidance to management than does social responsibility on the best strategies or policies to be adopted for library service. It appears that library personnel, by determining the degree of social responsiveness and the pressures to which they will respond, decide the meaning of the concept and what services will be developed as a result.

There is still a lack of moral principles or theory on which to base decisions. Societal pressures are assumed to exist, and libraries must respond to these in some manner. Social responsiveness assumes a passive attitude to such pressures. The concept of responsiveness provides no moral basis for information professionals to respond to social problems. There is no explicit moral or ethical theory and no specific values for personnel to follow in making responses to societal demands.

This position becomes quite evident when examining the statement of professional ethics developed by the American Library Association (ALA) in 1981 (ALA. Committee on Professional Ethics, 1981, p. 335). The 1981 statement makes no mention of the Library Bill of Rights nor any other philosophical statement as a source of the foundational ethics of library service. Although a 1980 draft spoke of the need for „participation in professional associations [and] community activity in support of library programs and legislation" (ALA. Committee on Professional Ethics, 1980), this point was left out of the adopted version.

Criticism of the draft document includes the assertion that, „it does not deal adequately with the ends and means of the library profession. Rather it is primarily a guide to attitudes toward work, without examining the mission of that work" (Du Mont, 1980, n.p.). While the presence of an ethical code can stimulate debate and strengthen professional autonomy, these results can only take place if the effect of the code is one of clarification of the practice of librarianship rather than a clarification of the appropriate demeanor of the professional (Kuhn, 1989, p. 25).

In responding to such criticism, the question of managerial guidelines and principles becomes relevant. What criteria, other than self-interest, are relevant to guide information professionals in the development of socially responsible strategies? Shall these strategies be judged solely on their short term effectiveness i.e., in helping a library respond to a patron who wishes to remove a certain book from the shelves? Can libraries retain their neutral posture and still support those government leaders who support the interests of libraries and share traditional values of intellectual freedom and access? The nagging question of defining the social good or, in a public policy context, of defining the public interest, appears. And finally, the absence of a clear moral underpinning for whatever strategies are determined continues to present a problem. If information professionals become proactive, does such behavior mean that they are attempting to minimize the impact of social change? Do not information professionals have a moral obligation that goes beyond their identified mandate to acquire and disseminate information? If information professionals do have social and political responsibilities as well as professional responsibilities, what is the moral basis for these responsibilities today?

Ethical Dimension of Decision Making

In answering the preceding questions, the major premise is that management is basically an ethical task, and that many management decisions have an ethical dimension. In general, an ethical decision is one that affects human welfare or human fulfillment in some significant manner (Bucholz, 1989):

> An ethical decision can be further defined as a decision where questions of justice and rights are serious and relevant moral considerations. These concepts are central ethical considerations in human affairs and an ethical decision is one where a consideration of them is an important dimension of the decision. Can the decision be defended on grounds of justice? Is it fair and equitable in some sense to all the parties affected? Does the decision violate some basic human rights, such that it could be labelled an immoral decision? These are the kinds of questions that must be asked. (p. 31)

Bucholz (1989) has identified three levels of ethical issues which vary in scope and breadth the individual level, the organizational level, and the system level (pp. 30-47). At the individual level, one makes day-to-day decisions that mostly involve the application of institutional policy to specific situations. When dilemmas arise, judgment must be made, some of which have ethical dimensions. At the organizational level, decisions are made for the organization that will guide the behavior of employees. These decisions may be broad in scope and involve consideration of social responsibility. At the system level, broad questions can be raised about the ethical foundations of information service; such questions are not tied to a particular organization.

The specific nature of the decisions involved at each of these levels can be seen if a concrete example is used. Information access issues are fraught with ethical dimensions and provide a useful vehicle to illustrate ethical dilemmas at each of these levels. Let us assume that the basic organizational policy in regard to access is one of „free access to all library materials for all individuals." Ethics enters into access decisions at the individual level in borderline or exceptional cases that policy does not seem to cover. For example, does free access really mean that a ten year old can take out an „R" rated video?

At the organizational level, the ethical dimensions of decision making come into play when selection decisions are made. Decision makers must make certain that the criteria and procedures that are established to make selection choices do not discriminate against certain writers nor points of view nor on the basis of irrelevant factors such as race, sex, or religious preference of either the author or selector. Self censorship of controversial materials is a constant problem that must be addressed.

At the system level, ethical questions relate to information dissemination. Who has access to information and at what cost? How does information form at affect access? Who is responsible for providing information for those who have limited skills to acquire it? These kinds of questions are settled through the public policy process and the eventual outcome is reflected in laws and regulations related to information access at local, state, and federal levels.

Figure 1 shows these various levels of decision making and the ethical issues relevant to each level. Potential clashes exist at all levels. Institutional policy may require that a decision maker go against his or her own ethical standards, producing significant internal conflict for one so involved. Institutional policy may not always reflect the ethical standards of the society at large, which may force society to develop laws and regulations to bring about change in institutional behavior.

Decision Rule: Select the best materials for the most people at the least cost.

Individual level: Borderline and extraordinary cases.

Organization level: Are selection criteria discriminatory?

System level: Is information access just and equitable?

Figure 1. Information access decisions

Another example can be taken from the hiring process for librarians (see Figure 2). Many libraries make an ALA-accredited degree an entry-level qualification for a professional librarian. Applicants for professional positions lacking this qualification are rejected. The ALA-accredited degree thus becomes a standard by which libraries hope to assure the recruitment of a high quality staff.

Ethics enters into a decision to hire at the indvidual level in borderline or exceptional cases where applying the policy in a mechanical fashion does not seem just or equitable. For example, if an applicant does not have an ALA-accredited degree, should he or she be automatically rejected without looking at other information such as previous work experience or other academic credentials? Such a decision may not seem fair given the subjective nature of the hiring process in general. Suppose a candidate with previous work experience, but without an ALA degree, is narrowly rejected for an academic library position and another candidate with an ALA-accredited degree, but no work experience, is accepted for a position. Is that fair considering that the work experience and academic credentials are not really comparable. And what about exceptional cases in which applicants may have other credentials, including doctorates? Should they be mechanically rejected without some special consideration?

At the organizational level, ethical considerations come into play when one considers justice and rights in relation to the hiring policy itself. Does a hiring policy discriminate unjustly on the basis of race or sex, or can it be defenedd as fair and equitable? Are written employment tests biased in favor of white middle class applicants due to the concepts and language used in examinations: Is an applicant's right to equal treatment violated by the use of such examinations? And, given the fact that grades mean different things depending on the school one attended, is it fair that grades are used as a factor in making employment decisions?

At the system level, questions can be asked about the justice of public service institutions such as libraries hiring only those who are citizens or legal residents of a given community. Do not all individuals have a right to apply for employment for which they feel qualified, regardless of their legal status or place of residence? These are serious ethical questions worthy of debate.

Decision Rule: Reject applicants who do not meet the standards.

Individual level: Borderline and extraordinary situations.

Organization level: Is the required ALA-accredited degree fair and equitable to all groups, including all races and both sexes?

System level: Is it fair and just for public service institutions to have legal qualifications for employment unrelated to individual expertise?

Figure 2. Hiring decisions

These examples serve to illustrate where ethical questions arise at different levels of decision making in libraries. The decisions made at all these levels benefit and burden individuals and groups differentially. Some individuals gain and others are affected adversely. Questions of justice and individual rights become relevant (MacCann, 1989, pp. 1-11). The question for the manager to answer is, Whose rights should be respected and what concept of justice is appropriate? (Bucholz, 1989, pp. 35-47).

Ethical considerations for managers in librarianship

Librarians as managers are constantly making ethical decisions whether they know it or not. They are constantly directing people toward or away from information resources that may directly impact their ability to enhance their lives or the life of their community. They are creating the future for their organizations, for their employees, for their users, for those who fund the service, and for society as a whole.

Decisions about information access can affect human well being and social welfare, having ethical impacts that are significant for all those touched by the decisions. A recent article in the *Chronicle of Higher Education* discussed „a revolution in the nature of resources that provide [political] power" (Coughlin, 1990, pp. 10-11). The suggestion is made that access to information resources must now be counted as a source of world power. As the ability to access information across the globe becomes possible through the use of technology, librarians will have more and more opportunity to influence decision making on a worldwide scale through appropriate information provision. This is an awesome responsibility and one that calls for ethical reflection of the highest order.

Librarians must be encouraged to think more broadly and highly of their task. They must recognize that libraries are multiple purpose institutions that have many impacts besides cultural enrichment or recreation. Moral leadership of such institutions means recognizing information agencies as part of an ethical system having various values that are important to human welfare. The challenge to librarians is to incorporate these values into routine decision making and develop methods of analysis that are applicable to identifying appropriate goals for themselves and their organizations.

An action plan

The implementation of an ethical vision in librarianship requires action in several areas. An ethical perspective must be incorporated into the workplace as well as into the curriculum through which future librarians are being educated. The following areas constitute what could be called an ethical agenda for librarians in both of these settings.

1. In the educational setting, such a plan calls for a thorough integration of moral and ethical concerns into the library/ information science curriculum. Although separate courses in ethics may also be offered, integration of ethical concerns into basic courses such as management or reference is essential to make ethics more directly related to the roles and responsibilities of information professionals.

2. Continuing education programs need to develop parallel efforts to maintain the work begun in the academic setting. Questions about ethics and moral aspects of librarianship must continue to be addressed as professionals move through their careers.

3. Library boards of trustees and/or advisory boards must demonstrate a concern about ethics by raising ethical questions when boards can acknowledge the significance of ethical issues by raising them in relation to goal setting and long-range planning.

4. Information professionals at all levels must recognize the important role they play in institutionalizing ethical responsibility throughout their organizations. Professional librarians have many channels open to them to shape the library/information center, including the setting of objectives for units and individuals, developing and implementing the reward structure of staff, modifying organisational structures to accomplish goals, and developing and utilizing appropriate measures of performance. Professional staff not only have responsibility for efficient and effective use of material and human resources but also must be willing to create a responsible institution that cares about and responds to the ethical and moral imperatives of its policies and actions.

5. Information policy-making by various government bodies must be considered from an ethical point of view. Librarians have a role to play in the debate; they can make contributions to the discussion and provide insight into the formation of regulations regarding the dissemination of information. Librarians must be given the freedom to respond to information policy issues out of a sense of ethical responsibility; rules and regulations for

the control of information flow must be evaluated as well as the inherent limitations of information dissemination systems.

6. More research must be considered by both library school faculty and professional librarians into the ethical aspects of decision making by librarians. One of the themes of this article is that many in the profession of librarianship are ignorant of ethical issues, not having a good understanding of how such matters should be analyzed and discussed. Research into ethical and moral issues can help overcome this ignorance. Scholars in the field need to apply their expertise to ethical questions and combine this with the work of those from other professional disciplines who have similar concerns.

This action plan suggests that a consideration of ethical issues must become a familiar comfortable part of librarians' thought processes. Ethical ambiguities are always present because no one can formulate policies that are going to be morally justified in all circumstances and in all places and times. It is important that those responsible for formulating, implementing, and evaluating policies should be made aware of these ambiguities and be ethically aware so as to act in a responsible and moral manner. Ambiguity, it should be noted, does not diminish the significance of ethical issues, which this discussion implies are pervasive in librarianship. In point of fact, the ethical dimension of librarianship represents a generalized concern for the improvement of quality of library service and professional conduct of librarians.

A final caveat is in order. Ethical behavior in librarianship does not mean that one should take no action, that is, avoid certain actions or books or ideas in an effort to keep out of trouble. On the contrary, the notion of ethics suggests that librarians take actions that are socially just. Only by actively pursuing social aims can librarians be ethically responsive. There is evidence to suggest that librarians choose not to choose, to „play it safe" with services and collections.

Instead, librarians ought to exercise ethical judgment in their duties. Only by demonstrating the highest standards of ethical decision making will librarians inspire confidence and respect in the information arena.

References

American Library Association. Committee on Professional Ethics. (1980). *Draft: state on professional responsibilities.* Unpublished manuscript.

American Library Association. Committee on Professional Ethics. (1981). On professional ethics. *American Libraries,* 12(6), 335.

Bucholz, R. (1989). *Fundamental concepts and problems in business ethics.* Englewood Cliffs, NJ: Prentice Hall.

Bundy, M. L. (1980). *Helping people take control: The public library's mission in a democracy.* College Park, MD: Urban Information Interpreters.

Bundy, M. L., & Stielow, F. J. (eds.). (1987). *Activism in American librarianship, 1962-1973.* New York: Greenwood Press.

Coughlin, E. K. (1990). The astonishing transformation of Eastern Europe upsets research agendas, intellectual assumptions. *Chronicle of Higher Education,* 37(January 3), 10-11.

Du Mont, R. R. (1977). *Reform and reaction: The big City public library in American life.* Westport, CT: Greenwood Press.

Du Mont, R. R. (1980). A comment on „The statement of professional responsibilities." Unpublished paper presented at the Council on Professional Ethics Forum, American Library Association annual conference, New York City, June 26.

Dwivedi, O. P. (1987). Ethics, the public service and public policy: Some comparative reflections. *International Journal of Public Administration,* 10(1), 21-50.

Hosmer, T. R. (1988). Adding ethics to the business curriculum. *Business Horizons,* 31(July-August), 9-15.

Kuhn, J. (1989). *The neutral librarian: An overview of the defense and critique of ethical neutrality in the profession.* Master's thesis, School of Library Science, Kent State University.

MacCann, D. (Ed.). (1989). *Social responsibility in librarianship: Essays on equality.* Jefferson, NC: McFarland.

McClure, C. R.; Owen, A.; Zweizig, D. L.; Lynch, M. J.; & Van House, N. (1987). *Planning and role setting for public libraries; A manual of options and procedures* (Prepared for the public library development project). Chicago, IL: American Library Association.

Martin, W. J. (1989). *Community librarianship: changing the face of public libraries.* London: Clive Bingley.

Pearce, J. A., & Robinson, R. B. (1989). *Management.* New York: Random House. Peattie, N. (1987). Intellectual freedom activities in the sixties: The defence of a professional standard. In M. L. Bundy & F. Stielow (Eds.), *Activism in American Librarianship, 1962-1973* (pp.43-57). New York: Greenwood Press.

Schermerhorn, J. R. (1989). *Management for productivity*, 3d ed. New York: Wiley.

Trevino, L. K. (1986). Ethical decision making in organizations: A person-situation interactionist model. Academy of Management Review, 11(July), 601-617.

Ethical Concerns in Librarianship: An Overview[*]

von Robert Hauptman

Introduction

The ways in which human beings interact are as perennial as the themes of Shakespeare's plays and as constant as well. Thus, the ethical problems and dilemmas that arise today are similar in kind to those that have arisen since humans first began to interact in a civilized manner. And I think that this is true despite Hans Jonas's perceptive insight that things are a bit different now that technology dominates our lives and a simple error may prove fatal for humankind generally. Jonas (see bibliography at end of this article) suggests that some of our earlier ethical imperatives, Kantian duty or Spinozean axioms, concepts that were so eloquently discussed by Diana Woodward just now, be replaced by what he called the „ethic of responsibility" (p. 178), a perspective that has played only a minimal role in ethical theories of the past (p. 123). I think that this can serve us well not merely in librarianship but in virtually any field.

If each person here today were to return home and visit his or her local supermarket, mall, public or even academic library and ask a number of arbitrarily chosen people what semiotics (or deconstruction) is, I think that you would discover that virtually no one has any idea. If, on the other hand, you ask what ethics is, almost everyone will have something to say. Most people know what ethics (or morality) entails, at least by exemplification. And, of course, most people know what is wrong - within their own society. But it is important not to forget that correct actions are culturally, temporally, and even sexually relative. What is good or right at one time, for example, may be unacceptable at another.

Overview

Ethical considerations have been fairly unimportant in traditional librarianship and more recently information dissemination. If one were to work one's way through *Library Literature*, from its inception until the mid-seventies, one would discover few listings under the heading „Ethics," and those pieces that do exist usually turn out to deal with decorum, etiquette, and other tangential matters. As an MLS candidate, I was surprised by this lack of interest in ethi-

---

[*] From Information Ethics: Concerns for Librarianship and the Information Industry. Ed. by Anne P. Mintz. © 1990 Rutgers Graduate School of Library and Information Studies Alumni Association by permission of McFarland & Co., Inc., Jefferson NC 28640

cal concerns, and so I devised what is now a rather infamous experiment. In the fall of 1975, I visited thirteen academic and public libraries and asked the reference librarians for help in constructing a small explosive device. I strongly implied that I was going to blow up a suburban home. I was appalled that none of the librarians refused to help on ethical grounds. The results of this experiment were published in the April 1976 *Wilson Library Bulletin* and apparently struck a sympathetic chord, because subsequently there has been a spate of publications on ethics and librarianship, the most important of which are the fourth issue of *The Reference Librarian* (which is entirely allocated to ethical concerns), Jonathan A. Lindsey and Ann E. Prentice's *Professional Ethics and Librarians*, and my recent Ethical Challenges in Librarianship. During the mid to late 1980s, interest in ethics has increased dramatically although not only in librarianship. Individual articles are appearing more and more frequently and I suspect that this will be a continuing trend.

Ethical dilemmas arise when two positive or necessary dicta conflict with each other. In librarianship this may occur when the demand for information clashes with an iconoclastic advocacy of individual decision making, the human necessity to bear responsibility, to be accountable for one's actions. This conflict between a broader social responsibility and what I have termed the „dubious professional commitment to dispense information" can be reduced to the insurmountable dichotomy that arises when one's personal and professional ethics conflict with each other. But it is important to bear in mind Stanley Fish's admonition that professional ethics (with few exceptions) must never supercede nor displace generally accepted ethical norms, one's general ethical responsibility to society. Consider the example discussed on the Public Television program, „Ethics in America": a journalist insisted that he would go to any lengths in order to ferret out information concerning a presidential candidate who was off on a tryst in a northern hideaway. He claimed that he would climb through windows, trespass, and hang around in the shrubbery; in other words, he would do things that were he not acting as a journalist, he would never do. From my perspective as well as that of Stanley Fish and others, one's personal or social ethic should supercede the ethic that journalists have created for themselves. Their ends (discovering information) do not justify the means (acting in an uncivilized or illegal manner). Or as Diana Woodward pointed out, in a consequentialist system, information must be disseminated: we simply ignore the possible harmful consequences, because there is some supervening professional principle or axiom that insists that information dissemination itself is an ethical imperative. This is unacceptable, since whenever there is a direct conflict between professional ethics and societal good, the latter must take precedence. A final example may help to clarify this. It is perfectly comprehensible why information obtained in the confessional must be absolutely confidential. If a confessor thought that the priest would reveal these innermost secrets, then he or she would not speak freely. But to insist that the revelations of a madman who promises to poison city's water supply and thereby kill millions of people must be protected regardless of consequences, is unacceptable. Each profession's ethical strictures must be respected, but when these conflict with normal ethics, it is the latter that must supervene.

The American Library Association promulgates its perspective through a number of polemical documents. The most important of these is the code, but unlike analogous documents in professions such as law or medicine, there is no operative force, neither state nor professional, neither legal nor ethical that mandates compliance, which occurs entirely at one's own discretion. And failure to comply with the code results in few detrimental consequences, unless one's actions are blatantly illegal. The specter of a malpractice suit, of course, always hangs over service personnel, but in the world of information dissemination, it is more likely that a suit will be brought for incompetence than for breaches of ethical conduct.

Applications

There are many areas in librarianship in which ethical considerations are necessary. I would like to briefly discuss a few of these. First, there is the selection process. Here one must guard against censorship, spend budgeted monies judiciously, and avoid purchasing reference tools that purposely duplicate information. Selection increases in importance as materials become more and more expensive, and although at first glance one might think that this does not have very much to do with ethics, it really does because the selector must choose one item to the exclusion of another that may be just as important simply because adequate funding is not available. In technical services, it is extremely important to protect uncataloged and unstripped items, not only from the dishonest but also from employees, professors, and administrators who may want to merely „borrow" materials for a short time. And catalogers must fight to change racist, sexist, and other offensive terminology; this is a task that requires great perseverence. Access services demand a great deal of human compassion from its workers, since it is here that fines are levied and reserve materials are often made available in academic libraries.

These functions create tension and anxiety in patrons and rules should be enforced with care and understanding. Most important, the confidentiality of patrons must be protected. The recent brouhaha over the Federal Bureau of Investigation's Library Awareness Program has made this patently clear to all people involved in the dissemination of information.

Ethical considerations probably have their greatest import in reference work because of the dichotomy between the ethical imperative to provide information (according to John Swan) and the need to question or refuse to cooperate in situations that may demand unethical activity. When foul play is merely suspected, one obviously must use discretion in refusing to help a patron. Consider the following case, related by Mary Prokop and Charles McClure. After John Hinckley shot President Reagan, a patron called the reference desk at a major university library and requested the phone numbers of all of the Hinckleys living in Ardmore, Oklahoma. The student who happened to be at the desk wondered whether the caller really was a journalist or whether she was planning to harrass these people. She may also have wondered whether she would be culpable or even legally liable in case something untoward did occur. When mere suspicion gives way to apodictic knowledge, when one knows with certainty that something socially detrimental will occur, then one must refuse to render assistance. Let me outline the hypothetical case that I created for *Ethical Challenges in Librarianship*. A distraught male approaches a reference librarian. He indicates that his wife has left him and is now at a local women's shelter. Since these organizations often keep their addresses secret (to protect the women and children who seek refuge there), he needs help in locating the address of the local shelter. He rants and raves that when he locates his wife, he will kill her. In a case such as this, one must refuse to render assistance; to aid and abet this person by helping him is morally reprehensible and a dereliction of both human and social responsibility. Instead of worrying about breaching the dubious professional ethic in such bizarre situations, reference personnel should concentrate on the quality and accuracy of the service they do render. Then perhaps the percentage of correct answers would improve from its current 50 percent rate.

The ubiquitous use of computer technology presents special problems for the librarian. The primary responsibility one has to all technological devices is to protect them from theft. This includes not only the hardward but all of the peripheral material as well. Software and CD-ROMs are especially susceptible to loss. Patron use of OPACs (online public access catalogs) demands infinite patience on the part of the librarian. This is especially true in public libraries, since patrons may be older, technophobic, or simply curmudgeonly and refuse to learn how to operate even truly user friendly systems. Online data base searching presents a group of interrelated problems. First, there is the question of fees. Despite the ALA's position that charging for services is always untenable, most institutions do charge for online searching. This is a service that would often be impossible to render without a fee of some kind. Nevertheless, charging for services demands constant consideration and policies can be revised depending on budgetary changes. This, by the way, is a superb indicator of ALA's power to regulate. ALA promulgates a code and takes stances on various issues, but there is no necessity to comply with ALA positions. Professionals who do not, suffer no adverse consequences. Whereas in law one may be disbarred or in medicine one may be prohibited from practicing, in librarianship unless one does something like punch the director in the nose, there are few negative consequences for breaches in behavior. Second, accuracy of results must be assured. If a searcher subsequently realizes that an error has been made, it is incumbent upon him or her to redo the search and get it to the patron. Third, it is an infringement of copyright law to maintain copies of searches in order to present them to subsequent patrons who require the same information. And fourth, despite positive theoretical admonitions concerning confidentiality, patrons' identities and informational needs are often unintentionally made available to a broad array of uninvolved people. The automation process itself is another area in which care and caution can help to forestall potential problems. Vendor infractions include lowballing (setting costs too low for the complete system, which thus forces the purchaser to buy more equipment and spend more money then was allocated) and making unfulfillable promises. Librarians may also be culpable here. Wiring, for example, is the practice of rigging things in such a way that only a single predetermined vendor can meet specifications (which makes a mockery of open bidding).

There are other areas in librarianship and information dissemination in which ethics can play an important role, but let me confine myself to briefly commenting on medical and legal reference work. One of the most difficult distinctions to make is that between giving medical or legal advice or interpreting cases or laws and merely guiding the patron. Advising and interpreting are illegal and unethical. It has been pointed out that librarians in public or academic libraries have neither the knowledge nor the materials to adequately answer complex medical or legal questions, the patrons are uninformed, and a public reference desk does not allow for the confidential transactions necessary for medical and legal advising. The implication is that in hospital, legislative, legal, and medical or law school libraries matters are somewhat altered. I think that one of the reasons that the legal profession is so adamant on this point is not to protect the client but rather to protect the guild, to protect the law profession and its individual members. If librarians disseminate free interpretive advice at the reference desk, then there is no need to consult a lawyer.

Law Librarianship

Now I would like to turn my attention to law librarianship. Consider the following scenario. Two friends, a doctor and a lawyer are strolling along a typical suburban street in, say, Highland Park or New Brunswick. A speeding automobile careens around a corner, hits a young woman walking on the opposite sidewalk, and smashes into a utility pole. The drunken driver emerges, shaken but unhurt. The woman, on the other hand, is badly cut and in shock. The doctor hurries over, stanches the bleeding, makes her comfortable, and reassures her. While waiting for an ambulance, the lawyer hands the woman his card and indicates that he specializes in liability suits and would be happy to represent her, once she has recovered enough to consider such matters.

Virtually everyone would praise the doctor for his actions, but the lawyer, despite recent changes in attitude toward professional advertising and related matters, might still be accused of ambulance chasing, an unethical and even illegal practice in some jurisdictions. Keep in mind that as recently as some ten years ago, it was unethical for lawyers to advertise. Now lawyers advertise just as automobile salesmen do. If you watch a lot of television, as I lamentably do, you will see Joel Hyatt and a bunch of other lawyers parading across the screen inviting the public into their offices: „You do not need any money; we will get as much compensation for you as possible and then you can pay us a small percentage, say, eighty percent." So it is a very fine line, and to know whether something is ethical or unethical in a given situation or even in a given culture is sometimes extremely traumatic. Is such activity deemed unethical because it harms clients or because it is detrimental to the profession? Some sociologists claim that codes are formulated to protect the practitioner, to keep fees inflated, to control and manipulate the client. Thus, even when the librarian holds a J.D. and is a member of the bar of the state in which he or she practices, even when the collection is adequate, and the patron happens to be a knowledgeable law student, professor, legislator, judge, or pro se litigant, it is still unethical to offer advice or interpretation. That confidentiality cannot be maintained at a public reference desk is hardly a valid excuse. The parties involved could simply repair to a nearby office, as they often do in the case of data base search interviews, and discuss the problem at length. That this type of service is considered unethical is indicative not of a caring attitude toward patrons' rights and needs, but rather of the profession's desire to protect billable hours and avoid malpractice suits against its members.

There are many ethical problems that deserve consideration here (some of which are not unique to law librarianship). Of primary concern are conflicts of interest. Vendors often subsidize potential customers by giving parties, presenting awards, and even lending money for legitimate reasons, e.g., publishing materials. Much of this activity is generally accepted, but quid pro quo relationships should be carefully avoided. A second area of danger occurs when a scholarly librarian becomes too involved in writing, editing, or free lance consulting. A modicum of such work is part of every professional's activity, but if editing or writing is overdone during work hours, it may supplant the librarian's normal obligations. A careful balance must be maintained. A third potential conflict occurs when a patron requests help at a reference desk and the librarian attempts to solicit business for his or her outside practice. Finally, consulting and developing materials for publishers for a fee may subsequently conflict with the need to decide whether these same often expensive items should be purchased for the collection.

As in all types of librarianship, confidentiality must be protected. Interestingly, there is one unusual situation that could occur in law librarianship. A public law librarian who happens to be helping opposing lawyers, has to be extremely careful not to inadvertently disclose confidential matters to either party. When developing the collection, the decision may be made to cancel subscriptions to certain serials or services because the same material is available online through Lexis or Westlaw. But if the use of these data bases is limited to certain groups, law students and faculty, for example, then vital information may be lost to all other patrons. Similarly, budgeting constraints may result in the cancellation of tools or the inability to purchase new monographs. Such failures to keep the collection up to date will again result in the loss of important information. Sometimes students provide services at the circulation counter or even in reference. They may be enrolled in the law school or merely work-study students from some other part of the university. In either case, they must be conscious of their limitations and careful to provide full and correct information. It is often difficult for a professional to render correct service here, so it is doubly hard for an inexperienced student. I have had varying degrees of success when interacting with student help in law libraries. There are other potential problems but I will limit myself to one final comment. I have heard of a case in which a librarian monitored the insider trading of a firm, managed to make some money, was discovered by the SEC, and prosecuted. There are obviously perils to be avoided on all fronts.

Many people have provided helpful suggestions for this presentation. I would especially like to thank four university law librarians: Maria Protti, University of Oklahoma; Susan Kiefer, Hamline University; Martha Dragich, Georgia State University; and Kathleen Price, University of Minnesota; and one county law librarian: Judy Zetterberg, Hennepin County (MN) Law Library.

Bibliography

Fish, Stanley. „Anti-Professionalism." *New Literary History, 17 (1)* (Autumn 1985): 89-107.

Hauptman, Robert. *Ethical Challenges in Librarianship.* Phoenix: Oryx Press, 1988.

„Professionalism or Culpability? An Experiment in Ethics." *Wilson Library Bulletin,* 50 (8) (April 1976): 626-627.

Jonas, Hans. *The Imperative of Responsibility: In Search of an Ethics for the Technological Age.* Chicago: University of Chicago Press, 1984.

Lindsey, Jonathan A. and Ann E. Prentice. *Professional Ethics and Librarians.* Phoenix: Oryx Press, 1985.

Prokop, Mary and Charles R. McClure. „The Public Librarian and Service Ethics: A Dilemma." *Public Library Quarterly, 3 (4)* (Winter 1982): 69-81.

The Reference Librarian. No. 4 (1982). (Entire issue).

Ethics Inside and Out: The Case of *Guidoriccio*[*]

von John Swan

Abstract

This is an examination of problems of oversight and responsibility arising from a case in which librarians are implicated at several levels. Two art historians, principals in a major controversy in which they are challenging the traditional attribution of a great Sienese fresco, discovered what they (and others) deemed to be a pattern of censorship of their point of view via card catalog indexing in an important Florentine research library. This article surveys their attempts to find redress and to gain a hearing for their case, and it attempts an analysis of the major hurdles they faced in the academic and research world, principally the „ethics of collegiability" which presumes against complaining outsiders. The implications of both the alleged misdeed of librarians and the actual lack of response of librarians are explored.

Information becomes entangled with ethics through two obvious paths by way of what people do with it, and by way of what they do not do with it. For librarians and others whose trade is information itself, this process begins when decisions are made as to how the information is to be dispensed in the first place. Thus, it is very early in the life of a piece of information that questions of action and its consequences gather around it - and for the purposes here we are ignoring many large related dilemmas, such as those involved in the choices that are made about just what information to generate - e.g., the morality of choosing to do the research necessary for the development of a plastic handgun, to name but one recent technological triumph.

That there are ethical connections between information and action is hardly startling news, but this does not establish any similarly obvious ethical dimension for those whose field of operation is the connection itself, the passage of information from its generators to its users. There is a character in a Flannery O'Connor (1971) story whose place in the moral scheme of things could be said to be parallel to that of the middle persons: „[she] had no bad qualities of her own but she was able to use other people's in such a constructive way that she never felt the lack" (p. 272). Neither the generators nor the users, neither the institutions that support us nor the patrons of our wares, fall under our ethical purview. As much as we are dependent upon and responsive to both, the ends to which they put our means do not play a part in the provision of those means. Or do they?

---

[*] Reprinted from Library Trends (Fall 1991) 40(2), 199-375. ©1991 by The Board of Trustees of The University of Illinois.

In the case examined here, that question arises in a rather specialized context, but its implications are broad and serious, especially within the world of research and scholarship. Librarians come into the picture first as alleged overt violators of what are presumably shared standards of professional ethics (codified and otherwise), then as professional colleagues within the academic establishment faced with the fallout from this transgression. In both phases of this event, which is still unfolding, we have faced multiple challenges; it will be argued here that, for reasons intimalely related to the nature of professional collegiality and our professional identity itself, librarians have failed to meet these challenges.

This inquiry begins with a specific instance of unethical behavior i.e., the apparent suppression of a controversial point of view through selective indexing of materials with important connections to the other side of the controversy. The word *apparent* is important here because this writer has not had the opportunity to examine the evidence first hand and is relying heavily on extensive correspondence with one of those whose published arguments were censored, as well as on the experience reported by others who encountered the selective pattern of indexing in the research institution.

It should be made clear that this author does find credible the charges leveled by my corresondent and his coauthor. Both have waged a long, tenacious, scrupulously documented, and, for the most part, thoroughly unrewarded campaign for redress. It is true that they have earned support and not a little sympathy from many along the way, and that is part of the point of this study. Just as this author must admit his own distance from the evidence for the accusation, despite the years of documentation arrayed before him, and his own impotence in terms of direct action, virtually everyone who has found the evidence compelling has nevertheless found it easy to express sympathy than to find a solution. And further, this is not necessarily a failure of will or personal ethics among those who see the problem but do nothing directly about it. It is a problem that attaches itself with peculiar force to this kind of ethical breach, a problem compounded by questions of responsibility, authority, evidence, and the very nature of the unethical deed itself.

The importance of focusing on this instance of suppression lies not so much in the particular variety thereof. Outside of states controlled overtly by censoring elites and exclusive ideologies, there is little recorded evidence of censorship specifically by indexing because it is usually accomplished much more efficiently long before this stage of the processing of materials. But censorship by index may be a general problem with broad consequences, unreported because it is difficult to detect and often practiced by those who are unaware that they are, in fact, erecting barriers to information in the very process of organizing it (see Intner, 1984). What is more significant is the fact that this apparent censorship occurred within an academic research environment, and the act and the responses to it reveal a number of uncomfortable truths about the nature of the communal trust that is supposed to be the very foundation of scholarship.

That deed and its background are set forth from the point of view of its victims in a paper delivered in 1986 at the Second European Conference of the Art Libraries of IFLA the International Federation of Library Associations being one of the organizations to which ist authors took their case. The elaborate title of the paper (which was published in the proceedings of the conference) is effectively a summary of the situation as they see it: 'Selective' Card Cataloging (or In-House Screening of Periodical Indexing) of Art History Articles in authors' Files, and the Potential Effects of this 'Selectivity' on the Bibliographical Entries Relating to Specific Art Historical Problems: A Case Study" (Moran & Mallory, 1986).

In the world of research and scholarship as well as any other, censorship is most likely to occur in a politicized environment. In this case, it is the politics of a major controversy in the world of Italian art, indeed, one which has repeatedly been called „the case of the century" (Watson, 1986). This is not the occasion for a recounting of this much recounted attribution debate, which is also treated elsewhere in this volume (for a convenient overview of the early literature thereof, see Wohl [1984] as well as Moran and Mallory [1986]; for a recent survey from particular points of view of salient portions of the evidence and arguments, see Mallory and Moran's [1986] Burlington article, as well as Polzer [1987] and Maginnis [1988]).

However, knowledge of the essentials of the controversy are necessary for an appreciation of the intensity of conflict that led to the „selective" indexing and other instances of (at least apparent) suppression such as the exclusion of Moran and Mallory from an important conference and the involvement in a letters to the editor fracas within the pages of a major art journal. This writer is, of course, in no position to take a stand in the original debate itself. Nor is that relevant to a brief account of the struggle of Moran and Mallory for what they consider to be a fair hearing within the scholarly establishment.

The RILA Editor, Allee Sedgwick Wohl (1984), is eloquent on the subject of the work of art that is at the center of all this:

> The fresco known as *Guidoricccio da Fogliano at the Siege of Montemassi* in the great council hall of the Palazzo Pubblico in Siena has long been famous both as an artistic masterpiece and as a proud political symbol of the Republic. To the Sienese it means what Michelangelo's David means to the Florentines. To art historians it represents a conerstone of the art of Simone Martini and the origin of the equestrian portrait. Solitary and powerful, baton in hand like a Roman conqueror, the condottiere rides his caparisoned horse along the fresco's frame, against a tawny and desolate landscape. In the background an undulating palisade encloses the scene of the siege... There is an eerie quality to the scene which makes it unforgettable. (p. 10)

Simone Martini, master of what some scholars call the „Sienese proto-Renaissance" and, like Giotto and Duccio, an Art eminence and one of the founding fathers of Western painting, was taken to the creator of the *Guidoriccio* by unquestioned consensus and multiple-century tradition until the appearence in 1977 of an article by Gordon Moran (1977) challenging that assumption. Basing his argument on a range of considerations, from the lack of mention of the *Guidoriccio* in contemporary documentation of payments to Martini or early descriptions of either Martini or the Palazzo Pubblico, to apparent incongruities and anachronisms in the costume and rank of the equestrian. Moran suggested that if there was originally a portrait of Guidoriccio by Simone Martini on that wall, it had been obliterated when the *capitano generale* was deposed in 1333 and forced to leave town in disgrace. When the redoubtable leader returned to rule again fifteen years later, Simone Martini was already dead. Moran originally argued that the Sienese likely commissioned a memorial portrait of Guidoriccio upon his death in 1352 added to the preexisting Simone Martini fresco of the castle of Montemassi; later, taking into account a decade of new evidence, Mallory and Moran (1986) suggested that the whole Guidoriccio fresco was probably painted much later than the mid-trecento, perhaps even in the sixteenth century.

The act of questioning the authenticity of one of the most famous and revered works of one of the most famous and referred artists of the early Renaissance produced a reaction that still seems to be growing, over a dozen years and many further developments later. The most striking of these developments came as a result of the official Sienese response to the Moran heresy. In Siena, as can be imagined, the issue has been, and continues to be, far more than a matter of scholarly dispute. The Mayor of Siena took the reasonable step of appointing a committee of experts to examine the Guidoriccio carefully and seek a resolution to the new controversy.

The resultant labor of studying, cleaning, and restoring the fresco led to the extremely important discovery and eventual uncovering in 1980-81 of a heretofore unknown fourteenth-century fresco directly below the Guidoriccio. This work, recognized immediately to be an outstanding example of trecento painting, depicts a castle and its palisade, its gates open perhaps to signify capitulation, with two figures standing at the left, both intentionally defaced with blue overpainting, apparently notions after they were painted in the first place.

The civic leaders of Renaissance Siena had a tradition of celebrating the city's conquests of important rival fortifications by commissioning their portrayal on the walls of the Palazzo Pubblico therefore, the identification of the subject matter of the newly uncovered fresco has become a controversy intimately connected to that involving the Guidoriccio, itself traditionally identified as the memorialization of the siege and conquest of Montemassi in 1328 indeed, in his detailed defense of the traditional attribution, Polzer (1987, p. 67) places great emphasis on the signal importance of Guidoriccio's triumph at Montemassi over the most famous and feared of Tuscany's military foes, Castruccio Castracani, as the reason for the fresco's prime location and its survival without the defacement posited by Moran and Mallory. The proper naming of the event portrayed on the other fresco, and the various possible alignments thereof with recorded commissions of Simone Martini (and others), have added a whole new dimension of the similar struggle concerning its famous wall companion.

Throughout the controversy, the Kunsthistorisches Institut in nearby Florence has played a number of vital roles. As one of the great centers of scholarship and research in the art of the Italian Renaissance, it has inevitably served as a major resource for all concerned, but the institute's members have also been more particularly involved. Max Seidel, president of its support organization and member of its governing Kuratorium, was also a member of the special Guidoriccio commission appointed by Siena's (then) Mayor Mauro Barni. Seidel was co-author of the official report of the commission and he has consistently argued for the traditional attribution of the fresco. Members of that supporting organization (Verein zur Förderung des Kunsthistorischen Instituts) also gave the funds necessary to uncover and restore the newly discovered fresco, which Seidel and co-commissioner Luciano Bellosi consider to be a portrayal of the submission of the town of Giuncarico in 1314 and painted by Duccio, another founding father. Moran and Mallory argue that it is, rather, the work of Simone Martini himself, a depiction of the surrender of Arcidosso to Guidoriccio done in 1331. (The commission had also originally identified the site as Arcidosso, but they changed their collective mind-according to Moran [G. Moran to G. Ewald, Kunsthistorisches Institut in Florence, personal communication, June 18, 1986], this was because they belatedly recognized that this position played havoc with the traditional view of the man on horseback as being Guidoriccio.) Each of these views has the expected implications for the identity of the fresco, of course.

Seidel and two other institute officials, Irene Hueck and Hans Belting, were also members of the organizing committee of a special conference devoted to the subject of Simone Martini. This convegno, which took place in Siena in March 1985, has a place in this complicated tale, because, according to Moran (personal communication, 1986) and backed by considerable documentation, this committee excluded Moran and Mallory from the speakers' program twice, at first upon their written request for the opportunity to present new evidence disputing the established view of the Guidoriccio, then (and more tellingly), after the local government of Siena negotiated to have them placed on the program at the last minute, in response to the local and even national outcry against their exclusion. (In fairness, it should be mentioned here that according to the institute, and specifically according to B. Döll [to G. Moran, personal communication, September 24, 1986 at the behest of Döll and copied to twenty others including this author], head of the Division for Humanities of the Bundesminister für Forschung und Technologie in Bonn, Seidel had no part in preparing the Simone Martini Congress, nor in excluding Moran and Mallory from it - „solely the Italian organizers were responsible for preparing and holding this congress." The West German government funds a number of research Centers in foreign countries, among which is the Kunsthistorisches Institut, and thus it became Döll's place to defend the institution and its officials against the accusations of censorship.)

In terms of both scholarly and political issues then, the Kunsthistorisches Institut, or at least key figures associated with it, has a place in this controversy that goes beyond its central function as a vital institutional resource. As an independent scholar and a resident of Florence, Gordon Moran has long made use of this great library for reasons quite unassociated with the controversy. His and Mallory's accusation of censorship by indexing and the article summarizing the case are based on their experience as patrons of the library, not on their role in that debate although for them as well as for the members of the institute, this background presses rather closely at times.

As Moran explains, the Kunsthistorisches Institut began indexing in the card catalog beyond the level of the monograph in the early seventies, producing card sets for articles from periodicals, conference proceedings, *Festschriften*, and other sources. He quotes Head Librarian Peter Tigler to the effect that this procedure covers „several hundred periodicals" and that „this coverage is far more extensive than that of the standard bibliographic tools such as *RILA*, *Art Index*, and *the Repertoire d'art et d'archeologie"* (Moran & Mallory, 1986, p. 123). Around 1980, this comprehensive indexing had to be curtailed because of a shortage of help. It was replaced by the practice of „selective" indexing of periodicals according to their „importance" - that is, whether their were „especially rich" in articles on Italian art or were otherwise regarded as significant according to the „special knowledge or interests" of those responsible for the indexing was begun (Moran & Mallory, 1986, p. 124).

The essence of the Moran/Mallory charge is that, starting in 1980, this „selective" indexing took on a particular ideological pattern that affected the treatment of articles dealing with the *Guidoriccio* affair. The year 1980 was also the time that these articles began appearing in larger numbers, reflecting the discovery of the other fresco. Before glancing at the evidence behind the charge, it is appropriate to quote at length from Döll's (1986) defense of the institute, as addressed to Moran, because it does provide useful coverage of the technical processing problems facing its catalogers and of the nature of the official response:

> With your indication of the delays in the cataloguing of journals, you, quite rightly, pointed to a major emergency impairing the use of these journals, which does exist unfortunately. The Kunsthistorisches Institut has a library of currently approx. 158,000 volumes, among them 1,082 journals which must be indexed. The number of visitors is very high for a research institution of the size of the Kunsthistorisches Institut. Only three scientists and one academically trained librarian are available for acquisition, cataloguing, maintaining and safekeeping the books and for attending to visitors. If this situation is compared with the proven standards existing for art libraries, namely that one librarian should be responsible for a maximum of 20,000 books, the acute shortage of personnel ... becomes clear. This shortage is particularly

painfully felt in the work-intensive indexing of the journal catalogues; it is the reason or the major backlog from 1980 onwards .... Because of the ban issued by the Federal Government for the purpose of consolidating the budget - on the recruitment of new staff, it has been impossible so far to remedy this unsatisfactory situation.

Yet it is the supreme aim to handle all journals as speeds possible. While this optimum cannot be reached, one must make do with makeshift measures, which are in the first place determined by internal technical aspects.

This shortage of staff is therefore the only reason why your essays ... have not yet been indexed. Your claim that your publications had been deliberately neglected in the indexing of journals is an insinuation which is explicitly rejected once again here. Indeed, no member of the Institute is concerned in their own research work with the Riccio controversy. If this were the case, they would strictly separate their tasks at the Institute from their own scientific work.... (pp. 2-3)

Although they reject much in the official defense here and elsewhere and present considerable evidence of evasion and misrepresentation, Moran and Mallory do not dispute some salient features of the above passage. The financial and staff workload difficulties faced by the institute have, in fact been very large. They constitute the essence of the defense offered by the institute - that is, by its Director, G. Ewald, and the Head Librarian, Tigler - as well as Döll; the response to the charge of censorious selectivity has been nothing but categorical denial. An addition to the workload defense, also undisputed, is ironically revealing from the point of view of librarians who worry about points of access. In response to Moran's accusations, that his and Mallory's publications were being suppressed, the library instituted the practice of collecting Moran's essays „in dailies and other ephemeral organs" and putting them in a folder under the title of „Miscellanea Moran," claiming „this folder can be used at any time by any visitor to the library" (Döll, 1986, p. 3). Since this folder was apparently unconnected by any cross reference to Simone Martini or the *Guidoriccio* issue, at least, between 1984 and early 1986, visitors may have had the right to use it, but they did not have the knowledge necessary to make use of that right. Indeed, the effectiveness of concealment by subject heading (whether or not it was intentional) was demonstrated in the fate of the February 1984 issue of *News from RILA* the issue containing Alice Wohl's summary of the controversy (quoted earlier), as well as her useful bibliography on the subject. When the issue arrived in the library, it was put into the „Miscellanea Moran" folder instead of being shelved with other issues of the title. This meant that not only were interested patrons unable to find it, but even an institute librarian failed to retrieve it when asked by visiting scholar Samuel Edgerton (Moran & Mallory, 1986, p. 127). After two years, the issue was finally reunited with other copies of the title, although the Wohl article therein remained unindexed long after that, and the problematic nature of „Miscellanea Moran" continued. It was further dramatized by the fact that, until early 1986, none of the twelve articles abstracted in the Wohl piece that disagreed with the traditional attribution of the *Guidoriccio* could be found in the Kunsthistorisches Institut's authors' catalog card indexing, although many contemporaneous articles that upheld the Simone Martini identification did receive prompt indexing. To quote (as do Moran and Mallory) Sheila Intner: „because the function of an index is to bring out ideas and materials from a mass of stuff, searchers rely on it and assume that an item not found in the index, for whatever reason, is missing..." (Intner, 1984, p. 106. Her specific reference is to printed indexes, but it applies to a card index as well).

Without repeating the sometimes grueling detail of the Moran/Mallory inventory of what articles expressing which points of view were indexed when, suffice it to say that they provide a thorough documentation of the charge that articles of the traditional persuasion received the thorough indexing that it was the institute's policy to provide selected titles, while articles challenging that view - even when they were from journals that heretofore had been indexed - did not. A number of the latter are, of course, by Moran and Mallory themselves but several are not.

The authors offer as evidence the difficulties experienced by other patrons of the institute, and Moran later pointed to the evidence of an article written in December 1987 by Nicole Squires, a California State University student, who went to the Kunsthistorisches Institut to study Simone Martini via its „fabulous collection of periodicals." As she tells it, the card catalog yielded some sixty articles on her subject but very few after 1983. After considerable struggle learning and relearning the library's systems (her first assumption, naturally, was that she was not using them properly), seeking staff help, and finally being told that the recent material she sought was not indexed because of the earlier-mentioned workload problem, she came to the following conclusions:

> Based on the catalogueing (sic)-indexing situation, people from the Kunst went against principles of some teaching in library science and left out, in an inconsistent manner, several crucial articles on Simone Martini having to do with Moran's side of the Guido Riccio controversy, giving the excuse that they were understaffed. If this was really true, then why were all existing articles written by the opposing side (their side) immediately filed in both author and subject indexes! As a result students like myself encounter some difficulties in using materials at the Kunst. Is such difficulty the case only in this particular situation, and thus limited to art history, or do such cases occur elsewhere in academia? (Squires, 1987, p. 11)

Whatever the truth in this particular case, her final question is extremely important and one that makes this incident, a small faced of a large controversy, relevant to all librarians.

Once they had uncovered what they perceived to be a pattern of censorship by indexing, Moran and Mallory were not reticent about seeking redress, both in person at the institute and by way of correspondence with a great many near distant connections with the institute and the art world, the library community, intellectual freedom groups, any organization or person who came to their attention who might be able to bring pressure to bear, or at least shed light upon, their case Gordon Moran is an indefatigable builder of epistolary networks who puts forth his case in long and detailed letters, often copied to many other parties. Sometimes he is rewarded with silence or even hostility (there is considerable potential for both contentiousness and defensiveness in this case, of course), or the kind of weary politeness expressed by Döll toward the end of the letter quoted earlier:

> If a visitor feels he has been treated unfairly, his criticism is heard, not only at the Institute but also in the Ministry. This obligingness ends, however, where the effort is disproportionate to the importance of the matter. Please consider this statement to be a conclusive answer to your numerous questions.... (p. 4)

However, just as his *Guidoriccio* position continues to gain ever awider notice, Moran has also attracted the sympathetic response of many who concern themselves with ethical issues in the worlds of scholarship and librarianship. The fact that he pours such energy with such effectiveness into letter writing (not word processed, which these days is further evidence of an unusually high level of energy) is not merely an observation of a personality quirk. It is thoroughly germane to this discussion, not only because without the major epistolary habit there would be no network and likely no broader case, but also because it bespeaks an „outsider's" style.

As an observer and (very minor) participant in this matter for a number of years, this writer has come to believe that one of the obstacles confronting Moran is the fact that he is an outsider who has become something of a major player in an insider's game. This is not to deny that „gentlemen scholars" and inspired amateurs have contributed mightily to scholarship, certainly in the field of art history, or that the professionals have been capable of acknowledging this in the past and no doubt will continue to do so in the future.

That Gordon Moran is a former stockbroker who has settled in Florence to pursue the life of the art historian is, then, only partly to the point - and his partner in the struggle, Michael Mallory, is, after all, a professional in the field, a bona fide member of the Brooklyn College faculty. More relevant is the fact that being an outsider to the academic establishments Moran acts like an outsider; that is, he writes long letters expressing and documenting his charge of injustice to a wide range of correspondents without regard to the protocols attendant upon academic hierarchies and turf. He is courteous, even referential, but he is also relentless and exhaustive in the support of his argument, and in effect he calls upon the wider world to bear witness to his cause. All of this is, it seems a considerable strain upon the politesse which is everywhere at the center of the academic style, both personal and institutional, even when academics are at each other's throats.

This flagrantly subjective point is insisted upon here because this author believes that there is such a thing as an „ethics of collegiality" that is at work in this case. It is not unique to academia, of course; just as the Greeks tended to regard fellow Greeks as somehow more civilized, more fully human, than the barbarians (which meant, in a simple and pejorative sense, non-Greek), People have always parsed the race into insiders and outsiders. But the world of research, scholarship, and higher education depends, at least in theory, upon uniquely high standards of mutual trust and openness, combined with an intricate, discipline-based meritocracy of knowledge, brains, and curriculum vitae. It is in many respects an open-ended democratic world in accordance with the dynamics of meritocracy, but once one is a member of the *collegium*, it becomes very natural to divide the world into those within and those without.

Thus, for example, when Serge Lang, the Yale mathematician, attacked the candidacy of Samuel Huntington for membership in the National Academy of Sciences on the grounds that the influential Harvard professor had presented a political view (that South Africa was measurably a „satisfied Society" before the „early 1960s") as if it were objective science, he was perceived as an insider betraying the insider's code. The fact that his campaign to block the membership of Huntington has (so far) been successful indicates that that code is not monolithic, but the fact that he has to resort to a paid advertisement to get his argument and defense on his action into print is but one indication of the price paid by one who behaves like an outsider. In that advertisement, he quotes from a letter to him by Yale's provost:

> We need to muster all the strength we have to combat the ignorance and superstition that prevails without our walls. Our Mission as an institution for the precious nourishment of ideas and scholars is badly bruised when we turn on our own, when we withhold that extra ounce of trust and forgiveness. (Lang, 1988, p. 4)

As this example should make clear, the „ethics of collegiality" is a genuine ethics, not just a Mafia code for scholars who seek to hide the misdeeds of their own. The provost, like Döll on behalf of the Kunsthistorisches Institut, is not seeking a coverup but urging cooperation. That the result is the same as a coverup is only the view of those who have taken the position of outsiders. There is a common presumption shared in one case by the provost and, among others, the Harvard colleagues who rushed to Huntington's defense, and in the indexing case, by offcials of the Institute and its governing ministry. That is, that their colleagues, as honest and proven insiders, are being attacked unfairly. The related assumption is, naturally, that their assailants are misguided at best, traitors to a higher cause at worst.

The well-known case of the examination of the effects of a proven case of laboratory fraud on the scientific literature by Walter Stewart and Ned Feder (1987) is very revealing in this regard. Their analysis of the 109 papers of Harvard researcher John Darsee (and his forty-seven variously attentive co-authors), exposing an extensive pattern of errors stemming from Darsee's original falsifications, was an insiders' attack concluding that „certain lapses from generally accepted standards of research may be more frequent than is commonly believed" (Stewart & Feder, 1987). This article encountered massive resistance even before finally being accepted for publication (in a form surrounded by hedging commentary and a negative responce), and even more hostility thereafter. Many scientists felt that Stewart and Feder were letting down the side, overreacting to an unfortunate but still uncommon incident; there was derogatory comment about their personal careers, and they also encountered difficulties at the National Institutes of Health (NIH), their place of employment (Greenberg, 1988).

It should also be noted that the scientific and scholarly community has responded to recent instances of fraud and allegations of misconduct with considerable worry and self-examination, including the establishment by the NIH of a special office to ferret out misconduct (Mervis, 1989). Additionally, the research community's fear of government interference in the laboratory is genuine and well-founded (Jaschik, 1989), and all agree that trust and collegiality remain essential to the research process. But the fact of fraud and dishonest behavior within this collegial, but very pressured, system has been established, and the fate of those who point this out is still often painful (see also the special section on „whistle-blowing" in *The Scientist* [„Special Section," 1987]).

The ethics of collegiality is not a universal ironclad code that renders all who abide by it capable of concealing what are genuine ethical transgressions, but it is, at the very least, a strong reference point quite independent of issues of guilt or innocence. Denial was sufficient defense for the institute librarians (that and at least some redress, after more than two years, in the form of some cataloging for some of the affected articles). Therefore, absent any independent investigation, the issues of evidence as well as turf came to the fore very early as part of the problem of seeking redress. Moran approached, among other groups, the American Library Association (specifically the Office for Intellectual Freedom, through them the Intellectual Freedom Committee, and the Intellectual Freedom Round Table [IFRT]), the International Federation of Library Associations (where they were given a place on the program of the Second European Conference of Art Libraries, if no other official support), and the College Art Association.

Although Moran's correspondence caused not a little discussion in all of these groups, none of them decided that it was appropriate to take specific action, either because they thought it was not their business (especially the American groups), or because of a lack of clarity (from a distance, anyway) about what the evidence proved and just what they were to do about it. As is apparent in the Moran/ Mallory charges, the „selective card cataloging" pattern is inextricably bound up with the larger Guidoriccio controversy, and (again, from a distance) this presents the possibility of motives not only for the censorship but also for the accusation of the misdeed. In the minds of people who may have a responsibility for ethics oversight but still do not know exactly what they are supposed to do anyway, this presents further hurdles. In the wake of the Stewart/Feder (1987) *Nature* article controversy, a number of scientists, including David Baltimore (not himself accused of actual fraud but involved in a controversy surrounding published work emanating from his lab), argue that significant discrepancies that may to outsiders look like fraud were the result of differences of opinion rather than misrepresentation. This is always a possibility in cases of heated controversy especially (again) from a distance. For Moran and Mallory, Stewart and Feder, the evidence may appear unmistakable, but there is a question as to how well some kinds of evidence travel.

The IFRT Executive Committee did approve a very general resolution on „Libraries and the Integrity of Research and Scholarship," inspired in part by the Moran/Mallory experience („be it resolved that the membership of the American Library Association work within and beyond our profession to further cooperation and vigilance in the affirmation of the highest standards of ethics in research and in the sharing of knowledge" [Approved January 8,1989]). This, however, was a very broad statement that did not find approval beyond the ALA round table. The cases and the issues that engendered it have resulted in some discussion about the place of librarians in all of this, however. While that is itself small comfort to Moran and Mallory or others who seek redress or at least support from organizations which are supposed to concern themselves with ethics oversight, it may be a sign that librarians are beginning to see that their role cannot be limited to that of passive shepherds of documents and data, even if this means addressing some very difficult questions surrounding their mediator's role.

Librarians have long involved themselves in the exploration of both the theory and practice of ethics, including the ethical aspects of intellectual freedom. The traditional professional commitment to the care and delivery of the information package, rather than to the nature of its contents, usually serves as an important limitation upon the range of that exploration. Professionals have been nervous, rightly, about any claim that they ought to have a share of responsibility for the actual quality of the information delivered beyond their training in and reliance upon review sources and collection development and organization tools. „Vigilance," the word used in the IFRT resolution on ethics quoted earlier, was chosen in an attempt to assert the responsibility of librarians to maximize access to the best information. However, it conjured up, for some, the old vision of the librarian as a gatekeeper of the House of

John Swan: Ethics Inside and Out. The Case of Guidoriccio 233

Knowledge, censor of that which does not meet a particular standard. This is a genuine danger that requires its own kind of perpetual vigilance, but it does not let librarians off the hook.

Moran and Mallory encountered a situation of a kind that is probably as old as libraries and academic politics, but when they sought an audience for their case, there was no mechanism in place within academia, librarianship, or otherwise adequate to their need adequate, that is, even to give them a forum with the proper authority and opportunity to judge the evidence, no matter what the outcome the reasons for this go beyond the specific problem of a lack of effective ethics oversight, of course; the controversy, of which the indexing issue is a part, is large and messy and getting messier. It has even reached into the latest guidebook for Italy-bound tourists, where the *Guidoriccio* is referred to as „attributed" to Simone Martini:

„In recent years a nasty squable has broken out among art historians," it says, with a quick summary of the Moran/Mallory Position (Hoefer & Barrett, 1989, p. 262). The nastiness now includes accusations of destruction of evidence in the process of restoration, accusations concerning the suppression of a letter to the editor (of *Burlington Magazine)* that was a response to another bitter attack, and many other signs of a scholarly war with more than its share of excesses. Meanwhile, whether or not there was an original intention to suppress their point of view, the co-authors have gained an ever wider following and not a few adherents in part, surely, because of the earlier mentioned „outsider's" persistence.

Whatever their ultimate success, however, librarians are still confronted with the issues of ethics and ethics oversight that Moran and Mallory raised. It may well be that this incident took a shape from the beginning that prevented an effective response by the library community; still it behooves us to examine our place, or lack of place, in the process of articulating and enforcing ethical standards in academic and research institutions. On the level of individual responsibility and practice, there are also important lessons to be learned from the frustrations of Moran and Mallory.

In a thoughtful article on the impact of information technology on professional ethics, Lawson Crowe and Susan Anthes (1988) addressed what they regard as an increase in this professional responsibility:

The academic librarian as information mediator must acquire deeper and broader subject expertise ... and prepare for new information storage and retrieval capabilities. In respect to both technique and substantive content, the mediator must be more directive in relationship to the user. The modern academic librarian must be client-oriented rather than medium-oriented ... in offering bibliographic services, and by discriminating among materials acquired, the academic librarian may stand in the midst of contending interests. It is at this confluence of values that ethical conflicts arise. (p. 126)

The authors are not addressing the kind of conflict examined here, and it could be argued that the responsibilities they describe as new should have always been part of the librarian's code of service, with the new technology only providing extra pressure down the paths of greater content mastery and stronger patron orientation. Their essential argument is very relevant here, however.

Academic librarians, even impressively pedigreed inhabitants of major research institutions, usually find themselves at the fringes of the circle of faculty collegiality. In this uncertain position (uncertain in most cases even if librarians do have „faculty status"), they are particularly vulnerable to the push and pull of the insider-outsider condition. Effectiveness and status increase with greater faculty recognition and cooperation, but it remains important to remember that the patrons are outsider as well as insiders, and professional priorities must take both into account. (A common, if not directly relevant, example is the widespread practice of granting faculty much longer check out periods than students and then charging overdue fines to students but not faculty; there are many who do not even regard this as an ethical issue, not to mention an unfair practice.)

If (and only if) the Moran/Mallory charges are true, the indexers involved arranged their indexing priorities in favor of the insiders in the Guidoriccio controversy. Librarians do receive complaints from faculty members for acquiring books inimical to views of the complainers - a rare occurrence, to be sure (in one of the few personal cases, the faculty member was abjectly apologetic some time after he realized the implications of what he was doing). Librarians are also sometimes under quite understandable pressure to spend more resources and energy in some areas than in others. This is a fact of life in every institution that must support a particular curriculum rather than the broad world of inquiry, but it becomes an ethical trap if it means supporting one side of a controversy within a given field more than another.

With the resources of modern information technology at hand, a librarian can compensate for virtually any under-representation of significant points of view in the local collection. But this presupposes an awareness that there are other points of view in the first place. As the experience of Nicole Squires (1987), described earlier, indicates, it is not enough to assume that the patron will have that awareness.

The difficult truth is that librarians must be both neutral champions of access to all points of view and advocates for the important views that are suppressed or unrepresented. This means that they must worry about the inside as well as the outside of the information package. In most cases the preparation given to become effective information providers is narrow and inadequate for these challenges. What people do or do not do with the information made available may be beyond the ethical purview (in the vast majority of cases, anyway), but there is a responsibility for the quality and comprehensiveness of the information upon which they do or do not act. If the immense fracas that began on an old wall, in Siena has no other relevance for librarians, it at least carries the vital lesson that this responsibility does indeed have serious ethical implications. More is expected of librarians than they are in the habit of giving.

References

Crowe, L., & Anthes, S. H. (1988). The academic librarian and information technology: Ethical issues. College & Research Libraries, 49(2), 123-130.

Greenberg, D. S. (1988). Lab-scam: How science goes bad. The Washington Post, Sunday, April 24, D3-D6.

Hoefer, H., & Barrett, K. (Eds.). (1989). Insight guides: Italy. Hongkong: APA Publicalions.

Intner, S. S. (1984). Censorship in indexing. The Indexer, 14(2), 105-108.

Jaschik, S. (1989). Congress's interest in ferreting out fraud is misinformed, harmful, say researchers. The Chronicle of Higher Education, June 7, A1, A25.

Lang, S. (1988). Academic, journalistic, and political problems (advertisement). The Chronicle of Higher Education, February 3, B4.

Maginnis, H. B. J. (1988). The „Guidoriccio" controversy: Notes and observations. RACAR, Revue d'art Canadienne. Canadian Art Review, 15(2), 137-144.

Mallory, M., & Moran, G. (1986). New evidence concerning Guidoriccio. Burlington Magazine, 128, 250-259.

Mervis, J. (1989). NIH establishes office to probe science misconduct. The Scientist, 3(10), 1, 6-7.

Moran, G. (1977). An investigation regarding the equestrian portrait of Guidoriccio da Fogliano in the Siena Palazzo Pubblico. Paragone, 28(333), 81-88.

Moran, G., & Mallory, M. (1986). „Selective card cataloging (or in-house screening of periodical indexing) of art history articles in authors' files, and the potential effects of this „selectivity" on the bibliographical entries relating to specific art historical problems: A case study. In K. Wynia (Ed.), Art periodicals: Papers of the 2nd European Conference of the Art Libraries of IFLA (13-17 October, 1986) (pp. 123-132). Amsterdam: Overleg Kunsthistorische Bibliotheken in Nederland.

O'Connor, F. (1971). Good country people. In The complete stories of Flannery O'Connor, New York: Farrar, Straus and Giroux.

Polzer, J. (1987). Simone Martini's Guidoriccio fresco: The polemic concerning ist origin reviewed, and the Fresco considered as serving the military triumph of a Tuscan commune. RAGAR, Revue d'Art Canadienne, Canadian Art Review, 14(1-2), 16-69.

Special section: Whistle-blowing. (1987). The Scientist, 1(27), 9-12.

Squires, N. (1987). Unpublished paper.

Stewart, W., & Feder, N. (1987). The integrity of the scientific literature. Nature, 325 (January), 207-214.

Watson, P. (1986). The well-shaken Martini. The Observer, (London), February 15, 4.

Wohl, A. S. (1984). In Siena, an old masterpiece challenged, a new one discovered. News from RILA, 2(February), 1, 11-13.

Infoethics for Leaders: Models of Moral Agency in the Information Environment[*]

von Martha Montague Smith

Abstract

Infoethics, the ethics of information systems, can offer insights and methods to understand the problems which leaders in the information professions face. As moral agents (ethical selves) who assume responsibility in their personal, private, professional, and public lives, information professionals balance conflicting loyalties. In the workplace, they negotiate between the ideals and realities of their institutions and of the profession in making decisions. In the global information environment, leaders will be needed to use the tools of ethical analysis for shaping policy.

In the title story of The Abilene Paradox, the author, Jerry Harvey (1988) his wife, his mother-in law, and his father-in-law go to Abilene, Texas, one hot July afternoon „in an unairconditioned 1958 Buick" (p. 13). They discover later that none of them had wanted to go. Why then did they go to Abilene? They went because they misunderstood each other. All had wanted to stay home, but they had not communicated their desires honestly. The author uses this story to illustrate the problem of managing agreement in organizational life. He says that agreement is much harder to manage than conflict because most people fear revealing their real opinions if they think that their views are contrary to those of the prevailing group. Too often, according to Harvey, members of „organizations fail to accurately communicate their desires and/or beliefs to one another" and thus there is a „misperceiving of the collective reality." In private, members may actually agree on the solution to a certain problem, but this is not communicated effectively (p. 16).

Harvey's story provides an appropriate introduction to the present discussion of ethics and leadership. Here it will be suggested that ethics offers traditions of analysis and methods which leaders can use in facing an uncertain future. The need to question assumptions and the shaping of intellectual tools for approaching controversial issues are both part of the rich heritage of ethics. In the past fifty years, for example, ethicists have confronted challenging new issues in medicine. More recently, the environment has become an arena for ethical inquiry. So too will the future of information and those who manage information resources be proper subjects for ethical analysis.

---

[*] Reprinted with permission from Library Trends, Vol. 40, No. 3, pp. 553-570. Copyright ©1992 by The Board of Trustees of the University of Illinois.

Ethics raises the big questions. What is good? What is just? Ethical analysis is designed for weighing competing factors. What is the best of the good? What is the worst of the bad? Ethical inquiry presses to the principles and foundations of both agreement and conflict. What are the goals? How are ends related to means? Applied ethics, such as bioethics or environmental ethics, moves these questions into the private and public arenas. Issues such as the right of an individual to refuse medical treatment or a company's responsibility to clean up an environmental pollutant illustrate the role of applied ethics in society. Similarly, as information has become a recognized commodity and source of power (Toffler, 1990), the need to address information issues, such as access and privacy, in a systematic way has been acknowledged by many. Thus, these are some of the questions which may be posed:

1.) What are the biggest questions concerning information? What is the relationship between information and the good of society? Justice? Who will decide the future of information?

2.) What should be the relationship between the many information professions and the public consumers of information? Is a new megaprofessional code needed? A new government information agency?

3.) How are codes and other statements of purpose and policy to be used in ethical inquiry and to address problems (Lindsey & Prentice 1985; Finks, 1991)?

4.) How shall professionals be prepared and sustained to ask the big questions about options for the future (White, 1989)?

5.) What sources can be used and what research can be encouraged to offer insights into these matters? (Ellul, 1964 and 1990; Florman, 1981)?

6.) Is it appropriate for information professionals to raise these questions in public forums (Doctor, 1991)?

That leaders in libraries and information services must be participants in planning for the future by asking such hard questions is the burden of this article. It is assumed that a better understanding of the field of ethics can help leaders ask better questions and make the best decisions.

Ethics, for the purpose of this discussion, does not refer to codes or to a particular morality but to a discipline of study and a process of reflection which leads to the clarification of assumptions and alternatives. The pursuit of ethical understanding, especially in applied areas, often calls for multidisciplinary approaches. One example of this is found in programs of Science, Technology, and Society (Cutcliffe, 1983; Reynolds, 1987) where engineers, physicists, theologians, and public administrators work together. Ethical concerns in library and information science (Brown, 1990) have been diverse and include issues of censorship (Demac, 1988), threats to privacy, (Gerhardt, 1990), reference service (Hardy, 1990), vendor relations, (Sugnet, 1986), questions of equity (Doctor, 1991), and access to government information (Schmidt, 1989). Hard issues such as defining areas of responsibility for electronic technologies (Jonas, 1984) and defining freedom in a new environment (Pool, 1983) have also been topics for ethical inquiry. All these areas are relevant to current discussions of democracy, literacy, and productivity - the theme areas for the 1991 White House Conference on Information and Library Service.

The field of ethics offers a variety of frameworks for examining information technology in relation to the future of humanity (Iannone, 1987). Diverse philosophical traditions, including the contributions of Bacon, Hume, Marx, Heidegger, Whitehead, and others have been explored in recent scholarship (Ferre, 1988). The many approaches provide no easy answers. Increasing activity in the philosophy and ethics of technology, however, suggests broad interest in these issues (Kranzberg, 1980; Durbin, 1987; Ihde, 1990).

The term *infoethics* is used here to unite under one term a wide variety of concerns. Like bioethics, which considers ethical issues and living systems, infoethics examines ethical issues and information systems. As, for example, bioethics addresses genetic engineering, infoethics addresses the engineering of information systems as these systems influence individual welfare and the public good. Like bioethics which moves beyond medical ethics and the professional ethics of doctors and nurses, infoethics includes but is not confined to the professional ethics of librarians, information specialists, and those in related fields. Infoethics encompasses computer ethics, (Johnson, 1985) media ethics, (Christians, 1987) library ethics, (Hauptman, 1988) and networking ethics, (Gould, 1989). To summarize, infoethics addresses the use of information in relation to human values. Who should control information? What is information justice? Is there a citizen's right to know? How are conflicting claims of personal privacy and public health to be mediated? Just as health professionals have a responsibility to participate in such debates, information professionals must also become involved.

Models of Moral Agency

The models presented here illustrate one way to understand the various roles which information professionals play. They present the individual and the organization as parts of a larger information environment. The purpose of these models is to show that each individual is a moral agent. The models highlight aspects of loyalty and show that both individuals and groups negotiate among several spheres of experience. A brief overview of the models begins with Model 1- *The Ethical Self,* which describes the information professional, as a moral agent, who has a variety of experiences which influence behavior and decision-making. Model 2 focuses on the loyalties of the information professional on the job. Model 3 explores the relationship between ideals and realities in the working world. Finally, Model 4 shows the Ethical Self and the Professional within the larger context of the Information Environment and the place of infoethics within this Infosphere.

These models, therefore, demonstrate the complex roles of the professional at various levels, including public policy making (Kelly, 1990). Again information professionals share with medical and other professionals the potential for conflicting loyalties. For example, in debates over abortion or the right to die physicians and other medical professionals are also citizens, parents, and mortal human beings. Their expertise is needed, but they can not be disinterested parties as they contribute to public debates. In addition, experts must be accountable to the public without sacrificing too greatly their responsibilities to their professions (Kultgen, 1988; Bayles, 1989). Information professionals' role in shaping policy may be an even more complex issue. Many more people in society claim expertise about libraries, education, or information. Others have money and power at stake in the controversies about access and control of information.

Librarians and Information Professionals as Moral Agents

As defined here, all information professionals are moral agents who think, make decisions, and act according to their self-understanding, which includes personal, private, professional, and public dimensions. Robert Coles, the Harvard child psychiatrist, (1986) argues for an awareness of the moral life of the professional. To illustrate, he recalls his experience as a medical student in analysis. Regularly, young Coles would go to the plain, sparsely furnished office of his analyst, who believed in a value-free, artifact-free setting, which was designed not to distract patients from their problems or give them any hints about the personality of the analyst. However, the office itself was located in the midst of expensive real-estate and was itself in a lavish high-rise apartment complex. Coles uses this example to explain why he disputes „the notion that our personal values, our moral ideals and ethical standards occupy a separate realm" (p. 38). Many others, from Harlan Cleveland (1985, 1986) and Robert K. Greenleaf (1977) to Max Depree (1989) and John Heider (1986) suggest that leaders are those whose own values, beliefs, and loyalties can be effectively translated into institutional form.

One way to describe these beliefs, values, and loyalties is presented in the model of *The Ethical Self.* (see Figure 1) This model was influenced initially by Ulric Neisser's analysis of the self and more recently by Joseph Margolis' description of the Technological Self (1989). Neisser, (1989) describes „five different kinds of information on which self-knowledge is based."

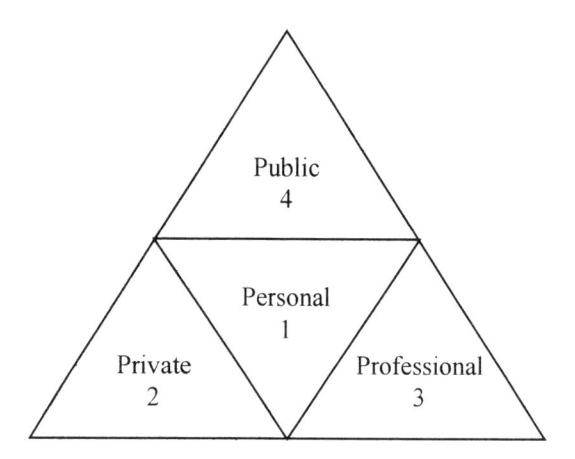

```
              /\
             /  \
            / Public \
           /    4    \
          /-----------\
         /\   Personal  /\
        /  \     1     /  \
       /Private\    /Professional\
      /    2    \  /      3       \
     /_____\/_____\
```

Figure 1. The ethical self

Neisser's view of self-knowledge includes 1.) „the ecological self, which is the self that we know through direct perception," 2.) „the interpersonal self, which we know through the immediate interactions we have with other people," 3.) „the extended self that we know as a result of information stored in memory about what we have done and expect to do," 4.) „the private self, which we know by virtue of internal mental experiences that no one else shares, and 5.) „the conceptual self, which is the self that we have concepts and theories about" (pp. 1-2).

In Model 1, The Ethical Self has four aspects - the Personal, the Private, the Professional, and the Public. The four aspects function together. The triangle of the Ethical Self fits into the larger world, represented by the circle, which for this discussion represents the Information Environment but also indicates that the self functions within the much larger world. Thus, Model 1 illustrates the four major areas of experience from which values arise. Harmony and congruence among the four areas is the ideal. However, in facing most decisions, persons must negotiate among conflicting claims. In a time of rapid change, the individual may have special difficulty maintaining the balance among the four parts. The individual must act as a unit, negotiating among the parts. The resulting psychic conflicts and how they are resolved would be a good starting point for further study. The concern here, however, is to provide a model which can be used by information professionals to understanding why some conflicts arise and to suggest resolutions through discussion and compromise among Ethical Selves.

As Personal Self, the self experiences the world as a person of a certain age and gender, with certain likes, dislikes, and feelings. As the Private Self, each person knows the world through relationships and affiliations, with family, friends, clubs, and support networks. As the Professional Self, a person identifies with the profession, its values and goals, and learns about the self in a professional group from the reactions of others. As the Public Self, each individual is a member of many public communities- the town or city, the state and nation. Thus, the individual occupies a place within the larger community, as, for example, a patron of the arts or sports enthusiast. As an ethical self who exerts moral agency through each of these dimensions of experience, the information professional will inevitably face conflicts. Model 2 (see Figure 2) illustrates in more detail the conflicting allegiances of the Professional Self.

The Professional Ethical Self: Conflicting Loyalties

Model 2 (see Figure 2) illustrates the multiple loyalties of the professional person.

1. *Loyalty to Self* - to personal integrity, to job security, to personal responsibilities, to social responsibilities defined by the individual.

2. *Loyalty to Clients/Patrons* - to clients' information and general welfare, to freedom of access, to patrons' privacy, to serving patrons' needs.

3. *Loyalty to the Profession* - to maintain professional standards of service, to promote the good of the profession as a whole by working to raise the status within society, to raise the awareness of the public to issues identified by the profession.

4. *Loyalty to the Employing Institution* - to uphold the goals and priorities of the institution, to honor contract obligations, to promote the good of the organization through loyalty to colleagues and administration.

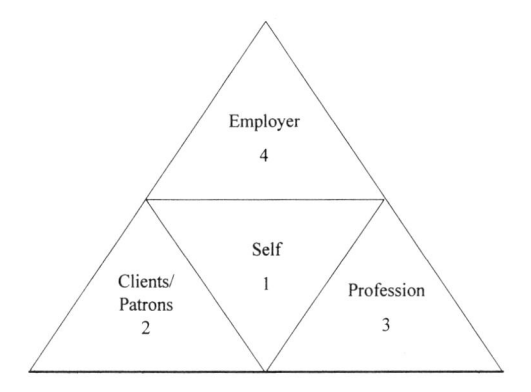

Figure 2. Loyalties of the information professional

Model 2 then presents the multiple loyalties of the person as a *Professional Ethical Self*. Again the triangle is divided into four parts, each impinging upon the others. This model was developed from reflection on The Potter Box (see Figure 5) presented by Clifford Christians and others in *Media Ethics* (1987). Originated by Dr. Ralph Potter of the Harvard Divinity School and named by Dr. Karen Lebacqz of the Pacific School of Religion, the box was created and has been elaborated to define „four dimensions of moral analysis" and serve as an „aid...in locating those places where most misunderstandings occur" (p. 3). This method of analysis also moves the person through the decision-making process even if the decision must be reassessed and the four steps taken again. The Potter Box includes four steps: 1.) defining the problem, 2.) identifying the values at stake, 3.) considering the ethical principles involved, and 4.) defining and prioritizing loyalties and reaching a decision (pp. 3-7).

Of particular usefulness in defining Model 2 (see Figure 2) is Step 4 of the Potter Box analysis (Figure 6). For example, if a librarian is asked by a city official to monitor circulation records to aid in the investigation of illegal manufacturing of drugs, then Steps 1, 2, and 3 of the Potter Box analysis can be quickly covered. The problem, the values, and the principles are quite familiar to most librarians. However, which loyalty will have priority? To the employing institution? Could the librarian loose the job? To the patron? To professional standards which defend the privacy of patron records? To the librarian himself or herself who is a citizen of the community and therefore potentially harmed by drug activity and also by unchallenged police policies? Model 2 and the Potter Box make clear the challenges of analysis and the necessity of discussion and debate (Hauptman).

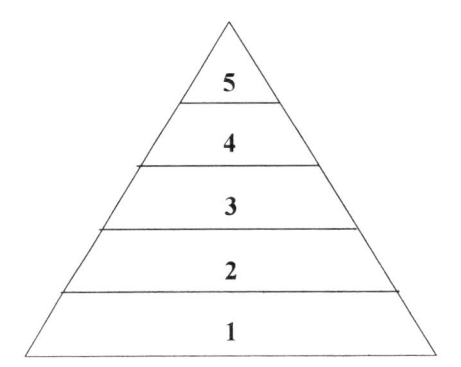

Figure 3. Levels of ethical orientation

In summary, Models 1 and 2 suggest that the processes of decision making are complex, involving the whole person, and resulting from combining the wisdom of the past, knowledge about the present, a realistic assessment of the self and others with balancing of loyalties. With the notion of the Ethical Self as Professional, the role of professional ethics and of statements which have long defined the commitments of the field are placed in the a larger context of the total environment of decisions and meaning. If indeed ethical selves are guided by personal, private, or public experiences and by loyalties to self, clients, and the employing institution, the role of professional ethics may appear to be smaller than when it is considered the main guiding force of the profession. However, as has been argued here, the best leaders may be those who act out of the totality of their experience and also encourage others to do so. Thus, the challenge for the future would be to help potential leaders integrate professional ethics into their Ethical Self-Concepts. This means that the profession should welcome persons with diverse backgrounds and strengths and should encourage efforts to present the claims of professional ethics in a way that encourages involvement with the issues and an openness to debate and even disagreements. The aim then is not to create clones but to nurture thinking, judgment, and integrity (Daniel, 1986). These leaders of the future would have knowledge and skill to enter persuasively into dialogues both within institutions and in the public arena.

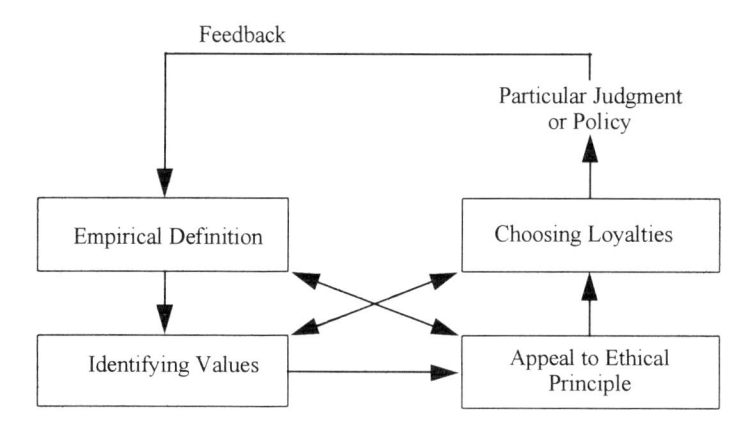

```
                    Feedback
         ┌─────────────────────────────┐
         │                             │
         ▼                  Particular Judgment
                               or Policy
                                    ▲
  ┌──────────────────┐      ┌──────────────────┐
  │ Empirical Definition │      │ Choosing Loyalties │
  └──────────────────┘      └──────────────────┘
         │     ╲       ╱            ▲
         │      ╳                    │
         ▼     ╱       ╲             │
  ┌──────────────────┐      ┌──────────────────┐
  │ Identifying Values │─────▶│ Appeal to Ethical │
  │                    │      │     Principle      │
  └──────────────────┘      └──────────────────┘
```

Figure 5. The Potter Box. *Source:* Media Ethics: Cases and Moral Reasoning (3d ed.) by Clifford G. Christians, Kim B. Rotzoll, Mark Fackler.

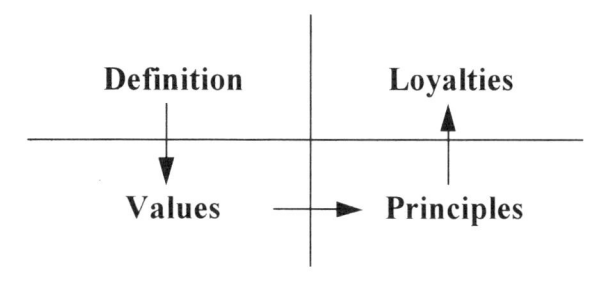

```
   Definition    │   Loyalties
        │        │        ▲
        ▼        │        │
   ─────────────┼─────────────
                 │
   Values    ───┼──▶  Principles
                 │
```

Figure 6. The Potter Box analysis. *Source:* Media Ethics: Cases and Moral Reasoning (3d ed.) by Clifford G. Christians, Kim B. Rotzoll, Mark Fackler.

Levels of Ethical Orientation in the Workplace

Model 3 (see Figure 3) describes possible relationships among various ethical selves in the workplace by defining five levels of ethical orientation. These levels of orientation focus on the interplay between the goals of the organization, such as those found in mission statements or codes of ethics, and the realities of working life. Model 3 is intended to be a very practical model which shows how vision statements and codes may become inoperative especially in uncertain times. It also shows how the value systems of individuals interact within the organization or profession. Like Models 1 and 2, Model 3 offers a framework to consider how and why decision are made and why there may be tensions within an organization or a profession. It also explains why there are so many different interpretations of goals and why mission statements or codes of conduct may need to be rethought and rearticulated as institutional life changes.

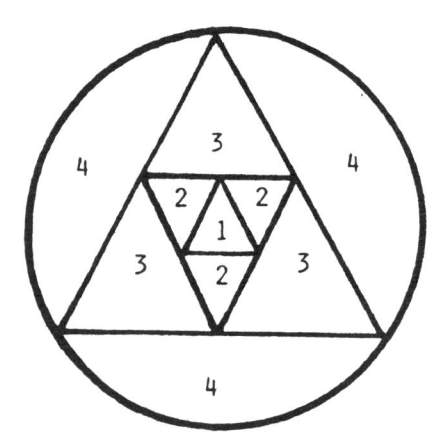

Figure 4. Ethical selves in the global information environment

Level 5 - Ideal Ethics. Highest goals and aspirations of a group or of an individual, ex. codes, mission statements, company goals and purpose statements; Harmony at all levels; Values affirmed by larger society. For example, many official statements and community policies address censorship issues. Librarians are expected to oppose censorship and most often receive professional support and general societal affirmation for doing so.

Level 4 - Practical Working Ethics. Not as grand as Ideal Ethics but consistent with high aspirations; Institutional objectives and personal/professional goals are mutually supportive; Practical orientation, can withstand the stresses of the workplace and the complexities of a changing environment; Flexibility and adaptability. For example, although librarians fight censorship and defend the patron's right to read, a librarian uses judgment both in selection and in promotion of materials. Influenced by community standards and personal beliefs, librarians can exert much influence in the selection and promotion process and may not balance collections appropriately. If personal factors impinge too greatly, it could be called „self- censorship" and be seen as contrary to professional ethics.

Level 3 - Pressure Ethics. Internal or external pressure begins to separate the institutional or professional purposes from the goals of the people on the job; Loyalty to institution/ profession remains but is strained, ex. potential layoffs, changes in ownership or management, introduction of new technologies. Temporary conflict between personal and professional or institutional values, such as a personal crisis such as a divorce or family illness with which the organization is unable to cope. For example, if severe budget pressure brought unusual scrutiny to each item purchased, then librarians might be much more reluctant to purchase controversial materials even if they were personally and professionally certain of its appropriateness for their patrons.

Level 2 - Subversive Ethics. A large or small group of people uphold what they perceive to be worthy goals for the profession or institution by working outside the system of stated or perceived goals. For example, librarians in charge of collection development order gay and Lesbian materials suggested by patrons' but against an unwritten but clear system policy against ordering materials for controversial groups. Or, for example, circulation librarians erase disks „by mistake" after they hear informally that the FBI will order their records to be surrendered.

Level 1 - Survival Ethics. In situations when institutional demands conflict with the basic requirements for employee safety and security or even integrity, individuals may isolate themselves from others in the institution or profession. If the situation worsens, employees will begin to leave or to become detached from the work, from clients, and from colleagues. For example, if librarians were asked to staff a branch library in a dangerous location and they believed that their requests for security personnel were not answered, they might look for other employment. In the meantime, they might come to work armed or keep the doors locked to the building rather than offering service to the clients. Or librarians might organize themselves to protest long hours sitting in front of computer terminals, because they fear the health risks.

In each of these cases, there are important values at stake and complex ethical issues to discuss. Each level upholds justifiable values. The tensions between Level 5 and the others arise out of real situations in the work place and can be the source of productive negotiation.

Model 3 follows the structure of Abraham Maslow's well-known hierarchy of needs (1954) and also reflect the influence of Michael Maccoby's value drives. Maslow's hierarchy includes 5.) Self-actualization needs; 4.) Esteem Needs; 3.) Social Needs; 2.) Safety Needs; and 1.) Physiological Needs. These are all important needs and to Maslow fulfillment of the higher needs usually depends upon the satisfaction of the lower needs.

Maccoby (1988) lists these eight value drives meaning, dignity, play, mastery, information, pleasure, relatedness, and survival. Like Maslow, Maccoby holds that all the needs are important. Model 3 suggests that in order to assure that codes and other statement of purpose are effective in institutions or professions, a variety of needs must be considered. Maccoby's list, Maslow's hierarchy, and Model 3 are not intended to oversimplify the behavior of the individual or the group. Rather they are designed to promote reflection on the relationships among the values and motivations which influence the achievement of the highest goals for all -institutions, professions, and individuals. In particular, Model 3 suggests that codes and similar documents are important but must continually be articulated and interpreted in light of changing conditions and experiences.

Ethical Selves in the Global Information Environment

Finally, as librarians and other information professionals understand themselves as moral agents- as ethical selves- working in complex environments, they can indeed expect to influence policy making both within and outside their organizations. As they perceive themselves as members of the larger Information Environment or Infosphere, they will need to negotiate among competing interests and to assert their professional expertise in a constructive and forceful manner.

In the future, will these professionals be regulated from the top by a megaprofessional organization, such as a combination of ALA, ASIS, and others? Probably not. The diversity of the issues suggest a much more fluid model, with competing and cooperating groups seeking to build consensus among diverse interest groups. With rigorous education in the traditions of librarianship and in the complexities of the information environment, Ethical Selves as information professionals should be well prepared to examine conflicting claims and balance complex objectives. Knowing that the good and the beautiful may appear in many forms to many people and that justice is an illusive goal, the professional of the future may need imagination as well as analysis. Already rich resources are appearing to stimulate debate and to encourage librarians, (Lancaster, 1991) computer specialists, (Forester, 1990) and other information professionals (Mintz, 1990) to join in the conversations.

In closing, the work of Robert Coles (1988) again provides insight. This time Coles makes the case for using fiction in teaching ethics in professional education. For example, Coles uses the novels of Charles Dickens with the law students, the poetry of William Carlos Williams with the physicians, and writers like Walker Percy and Flannery O'Connor with others. Fiction, for Coles, frees the mind and the heart so that students can identify with others and with their own inner selves. In this way, they learn to raise unanswerable questions and to struggle with meaning beyond the bottom line. Coles' work suggests that those who aspire to be leaders or to prepare leaders for the libraries and information field might do well to sink deeply into poetry, novels, and short stories and to ponder quietly before moving on to action. Just as the ethical heritage can contribute to current understanding so too can the literary heritage (Booth, 1988; Gardner, 1978). These ideas were embodied not long ago in a speech by a young professor from Africa who had come to this country to prepare himself to be an international spokesperson for librarianship. His father, a tribal storyteller, who could not read, kept books in many languages in his home for the children (Abdullahi, 1989). In this setting, linking past and present, a future leader was nurtured. The books in many languages pointed this young man toward a future which continues to unfold. They are treasures and so too is he.

References and Additional Bibliography

Abdullahi, I. H. (1989). Why choose librarianship: An international perspective. Speech delivered at the Golden Anniversary Celebration of the School of Library and Information Sciences. North Carolina Central University, Durham, North Carolina. Fifty years of contributions to North Carolina and the nation, 1939-1989 (September 28-30, 1989).

ALA. Office for Intellectual Freedom and the Intellectual Freedom Committee. (1989). *Intellectual freedom manual.* (3rd Ed.) Chicago: ALA.

Anderson, A. J. (1989, June 15). The FBI wants you-to spy. *Library Journal,* 114, 37-39.

Apel, K. O. (1979). The common presuppositions of hermeneutics and ethics. *Research in Phenomenology, 9,* 35-53.

Barnes, R. F. (1986, April/May). Some thoughts on professional ethics codes. *Bulletin of the American Society for Information Science, 12*(4), 19-20.

Barnes, R. F. (1986, August/September). Professional ethics for information science. *Bulletin of the American Society for Information Science, 12*(6), 23.

Bayles, M. D. (1989). *Professional Ethics.* (2nd ed.) Belmont, CA: Wadsworth.

Bekker, J. (1976). *Professional ethics and its application to librarianship.* Unpublished dissertation, Case Western Reserve University.

Bennett, G. E. (1988). *Librarianship in search of science and identity: The elusive profession.* Metuchen, NJ: Scarecrow.

Berry, J. N. (1987, December). A new social concern of ASIS (Technology is not ethically neutral). *Library Journal, 112*(12), 79-81.

Blixurd, J. C. & Sawyer, E. J. (1984, October). A code of ethics for ASIS: The challenge before us. *Bulletin of the American Society of Information Science, 11*(1), 8-10.

Bolter, J. D. (1984). *Turing's man: Western culture in the computer age.* Chapel Hill, NC: University of North Carolina.

Booth, W. C. (1988). *The company we keep: The ethics offiction.* Berkeley, CA: University of California.

Borchert, D. M. & Stewart, D. (Eds.). (1979). *Being human in a technological age.* Athens, OH: Ohio University.

Borgman, A. (1984). *Technology and the character of contemporary life: A philosophical inquiry.* Chicago: University of Chicago.

Bozeman, P. (Ed.). (1990). *Forged documents: Proceedings of the 1989 Houston conference.* New Castle, DE: Oak Knoll.

Brichford, M. J. (1980). Seven sinful thoughts. *The American Archivist, 43*(1), 13-16.

Brown, G. (1990). *The information game: Ethical issues in a microchip world.* Highlands, New Jersey: Humanities.

Byrne, E. F. & Pitt, J. C. (Eds.). (1989). *Technological transformation: Contextual and conceptual implications. Philosophy and technology*, 5. Boston: Kluwer Academic.

Callahan, D. & Jennings, B. (Eds.) (1983). *Ethics, the social sciences, and policy analysis.* New York: Plenum.

Capurro, R. (1985, August). *Moral issues in information science.* Stockholm: KTH Library.

Cappuro, R. (1987). Technics, ethics, and the question of phenomenology. *Analecta Husserliana, 22,* 475-481.

Christians, C. (1986). Books in media ethics. In *Two bibliographies on ethics,* by C. Christians and V. Jenson. Minneapolis, MN: Silha Center for the Study of Media Ethics and Law. School of Journalism and Mass Communication. University of Minnesota.

Christians, C. G., Rotzoll, K. B. & Fackler, M. (1987). *Media ethics: Cases and moral reasoning.* (2nd ed.) New York: Longman.

Clarke, J. (1982, Summer). Reference ethics: Do we need them? *The Reference Librarian* (Special issue on Ethics and reference service), *4,* 25-30.

Cleveland, H. (1985). *The knowledge executive: Leadership in an information society.* New York: Truman Talley.

Cleveland, H. (1986). Educating for the information society. In H. F. Didsbury, Jr. (Ed.) *Challenges and opportunities: From now to 2001.* Bethesda, MD: World Future Society.

A code of ethics for archivists. (1980). *The American Archivist, 43*(3), 414-415.

Coles, R. (1986, May/June). Our moral lives. *Society,* 23(4), 38-41.

Coles, R. (1989). *The call of stories: Teaching and the moral imagination.* Boston: Houghton Mifflin.

Crawford, H. (1978). In search of an ethic of medical librarianship. *Bulletin of the Medical Library Association, 66*(3), 331-337.

Crowe, L. & Anthes, S. H. (1988, March). The academic librarian and information technology: Ethical issues. *College and Research Libraries, 49*(3), 123-130.

Cutcliffe, S. H. (Ed.). (1983). *The machine in the university: Sample course syllabi for the history of technology and technology studies.* Bethlehem, PA: Lehigh University, Science Technology, and Society Program.

Daniel, E. H. (1986). Educating the academic librarian for a new role as information resource manager. *Journal of Academic Librarianship, 11*(6), 360-364.

Demac, D. A. (1990). *Liberty denied: The current rise of censorship in America.* (Rev. Ed.) New Brunswick, NJ: Rutgers.

Dennett, D. C. (1986). Information, technology, and the virtues of ignorance. *Daedalus, 115*(3), 135-153.

Depree, M. (1989). *Leadership is an art.* New York: Doubleday.

Doctor, R. D. (1991). Information technologies and social equity: Confronting the revolution. *Journal of the American Society for Information Science, 42*(3), 216- 228.

Drabenstott, J. (Ed.). (1986, Winter). The consultant's corner: A forum on ethics in the library automation process. *Library Hi Tech, 4*(4), Issue 16, 107-119.

Durbin, P. (Ed.). (1987). *Technology and responsibility. Philosophy and technology,* 3. Boston: Reidel.

Durkheim, E. (1958). *Professional ethics and civic morals.* New York: Free Press.

Durrance, J. C. (1983, Spring). The generic librarian:Anonymity vs. accountability. *RQ, 22*(3), 278-283.

Ellul, J. (1964). *The technological society.* New York: Knopf.

Ellul, J. (1990). *The technological bluff.* Grand Rapids, MI: Eerdmans.

Erlich, M. (1955). A puzzling problem. (Crossword puzzles and other contests). *Wilson Library Bulletin, 30*(4), 326-333.

Ferré, F. (1988). *Philosophy of technology.* Englewood Cliffs, NJ: Prentice-Hall.

Finks, L. W. (1991, January). Librarianship needs a new code of professional ethics. *American Libraries, 22*(1), 84-88.

Florman, S. C. (1981). *Blaming technology: The irrational search for scapegoats.* New York: St. Martin's.

Forester, T. & Morrison, P. (1990). *Computer ethics:Cautionary tales and ethical dilemmas in computing.* Cambridge, MA: MIT.

Frankel, M. S. (Ed.). (1988). *Science, engineering and ethics: State-of-the-art and future directions.* Washington, DC: Office of Scientific Freedom and Responsibility, American Association for the Advancement of Science.

Gardner, J. (1978). *On moral fiction.* New York: BasicBooks.

Gerhardt, L. N. (1990, June). Ethical back talk, III:Librarians must protect each user's right to privacy with respect to information sought or received, and materials consulted, borrowed, or acquired (fending off the FBI is easier than stonewalling a concerning parent or teacher). *School Library Journal, 36,* 4.

Gould, C. C. (Ed.). (1989). *The information web: Ethical and social implications of computer networking.* Boulder, CO: Westview.

Greenleaf, R. (1977). *Servant leadership.* New York: Paulist.

Greiner, J. M. (1989, March/April). Professional views:Intellectual freedom as a professional ethic. *Public Libraries, 28*(2), 69-72.

Gurnsey, J. (1986, Winter). A U.K. code of practice for consultants: A partial solution. *Library HiTech, 4* (4), Issue 16, 59-62.

Haines, H. E. (1946, June 15). Ethics of librarianship. *Library Journal, 71*(12), 848-851.

Hardy, G. J. & Robinson, J. S. (1990, Fall). Reference service to students: A crucible for ethical inquiry. *RQ, 30* (1), 82-87.

Harvey, J. B. (1988). *The Abilene paradox and other meditations on management.* Lexington, MA: Lexington.

Hauptman, R. (1976). Professionalism or culpability? An experiment in ethics. *Wilson Library Bulletin, 50* (8), 626-627.

Hauptman, R. (1987, May/June). Iconoclastic education: The library science degree. *Catholic Library World, 58*(6) 252-253.

Hauptman, R. (1988). *Ethical challenges in librarianship.* Phoenix, AZ: Oryx Press.

Heidegger, M. (1977). *The question concerning technology and other essays.* W. Lovitt (Trans.) New York: Harper Torchbooks.

Heider, J. (1986). *The Tao of leadership: Leadership strategies for a new age.* New York: Bantam.

Holleman, M. (1989). Professional ethics and community college librarians. *Community and Junior College Libraries, 6*(2), 1-7.

Horn, D. E. (1989, Winter). The development of ethics in archival practice. *American Archivist, 52*(1), 64-71.

Iannone, A. P. (Ed.). *Contemporary moral controversies in technology.* New York: Oxford University.

Ihde, Don. (1990). *Technology and the lifeworld: From garden to earth.* Bloomington, IN: University of Indiana.

Johnson, D. G. (1985). *Computer ethics.* Englewood, NJ: Prentice-Hall.

Johnson, D. G. & Snapper, J. W. (1985). *Ethical issues in the use of computers.* Belmont, CA: Wadsworth.

Jonas, H. (1984). *The imperative of responsibility: In search of an ethics for the technological age.* Chicago: University of Chicago Press.

Kelly, M. (Ed.). (1990). *Hermeneutics and critical theory in ethics and politics.* Cambridge, MA: MIT.

Knoll, S. B. (1982). The responsibility of knowledge: Humanistic perspectives in information management. In E. H. Boehm and M. K. Buckland (Eds.) *Education for information management.* Santa Barbara, CA: International Academy.

Kostrewski, B. J. & Oppenheim, C. (1980). Ethics in information science. *Journal of Information Science, 1* (5), 277-283.

Kranzberg, M. (Ed.). (1980). *Ethics in an age of pervasive technology.* Boulder, CO: Westview.

Kultgen, J. H. (1988). *Ethics and professionalism.* Philadelphia: University of Pennsylvania.

Lancaster, F. W. (Ed.). (1991). *Ethics and the librarian. Allerton Park Institute,* 31. Urbana-Champaign, IL: University of Illinois.

Libraries in the Tradition of Freedom of Expression. (1989, Winter) Special Issue of *The Bookmark,* 47(2), State Library of the State of New York.

Lindsey, J. A. & Prentice, A. E. (1985). *Professional ethics and the librarian.* Phoenix, AZ: Oryx.

MacCormac, E. R. (1983). Values and technology: How to introduce ethical and human values into public policy decisions. *Research in Philosophy and Technology.* (Vol. 6, pp. 143-156). Greenwich, CT: JAI.

McCoy, M. (1982, Summer). Bibliographic overview: The ethics of reference service. *The Reference Librarian* (Special issue: *Ethics and reference service*), *4*, 157-162.

Maccoby, M. (1981). *The leader: A new face for American management.* New York: Ballantine Books.

Maccoby, M. (1988). *Why work: Leading the new generation.* N.Y.: Simon and Schuster.

Margolis, J. (1989). The technological self. In E. F. Byrne & J. C. Pitts (Eds.). *Technological transformation: Contextual and conceptual implications.* (pp. 1-15) The Netherlands: Kluwer Academic. Also in Margolis, J. (1989). *Texts without referents: Reconciling science and narrative.* New York: Oxford.

Maslow, A. (1954). *Motivation and personality.* New York: Harper and Row.

Meadows, J. (1983). Social limitations on the use of new information technology. *Journal of Information Science*, *6*(1), 11-20.

Miller, J. H. (1987). *The ethics of reading.* New York: Columbia University.

Mintz, A. P. (1984). Information practice and malpractice: Do we need malpractice insurance? *ONLINE*, *8*(4), 20-26.

Mintz, A. P. (Ed.). (1990). *Information ethics: Concerns for librarianship and the information industry.* (Proceedings of the twenty-seventh annual Symposium of the Graduate Alumni and Faculty, Rutgers School of Communication, Information, and Library Studies, April 14, 1989.) Jefferson, NC: McFarland.

Mitcham, C. & Huning, A. (Eds.). (1986). *Philosophy and technology II: Information technology and computers in theory and practice. Boston studies in the philosophy of science*, 90. Dordrecht, Holland: D. Reidel.

Neisser, U. (1989). The ecological approach to cognitive psychology. III. Concepts and self-concepts *Communicationi Scientifiche 1: Psicologia Generale.* (pp. 1-29). Rome.

1984: Challenges to an Information Society. (1984).(Proceedings of the 47th ASIS Annual Meeting, Philadelphia, Pennsylvania, October 21-25, 1984) (Volume 21). White Plains, NY: Knowledge Industry.

Peterson, K. G. (1983, July). Ethics in academic librarianship: The need for values. *The Journal of Academic Librarianship*, *9*(3), 133-137.

Pool, I. de S. (1983). *Technologies of freedom.* Cambridge, MA: Press of Harvard University.

Rainey, N. B. (1988). Ethical principles and liability risks in providing drug information at the Philadelphia College of Pharmacy and Science. *Med.. Ref. Service Quarterly*, *7*(3), 59-67.

Rawls, J. (1971). *A theory of justice.* Cambridge, MA: Harvard University.

Reynolds, T. S. (Ed.). (1987, March). *The machine in the university: Sample course syllabi for the history of technology and technology studies.* (2nd Ed.) Bethlehem, PA: Science, Technology, and Society Programs of Michigan Technological University and Lehigh University.

Roszak, T. (1986). *The cult of information: The folklore of computers and the true art of thinking.* New York: Pantheon.

Schmidt, C. J. (1989). Rights for users of information conflicts and balances among privacy, professional ethics, law, national security. In *Bowker Annual of Library and Book Trade Annual, 1989-1990* (pp. 83-90). New York: Bowker.

Shields, G. R. (1990). Ethics and the librarian: Taking stock at Allerton. In *The ALA yearbook of library and information services 1990.* (Volume 15, pp. 1-10). Chicago: American Library Association.

Stahl, W. M. (1986, Winter). Automation and ethics: A view from the trenches. *Library Hi Tech, 4* (4), Issue 16, 53-57.

Sugnet, C. (1986, Winter). The vendor's corner: A forum on ethics in the marketplace. *Library Hi Tech, 4*(4), Issue 16, 96-106.

Swan, J. & Peattie, N. (1989). *The freedom to lie: A debate about democracy.* Jefferson, N C: McFarland.

Toffler, A. (1990). *Powershift: Knowledge, wealth,* and *violence at the edge of the 21st century.* New York: Bantam.

Traber, M. (1986). *The myth of the information revolution: Social and ethical implications of communication technology.* Beverly Hills, CA: Sage.

Turkel, S. (1984). *The second self: Computers and the human spirit.* New York: Simon and Schuster.

Watt, T. J. (1987). *Ethics of information science.* (P 2092) Monticello, IL: Vance Bibliographies.

Webster, F. & Robins, J. (1986). *Information technology: A Luddite analysis.* Norwood, NJ: Ablex.

White, H. S. (1989). *Librarians and the awakening from innocence: A collection of papers.* Boston: G.K. Hall.

White, H. S. (1990, January). My truths are more moral than your biases (Reply to H. T. Blanke). *Library Journal 115*(1), 72.

Woodward, D. (1989, Fall). Teaching ethics for information professionals (Developed and taught at Drexel University). *Journal of Education for Library and Information Science, 30*(2), 132-135.

Zimmerman, J. (Ed.) (1983). *The technological woman: Interfacing with tomorrow.* Westport, CT: Praeger/Greenwood.

3. Ethische Fragen in der Informationpraxis

3.3 Ethische Fragen in Lehre und Forschung

Ethics in information science[*]

von B.J. Kostrewski und Ch. Oppenheim

Ethical questions in information science research, teaching and practice are considered. It is recommended that supervisors of research make clear their publication policies before a piece of research is undertaken and if they don't wish to publish, then the junior author should have the right to write up the work. In any case, papers should be in alphabetical order of authors. Certain areas of research should possibly not be attempted because of their possible implications. Bias in teaching is considered. The following problems in information work are considered: the unauthorised use of work facilities, the confidentiality of inquiries, bias in results presented and many aspects of the social responsibility of an information scientist. It is concluded that inquiries should always remain confidential, but that information scientists should be willing to divulge non-confidential matter to bonafide third parties and should be prepared to reveal confidential matter if the public interest warrants it. No information scientist should be asked to present biased or misleading results. There is a need for a code of ethics for information scientists, and information scientists need to be far more aware of ethical questions.

Background

American librarianship journals devote a considerable proportion of their text to questions of professional responsibility and ethics, but the literature of information science shows no such preoccupation. Before discussing the question of ethics in information science, the literature relating to ethics in librarianship and information work is reviewed.

We would like to thank Maureen Nolan, Paul Randall and Martin White for their comments on an earlier draft of this paper. We would also like to thank Baba Adenaike, Lesley Dunlop, Jennifer Eaton, Pamela Harling, Helen Minter, Stephen Robertson and Katy Zammarano for helpful discussions.

Fetros [1] discussed the work of the American Library Association's Code of Ethics Committee. The first code of ethics to be developed appeared in 1938 and since then many follow-up statements and drafts of new codes have been published. Fetros pointed out that the old 1938 code is filled with banalities and platitudes and was generally ignored by most librarians in the USA. It is also far more concerned with keeping all criticisms of library policy to acceptable channels, than in the librarian's duty to society. It does state that a librarian is obliged to treat as confidential any private information obtained from patrons and that a librarian should never use his library's resources to the detriment of the services to its patrons. Finally, the code stresses that impartial service should be rendered to all who use the library [2].

---

[*] Reprint from North Holland Publishing Company; Journal of Information Science 1(1980) 277-283.

Since Fetros wrote this review, the American Library Association has published a new 1975 code of ethics [3]. This code places more emphasis on the free flow of information than the previous code and states that every citizen has a right to free expression and free access to ideas. It reiterates the right to privacy of patrons, and thus circulation records or any other information gained by a librarian in serving a patron is deemed confidential, as in the cases of lawyers and doctors. Confidential information should only be released by court order or with the written permission of the patron(s) concerned. It emphasises the need to avoid personal financial gain at the expense of the employing institution. The code is also concerned with promotions and reference writing.

For a while in the early 1970's, the American Library Association was also concerned with the removal of censorship applied by the US Government and its agencies on publications claimed to be prejudicial to security [4,5]. Since the Watergate scandal and the Freedom of Information Act, these fears seem to have subsided.

The American Library Association is not the only body to have concerned itself with professional ethics; several state library associations have also done so, and the California Library Association draft statement is of interest because it specifically included information scientists in its code of ethics [6]. This statement is primarily concerned with professional standards and in improving libraries, library systems and the profession. It states that the aim of a librarian's activities is to make information accessible to users. In the case of medical, legal or political queries, the librarian has an obligation to provide the patron with information with which he can form a considered opinion. Personal interests or opinions should not be allowed to interfere with the provision of responses and on no account should a query be unanswered. Information services should not be limited to answering questions on demand, and methods such as S.D.I. should further patron's awareness. The draft code also emphasises that a librarian should preserve the confidences and respect the privacy of each client. No judgement should be made on clients' requests and circulation systems should be administered to protect privacy. Another body concerned with ethics is the American Association of Law Libraries. At their 67th Annual Meeting, they devoted a session to the ethical problems of law librarianship [7]. Most of the points made were analogous to those that have been made for other librarians - the need to create a good collection, to maintain financial integrity, no to restrict access to materials, denying access to third parties of circulation records and personnel selection, promotion and training. Difficulties arise on the question of legal advice to third parties and it is emphasised that a law librarian should not engage in the practice of the law. All information given to or requested by third parties should remain confidential.

These are all high ideals, and if they were to be carried out to the letter, then libraries would become the 'convivial tools' that Illich believes they ought to be [8]. In practice, though, many librarians exercise censorship on texts they consider to be morally or politically dubious. Even scientific texts are not immune; what would a librarian do if a user came to him and asked for information on making an explosive device powerful enough to blow up a house? This question was posed to 13 librarians in the USA [9], and interestingly, none refused to supply the information on ethical grounds. The patent literature is known to abound with detailed instructions on, e.g. how to make napalm or nerve gases [10]. How would patent library staff react to a request for such information?

The above discussion should make it clear that ethics for librarians is a subject of considerable interest in the USA, although not elsewhere. However, as we indicated before, little discussion on ethics for information scientists has appeared in print. Rovira and his coworkers [11] wrote an appeal, in Spanish, to the consciences of all information scientists in 1975. They want a code for all those working in information science so that information is circulated honestly and accurately. They also state the principle whereby the professional must not exploit the 'machine' for his own gain and must guarantee the data provided. Stern [12] has argued for the need of information scientists to prevent potential infringement of personal privacy and the dangers of computerised information retrieval systems restricting the free flow of information have been discussed [13-15]. A draft ethics of Service statement appeared in the journal *RQ* recently [16]. It states that information provided to a user shall be as accurate as possible and must be provided impartially. All contacts with users should be treated in confidence and no direct financial gain should accrue to the librarian or information scientist providing the information. No attempt has been made beyond these works to formulate a code of ethics for information scientists.

Ethics in research

„Cheating" in research

It seems to us that in the field of information science, cheating is much less likely to occur than, say, in the biological and physical sciences. For one thing, information science may not be as afflicted by the 'publish or perish' syndrome (or the related 'be cited or perish' syndrome) as some of the harder sciences have been. This is partly because there are simply fewer academics and researchers in information science, but also because information has a much narrower research base than the physical sciences. Because information science is essentially an art and one learns the tricks of the trade, publications based on research findings are relatively few. Furthermore, the theoretical foundations of information science are not well developed and what theories have appeared have been largely borrowed from other disciplines.

Clearly, intellectual dishonesty is not productive in the long term; it leads researchers up false paths and thereby hinders the development of the theoretical basis of the science. Furthermore, at the individual level it impairs career prospects!

Giving credit to co-workers

On the other side of the coin of researchers who cheat in their research is the problem of publications resulting from a piece of work involving senior and junior authors. There are two ethical questions here: should a worthwhile piece of research be written up at all, and if so, by whom? We think that if a supervisor does not wish to publish, then the junior author, i.e. the person who actually carried out the research, should have the right to write up one or more articles based on the research in his/her name *alone*.

The second question concerns the authorship of an article which is published. Acknowledgement of the co-operation of co-workers, regardless of their status is an essential component of the integrity of all types of research. Thus, student projects which are of sufficient substance to warrant publication should give principal credit to the student rather than the supervisor. One simple method is to place the authors in alphabetical order of surname. Indeed there is some evidence that senior authors who adopt this practice are more likely to be awarded a Nobel Prize than those who don't [17].

Areas of research that should not be attempted

Belkin and Robertson [18] have argued strongly that there are certain areas of information science that should not be researched because of their possible implications. In particular they are concerned that the results of research in information science are not transferred into such areas as propaganda, advertising and education in which information is sender-oriented rather than user-oriented. Theoretically it can be argued that once the nature of information transfer is understood and the mechanisms for altering the recipient's image established, this knowledge can then be put to morally undesirable ends, e.g. in the realms of propaganda and manipulation and thus have a profound effect on personal freedom and choice. They consider that influencing people's images without their consent or knowledge is unethical, and that as soon as information science begins to concern itself with questions of changes in the recipient's image, its results become possibly applicable to sender-oriented activities. However, Belkin and Robertson express the hope that in fact information research will not be of any use to sender-oriented systems, but nonetheless they are concerned in case their optimism is unfounded.

They conclude that if need be, theoreticians in information science must be willing to limit their inquiry according to public interest and before developing theories reach a point at which they might be misapplied.

The argument that theoretical research should not be undertaken is, of course, highly debatable, as it is difficult to predict the long-term consequences of particular theoretical advances.

One other point should be made about research in information science. A number of studies involve observing information transfer processes in action or involve questionnaires. In the former case, the researcher should inform whoever he is observing that he is carrying out observations on that person's behaviour. In the second case, results from the questionnaires should be published only in such a way that responses cannot be identified with particular individuals.

Ethics in teaching of information science

A lecturer in any subject is in a unique position to influence his or her students by presenting the information in a biased manner. Perhaps the surest defence against such bias is the long term one of ex-students going into the information science profession and becoming aware that their education has been biased in some way. It must also be said that lectures would be dull indeed if the lecturer did not inject some personal asides and commentary on other people's work.

The above remarks apply to all subjects, of course. Information science at present lacks the theoretical framework which could act as a template against which intellectual dishonesty could be checked, and is in this respect particularly vulnerable. Furthermore, because the subject is so wide-ranging, a teacher has a responsibility to present as total a picture as possible, since witholding information is a form of bias.

Ethics in information work

Use of work facilities

Industry suffers considerable losses each year through theft by its employees. In the field of information work, the possibilities for theft are legion. An information scientist could make use of the information retrieval facilities within his organisation to answer queries wanted for personal reasons, or for paid freelance work. If, say, a particular information officer has access to on-line databases and if he is unlikely to be disturbed when using them, he could carry out searches for other people using his company's password. Such abuse would only be likely to be noticed if the monthly bills showed a sharp rise, or if databases not usually required for company searches were found to be used.

We are sure such unauthorised use of facilities goes on, and we do not see any easy way of controlling such abuse. Any code of ethics should condemn ,any unauthorised use of work facilities.'

Confidentiality of information

Information officers are in a unique position to know their company's current research interests and are also privy to much confidential information on their company's financial interests. It goes without saying that the nature of inquiries should always remain confidential and should not be passed on to any third party without the original requestor's permission. As a general rule *all* requests for information must be regarded as confidential. Equally, an information officer should not be prepared to answer any request for confidential information which originates from outside the company without permission from someone in authority. However, we stress the term confidential. Some firms have adopted a highly unco-operative attitude to the revealing of published information (e.g. the patent number relating to one of their products). Such information could always be obtained by the outside requester, but at some effort. Unless the request involves the information officer in a lot of work, we do not see why such a request should be refused, and co-operation at this level should be encouraged.

A particularly difficult problem arises in the pharmaceutical industry. Frequently, medical information departments in this industry are approached by third parties with questions about side-effects of drugs, recommended dosages, etc. As a general policy, medical information departments decline to issue any such information to third parties without clearance from a senior person within the organisation. In any case, members of the public are never told about, for example side-effects of drugs and the person is advised to consult his doctor instead. Unfortunately, many doctors are not prepared to divulge such information either. The fact remains that in theory a member of the public can get hold of all the published literature of a given drug through his local public library or by paying for on-line searches. We have carried out such searches on particular drugs prescribed by doctors who declined to describe side-effects. It seems very unfair that people trained in searching the literature should be placed at a very considerable advantage over the rest of the public in such an important respect. Should we accept the argument that to provide such information would only cause the spread of alarm because the public won't understand or appreciate the information they are given? Should there be any reason why, if a person is administered a drug, he should not be told what is known about it if he wants such information? If his GP isn't prepared to provide such information, should the pharamceutical company marketing the drug be obliged to?

Bias in information presented

An information scientist may be asked to find some information for the sole purpose of 'knocking' a rival firm or one of its products. What if in the course of his search he finds the product isn't that bad, or, indeed, his company's product is clearly inferior? Information scientists should never be asked to employ their expertise to present biased results, and they should always strive to present a balanced picture evaluating all the literature that is available. If the company objects to such 'balanced' reports and insists on being told only about the material damaging to the rival firm, then the information scientist ought to leave that particular job as soon as possible. A code of conduct should be introduced, which requires an information scientist to present to the best of his ability a balanced picture of the literature he has read, irrespective of how uncomfortable such a picture may be for his employers.

Problems of information brokers

Information brokers, i.e. people who carry out searches (often on-line) for a variety of clients in a variety of organisations and who are paid a fee for each search they do, face some particular ethical problems. Consider a case where such a broker is approached independently by two clients for the same information. Two problems arise here. Firstly, should both firms be charged the full price, should the second client get the report at a reduced price, or should both get the information at reduced price? In both the latter cases it is then evident to each client that someone else has asked for that piece of information. Secondly, some clients insert exclusion clauses whereby information supplied by the broker may not be passed on to third parties. Such exclusion causes could damage the broker's business in that he may have to turn away a potential client.

A second problem for information brokers is pricing policy. In the UK there are a number of bodies (e.g. Aslib and the Science Reference Library) who offer on-line searches at virtually cost price. A commercial information broker has to cover overheads and make a profit and his prices are therefore inevitably higher. On the face of it there might appear to be arguments for prohibiting any body offering on-line searches at anything less than true cost price, including costings for overheads. However, in practice information brokers gain particular areas of expertise in which the more general services cannot compete.

Some on-line database suppliers insist that results obtained on-line may not be passed on to third parties without permission. Such restrictions are unlikely to hamper brokers, as they can often get such permission or even if they cannot, they can always claim they obtained the information from other sources, or from the printed equivalent to the on-line service.

Ethical problems for on-line vendors

Any on-line service faces particular problems regarding confidentiality. Each should ensure, for example, that off-line prints always get sent to the correct address and that records of searches carried out by clients are not maintained. We do know of case where safeguards do not exist.

Some companies protect themselves by surrounding 'sensitive' searches with a number of low priority searches, or by adjusting their search strategy to be close to, but not precisely what their interest is. It is best not to be complacent about this, and firms should continue to protect their interests if they feel this is desirable. We believe any code of ethics should require that on-line vendors be obliged to inform their customers of the sorts of records they keep.

Information as power

There can be no question that some individuals have access to a greater amount of information than others. This applies particularly to large corporations, which, by virtue of their ability to spend money on information are better placed than smaller corporation or individuals. Furthermore, some people are better able to process and assimilate information than others. One implication of the large scale advent of on-line information retrieval is the possibility that on-line vendors or governments would find it easier to restrict or distort the flow of information to some or all of the public [18]. Print on paper is widely available in libraries, is easy to reproduce and a government (even the most repressive) would find it difficult to keep track of who is reading what; equally it would find it difficult to control the spread of such documents. By contrast, computerised systems,being more centralised, allow for the possibility of the recording of search strategies and /or distorting the information flowing to particular customers. The sophistication of such processes also means that relatively poor members of society will find it harder to access such information or to reproduce it. Kent [19] has discussed some of these points and has argued that the way to reduce these dangers is not to turn the clock back, but to develop a profession of information management which will make information and the mechanisms for processing it as widely available as possible. To that end he suggests information scientists should concern themselves not only with technical and economic aspects, but also with political, social and ethical matters. Cawkell has argued on similar lines [20]. We fully endorse Kent's and Cawkell's views. It is time information scientists realised that information, like science is not neutral; in that it can be abused and distorted. In the next section we discuss some specific instances of how information scientists can become more involved in such matters.

Before we leave the question of information as power, one particular area of underprivileged information users should be mentioned. The developing countries have an urgent need of more information to raise their standards of living. This problem is rarely discussed in the information science literature, although the December 1976 issue of *The Information Scientist* created an honourable exception. What the developing countries do not need is highly sophisticated computerised systems without the personnel to handle such systems or the R&D effort to make use of them. They have a need for information that has been analysed and digested and is of immediate value to them and in printed form. There is a need for information scientists in the developed countries to get involved in such work as a matter of urgency.

Does an information scientist have responsibilities to society?

In the course of his duties, an information scientist may be asked to carry out a search on, say, the safety of a particular effluent from one of his company's factories. He may find that his effluent has many dangers and/or that the amounts being discharged exceed legal limits. Has the information scientist any duty to society in such cases? One of us (C.O.) thinks he has, and indeed should feel obliged to make the results known (by anonymous means if need be) to the public. Even if the data includes material which is unpublished and which is (say) held in confidential company files, there is a public duty which overrides the duty of the employee to his company. However this argument is clearly debatable, and indeed one of us (B.J.K.) would not subscribe to the views started here. We both agree that an information scientist has a duty to draw attention to possible consequences to those responsible for these actions. Thus memoranda or notices drawing attention to research results providing evidence of the dangers of a particular product or process should be made. Honesty and integrity demands that views should be made known and that there should be a mechanism which would allow an information scientist to make his fears known both within his company and within the profession. For too long, information scientists in their work have tended to disassociate themselves from the outside world. They need to realise that the consequences of actions taken by their organisations can, and often do, have far-reaching effects on society at large and it is their duty to be aware of such consequences. Information scientists are in a unique position to do this as they are well used to collecting and evaluating scientific information and to summarising it in a concise and readable fashion. We would also like to emphasise a point which is not often made about information science. The information worker is in a unique position in industry. He handles knowledge and has a specialist background, and he is in a position to manipulate the course of research and development. The need for information scientists to have integrity has frequently been underestimated and needs to be stressed.

Conclusions and summing up

Thus the major recommendations in this paper are as follows:

(1) There may be certain areas of information science research, particularly in the area of cognition, where results have the potential to be abused. It could be argued that researchers in such areas should not continue to carry out such research until the possible implications of such research are better understood.

(2) Information scientists should never reveal the nature of any inquiry passed on to them without the express permission of the requestor.

(3) Information scientists should be prepared to give assistance on non-confidential inquiries to outside bodies. They should not be prepared to pass on confidential information if requested by a third party without authority.

(4) Information scientists should never present biased reports or ignore material damaging to their employer's interests.

(5) Information scientists should know that they have a duty to the public as well as to their employer and should be prepared to exercise that duty.

One final question needs to be considered. Should there be a code of ethics for information scientists and, if so, who should administer it and what should be the penalties for failing to abide by this code? A cursory examination of codes of ethics in the world demonstrates that only one sort of code of ethics is enforceable, i.e. those codes prepared by the controlling body of a true profession. By a 'true profession' we mean a group of practitioners, such as lawyers, who have a controlling body which awards some mark of approval without which it is impossible to carry on that practice. Such professional bodies grant exemption to approved courses in their topics, and are usually chartered bodies which allow their members to add letters after their name. These bodies employ codes of ethics and a breach of such a code can, and sometimes does, lead to a practitioner losing his livelihood. The code is meant to ensure that the public can be certain that anyone carrying out that profession maintains high professional standards. Information science is not a profession, and may never be. In no country in the world is it necessary to belong to a given professional society to practice information science. Thus, it would be naive to assume that if a body such as the Institute of Information Scientists were to publish a code of ethics that all members of the Institute would automatically follow it on pain of expulsion from the Institute. However, we do believe the Institute could, and should, prepare a code of ethics in information science. This code would have to be fairly general in its wording, and we hope it would be on the lines we have outlined above, with special sections for on-line vendors, information brokers, etc. Failure to conform to such a code would lead to ostracisation rather than. expulsion. However, the real point of the code would be to commit the Institute to a certain stance in the case of a dispute between an information scientist and his employer on, for example, the question of the presentation of biased information. Also, whatever committee was delegated to prepare a code of ethics, should be available thereafter for advice for any member who approached it. We believe that by taking such a lead, the Institute of Information Scientists will create an awareness of ethics amongst information scientists and will encourage equivalent bodies in other countries to create their own codes of ethics, and thus create a path towards a truly committed profession.

References

[1] J.G. Fetros, The search for a code of ethics, American Libraries 2 (1971) 743-746.
[2] D.R. Brink, Letter to the Editor, RQ 14 (1975) 86.
[3] Anon., 1975 Statement on professional ethics, American Libraries (1977) 500-501.
[4] Anon., Intellectual freedom and the jurisdictional jungle, Library J. 64 (1971) 925-931.
[5] Anon., Intellectual freedom in Chicago, Library J. 65 (1972) 2531-2534
[6] Anon., Draft statement of professional responsibility, RQ 15 (1976) 241-244
[7] Anon., Ethical Problems of law librarianship, Law Library J. 67 (1974) 528-540.
[8] I. Illich, Tools for Conviviality (Fontana, London, 1975)
[9] R. Hauptmann, Professionalism or culpability, Wilson Library Bull. 50 (1976) 626-627.
[10] B. Beckett, Chemical warfare is available to terrorists, New Scientist 80 (1978) 100-102.
[11] C.R. Rovira et al, A basic code of ethics for information science. Informatico e Diritto 1 (1975) 454-475.
[12] D.L. Stern, Computer privacy: issues and analysis, Inform. Scientist 12 (1978) 100-102.
[13] C. Oppenheim, Data banks and democracy, Information Scientist 10 (1976) 166-168
[14] A.E.Wessel, Social use of information (Wiley, New York), (1976).
[15] C. Oppenheim, Essay review, Information Scientist 11 (1977) 32-35.
[16] Anon., Ethics of service draft, RQ 18 (1978), 57.
[17] S.V. Ashton, and C. Oppenheim, A method of predicting Nobel price winners in chemistry, Social Studies in Science 8 (1978) 341-348.
[18] N.J. Belkin and S.E. Robertson, Some ethical and political implications of theoretical research in information science, Paper presented at ASIS Annual Meeting, 1976.
[19] A.K. Kent, Information as power, Aslib Proceedings 31 (1979) 16-20.
[20] A.E. Cawkell, The paperless revolution, Wireless World 84 (1512) (1978) 69-74.

Knowledge and power in information science: toward a discourse analysis of the cognitive viewpoint[*]

von Bernd Frohmann

Abstract

A discourse analysis of the cognitive viewpoint in library and information science (LIS) identifies seven discursive strategies which constitute information as a commodity, and persons as surveyable information consumers, within market economy conditions. These strategies are: (a) universality of theory, (b) referentiality and reification of „images", (c) internalization of representations, (d) insistence upon knowledge, (e) constitution of the information scientist as an expert in image negotiation, (f) radical individualism and erasure of the social dimension of theory, and (g) instrumental reason, ruled by efficiency, standardization, predictability, and determination of effects. The discourse is guided throughout by a yearning for natural-scientific theory. The effect of the cognitive viewpoint's discursive strategy is to enable knowledge acquisition of information processes only when users' and generators „images" are constituted as objectively given natural scientific entities, and to disable knowledge of the same processes when considered as products of social practices. By its constitution of users as free creators of images, of the information scientist as an expert in image interpretation and delivery, and of databases as repositories of unmediated models of the world, the cognitive viewpoint performs ideological labour for modern capitalist image markets.

Introduction: Discourse Analysis

The continuing debate about theory in library and information science (LIS) has, by now, sufficient history to establish „foundations of LIS" as a distinct subject, practiced by a specific coterie of researchers from authorized institutional sites (e.g., the ASIS SIG „Foundations of Information Science"). This debate has often been waged as a confrontation between rival epistemological positions, each claiming to provide the most fruitful theoretical foundation for knowledge production in LIS. This paper deliberately abstains from adjudicating candidates for LIS's most productive knowledge base. Instead, my aim is to contribute, by a discourse analysis of a recent contender in these epistemological rivalries, to an improved understanding of LIS theory.

In her *Powermatics: A Discursive Critique of New Communications Technology*, Marike Finlay provides a useful description of discourse analysis:

> ...discourse analysis is the study of the way in which an object or idea, any object or idea, is taken up by various institutions and epistemological positions, and of the way in

---

[*] Prev. published from ASLIB, London EC1V 9AP in: J. of Documentation, Vol.48 No.4, Dec. 1992, pp.365-386. B. Frohmann: The power of images: a discourse analysis of the cognitive viewpoint.

which those institutions and positions treat it. Discourse analysis studies the way in which objects or ideas are spoken about. (Finlay 1987, 2)

Information, of course, is the chief „object or idea" taken up and spoken about by the various institutions and epistemological positions of LIS. Discourse analysis seeks to reveal hither to unnoticed connections between the ways in which a specific discourse is configured, and identifiable relations of power. This methodology assumes that power operates through and upon discursive formations. In this paper, I suggest that the manner in which information is articulated within LIS theory inscribes specific and identifiable power relations. More precisely, my aim is to show that the recent candidate for theoretical supremacy in LIS, known as the „cognitive viewpoint", consolidates on academic terrain those power relations which constitute information as a commodity, and persons as surveyable information consumers, within market economy conditions. In brief, the claim put forward here is that the cognitive viewpoint performs ideological labour (to borrow a term from Kevin Wilson; Wilson 1988, 4, footnote) for corporate interests.

The Cognitive Viewpoint in LIS Theory

The main features of the cognitive viewpoint can be briefly summarized. It is the view that central theoretical consideration ought to be given to the „cognitive processes" that occur at each pole of typical information-retrieval systems. Information is produced by „generators", each with their „world images", or „knowledge structures". They produce texts with the intention of changing the „„world images" of the recipients who, for their part, pursue information as a result of a perceived „gap" in their own image-structure. Information scientists bring the two together by virtue of their knowledge of both the recipient's need and the information available in the „knowledge store". The generation of this knowledge is the mandate of LIS theory. The following is one of many passages which includes most of these features:

> ...a generator, such as an author, decides to communicate ...his or her state of knowledge or „image" of the world. What the generator knows ... is modified by beliefs, intentions, values ...This modified state of knowledge, the information, is further amended by linguistic and pragmatic rules to become the text ... a user decides to investigate or use some part of his or her state of knowledge with respect to the problem faced. This realization ... becomes a request put to the IR system ... (Belkin 1980a, 135)

Further features of the cognitive viewpoint will become apparent in the following sections of this paper.

The Discursive Context of the Cognitive Viewpoint: Theoretical Desire Speaks Natural Science

The cognitive viewpoint fits a discursive space already prepared for it by a wider discursive context which sets out the appropriate general form of LIS theoretical discourse.

The discursive features of this wider context are available in seven papers by Brookes (1975, 1975a, 1977, 1980, 1980a-b, 1981). He first sets theory firmly within a natural-scientific paradigm by identifying the „four basic needs" of theory as (i) a unique subject area, (ii) a set of basic concepts, (iii) a set of fundamental laws, and (iv) an explanatory theory (Brookes 1975, 115). He then presents a series, an order, a hierarchy, a teleology, and an evolution, referred to as „a continuous spectrum of information processes" (ibid., 119). The dominant metaphor is Shannon's: the elements of the series are variations on the figures of „message stores", „encoding devices", „transmitters", „detectors", „decoders", and „receptors". Throughout, information is spoken of as a natural process, whether the „transmission" of „neural electrical pulses" (Brookes 1975a, 118), or „biochemical transmissions that occur in the cell" (ibid.), or „ranges of physical signals" impinging upon sensory organs. The evolutionary series begins with „physical processes", not excluding „the absorption of energy and nutrients". Food consumption by „simple unicellular creatures" becomes the figure of a primitive information process „the basic Shannon information system limited to two possible discrete signals" (Brookes 1975, 120). When „eventually man emerged from among the higher animals" (ibid., 121), the natural-scientific metaphors continue; human understanding is conceived as a higher-order „information process", a „cognitive interpretation" of „signals" by a „cortex" (ibid., 118; 1975a, 46). The apogee and final telos of this naturalistic movement is the metaphor of the computer as an „exosomatic brain" (ibid., 122), presenting a parallel, in the cognitive realm, to such previously enumerated extensions of sensory faculties as the microscope and telescope (ibid., 122; 1975a, 47). These latter technologies are themselves spoken of as products of a natural evolution of information processes. Indeed, evolution itself is spoken of as „more effective information-gathering, processing and exploiting" (ibid., 121).

The essential rhetorical move in this otherwise harmless and rather quaint narrative is the assimilation of human understanding, and especially the production and use of documents, to processes theorized as natural objects and events. The rhetorical segue from impulses, transmitters, receivers, decoders, and the like, to human uses of documents, and from unicellular creatures to homo erectus to the exosomatic brain, functions not as convincing scientific research, but as the constitution, by means of its position in a specific series and hierarchy, of stable and objective „knowledge structures", analogous to the stable and objective elements of the evolutionary series.

Taking Belkin and Robertson's „Information Science and the Phenomenon of Information" (1976) as a paradigmatic text of the cognitive viewpoint, we find a reprise of this natural-scientific narrative, but this time in terms of the cognitive viewpoint's special theoretical contribution, the notion of „structure", or „image". The primary figures of Brookes's series of information processes are replicated: biological information, noiseless and noisy channels, sense organs at work structuring incoming data, single-celled organisms with their simple binary classifications, and, at the later stages of the hierarchy, the creation and use of documents. What is new is the insertion of „images" into this discourse. Talk of transmission through channels now becomes talk of images acting upon images. There is the cat's image of its surroundings, generated by optical systems and „a sophisticated set of traps" (Belkin & Robertson 1976, 199), the sensual and conceptual images „inside the mind of the organism", especially the „higher animals" (ibid.), which act upon each other by a process of „cogitation" to generate new images (ibid.). The cognitive viewpoint thus constitutes its primary theoretical object entirely within the natural-scientific discourse it so faithfully repeats. The important rhetorical move, as in Brookes and true to the form of the discursive space prepared for it, is the segue from natural-scientific objects to document production and use. This time the move is accomplished by shortening the discursive distance between amoeba absorbing nutrients and people reading books by a uniform application of a natural-scientific language of images. A place for meaningful theory is thus carved out: document production and use will be spoken of in the language of images, which in turn are spoken of as natural-scientific entities.

The following discussion of some of the discursive procedures specific to the cognitive viewpoint will amplify and reinforce this conclusion.

Discursive Features of the Cognitive Viewpoint

Theoretical Imperialism

The cognitive viewpoint is proposed neither as one theory among many, nor as a local theory for a specific set of problems, but as a total theory for LIS, and as the only theory. It claims to enable „the integration of various now more-or-less autonomous aspects of information science into a coherent whole" (Belkin & Robertson 1976, 202); it unites problems „within a single theoretical framework ... allowing results from one of the problem areas to be applicable to investigations in the others" (ibid., 203). The fundamental theoretical task becomes translation and redescription, as befits the development of a discursive formation: „defining and relating these phenomena in terms [my emphasis] of structure does lead to something new..." (ibid., 202). The strength of the discursive imperative to privilege a totalizing theory over empirical results can be measured by the cognitive viewpoint's hospitality to conclusions based upon just two cases (Belkin 1984).

The colonization of all LIS territories through the imposition of a universal and unifying discourse requires the constitution of stable, objective, knowable, and fundamental theoretical objects. It can promise a unified knowledge of „a continuous spectrum of information processes" because it first constructs fixed, stable mental image-structures. A discourse of fragmented, conflicted, or contradictory mental contents could offer no stable „image-structures" for objective investigation. A discourse of social constitution of „images" or „models of the world" could not offer fundamental theoretical entities. A discourse of „information processes" as social practices played out on an agonistic field of conflicting and shifting historical forces, instead of mental events inside individual minds, could not issue guarantees of explanatory theory. The cognitive viewpoint's talk of image-structures as natural objects, of „information" as a change in „structure", is an essential part of its universalist and totalizing discursive strategy.

Referentiality and Reification

A single theory of the countless „information processes" of our planet's advanced civilization is clearly a tall order. The cognitive viewpoint effects an extraordinary discursive economy through the deployment of a very limited number of key referring expressions. These are used in a strategy of reification to stabilize the volatile mass of phenomena of possible interest, thereby constituting a limited number of key structures as investigable objects of an objective world. Among the most important of these are „image", „model", „picture", „knowledge structure", and „knowledge store". Reification of the image is established by procedures of investigation, identification and classification. Once users' images are identified as Anomalous States of Knowledge (ASKs), for example, procedures of classifying „the range of possible ASKs" (Belkin 1980, 193) can be mobilized and descriptive notations legitimated. Thus the image is „a highly complex network"; „partitions of the image are possible and reasonable"; they can be „roughly grouped into two basic types: vertical and horizontal" (Belkin 1977, 189). „Image-" or „model-building" is supported by „functional codes", statistical methods, and graphic representations (Belkin 1984). The discursive effect of a strategy of reification of images is a reduction of a complicated field of conflicting and contradictory social forces which configure information processes to the interaction of two primary „structures": the user's „image", conceived as a mental representation, and the „knowledge store", conceived as a repository of similar images in the form of graphic records.

Interiors: Representations and Processing

The cognitive viewpoint's discourse about images imposes a grammar of representations, reflections, or appearances. Users represent the world, generators represent the world aided by their images of the users, information scientists represent both users and the knowledge store, the knowledge store represents just about anything. A telling statement is the following: „We ... start from the image (...the mental conception that we have of our environment and ourselves in it), and consider the structures of the image itself. These structures may or may not represent reflections of real-world structures" (Belkin & Robertson 1976, 198). Here the image has elements, called „structures", which themselves are capable of representing. But they represent entities that are also capable of representing, i.e. „reflections". Images have structures which represent reflections which themselves may or may not mirror „real-world structures". Representation is piled upon representation, until, under the appropriate heading „Why the Information System is Problematic", no fewer than seventeen types of representations are identified, albeit with the proviso that there are yet others which must be excluded in order to manage an already „highly complex situation" (Belkin 1984, 115).

Furthermore, representations generate other representations. The metaphor is of a set of rules and procedures (a program) for processing „input", so that the „output" of an „information-processing device" is a function not merely of its input but also of its program. Not only is the output a representation, but so is the program, which is said to be „a system of categories or concepts which, for the information-processing device, are a model of the world" (De May 1980, 48).

Thus LIS theory is to concern itself exclusively with representations, reflections, and appearances. Information processes are understood by „assessing the 'cognitive maps or pictures' of an individual. What kind of picture does this person have of his situation? What kind of picture is he trying to make? What kind of picture does he require..." (Dervin 1977, 22).

Knowledge

Talk about knowledge is ubiquitous. For example, a criticism of traditional information retrieval is followed immediately by the claim that „cognitive states of knowledge" underlie the „communication system" of retrieval (Belkin 1980, 191). The benefit of a proposed IR method is that „it allows one to take advantage of the cognitive viewpoint, for the system can now be interpreted in terms of the general idea of states of knowledge" (Belkin 1977, 189). No justification is provided in either case for the restriction of IR to knowledge retrieval. At another point, the user's image is said to include „all of his or her knowledge and prejudices" (ibid.; my emphasis), yet in the following paragraph, the image is described exclusively in terms of knowledge. No mention is made of the discrepancy.

More examples could easily be adduced, but the general discursive strategy is plain. The term „knowledge" has unrestricted access to the discursive terrain occupied by the term „information". Image, representation, world model, information, and knowledge become interchangeable discursive elements. The effect of this procedure is twofold. First, the silent graft of the language of knowledge onto the language of information displaces doubts about the legitimacy of theory. Theory is firmly positioned beyond criticism within the familiar „quest for knowledge". Second, the language of knowledge supports talk about structure. Metaphors of structure have a far stronger intuitive appeal for images or representations of knowledge than of ignorance, fiction, or error. Since the world is not chaotic or contradictory, the knowledge of it which we store in our images, models, and representations must itself be somehow similarly structured. The cognitive viewpoint need perform little discursive labour to establish its grammatical connections between world, structure, knowledge, and science, for they are readily available; its achievement is to insert talk about information, image, and representation into a space where those notions are already contiguous.

Expert Intervention

The cognitive viewpoint distributes knowledge and ignorance unequally among the three major actors in its drama of information processes. Only the information scientists enjoy the clarity of complete knowledge. Their expertise is based upon methodologies of image analysis and harmonization. They discern the contours, the configurations, of the gaps in users' „knowledge structures", or world-models. They discover exactly what it is that the user cannot know. They use this discovery to interrogate a „knowledge store" with an expertise denied the user in principle, due to the user's essential ignorance about that which is employed to interrogate it. The information scientist's expertise reaches into recesses of the human mind inaccessible to users themselves. Information scientists discover the user's „internal program" or „sense-making processes"; they investigate the users' „images", „world models", „cognitive maps", or „internal realities". Reification of representations and imperialism of theory combine to constitute LIS professional expertise as a colonization of individual and group minds.

Radical Individualism: Erasure and Reconstruction of the Social

According to the cognitive viewpoint, „each individual must make his own sense. No outsider can impose sense" (Dervin 1977, 28). This constitution of free individual image generators and recipients inscribes a discourse of radical individualism, which is underwritten by a discursive opposition between inner and outer. The cognitive viewpoint's territory is the inner, hidden, interior individual reality, the „inner worlds of users, where most of the important acts of communicating interrogating, planning, interpreting, creating, resolving, answering are performed" (Dervin 1989, 217). The cognitive viewpoint deploys categories which „involve entering the world of users from actors' perspectives, from the inside" (ibid., 222). In line with its theoretical imperialism, the theory seeks to „formalize into system design..."universal aspects of the human experience", or „the universal human mandate to make meaning" (ibid., 224), and to investigate the „acts of meaning that are necessary to the human condition" (ibid., 226, footnote). Thus the outer is the epiphenomenal, the defective, the product of categories which are „inventions or constructions" (ibid., 217). The inner is the real, the true, the essential, and the universal; its categories put theory in touch with mental processes of individual sense making and development of interior world-pictures. Since the activities valorized by the cognitive viewpoint take place inside individual minds, the erasure of the social becomes one of its discursive achievements.

Having erased the social, the cognitive viewpoint can reinvent it only within individual psyches. Social factors are mere agents of cognitive effects; in some cases, society is constituted through a „world view", or „public image" (Rennie 1977, 221) common to several individuals. Social practices have but a noumenal reality, accessible to LIS theory only through their miniaturized effects in individual minds.

Instrumental Reason

By constructing information production and reception as independently motivated processes within individual „information-processing devices", the cognitive viewpoint restricts LIS theory to a discourse of instrumental reason. Its keywords become efficiency, standardization, predictability, and determination of effects. It submits to a master narrative whose controlling metaphor is the Shannon model of information transfer. Progress beyond this model on the grounds that it ignores the meaning of messages has become a truism of much LIS theorizing, but to introduce meaning through talk of images, representations, pictures, or cognitive maps, while at the same time accepting a discursive construction of two devices, a generator and a recipient, whose operations are understood as objective, given, natural world processes, fails to escape the dominance of the model's most powerful metaphor. Since information transfer is conceived as an alteration of internal representations, rather than, for example, as a social practice, the cognitive viewpoint bars LIS theory from investigation of the social, political, and economic forces which configure each pole of the information system.

Conclusion: A Discourse of Commodification

The cognitive viewpoint offers a specific way of talking about information processes. In public-relations jargon, it puts a certain „spin" upon our talk about information. The discursive strategies surveyed here impose a „grammar" by achieving a specific economy of discourse. „Images", for example, are not the discovery of the cognitive viewpoint, but its construct, its discursive achievement. The analysis presented here aims to reveal the specific enablings and disablings of the cognitive viewpoint, and to identify the institutional power sites which speak its language.

Discourses are analogous to technologies; their practice yields a specific product. The discourse of the cognitive viewpoint enables the production of a specific kind of knowledge. Discourse analysis practices no a priori skepticism about the possibility of devising an analysis in which „representations of a user's world model" are stabilized, nor about the possibility of using that analysis to deliver documents providing greater user satisfaction than hitherto. Indeed, the aim of discourse analysis is to show that the cognitive viewpoint constitutes its objects and methods such that this sort of knowledge may be obtained. But the cognitive viewpoint's discursive economy operates to restrict knowledge acquisition to what can be known of information processes when users' and generators „images" are constituted as objectively given natural scientific entities, rather than, for example, as determined by social practices.

The power relations which maintain the discourse of the cognitive viewpoint not only enable a technology of knowledge acquisition, but also disable others. Through its discourse of information processes as natural-scientific cognitive events taking place within radically individualized „information processing devices", the cognitive viewpoint relegates the social processes of information production, distribution, exchange and consumption to a noumenal realm, indicated only by their effects on the representations of atomized image-generators. The social construction of information processes, that is, the social constitution of „user needs", „knowledge stores", and patterns of image production, transmission, distribution, and consumption are thereby excluded from LIS theory. The theoretical supremacy of the cognitive viewpoint would disable the production of knowledge of information processes conceived as social practices.

A full investigation of the institutional sites of power which give the discourse of the cognitive viewpoint its meaning by applying it in specific social practices is beyond the scope of this paper. But some speculations may be made regarding the institutions likely to find in the cognitive viewpoint a congenial and obliging discourse of information processes.

Referentiality and reification support, as Finlay reminds us (Finlay 1987, 35), a discourse of exchange. Reification of users' „images" as objects to be „harmonized" with images in a „knowledge store" enables a discourse of image delivery and exchange which is happily wed to a market economy of images as consumer goods. Peculiar to advanced global capitalism is the scale of an expanding domestic and global market in images and representations. This market benefits from any discourse which can speak the language of freely expressed natural needs and free product production in terms of image need, production and delivery. Modern capitalism's image economy, or „consciousness industry" depends upon constructing fantasies of image needs for image consumers, and therefore upon methodologies for identifying products to fulfill those fantasies through consumption. The cognitive viewpoint provides an obliging discourse for capitalist image markets by its constitution of users as free creators of images, of the information scientist as an expert in image interpretation and delivery, and of databases as repositories of unmediated models of the world.

Promotion of information commodities as meeting deep-seated needs depends in no greater degree upon the truth of the cognitive viewpoint's theoretical elaborations than promotion of perfume depends upon the advertising claim that a specific scent is „the real me". But we know that a commodity represented as individual, essential and inner generally sells quite well. (So: how can we negotiate this vale of tears with gap-riddled world-images?) Successful promotion of any commodity depends, first, upon its construction, second, upon its representation as somehow important, or even better, as essential, and finally upon a methodology of consumer profile construction to determine how best to target its delivery. The cognitive viewpoint provides all three: it reifies information as a surveyable, objective entity which circulates from knowledge stores to individuals, it represents this entity as essential, inner and individual by locating it in „minds", and it offers to experts a technique of „harmonizing" „fundamental needs" with an information commodity.

The cognitive viewpoint presents itself as „user-centered", suggesting an appealing move away from system domination to „people power". Yet it is difficult to reconcile the talk of „user-directedness" with discursive procedures that disempower users by (i) limiting their information activities to internal cognitive processes and their information acquisition to image modification, (ii) atomizing the social world into a dispersion of „inner realities", (iii) limiting their access to their own inner worlds to the perception of a „gap", and (iv) yielding themselves up to a technology of surveillance administered through expert procedures of image harmonization. The theoretical erasure of social practices of individual and collective image manipulation in the interests of an image market also raises doubts about the „user-directedness" of a viewpoint which fails to recognize that an image without a gap may mask a dire need. Thus Dervin's claim that no outsider can impose sense on another (Dervin 1977, 28) becomes an extraordinary statement, indeed necessarily an ideological statement, in a society, to borrow from Chomsky, of necessary illusions and manufacturing consent. If Baudrillard is right in characterizing our modern world as a „hyperreality of communication and meaning" in which, by dint of being „more real than the real itself", „reality is destroyed", to be replaced by chimera, by simulation (Baudrillard 1973, 139) in the interests of a market economy, then a hypothesis perhaps worth further exploration is that the cognitive viewpoint, far from delivering „user-directedness", instead provides ideological labour for the commodification of information.

Bibliography

Baudrillard, Jean, 1973. „The Implosion of Meaning in the Media and the Implosion of the Social in the Masses". In: Kathleen Woodward, ed. The Myths of Information: Technology and Postindustrial Culture. Madison: Coda.

Belkin, Nicholas J., 1977. „Internal Knowledge and External Information". In: International Workshop on the Cognitive Viewpoint. Ghent: University of Ghent.

Belkin, Nicholas J., 1980. „The Problem of 'Matching' in Information Retrieval". In Harbo and Kajberg 1980.

Belkin, Nicholas J., 1980a. „Anomalous States of Knowledge As a Basis for Information Retrieval". The Canadian Journal of Information Science, 5: 133-43.

Belkin, Nicholas J., 1984. „Cognitive Models and Information Transfer". Social Science Information Studies, 4: 111-29.

Belkin, Nicholas J., and Stephen E. Robertson, 1976. „Information Science and the Phenomenon of Information". Journal of the American Society for Information Science, 26: 197-204.

Brookes, B. C., 1975. „The Fundamental Equation of Information Science". In Problems of Information Science. F.I.D. 530. Moscow: VINITI.

Brookes, B. C., 1975a. „The Fundamental Problem of Inform. Science". Informatics, 2: 42-9.

Brookes, B. C., 1977. „The Developing Cognitive Viewpoint in Information Science". In International Workshop on the Cognitive Viewpoint. Ghent: University of Ghent.

Brookes, B. C., 1980. „The Foundations of Information Science. Part I. Philosophical Aspects". Journal of Information Science, 2: 125-33.

Brookes, B. C., 1980a. „The Foundations of Information Science. Part II. Quantitative Aspects: Classes of Things and the Challenge of Human Individuality". Journal of Information Science, 2: 209-21.

Brookes, B. C., 1980b. „The Foundations of Inform. Science. Part III. Quantitative Aspects: Objective Maps and Subjective Landscapes". Journal of Information Science, 2: 269-75.

Brookes, B. C., 1981. „The Foundations of Information Science. Part IV. Information Science: The Changing Paradigm". Journal of Information Science, 3: 3-12.

De May, Marc, 1980. „The Relevance of the Cognitive Paradigm for Information Science". In: Harbo and Kajberg 1980.

Dervin, Brenda, 1977. „Useful Theory for Librarianship: Communication, Not Information". Drexel Library Quarterly, 13 (3): 16-32.

Dervin, Brenda, 1989. „Users as Research Inventions: How Research Categories Perpetuate Inequities". Journal of Communication, 39: 216-232. Reprinted in Marsha Siefert, George Gerbner, and Janice Fisher, eds. The Information Gap: How Computers and Other New Communication Technologies Affect the Social Distribution of Power. New York, Oxford: Oxford University Press, 1989.

Finlay, Marike, 1987. Powermatics: A Discursive Critique of New Communications Technology. London and New York: Routledge & Kegan Paul.

Harbo, Ole, and Leif Kajberg, eds., 1980. Theory and Application of Information Research: Proceedings of the Second International Research Forum on Information Science, 3-6 August 1977, Royal School of Librarianship, Copenhagen. London: Mansell.

Rennie, Janet, 1977. „The social dimension of information transfer". In International Workshop on the Cognitive Viewpoint. Ghent: University of Ghent.

Wilson, Kevin G., 1988. Technologies of Control: The New Interactive Media for the Home. Madison: University of Wisconsin Press.

4. Ein- und Weiterführende Bibliographie

Adam, R.: Laws for the lawless: ethics in (information) science. In: Journal of Information Science 17 (1991) 357-372.

Becker, J., Bickel, S.: Datenbanken und Macht. Konfliktfelder und Handlungsräume. Opladen 1992.

Bougnoux, D.: Sciences de l'information et de la communication, collection „Textes essentiels", Paris 1993.

Capurro, R.: Hermeneutik der Fachinformation. Freiburg, München 1986.

Capurro, R.: Leben im Informationszeitalter. Berlin 1995.

Finks, L.W.: Librarianship needs a new code of professional ethics. In: American Libraries, January 1991, 84-92.

Floyd, Ch.: Wo sind die Grenzen des verantwortbaren Computereinsatzes? Informatik-Spektrum (1985) 8: 3-6.

Foskett, D.J.: The Creed of the Librarian: No Politics, No Religion, No Morals. London 1962.

Froehlich, Th.J.: Ethical Considerations of Information Professionals. In: M.E. Williams, Ed.: Annual Review of Information Science and Technology, Vol. 27, 1992, S. 291-324.

Gould, C.C. (ed.): The Information Web - Ethical and Social Implications of Computer Networking. Boulder, San Francisco, London 1989.

Hauptman, R.: Ethical Challenges in Librarianship. Phoenix, AZ 1988.

Hauptman, R., Issue Editor: Ethics and the Dissemination of Information. In: Library Trends, Fall 1991.

Hauptman, R. Editor: Journal of Information Ethics, North Carolina (1994 ff.).

Johnson, D.G.; Snapper, J.W. (eds.): Ethical Issues and the Use of Computers. Belmont, Wadsworth 1985.

Katz, B., Fraley, R., Issue Editors: Ethics and Reference Services. In: The Reference Librarian 1982.

Kornwachs, K.: Kommunikation und Information. Zur menschengerechten Technikgestaltung. Berlin 1993.

Lancaster, F.W., Ed.: Ethics and the Librarian. Proceedings of the Allerton Park Institute: Vol. 31, 1989. Monticello,IL. Urbana-Champaign, IL: University of Illinois, Graduate School of Library and Information Science, 1991.

Lenk, H.: Können Informationssysteme moralisch verantwortlich sein? in: Informatik-Spektrum (1989) 12: 248-255.

Lyotard, J. F.: Das postmoderne Wissen. Wien 1986.

McBride, S. ed.: Many Voices One World. Report of the International Commission for The Study of Communication Problems. New York, NY, UNIPUB 1980.

Mintz, A.P. ed.: Information Ethics: Concerns for Librarianship and the Information Industry. New Brunswick, NJ. 1990.

Mintz, A.P.: Ethics and the News Librarian. In: Special Libraries 82 (1991) 1, 7-11.

Postman, N.: Das Technopol. Frankfurt 1992.

Roszak, Th.: Der Verlust des Denkens. München 1988.

Rubin, R.: Ethical Issues in Library Personnel Management. In: Journal of Library Administration. 1991 (14) 4: 1-16.

Schmidmaier, D.: Ethik in der Nutzerschulung. In: Zentralblatt für Bibliothekswesen 103 (1989) 7, 297-301.

Shaver, D. B., Hewison, N. S., Wykoff, L.W.: Ethics for Online Intermediaries. In: Special Libraries 76 (Fall 1985), 238-245.

Slack, J. D., Fejes, F. (eds.): The Ideology of the Information Age. Norwood, N.J. 1987.

Spinner, H.: Die Wissensordnung. Ein Leitkonzept für die dritte Grundordnung des Informationszeitalters. Opladen 1994.

Steinmüller, W.: Informationstechnologie und Gesellschaft. Darmstadt, Wissenschaftl. Buchgesellschaft, 1993

Sugnet, Chr., Issue Editor: Ethics in the Marketplace. In: Library Hi Tech, 6, 1986.

Swan, J.C., Peattie, N.: The Freedom to Lie: A Debate about Democracy. Jefferson, NC 1989.

Weizenbaum, J.: Die Macht der Computer und die Ohnmacht der Vernunft. Frankfurt Suhrkamp 1977.

Wersig, G.: Faktor Mensch: Bezugspunkte postmoderner Wissenschaft. Wissen, Kommunikation, Kultur. Frankfurt a.M.: 1993.

Woodward, D., Issue Editor: Intellectual Freedom/Parts I & II. In: Library Trends 39, 1990.

5. Ethik-Kodizes

ASIS Professional Guidelines

Dedicated to the Memory of Diana Woodward

The following set of „Professional Guidelines" was adopted for the ASIS membership by the Board of Directors in July 1993, finalizing a process involving Professionalism Committees, the ASIS Board of Directors and ASIS' legal counsel for more than a decade.

ASIS recognizes the plurality of uses and users of information technologies, services, systems and products, as well as the diversity of goals or objectives, sometimes conflicting, among producers, vendors, mediators and users of information systems.

ASIS urges its members to be ever aware of the social, economic, cultural and political impacts of their actions or inaction.

ASIS members have obligations to employers, clients and systems users, to the profession and to society, to use judgement and discretion in making choices, providing equitable service and in defending the rights of open inquiry.

Responsibilities to Employers/Clients/System Users

- To act faithfully for their employers or clients in professional matters.
- To uphold each user's, provider's or employer's right to privacy and confidentiality and to respect whatever proprietary rights belong to them by limiting access to, providing proper security for and ensuring proper disposal of data about clients, patrons or users.
- To treat all persons fairly.

Responsibility to the Profession

- To truthfully represent themselves and the information systems which they utilize or which they represent by
  - not knowingly making false statements or providing erroneous or misleading information
  - informing their employers, clients or sponsors of any circumstances that create a conflict of interest.

- not using their positions beyond their authorized limits or by not using their credentials to misrepresent themselves
- following and promoting standards of conduct in accord with the best current practices
- undertaking their research conscientiously, in gathering, tabulating or interpreting data; in following proper approval procedures for subjects; and in producing or disseminating their research results
- pursuing ongoing professional development and encouraging and assisting colleagues and others to do the same
- adhering to principles of due process and equality of opportunity.

Responsibility to Society

– To improve the information systems with which they work or which they represent to the best of their means and abilities by

- providing the most reliable and accurate information and acknowledging the credibility of the sources as known or unknown
- resisting all forms of censorship, inappropriate selection and acquisition policies and biases in information selection, provision and dissemination
- making known any biases, errors and inaccuracies found to exist and striving to correct those which can be remedied.

– To promote open and equal access to information, within the scope permitted by their organizations or work, and to resist procedures that promote unlawful discriminatory practices in access to and provision of information by

- seeking to extend public awareness and appreciation of information availability and provision as well as the role of information professionals in providing such information
- freely reporting, publishing of disseminating information subject to legal and proprietary restraints of producers, vendors and employers, and the best interests of their employers or clients.

Information professionals shall engage in principled conduct whether on their own behalf or at the request of employers, colleagues, clients, agencies or the profession.

(Bulletin of the American Society for Information Science 20(2): 4 (December/January), 1994)

American Library Association Code of Ethics

Librarians must provide the highest level of service through appropriate and usefully organized collections, fair and equitable circulation and service policies, and skillful, accurate, unbiased, and courteous responses to all requests for assistance.

Librarians must resist all efforts by groups or individuals to censor library materials.

Librarians must protect each user's right to privacy with respect to information sought or received, and materials consulted, borrowed, or acquired.

Librarians must adhere to the principles of due process and equality of opportunity in peer relationships and personnel actions.

Librarians must distinguish clearly in their actions and statements between their personal philosophies and attitudes and those of an institution or professional body.

Librarians must avoid situations in which personal interests might be served or financial benefits gained at the expense of library users, colleagues, or the employing institution.

(Adopted June 30, 1981 by ALA Membership and ALA Council) American Libraries, 13: 595 (October 1982)

Ethische Leitlinien der Gesellschaft für Informatik

Präambel

Das Handeln von Informatikerinnen und Informatikern steht in Wechselwirkung mit unterschiedlichen Lebensformen und -normen, deren besondere Art und Vielfalt sie berücksichtigen sollen und auch wollen. Dementsprechend sind diese Leitlinien nicht nur ethische Forderungen; sie sind zugleich Ausdruck des gemeinsamen Willens, diese Wechselwirkungen als wesentlichen Teil des eigenen individuellen und institutionellen beruflichen Handelns zu betrachten. Der offene Charakter dieser Forderungen wird mit dem Begriff Leitlinien unterstrichen.

Die Gesellschaft für Informatik (GI) will mit diesen Leitlinien bewirken, daß berufsethische Konflikte Gegenstand gemeinsamen Nachdenkens und Handelns werden. Ihr Interesse ist es, ihre Mitglieder, die sich mit verantwortungsvollem Verhalten exponiert haben, zu unterstützen. Vor allem will sie den Diskurs über ethische Fragen in der Informatik mit der Öffentlichkeit aufnehmen und Aufklärung leisten.

Handlungsalternativen und ihre absehbaren Wirkungen fachübergreifend zu thematisieren, ist in einer vernetzten Welt eine notwendige Aufgabe; hiermit sind einzelne zumeist überfordert. Deshalb hält die GI für unerläßlich, die Zusammenhänge zwischen individueller und kollektiver Verantwortung zu verdeutlichen und dafür Verfahren zu entwickeln. Im Sinne dieser Ausführungen bindet sich die GI an die folgenden Leitlinien.

Das Mitglied

Art. 1: Fachkompetenz

Vom Mitglied wird erwartet, daß es seine Fachkompetenz nach dem Stand von Wissenschaft und Technik ständig verbessert.

Art. 2: Sachkompetenz

Vom Mitglied wird erwartet, daß es sich über die Fachkompetenz hinaus in die seinen Aufgabenbereich betreffenden Anwendungen von Informatiksystemen soweit einarbeitet, daß

Ethik-Kodizes

es die Zusammenhänge versteht. Dazu bedarf es der Bereitschaft, die Anliegen und Interessen der verschiedenen Betroffenen zu verstehen und zu berücksichtigen.

Art. 3: Juristische Kompetenz

Vom Mitglied wird erwartet, daß es die einschlägigen rechtlichen Regelungen kennt, einhält und an ihrer Fortschreibung mitwirkt.

Art. 4: Kommunikative Kompetenz und Urteilsfähigkeit

Vom Mitglied wird erwartet, daß es seine Gesprächs- und Urteilsfähigkeit entwickelt, um als Informatikerin oder Informatiker an Gestaltungsprozessen und interdisziplinären Diskussionen im Sinne kollektiver Ethik mitwirken zu können.

Das Mitglied in einer Führungsposition

Art. 5: Arbeitsbedingungen

Vom Mitglied in einer Führungsposition wird zusätzlich erwartet, daß es für Arbeitsbedingungen Sorge trägt, die es Informatikerinnen und Informatikern erlauben, ihre Aufgaben am Stand der Technik kritisch zu überprüfen.

Art. 6: Beteiligung

Vom Mitglied in einer Führungsposition wird zusätzlich erwartet, daß es dazu beiträgt, die von der Einführung von Informatiksystemen Betroffenen an der Gestaltung der Systeme und ihrer Nutzungsbedingungen angemessen zu beteiligen. Von ihm wird insbesondere erwartet, daß es keine Kontrolltechniken ohne Beteiligung der Betroffenen zuläßt.

Art. 7: Organisationsstrukturen

Vom Mitglied in einer Führungsposition wird zusätzlich erwartet, aktiv für Organisationsstrukturen und kommunikative Verfahren einzutreten, die die Wahrnehmung von Verantwortung im Sinne kollektiver Ethik ermöglichen.

Das Mitglied in Lehre und Forschung

Art. 8

Vom Mitglied, das Informatik lehrt, wird zusätzlich erwartet, daß es die Lernenden auf deren Verantwortung sowohl im individuellen als auch im kollektiven Sinne vorbereitet und selbst hierbei Vorbild ist.

Die Gesellschaft für Informatik

Art. 9: Zivilcourage

Die GI ermutigt ihre Mitglieder in Situationen, in denen deren Pflichten gegenüber ihrem Arbeitgeber oder einem Kunden im Konflikt zur Verantwortung gegenüber Betroffenen stehen, mit Zivilcourage zu handeln.

Art. 10: Mediation

Die GI übernimmt Vermittlungsfunktionen, wenn Beteiligte in Konfliktsituationen diesen Wunsch an sie herantragen.

Art. 11: Interdisziplinäre Diskurse

Die GI ermöglicht interdisziplinäre Diskurse zu ethischen Problemen der Informatik; die Auswahl der Themen wird selbst in solchen Diskursen getroffen. Vorschläge hierzu können einzelne Mitglieder und Gliederungen der GI machen. Die Ergebnisse der Diskurse werden veröffentlicht.

Art. 12: Fallsammlung

Die GI legt eine allgemein zugängliche Fallsammlung über ethische Konflikte an, kommentiert und aktualisiert sie regelmäßig.

Art. 13: Ehrenrat

Die ethischen Leitlinien unterstützen den Ehrenrat nach § 11 der Satzung der GI in seinen Aufgaben und Entscheidungen.

Art. 14: Fortschreibung

Die ethischen Leitlinien werden regelmäßig überarbeitet.

Erläuterungen

Betroffener

Der Begriff wird in den Datenschutzgesetzen definiert als die natürliche Person, über die Daten etwas aussagen. Er umfaßt sowohl organisationsinterne (Beschäftigte, Nutzer) als auch organisationsexterne Personen (Bürger, Kunden). Es empfiehlt sich, diesen eingebürgerten Begriff für jegliche Form des Einsatzes von Informatiksystemen zu übernehmen. Die im englischen Sprachraum gebräuchliche Unterscheidung von „useyr" (intern) und „usee" (extern) hat sich in Deutschland bis jetzt nicht durchsetzen können.

Diskurs

Diskurse sind Verfahren gemeinschaftlicher Reflexion von Problemen mit einem normativen, d.h. wertbezogenen Hintergrund, die vom einzelnen oder einer einzelnen Fachdisziplin nicht überschaut werden können. Ihre wesentliche Leistung liegt darin, in der fachübergreifenden Kommunikation Erkenntnis- und Verständnisgrenzen zu überwinden sowie Vor-Urteile zu hinterfragen und im Licht anderer Positionen zu rechtfertigen oder zu modifizieren, um Verständigung zu ermöglichen. Allein die Überwindung der Sprachbarrieren erweist sich als langwieriges Problem. Deshalb sollen Diskurse auf eine mittelfristige Dauer angelegt sein.

Fallsammlung

Unter Fallsammlung wird eine Zusammenfassung von wirklichen Begebenheiten verstanden, in denen Beschäftigte (vorzugsweise Informatikerinnen und Informatiker) durch die ihnen übertragenen Aufgaben in ethische Konflikte geraten sind. Der Arbeitskreis „Informatik und Verantwortung" der GI wird diese Fälle zusammentragen und kommentieren. Die Sammlung hat den Sinn, diese Leitlinien zu konkretisieren und sie anhand praktischer Beispiele besser vermittelbar zu machen. Einzelne können diese Beispiele in vergleichbaren Situationen als Leitlinie für ihr Verhalten zu Rate ziehen.

Informatiksystem

Unter einem Informatiksystem wird die Einheit von Hard-, Software und Netzen einschließlich aller durch sie intendierten oder verursachten Gestaltungs- und Qualifizierungsprozesse bezügl. Arbeit und Organisation verstanden.

Kollektive Ethik

Ethik befaßt sich mit dem vorbedachten Verhalten von Menschen, die die Folgen ihres Verhaltens für andere Menschen, ihre Mitgeschöpfe und die Umwelt in noch unerfahrenen, durch Sitten und Rechtsnormen noch nicht geprägten Situationen bedenken (reflektieren). Hierbei können die Folgen des Verhaltens unmittelbar oder über längere Zeiten und größere Räume zu bedenken sein. Was der einzelne Mensch hinsichtlich dieser Verhaltensfolgen bedenken kann, umfaßt die individuelle Ethik.

Für den einzelnen Menschen sind aber nicht immer die Folgen von Verhalten in Kollektiven (Organisationen, Gruppen, Wirtschaften und Kulturen) überschaubar. Kollektives Verhalten bedarf deshalb zusätzlich zur individuellen der kollektiven Reflexion. Kollektive Ethik beruht auf der Möglichkeit, mit „Vorsicht" künftige kollektive Handlungen, die sich nicht an Erfahrungen und daraus entwickelten Normen orientieren können, gemeinschaftlich zu bedenken. Eine besondere Notwendigkeit solcher Reflexion ergibt sich immer dann, wenn individuelle Ethik oder Moral mit der kollektiven Ethik in Konflikt geraten.

Kontrolltechnik

Unter Kontrolltechnik werden analog zum Betriebsverfassungsgesetz „technische Einrichtungen" verstanden, die objektiv geeignet sind, „das Verhalten oder die Leistung der Arbeitnehmer zu überwachen" (§ 87 Abs.1 Nr.6 BetrVG). Bei der Einführung solcher Systeme steht den Interessenvertretungen ein Mitbestimmungsrecht zu.

Mediation

Unter Mediation werden Verhandlungsprozesse verstanden, mit deren Hilfe Interessenkonflikte zwischen zwei oder mehreren Parteien unter Hinzuziehung eines neutralen Dritten (Mediator) beigelegt werden. Das Ziel sind Problemlösungen, die von allen am Prozeß Beteiligten akzeptiert werden. Der Mediationsprozeß ist durch die Suche nach neuen Lösungen gekennzeichnet. Die Ergebnisse sind nicht rechtlich verpflichtend; als erfolgreich erweisen sich allgemein „jeder-gewinnt-Lösungen".

Rechtliche Regelungen

Rechtliche Regelungen, die für die Gestaltung von Informatiksystemen bedeutsam sind, finden sich inzwischen an zahlreichen Stellen der Rechtsordnung. Die wichtigsten sind:

- Allgemeiner und bereichsspezifischer Datenschutz, einschließlich Arbeitnehmerdatenschutz
- Freedom of information Gesetzgebung (Informationszugangsgesetze, z.b. für den Umweltbereich)
- Computerstrafrecht
- Gewerblicher Rechtsschutz, insbesondere Urheber- und Patentrecht
- Allgemeine zivilrechtliche und strikte Produkthaftung
- IT-Sicherheitsrecht
- Telekommunkationsrecht

In vielen, bei weitem aber nicht in allen Fällen begründet die Einhaltung technischer Normen und Standards (DIN, EN, ISO) die Vermutung der Rechtstreue.

Stand der Wissenschaft und Technik

Die Leitlinien wären schon bei ihrer Verkündung veraltet, wenn man sie auf eine schon bekannten Wissensfundus in der Informatik bezöge. Statt starrer Verweise bietet sich als Ausweg an, das Prinzip der sog. offenen normativen Standards zu übernehmen, für das sich das deutsche technische Sicherheitsrecht entschieden hat. Das Bundesverfassungsgericht hat dieses Prinzip in mehreren Grundsatzentscheidungen zu einer sog. „Dreistufenlehre" konkretisiert (BVerfGE 49,89ff., BVerfGE 53,30ff., BVerfGE 56,54ff.):

1. Stufe: Allgemein anerkannte Regeln der Technik

Eine Regel ist dann allgemein anerkannt, wenn die herrschende Meinung der Praktiker eines Fachgebiets von ihrer Richtigkeit überzeugt ist und dies auch dokumentiert hat. Die Regel muß in der Fachpraxis bewährt und erprobt sein. Maßgebend ist die Durchschnittsmeinung der Praktiker, abweichende Auffassungen von Minderheiten sind unerheblich. Eine starke faktische Vermutung für die allgemeine Anerkennung besteht, wenn z.B. DIN- oder ISO-Normen für das Problem existieren.

2. Stufe: Stand der Technik

Der Maßstab für das Gebotene wird an die Front der technischen Entwicklung verlagert, für die die allgemeine Anerkennung und die praktische Bewährung alleine nicht ausreicht. Bei dieser Formel müssen Meinungsverschiedenheiten unter technischen Praktikern ermittelt werden. Die meisten Datenschutzgesetze enthalten in ihren Datensicherungsvorschriften einen Hinweis auf den „Stand der Technik (und Organisation)".

3. Stufe: Stand von Wissenschaft und Technik

Mit der Bezugsnahme auf diese Formel wird ein noch stärkerer Zwang dahin ausgeübt, daß eine Regel mit der wissenschaftlichen und technischen Entwicklung Schritt hält. Geboten ist, was nach neuesten wissenschaftlichen Erkenntnisssen für erforderlich gehalten wird. Das jeweils Erforderliche wird also nicht durch das technisch gegenwärtige Machbare begrenzt. Einen Verweis auf den „Stand von Wissenschaft und Technik" enthält z.B. das Produkthaftungsgesetz von 1989, das zumindest für Standardsoftware anwendbar ist. Es bietet sich an, an die Fachkompetenz der Informatiker besonders hohe Maßstäbe anzulegen (3. Stufe). Bei der Realisierung von Informatiksystemen müßte es im allgemeinen ausreichen, die Erwartungen, wie sie z.B. Datenschutzgesetze an Informatiker haben, jedenfalls nicht zu unterschreiten.

(Informatik-Spektrum 16 (1993) 4, 239-240).

Ethik-Kodizes

Europäischer Verhaltenskodex für Informationsvermittler der EUSIDIC (Auszug)

A: Ethische Grundsätze

A.1 Moralische Anforderungen

Der Informationsvermittler ist verpflichtet,

- das Ansehen des Berufsstands zu wahren;
- redlich in der Erbringung seiner beruflichen Leistungen zu sein;
- seine Tätigkeit zuvorkommend und unter Achtung der Grundsätze von Moral und Menschlichkeit auszuüben;
- Kollegen, Kunden, andere Personen, die Kenntnisse und Fähigkeiten anderer und das Gesetz zu achten.

Der Informationsvermittler darf nicht:

- wissentlich Diskriminierung aufgrund von Rasse, Religion, Geschlecht oder sexueller Orientierung begünstigen;
- mit Leistungen werben, die er nicht selbst erbringen kann;
- zu welchem Zweck auch immer falsche Angaben machen.

A.2 Diskretion

Der Informationsvermittler ist verpflichtet,

- die Angelegenheiten seiner Kunden mit absoluter Vertraulichkeit zu behandeln, soweit nicht eine gesetzliche Pflicht zur Offenlegung besteht;
- Interessenkonflikte zu offenbaren, wenn sie die Vertraulichkeit gefährden können;
- Information, von der er in Ausübung seiner Tätigkeit Kenntnis erhält, nicht zu seinem persönlichen oder geschäftlichen Vorteil wiederzuverwenden oder zu mißbrauchen.

A.3 Geschäftsmoral

Der Informationsvermittler ist verpflichtet,

- vertragliche und gesetzliche Pflichten zu erfüllen;
- Information nur mit rechtmäßigen Mitteln zu beschaffen;
- die Eigentumsverhältnisse in seinem Betrieb sowie Höhe und Zweck etwaiger öffentlicher Beihilfen offenzulegen, mit denen seine Tätigkeit unterstützt wird;
- das Datenschutz- und das Urheberrecht zu beachten;
- die ethischen Grenzen anzugeben, innerhalb derer er bereit ist, Information zu beschaffen.

A.4 Objektivität

Der Informationsvermittler ist verpflichtet,

- fair und objektiv zu sein; er darf sich in seinem Handeln nicht von Voreingenommenheit und Einflüssen anderer leiten lassen;
- bei der Übergabe der Information an den Kunden eindeutig anzugeben, nach welchen Kriterien die Recherche durchgeführt wurde.

B. Qualität der Dienstleistungen

B.1 Regeln für die Geschäftspraxis

Der Informationsvermittler hat sich vor Auftragsannahme mit seinem Kunden über das gewünschte Ergebnis zu einigen.

Der Informationsvermittler ist verpflichtet,

- den Kunden zu verständigen, wenn das gewünschte Ergebnis seiner Ansicht nach auf andere, wirtschaftlichere Weise erzielt werden kann;
- sich an das geltende Recht zu halten;
- seine urheberrechtlichen Verpflichtungen gegenüber dem Informationslieferanten zu klären und den Kunden auf dessen urheberrechtliche Verpflichtungen bezüglich der beschafften Information hinzuweisen;

- seine datenschutzrechtlichen Verpflichtungen zu klären und den Kunden entsprechend zu informieren;
- bei der Vorlage der Ergebnisse klar zwischen den eigentlichen Ergebnissen und seiner Interpretation der Ergebnisse und den daraus abgeleiteten Empfehlungen zu unterscheiden;
- die Originalität fremder Werke zu respektieren;
- deutlich anzugeben, ob er ein Werk wörtlich zitiert oder dessen Inhalt frei wiedergibt;
- die Quellen der von ihm verwendeten Daten und Informationen anzugeben.

Der Informationsvermittler darf nicht:
- Arbeiten übernehmen, für die er nicht hinreichend befähigt ist;
- unter Vorspiegelung falscher Tatsachen versuchen, Information zu erlangen, die anders nicht zu erlangen wäre;
- unter Vorspiegelung falscher Tatsachen versuchen, einen Auftrag zu erlangen;
- fremde Arbeit für seine eigene ausgeben;
- falsche Angaben über den Wert der von ihm beschafften Information machen.

Die Geschäftsbedingungen und die Verfahren der Preisberechnung sind eindeutig zu formulieren.

Der Informationsvermittler ist verpflichtet,
- die Anweisungen des Kunden festzuhalten und zu befolgen;
- dem Kunden auf Verlangen einen Kostenvoranschlag anzufertigen, ehe er mit der Arbeit beginnt;
- auf Verlangen eine nach Einzelposten aufgegliederte Rechnung auszustellen.

Innerhalb des vom Kunden vorgegebenen Kosten- und Zeitrahmens hat der Informationsvermittler:
- dem Kunden eine realistische Schätzung der Information zu geben, die voraussichtlich beschafft werden kann;
- in den Informationsquellen zu recherchieren, aus denen er am ehesten aktuelle und richtige Information gewinnen kann;
- den Kunden auf Verlangen über den Fortgang der Recherche auf dem laufenden zu halten.

B.2 Berufliche Fähigkeiten

Der Informationsvermittler ist verpflichtet, sein Fachwisssen auf dem neuesten Stand zu halten und seine beruflichen Fähigkeiten laufend zu verbessern.

Der Informationsvermittler hat sicherzustellen, daß alle Personen, die mit ihm oder für ihn arbeiten, zur Durchführung der ihnen anvertrauten Recherchen hinreichend befähigt sind.

In der Regel steht der Kunde nur mit dem Informationsvermittler selbst in Geschäftsbeziehung.

Der Informationsvermittler

- kann mit Einverständnis des Kunden Recherchen, für die er selbst nicht befähigt ist, im Unterauftrag an entsprechend qualifizierte Personen vergeben;

- haftet für die Leistungen seiner Unterauftragnehmer;

- hat dem Kunden die Gründe für die Inanspruchnahme eines Unterauftragnehmers mitzuteilen;

- hat dem Kunden gegebenenfalls den Namen seines Unterauftragnehmers zu nennen.

Der Informationsvermittler ist verpflichtet,

- eindeutig anzugeben, welche Leistungen er auf welchen Gebieten erbringen kann;

- bei der Übergabe der Information an den Kunden eindeutig anzugeben, nach welchen Kriterien die Recherche durchgeführt wurde.

B.3 Diskretion

Der Informationsvermittler hat alle Geschäftsangelegenheiten vertraulich zu behandeln.
Er hat Vertraulichkeit zu wahren:

- gegenüber anderen Stellen in dem Betrieb, in dem er tätig ist;

- gegenüber seinen anderen Kunden.

Soweit nicht anders vereinbart bleibt jede in Auftrag gegebene Recherche und jeder Bericht an einen Kunden vertraulich. Jede Arbeit, die ein bestimmter Kunde in Auftrag gegeben hat, ist allein für diesen Kunden anzufertigen, auch wenn das dafür verwendete Quellenmaterial frei zugänglich ist oder nicht ausschließlich für diesen Kunden beschafft wurde. Die Vertraulichkeit von in Auftrag gegebenen Recherchen kann durch individuelle vertragliche Vereinbarung aller Parteien geregelt werden.

B.4 Haftung

Der Informationsvermittler hat seine Tätigkeit mit angemessener Sorgfalt auszuüben. Der Informationsvermittler ist verpflichtet,

- deutlich auf die Grenzen der Verläßlichkeit der beschafften Information hinzuweisen, soweit er im Rahmen seiner Fachkunde und der verfügbaren Quellen dazu in der Lage ist;
- deutlich auf seine Haftung hinzuweisen und auf völligen Haftungsausschluß zu verzichten;
- die für ihn geltenden gesetzlichen Bestimmungen für Haftung, Schiedsgerichtsbarkeit und Fahrlässigkeit in der Berufsausübung zu beachten;
- eine Haftung bis zum Wert des für den Kunden ausgeführten Auftrags zu übernehmen;
- in seinen Geschäftsbedingungen das anzuwendende Schiedsgerichtsverfahren anzugeben.

B.5 Werbung und Wettbewerb

Der Informationsvermittler darf im Rahmen der für ihn geltenden Gesetze für sich werben, hat sich aber jeder Art von unlauterem Wettbewerb zu enthalten. Unzulässig ist insbesondere vergleichende Werbung, in der die fachliche Befähigung anderer Informationsvermittler in Frage gestellt wird.

6. Die Autoren

Robert F. Barnes, geb. 1931; 1957 M.A. in Mathematik am Dartmouth College (USA); 1966 Ph.D. in Logik und Methodologie der Wissenschaften an der University of California, Berkeley. Lehrt als Professor of Computer Science and Philosophy an der Lehigh University (USA).
Veröffentlichungen u.a.: Some Thoughts on Professional Ethics Codes. In: Bulletin of the ASIS, 12 (4) 1986.

Daniel Bougnoux, Studium und außerordentliche Professur (agrégé) für Philosophie an der Ecole Normale Supérieure. Lehrt als Professor der Kommunikationswissenschaften an der Université Stendhal in Grenoble.
Veröffentlichungen u.a.: La Communication par la bande, introduction aux sciences de l'information et de la communication, Paris 1991; Sciences de l'information et de la communication, collection „Textes essentiels", Paris 1993.

Andreas Brellochs, geb. 1962 in Weinstadt, ursprünglich gewerbliche Berufsausbildung, kam nach langjährigen, verschiedenen Tätigkeiten in Industrie und Handel über den zweiten Bildungsweg zum Hochschulstudium. 1995 Diplom in *Dokumentation* an der Hochschule für Bibliotheks- und Informationswesen (HBI), Stuttgart.

Rafael Capurro, geb. 1945 in Montevideo; Studium der Philosophie und der Geisteswissenschaften in Chile und Argentinien; Ausbildung als wissenschaftlicher Dokumentar in Frankfurt/M.; 1978 Promotion in Philosophie an der Universität Düsseldorf, 1989 Habilitation an der Universität Stuttgart. Lehrt als Professor für Informationswissenschaft an der FH Stuttgart sowie am Institut für Philosophie an der Universität Stuttgart.
Veröffentlichungen u.a.: Information, München 1978; Hermeneutik und Fachinformation, Freiburg/München 1986; Leben im Informationszeitalter, Berlin 1985.

Ronald D.Doctor, geb.1935 in Brooklyn, New York; Masters und Ph.D. in Ingenieurwissenschaften an der University of Los Angeles; Masters in Library and Information Science an der School of Library and Information Science der University of Washington; verschiedene

Managementtätigkeiten. Lehrt als Professor an der School of Library and Information Studies der University of Alabama.

Veröffentlichungen u.a.: Seeking equity in the National Information Infrastructure, Internet Research, v.4(3), Okt.1994; Justice and social equity in cyberspace, Wilson Library Bulletin, v.68(5), Jan.1994.

Thomas J.Froehlich, geb.1941 in Johnstown, Pennsylvania; 1975 Ph.D. in Philosophie an der Duquesne University (USA); 1982 Master der Informationswissenschaft an der University of Pittsburgh. Lehrt als Professor an der School of Library and Information Science der Kent State University, Ohio.

Veröffentlichungen u.a.: Ethical Considerations of Information Professionals, Annual Review of Information Science and Technology, vol.27, 1992; Ethical Aspects of Library and Information Science (zus. mit Richard Rubin), Encyclopedia of Library and Information Science, 1995.

Bernd Frohmann, geb. 1946 in Karlsruhe; 1982 Ph.D. in Philosophie an der University of Toronto. Lehrt als Professor an der Graduate School of Library and Information Science an der University of Western Ontario (Kanada).

Veröffentlichungen u.a.: The Social and Discursive Construction of New Information Technologies, in: Rauch/Strohmann/Hiller/Schlögl (Hg.), Mehrwert von Information - Professionalisierung der Informationsarbeit, Konstanz 1994; Playing with Language, In: Canfield/Shanker (eds.): Wittgenstein's Intentions (Garland 1995).

Robert Hauptman, Ph.D. in Komparatistik. Lehrt als Professor an der St.Cloud State University (USA). Herausgeber der Zeitschrift: Journal of Information Ethics.

Veröffentlichungen u.a.: Ethical Challenges in Librarianship, Phoenix/New York 1988; Ethics and the Dissemination of Information. Library Trends, 1991 Fall, 40(2).

Norbert Henrichs, geb. 1935; Studium der Philosophie, Theologie, Psychologie und Geschichte in Bonn, München und Köln; Promotion und Habilitation in Philosophie. Seit 1974 Professor für Philosophie und Informationswissenschaft an der Heinrich-Heine-Universität Düsseldorf und Leiter der Forschungsabteilung für philosophische Information und Dokumentation des Philosophischen Instituts. Herausgeber verschiedener philosophischer Informationsdienste.

Die Autoren

Veröffentlichungen u.a.: ALBUM: Ein Verfahren für Literaturdokumentation. (mit H. Rabanus). München: Siemens-Aktiengesellschaft, 1971.

Barbara J.Kostrewski, Centre for Information Science, The City University, London. Veröffentlichungen u.a.: Education in medical documentation in West Germany. In: Journal of Information Science 3 (2) 1981; Biomedical information, education and decision support systems. In: Journal of Information and Image Management 12 (1/2) 1986.

Charles Oppenheim, Zwischen 1976 und 1980 Lecturer in Information Science an The City University, London; Lehrt als Professor und Head of the Department of Information Science an der University of Strathclyde, Glasgow.
Veröffentlichungen u.a.: Ethics of Information supply. London. Library Association 1981. In: ASLIB/IIS/LA Joint Conference, 15-19 Sept. 1980; Librarianship and information work in context. In: Librarianship and Information Work Worldwide 1991: an annual survey.

Rosemary Ruhig-Du Mont, geb.1947 in Chicago; 1969 Master in Library Science an der Syracuse University, New York; 1975 Ph.D. in Library and Information Science an der University of Pittsburgh, Pennsylvania. Lehrt als Professor an der School of Library and Information Science der Kent State University, Ohio; Herausgeberin der Zeitschrift: Journal of Education for Library and Information Science (1986ff.).
Veröffentlichungen u.a.: Cultural Diversity in Libraries, Greenwood Press 1994 (mit Lois Buttlar).

Martha Montague Smith, geb.1945 in Jacksonville, Florida; 1980 Ph.D. in Religion an der Duke University; langjährige Tätigkeit als Bibliothekarin, seit 1984 Head Librarian am Saint Mary's College.
Veröffentlichungen u.a.: Seit 1993 Ständige Kolumne: Educating for Information Ethics, in: Journal of Information Ethics.

John Swan, 1945 - 1994; Masters in Library Science am Simons College (USA), Ph.D. in Englischer und Amerikanischer Literatur an der Tufts University; langjährige Tätigkeit als Bibliothekar; erhielt u.a. 1986 den State Intellectual Freedom Committee Program Award der American Library Association.

Veröffentlichungen u.a.: The Freedom to Lie: A Debate about Democracy (zus. mit Noel Peattie), McFarland 1989.

Klaus Wiegerling, geb 1954 In Ludwigshafen/Rh. Studium der Philosophie, Komparatistik und Dt.Volkskunde an der Johannes-Gutenberg-Universität Mainz. 1983 Promotion. Freier Schriftsteller und Lektor; Lehrt an der FH Stuttgart, der Universität Stuttgart und der Universität Kaiserslautern.

Veröffentlichungen u.a.: Husserls Begriff der Potentialität, Bonn 1984; Die Erzählbarkeit der Welt, Lebach 1989; Das Ende der moralischen Instanzen, in: Terror 93, Landeszentr. f. polit.Bildung RLP, 1993.

Für Forschung,

Band 2
Harald Killenberg,
Rainer Kuhlen,
Hans-Jürgen Manecke (Hg.)
**Wissensbasierte
Informationssysteme und
Informationsmanagement**
Proceedings des 2. Internationalen Symposiums für Informationswissenschaften (ISI '91) zusammen mit dem 17. Internationalen Kolloquium für Information und Dokumentation
1991, 500 S., br.
DM 128,–/öS 999/sFr 128,–
ISBN 3-87940-412-7

Band 3
Rainer Kuhlen (Hg.)
**Experimentelles und
praktisches Information
Retrieval**
Festschrift für Gerhard Lustig
1992, 334 S., gb.
DM 89,–/öS 694/sFr 89,–
ISBN 3-87940-417-8

Band 4
Elisabeth Vogel
Informationsmanagement
Berufliche Anforderungen und Konsequenzen für die Ausbildung
1992, 260 S., br.
DM 74,–/öS 577/sFr 74,–
ISBN 3-87940-434-8

Band 5
Achim Oßwald
**Dokumentlieferung im
Zeitalter Elektronischen
Publizierens**
1992, 265 S., br.
DM 74,–/öS 577/sFr 74,–
ISBN 3-87940-447-X

Band 6
Anna-Maria Waibel
**Computerfrauen
zwischen Hackerkultur und
Technologiekritik**
1992, 212 S., br.
DM 64,–/öS 499/sFr 64,–
ISBN 3-87940-448-8

Band 7
Harald H. Zimmermann,
Heinz-Dirk Luckhardt,
Angelika Schulz (Hg.)
**Mensch und Maschine –
Informationelle Schnittstellen der Kommunikation**
Proceedings des 3. Internationalen Symposiums für Informationswissenschaft (ISI '92)
1992, 394 S., br.
DM 108,–/öS 843/sFr 108,–
ISBN 3-87940-449-6

Band 8
Angelika Glöckner-Rist
**Suchfragen im
Information Retrieval**
Eine empirische Untersuchung zum Rechercheverhalten von Informationsvermittlern und Endbenutzern
1992, 292 S., br.
DM 78,–/öS 609/sFr 78,–
ISBN 3-87940-453-4

Band 9
Gertrud Otremba,
Werner Schwuchow
**Elektronische
Informationsdienste**
Der deutsche Markt im Kontext Europas
1993, 104 S., br.
DM 38,–/öS 297/sFr 38,–
ISBN 3-87940-461-5

Band 10
Eva Mittermaier
**Planbasierte intelligente
Hilfe**
Design und empirische Fundierung auf der Basis eines symbiotischen Gesamtsystems
1995, 218 S., br.
DM 68,–/öS 531/sFr 68,–
ISBN 3-87940-508-5

Band 11
Fabian Glasen
**Wissensbasiertes
Informationsressourcen-
Management zur
Kreditwürdigkeitsprüfung**
Ein System zum Erarbeiten von Information aus heterogenen Wirtschaftsdatenbanken
1993, 360 S., br.
DM 89,–/öS 694/sFr 89,–
ISBN 3-87940-469-0

Band 12
Gerhard Knorz, Jürgen Krause,
Christa Womser-Hacker (Hg.)
Information Retrieval '93
Von der Modellierung zur Anwendung
Proceedings der 1. Tagung »Information Retrieval '93«
1993, 258 S., br.
DM 78,–/öS 609/sFr 78,–
ISBN 3-87940-473-9

Band 13
Josef Herget (Hg.)
**Neue Dimensionen in der
Informationsverarbeitung**
Proceedings des 1. Konstanzer Informationswissenschaftlichen Kolloquiums (KIK '93)
1993, 282 S., br.
DM 89,–/öS 694/sFr 89,–
ISBN 3-87940-475-5

Ausbildung und Praxis

UVK
Informations-wissenschaft

Band 14
A. Boehm, A. Mengel,
T. Muhr (Hg.)
Texte verstehen
Konzepte, Methoden,
Werkzeuge
1994, 384 S., br.
DM 89,–/öS 694/sFr 89,–
ISBN 3-87940-503-4

Band 15
Rainer Kuhlen
Informationsmarkt
Chancen und Risiken der
Kommerzialisierung von Wissen
1995, 624 S., mit zahlreichen
Tabellen und Abbildungen,
ausführlicher Bibliographie und
Stichwortregister
broschierte Ausgabe:
DM 98,–/öS 765/sFr 98,–
ISBN 3-87940-528-X
gebundene Ausgabe:
DM 128,–/öS 999/sFr 128,–
ISBN 3-87940-529-8

Band 16
W. Rauch, F. Strohmeier,
H. Hiller, Ch. Schlögl (Hg.)
**Mehrwert von Information –
Professionalisierung der
Informationsarbeit**
1994, 628 S., br.
Proceedings des 4. Internationalen Symposiums für
Informationswissenschaft
(ISI '94) vergriffen

Band 17
Erich Schoop,
Ralf Witt,
Ulrich Glowalla
**Hypermedia in der
Aus- und Weiterbildung
(HIM 95)**
Dresdner Symposion zum
computerunterstützten Lernen
1995, 316 S., br.
DM 89,–/öS 694/sFr 89,–
ISBN 3-87940-532-8

Band 19
Josef Herget,
Werner Schwuchow (Hg.)
Informationscontrolling
1995, 200 S., br.
DM 64,–/öS 499/sFr 64,–
ISBN 3-87940-510-7
Proceedings der 8. Internationalen Fachkonferenz der
Deutschen Gesellschaft für
Dokumentation e.V. (DGD) in
Zusammenarbeit mit der
Gesellschaft für Informatik e.V.
(GI), Schweizerischen Vereinigung für Dokumentation (FID),
Fachgruppe Informationswissenschaft an der Universität
Konstanz, Österreichischen
Gesellschaft für Dokumentation
und Information (ÖGDI) und
dem Hochschulverband für Informationswissenschaft e.V. (HI)

Band 20
Rainer Kuhlen,
Marc Rittberger (Hg.)
**Hypertext – Information
Retrieval – Multimedia
(HIM 95)**
Synergieeffekte elektronischer
Informationssysteme
Proceedings der 2. Tagung
Information Retrieval '95, der
2. Tagung Multimediale elektronische Dokumente und der
5. Tagung Hypertext, 5.–7. April
1995, Universität Konstanz in
Zusammenarbeit mit der Gesellschaft für Informatik (GI),
Fachgruppe 2.5.4/4.9.3. Information Retrieval, 2.5.4/4.9.1.
Hypertext, 2.5.4/4.9.2 Multimediale elektronische Dokumente,
der Österreichischen Computer
Gesellschaft (OeCG),
der Schweizer Informatik Gesellschaft (SI) und dem Hochschulverband für Informationswissenschaft e.V. (HI)
1995, 342 S., br.
DM 98,–/öS 765/sFr 98,–
ISBN 3-87940-509-3

Die Bände sind erhältlich in Ihrer Buchhandlung.

Gern senden wir Ihnen unseren Fachprospekt »Informationswissenschaft«
und/oder unser aktuelles »Gesamtverzeichnis« zu:
UVK · Universitätsverlag Konstanz · Postfach 10 20 51 · D-78420 Konstanz
Tel.: 0 75 31/90 53-0, Fax: 0 75 31/90 53-99